# Global Migrants, Local Culture

*Also by Laura Tabili*

'WE ASK FOR BRITISH JUSTICE': Workers and Racial Difference in Late Imperial Britain

# Global Migrants, Local Culture

## Natives and Newcomers in Provincial England, 1841–1939

Laura Tabili
*Associate Professor of Modern European History, University of Arizona, USA*

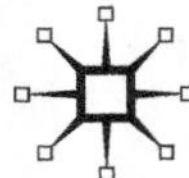



First published 2011 by
PALGRAVE MACMILLAN

Palgrave Macmillan in the UK is an imprint of Macmillan Publishers Limited, registered in England, company number 785998, of Houndmills, Basingstoke, Hampshire RG21 6XS.

Palgrave Macmillan in the US is a division of St Martin's Press LLC, 175 Fifth Avenue, New York, NY 10010.

Palgrave Macmillan is the global academic imprint of the above companies and has companies and representatives throughout the world.

Palgrave® and Macmillan® are registered trademarks in the United States, the United Kingdom, Europe and other countries.

ISBN 978–0–230–29133–1 hardback

This book is printed on paper suitable for recycling and made from fully managed and sustained forest sources. Logging, pulping and manufacturing processes are expected to conform to the environmental regulations of the country of origin.

A catalogue record for this book is available from the British Library.

Library of Congress Cataloging-in-Publication Data
Tabili, Laura.
Global migrants, local culture : natives and newcomers in provincial England, 1841–1939 / Laura Tabili.
p. cm.
Includes index.
ISBN 978–0–230–29133–1 (hardback)
1. Emigration and immigration—England—South Shields—History. 2. Migrants—England—South Shields—History. 3. South Shields (England)—Population—History. I. Title.
JV7695.S68T33 2011
305.9′06912094287509034—dc22 2011002017

10 9 8 7 6 5 4 3 2 1
20 19 18 17 16 15 14 13 12 11

Printed and bound in Great Britain by
CPI Antony Rowe, Chippenham and Eastbourne

# Contents

# List of Maps



Note: Maps in Chapter 3 are based on Ordnance Survey maps for 1858 and 1898; maps in Chapter 8 drawn by B. Eden, ward maps based on Henry Mess, *Industrial Tyneside: A Social Survey* (London: Ernest Benn, 1928) 105.

# List of Tables

# Acknowledgements

This book grew from an enquiry into economic and political processes dividing a global working class into competing 'races'. People stubbornly evaded these coercive measures, forging multiracial and multicultural organizations, families and communities, most visible in seaports. This drew me to South Shields in Northeast England: windswept, rainwashed, but never cheerless. The time has arrived to thank those who helped along the way.

In South Shields, local history librarians Doris Johnson, Keith Bardwell and Anne Sharp graciously indulged my extended sojourns and random reappearances at the South Tyneside Central Library. Steeped in the region's history as I never can be, all offered ready assistance and expert advice. I hope they will recognize something of what they know in these pages. Peter Hepplewhite, Education Officer at the Tyne and Wear Archives Service, not only offered expertise and assistance beyond all reasonable expectation, but also shared his love of the rugged hills, coasts and castles of Durham and Northumberland. Other staff at the now Tyne and Wear Archives and Museums and other repositories proved unfailingly helpful. Douglas Campbell generously shared his workspace and knowledge of the archives and library at the *Shields Gazette*. David Mole, Geoff Baxter and other Special Productions staff at the Public Record Office and David Gale, Roby Bose and Jacqueline Mitchell at the Home Office arranged for access to closed documents. Professor David Cannadine and the Advisory Council on Public Records negotiated access to 'lost' records. Ron and Elaine Freeman, Siobhan, Michael and Rebecca Hearn and Ann and Joe Foster offered not only lodging but also the unexpected gift of friendship.

I wish to thank the South Tyneside Metropolitan Borough Council, E. Rees of the Tyne and Wear Archives and Museums, and the British Library for permission to cite and quote from documents in their care. Financial assistance is gratefully acknowledged from the German Marshall Fund of the United States and the American Philosophical Society, the Udall Center for the Study of Public Policy of the University of Arizona, and the Social and Behavioral Sciences Research Institute at the University of Arizona. Thanks also to Helen Nader, Richard Cosgrove and Kevin Gosner for agreeing to and supporting the requisite leaves and sabbaticals.

Thanks are also due to my fearless readers, Kelly Boyd, Rohan McWilliam, Allen Howard and especially David Ortiz, who endured draft chapters with grace and forbearance. The book is better for their criticism and would be better still had I found a way to meet it all. Invitations from Clare Midgley enabled me to try out ideas at the 2005 Reconfiguring the British seminar at the Institute of Historical Research and at a postgraduate seminar at Sheffield Hallam University in 2008. Thanks also for the practical and moral support of Sonya Rose, Dana Frank, Antoinette Burton, Chris Waters, Julia Clancy-Smith and Linda Darling. Pamela Stewart helped collate census data at a crucial stage. Helen Nader, Susan Karant-Nunn and Philippa Levine generously offered the benefit of their experience at another. Jim Cronin tried to dissuade me from this project, saying it would take forever: as ever, Jim, you were right. In Tucson, Katja Schulz did her best to keep me from degenerating into a boring old poop. Linda Darling listened patiently to my stream of consciousness over countless plates of enchiladas. Lily, Alfie and Rosie assisted at every stage, sitting firmly on key passages and insisting that even humans need to play sometimes. Charles Beem, Bill Mericle, Paul Sachelari and Kristin, Jodie Kreider, Jeff Glasco and Sharon Bailey-Glasco looked after my kitties and home during several extended absences. In England, Ken and Liz Mosley, Keith and Pat Rowley, Kelly Boyd and Rohan McWilliam, and Clare Midgley and Norris Saakwa-Mante continue to offer precious friendship. Friends, family and colleagues in Tucson, Wisconsin, Britain and elsewhere bore with the project when it seemed endless. Finding the journey far from over, but merely changing course, I remain grateful to them all.

In a time and place where xenophobia again appears ascendant, this book is offered as evidence that it need not be so.

Laura Tabili
Tucson, Arizona
August 2010

# Introduction: Migration and Cultural Change

South Shields has been a crossroads of population since before recorded history. On a wind-scoured headland where the River Tyne joins the sea, the outermost reaches of the ancient world, Roman colonizers built a fort, securing their northern frontier in Britain.[1] Yet frontiers imply not only border control but also border crossing.[2] This border outpost stimulated migration and processes of cultural exchange that continue today. For two millennia, invaders and missionaries, merchants and other migrants circulated through South Shields, continually reshaping language, custom and landscape. Bearing goods and artifacts, ideas and practices from the Baltic, the Mediterranean, the Red Sea and beyond, they wove South Shields into a widening world. In the past two centuries the insistent yet capricious demands of an industrializing global economy have reconfigured the town's population anew.

Between 1850, when the port of South Shields gained autonomy from Newcastle, and the world depression of the 1930s, Tyneside's economy boomed and slumped, bound to the fortunes of a handful of major industries. Principal sources of local wealth and employment, coalmining, shipbuilding and repair, iron and steel manufacturing, engineering and merchant shipping became highly unstable appendages of the world economy.[3] These volatile industries attracted migrants from elsewhere in England as well as Scotland, Ireland, Wales, Scandinavia, Germany and the Baltic, the Mediterranean, the Americas, and the colonized world. Thousands converged on South Shields, yielding a diverse local population. They included, by the 1920s and 1930s, one of Britain's earliest and largest Arab or Muslim communities. In its rapid industrialization, its cultural, racial and confessional diversity, and its vulnerability to global market forces, South Shields became a microcosm of industrial societies also forming on the European Continent, in the Americas, in Japan and elsewhere. The erasure of these historical migrations from scholarly and popular consciousness has exacerbated controversies over recent migration to Britain.

Since the 1950s, political conflicts have produced a view of British society and culture as static and insular, unreceptive to and threatened by migration. Those seeking to exclude postwar migrants from former colonies in the Caribbean, Africa and Asia have depicted them as disruptive to the harmony of a previously culturally and racially homogeneous society.[4] This view has justified curtailing migration from the former empire through immigration Acts in 1962 and 1968, and even redefining British nationality. Corrosive rhetorical assaults on post-imperial migrants have included Conservative leader Margaret Thatcher's prediction that Britain would be 'swamped by people with a different culture', and her colleague Enoch Powell's infamous 'rivers of blood' speech proposing insuperable and lethal incompatibilities between migrants and natives.[5] Institutional racism, adversarial policing, and state and media rhetoric of cultural dissonance have continued in xenophobic responses to asylum seekers, migrants from Eastern Europe and even British-born Muslim youth.[6] Politicians, academics and pundits struggle to define Britishness and enforce cultural conformity.[7] In the process, the label 'immigrant' has become racialized, negative, even criminalizing, placing whole communities on the defensive.[8]

The history of migration to, from and through South Shields challenges the view of Britain as a culturally and racially homogeneous society disrupted only recently by exotic intruders creating unprecedented cultural change. First, it shows efforts to preserve Britain's cultural purity or demographic homogeneity have been and remain misguided, as such purity never existed.[9] Second, efforts to capture and define 'British cultural identity' around a stable and easily defined population must founder: Britain's population has historically proven kaleidoscopically fluid, the culture they created and inhabited plural and protean.[10] Third, British society before 1945 was already culturally and racially heterogeneous, following at least a century of substantial migration within the British Isles, from Europe to Britain, and from the colonized world to Britain.

## Cultures of migration

Recognizing migration as a constant of human history and a distinguishing feature of the industrial era demands reconsidering static and ahistorical views of culture. Antagonists of recent migrants lament erosion of British culture as if that culture were homogeneous, monolithic and firmly bounded.[11] Even liberal political figures and scholars have eulogized cultures as unitary, totalizing, a common way of life.[12] Echoing colonialist discourses, such understandings depict British culture as rigid and timeless, yet fragile and easily destabilized by change or challenge.[13] Detaching culture from other historical processes, such approaches treat as if natural and given what actually developed contingently, over time. Prevalent conceptions of British culture and British identity originated as elite gambits in ongoing struggles with explicit political agendas.[14] Assumptions of cultural unity and consensus slight class, gender, religion, region, politics, and other stratifications and marginalizations fissuring Britain like other societies. These yielded multiple and mutable British cultures.[15]

Scholars understand cultures not as static, closed and bounded, but continually reproduced and reinvented through an unstable dialectical circuit of belief and social practice. People recreate cultures through everyday relations including work, kinship, marriage, social interaction and of course migration.[16] Cultures and human existence itself have taken shape not in isolation but through global interactions and interpenetration.[17] Even localities acquire their unique character through intersecting, regional, national and global processes.[18] Cultures remain terrains of human negotiation and struggle rather than consensus, shaping and shaped by political and economic change as well as other historical processes.[19] Fears of cultural change prove unwarranted, for all cultures have changed continually, reshaped by migrants, natives, and the global, regional and local economic and political shifts they responded to and initiated.

Despite cultural fictions depicting Britain's island geography as a bulwark against external influences, scholars have re-envisioned the sea, not as a barrier to migration and cultural fluidity, but a 'contact zone', a pathway or borderland permitting populations, cultural practices, artifacts and ideas to converge and mix.[20] Drawing on these lessons, others have rediscovered the continuous exchange of people, ideas and cultural practices between colonies and metropoles. From Kashmir shawls and gooseberry chutney to ideologies of race, class and gender, colonizers and colonized shaped a common culture experienced in radically different ways depending on power and position.[21]

While colonial subjects in Britain have begun to receive due recognition, the peopling of South Shields reveals this mutual exchange of people and cultural practices was preceded and shaped by cross-currents from Europe and elsewhere in the British Isles as well as further afield. Longstanding maritime and commercial links to the North Sea, the Baltic and beyond made Tyneside a place where everyday relations dissolved boundaries between migrants and natives.[22] Colonial subjects formed but part of a continually shifting population that yielded a diverse and dynamic society and culture. Analysing migration to, from and through South Shields reinforces understanding of cultures as processual, continually reconfigured through agency and practice and through interpenetrations between the local and global, national and regional.[23] Migrants and natives alike took part in industrial expansion, empire building and war, global processes sprawling across boundaries and borders, seas and oceans. Understanding how diverse populations came together to interact, coexist or conflict can help re-envision cultures themselves as products of ongoing historical change.

## Migration in European and global context

The history of South Shields, its people and culture remains inseparable from those of global economic transformation, class experience and class struggle, and the massive movement of population characterizing the past two centuries. This enquiry thus rests on a substantial and distinguished scholarship on British, European and global migration.[24] Scholars have repainted our picture of pre-industrial Europe to stress population mobility and fluidity, undermining views of rural life as timeless and unchanging, or premodern people as sedentary and isolated. Hardly an unprecedented and disruptive effect of industrialization, the circulation of people, artifacts and practices began with human history.[25] A ubiquitous cultural practice among rural as well as urban populations, migration affected those who stayed as well as those who moved. Individual, short-distance and quotidian 'mundane movements' predominated, often seasonal or circular, among villages, towns and regional centres.[26] Still, internal migration and emigration overseas proved complementary, exhibiting fundamental continuities between shorter and longer distance, temporary and permanent migrations, pre-industrial and industrial-era patterns.[27] Together these millions of mundane movements produced the massive population shifts and displacements attending commercialization and industrialization.[28]

Europe's industrial workforce proved heterogeneous in origin and globally migratory.[29] In the most vigorous Continental industrial systems, transborder migrants made up substantial proportions of working people: Poles, Russians, Austrians, Italians, Dutch, Danes and Belgians in Germany; Belgians, Italians, Algerians, Poles and Spaniards in France.

In the late nineteenth century, one-third of Ruhr miners originated in Eastern Europe: Polish and Masurian labour sustained Germany's iron and steel industries.[30] Yet corresponding populations in industrial Britain remain virtually unresearched.

Quotidian and mundane migration collapsed dichotomies between local and international migration, for short-distance moves might cross political, linguistic and cultural boundaries: Belgians and Italians migrated to France, and Scots to Tyneside.[31] Further, mixed with short-distance migrants appeared a leaven from further afield: Constantinople and Bengal as well as Ireland, Scotland and Wales. European migration systems thus extended to the Antipodes, the Americas and the colonized empires, articulating with Atlantic, Indian Ocean and other migration systems. Between 1815 and the Great War, cheap steamship fares enabled European migrants' incorporation into a globally mobile working class, in agriculture, construction, industry and mining.[32] Simultaneously, hundreds of thousands of Asian and African slaves and contract workers dispersed to far-flung sites of colonial production.[33] Migrants disseminated ideas, information, norms and practices critical to working-class formation.[34] Problematizing distinctions between migrants and immigrants, these findings also invite reconsidering the role global migration played in British history and cultural formation.[35]

## A closed society?

Internal migration has long been recognized as integral to British industrialization and class formation. Scholars examining rural-to-urban migration in the first stages of British industrialization found high rates of mobility and patterns of migration structured by kin and village networks not essentially different from those of transatlantic migrants.[36] Correcting the view of British society as static and homogeneous, migration scholars offered an account of nineteenth-century industrial populations as dynamic, protean and far from monolithic.

Such observations ill fit assumptions of cultural fixity and homogeneity, especially those based on the identity of population and place. Nor have scholars much considered the cultural and social dimensions of these massive population movements. While overseas migration has been treated extensively as both product and shaper of the United States as well as African and Latin American societies, historians of Britain have given it little attention. Britain has not been recognized as a major country of immigration, thus migrants from overseas have been treated as extraneous or counterproductive to class and cultural formation.[37]

Historians have neglected foreign nationals as well as colonized populations, considering them numerically, thus historically insignificant. As early as 1851, however, overseas migrants outnumbered Scots and/or Welsh in Birmingham, Bristol and London.[38] By 1881 the population of colonials and foreign nationals added together outnumbered Scots in England and Wales, and by 1901 even the Irish.[39] Few would dispute Irish or Scottish impact, and they enjoy a robust literature. Attention is thus long overdue to the increasing numbers of overseas migrants who contributed to British society and culture in the century before 1945.

In spite of this marginalization, painstaking recuperative research has sketched in broad outlines two millennia of overseas migrants, beginning with the Romans, Anglo-Saxons, Danes and Normans. Contesting anti-Semitic xenophobia at the turn of the century, an early work documented migrants' contributions to British commerce, technology and culture, from Lombard bankers and Flemish weavers to religious refugees such as Huguenots in the seventeenth century and European Jews in the nineteenth and twentieth centuries.[40] Combatting the view of recent migrants as anomalous intruders, subsequent historians have documented discontinuous migrations enriching British societies throughout the centuries.[41] Scholars trace the African and Asian presence to the earliest times, while people from the Caribbean, Africa, the Indian Ocean region and elsewhere increasingly passed through or settled in Britain as it became the hub of a global empire.[42] Invoking, even celebrating, this multicultural legacy to counter xenophobia, scholars have yet fully to digest its implications. The unstated corollary must be the ongoing integration of long-distance migrants and the continual transformation of British culture.[43]

Despite more than a century of scholarship on overseas migrants the picture remains far from complete. The extant narrative remains unavoidably fragmented, based on evidence about visible groups or individuals widely scattered in time and place. Scholars have yet substantially to reconstruct where migrants came from, how many there were and where in Britain they settled. We know much more about some groups, times and localities than others. While some visible groups, particularly the Irish and Jews, have generated significant scholarly interest, no comprehensive survey of any modern British town's overseas-born population has yet been attempted.[44] Notorious episodes of conflict continue to capture scholars' imagination, to the neglect of community formation and internal dynamics, or even daily interactions between migrants and natives.[45] Scholarship has barely engaged why some native

Britons, and which ones, attacked migrants at some times and not others.[46]

Overseas migrants have been dismissed too easily as exceptional, the populations involved deprecated as numerically and thus historically insignificant. Contradictorily, antagonism to the same people has been attributed to intolerably large numbers. While intolerance must be confronted, relying on conflict to detect migrants' presence has allowed the most xenophobic and racist of historical actors to stand for all Britons. Decontextualized focus on spectacular episodes of violence has represented migrants as perpetual victims, neglecting broader contexts and communities in which everyday relations occurred. Portraying 'the British' as monolithic, stressing barriers between rather than dialogue among British cultures and peoples, has isolated migrants analytically from British society and history, reproducing racists' and xenophobes' own rigid and naturalized categories. According to primary agency to racist aggressors, emphases on 'othering' and polarization neglect migrants' participation in shaping British culture itself.[47]

Analysing South Shields reveals migrants more numerous and intercultural contact more widespread than previously acknowledged. It uncovers flexibility in local as well as migrants' cultural practices, and exposes hitherto discounted British customary practices of inclusion and integration. Examining this history over a century shows changing relations between migrants and natives make sense only when located within historical and global contexts. These relations reflected and could be mitigated by class schisms and solidarities, gender and sexual relations, and broad historical processes such as economic boom and bust, empire building and imperial crisis, world war and global depression.

## South Shields and the world

Studying migration and its impact on a single town can illuminate the local and interpersonal impacts of world-scale movements of population and wealth. Migration to, from and through South Shields, conversely, can be understood only in the context of local and global as well as national and imperial dynamics that shaped and sustained it.

Although South Shields has been a port since ancient times, and an industrial centre since the Middle Ages, its most spectacular economic and population growth occurred in the late nineteenth century.[48] The global shift to technological innovation and heavy industry culminating in the First World War enmeshed South Shields with other economies through ongoing exchanges of goods and people, ideas and practices.[49] Yet the town's distinctive patterns of migration, settlement and social relations remain neglected relative to better-known locales such as Liverpool, Cardiff and London.[50] So have the lessons South Shields might hold for other places undergoing rapid economic, demographic, social and cultural change through processes currently styled globalization.[51]

To get beyond the black-white polarity structuring post-1945 debates, and often approaches to racial and ethnic conflict generally, this investigation begins in the mid-nineteenth century. Whether from the surrounding countryside or half a world away, migrants then made up the bulk of urban populations.[52] It finishes in the 1930s, as global economic crisis eventuated in world war and a dramatically altered postwar order. Taking this longer view reveals migration to Britain as an ongoing process: successive historical contexts continually reshaped relations between and definitions of migrants and natives.

Beginning at mid-century is apt for several reasons. The Tyne Improvement Act, 1850, freeing the port of South Shields from Newcastle's domination, proved a major stimulus for the industrial expansion drawing migrants to South Shields and the Northeast. The 1850s formed the seed-bed for the 'second' Industrial Revolution of the late nineteenth century, exemplified in South Shields' pattern of economic boom and decline described in Chapter 1. This chapter shows that even before the mass migrations of the industrial era, South Shields, like much of Britain and Europe, took shape through ongoing processes of migration and settlement. It locates the town's economic and demographic development temporally, within the history of two millennia, and spatially, within an ever-widening network of economic exchanges and migrant flows. Originating with ancient economic and cultural ties to the North Sea, the Baltic and the Mediterranean, the town became increasingly dependent on exports to global markets. This rendered South Shields and its people vulnerable to competition, technological change and geopolitics far beyond local control, while attracting a labour force from equally far-flung locales.

Chapters 2 and 3 show migrants displaced by nineteenth-century economic and political upheaval contributed to workforces local and distant, linking South Shields with the Americas, India, Africa and Latin America as well as the European Continent. Chapter 2 presents and analyses the first 100 per cent sample of overseas-born residents for any town in modern British history. Compiled from the seven censuses between 1841 and 1901 as well as other records, it reveals a surprising volume and variety of people originating abroad passed through or settled in Victorian South Shields. Each successive census revealed overseas migrants living in the town, their numbers and proportion increasing steadily throughout the century. Comparative analysis of this evidence shows neither South Shields nor its migrant population proved atypical of industrial towns elsewhere in Britain and Europe, lending the case broad relevance.

Migration histories have stressed migrants' formation of and reliance on networks of relatives and co-villagers: fewer inquired, as this work does, into everyday relations between migrants and natives. Analysing the whole migrant population rather than visible 'ethno-cultural groups' shows multifarious relationships formed between migrants and natives, integrating newcomers into local society.[53] Census data permit microhistorical reconstruction of families, households and social networks, sometimes over several decades.[54] Chapter 3 examines migrant households, showing Germans, Jews, Norwegians and others, like migrants in the United States and elsewhere, reconstructed their communities in South Shields through chain migration, compatriot networks, co-residence, endogamy and institution building. More surprising, little evidence appears of spatial or other segregation or enclavement. Whatever cultural and linguistic differences overseas origin implied, they proved insufficient to create social, occupational or geographical segregation in Victorian South Shields. Instead, the data reveal a high degree of residential and marital integration with the native population. Numerous overseas-born householders married, fathered, housed and employed native Britons as well as compatriots and other overseas migrants, confounding views of migrants and natives as discrete and bounded populations. The vast majority of overseas migrants lived in households with British-born people, exposed to local custom and culture in the intimate realm of private life.

Chapter 4 reveals global mobility and cosmopolitanism even among native-born Britons living in provincial England, belying their stereotyped portrayal as unworldly, isolated and hostile to newcomers. Many had apparently worked and travelled abroad, returning to South Shields with spouses, children and other kin originating overseas. This complicates views of migrants and natives as mutually exclusive populations. Other local people opened their homes to lodgers and boarders from overseas. This analysis recasts South Shields as a crucible of multicultural and transcultural class and social formation, not only due to the emergence of migrant communities, but to co-residence among migrants and natives, return of emigrants, often with family members acquired abroad, and exogamous marriages.

The quality and content of such relationships emerges in a second body of evidence derived from naturalization case files. Between 1879 and 1939, hundreds of migrants who settled in South Shields applied for and received naturalization as British subjects. Chapter 5 analyses how these formal, state-sanctioned transitions from alien to subject rested on prior, informal mechanisms of integration through personal relationships and cultural practices such as work, marriage and kinship. Rich qualitative evidence of local cultural traditions of inclusion voiced by migrants and natives alike contrasts with the pioneering work of John Foster. He found high rates of residential segregation between the Irish and natives in mid-century South Shields, and low rates of intermarriage.[55] This difference exposes the impact of class and colonialism on migrants' reception.

Chapter 6 shows local and migrant women played a variety of crucial roles in these mostly male migrants' survival. Wives and other women proved integral to migrants' integration into local families and networks, as well as stabilizing culturally distinct German and Jewish communities. Landladies who welcomed migrants into their homes, native women who married migrant men, migrant women who married native men and women who arrived in South Shields with their families all proved critical. Differential rates of exogamy and endogamy suggest intermarriage functioned as an important if not decisive variable in migrants' acculturation and incorporation into local society. In turn, the state relied on local women to act as gatekeepers into British society.

Although explanations for conflict have often rested on the premise of insuperable differences between migrants and natives, Chapters 7 and 8 show that a diverse array of people found themselves excluded at one time or another. Individuals and groups could move from exclusion to inclusion—and back again—in particular historical contexts. Chapter 7 documents how, with the new century, the town's social fluidity diminished due to deepening imperial crisis. Economic contraction stimulated intensified scrutiny of migrants generally. Shifting state and economic policies, driven by global competition for imperial and industrial advantage, increasingly impinged on local social relations. This conflicted with the survival strategies as well as the loyalties and sensibilities of local people. The state removed discretion over naturalization from local residents to industry and the military. Mariners, who accounted for a large proportion of overseas migrants in this seaport town, became subject to increasing surveillance, policing and manipulation. They became segregated from land-based society, curtailing their freedom of movement, and inhibiting their integration. The First World War, climaxing

Anglo-German imperial rivalry, overnight made enemy aliens of long-standing German residents and their families. They became subject to internment, press calumny, mob violence and ultimately deportation. Jews and other longstanding residents also met harassment and threats of exclusion, not due to their personal or cultural characteristics, but to a transformed geopolitical context and its local effects.

Before and during the war, as Chapter 8 describes, a new group of migrants became visible in South Shields: mariners from Britain's recently acquired possessions in Aden, the Yemen and East Africa. South Shields' Arab community, as it was called, formed in the same decades as Britain became increasingly inhospitable to overseas migrants and mariners due to imperial and industrial crises. Intensive national and local state surveillance of this population yields a rich documentary record to compare with that of nineteenth-century migrants. It discloses continuing mutual cultural accommodation as well as a settled Arab population two to four times larger than previously thought. State-instigated policing and global crises, rather than migrants' culpable 'difference' or British intolerance, created the historical context for attacks on Arabs, like Germans and other migrants. Yet some processes of integration and incorporation, such as intermarriage, co-residence and naturalization, remained available to Arabs in the 1920s and 1930s as they had to previous migrants.

Analysis will show that migrant-native relations hardly reflected rigid insider-outsider binarisms created by cultural, confessional or racial differences. Relations responded to class, gender, social and sexual dynamics as well as local, national, imperial and global ones. Ongoing discursive construction and reproduction of familiar and foreign cultural identities occurred through census procedures, housing policies, labour market shifts, state formation, economic expansion and instability, empire building and imperial decline, world war and global depression. Individuals might in the course of events exchange one identity for another, perhaps repeatedly. As wartime attacks on Germans who had lived for decades in South Shields suggest, geopolitical contexts could dramatically and unexpectedly alter local relations. Such events, although national or even global in scope, still reflected local contexts as well.

Reconstructing and analysing overseas migration reveals continual circulation of overseas migrants to and through South Shields and commensurate movement of local men and women into the wider world and back again. Analysis will show how migrants became integrated into local society through work, marriage, civil engagement and other social relations. Local cultural practices of inclusion, permeability and fluidity belie fictions of cultural stasis, purity, fragility and defensiveness. Traditions of openness and tolerance did not operate in a vacuum however. Geopolitical shifts such as imperial competition, empire building, industrial boom and bust and global war impinged on and transformed local cultures.

The history of South Shields suggests Britain never was a homogeneous, closed society, detached from global flows of population or cultural influence. Instead, it reveals British society and culture as plural, protean, contested and changeable, embedded in circuits of people, goods, ideas, power and interest, local and global as well as national and imperial.

# 1
# Aal Tegither, Like the Folks O'Sheels: Colonizers, Invaders, Settlers and Sojourners in the Making of an Industrial Town

'Who says there is no beauty nor poetry in coal and grime and smoke, in huddled tenements, high chimneys, and such things?' So W. Clark Russell, a visitor in the 1880s, captured the prospect greeting travellers, sojourners and migrants disembarking in Victorian South Shields. 'Viewed from the rushing, broken, tossing river', the landscape Russell celebrated bore marks of the town's integration into an industrializing world: 'screw-ships with volumes of steam blowing from their sides... tugs rapidly darting to and fro or toiling along with a string of barges in their wake', steamships looming 'tall, gaunt and bare' and 'colliers... lifting their ill-stayed spars into the whirling gloom'. Iron foundries, shipyards, chemical and cement factories lined the river on either side, along with 'timber yards, warehouses, wharves—leagues of them stretching in one long unbroken chain'. All, to Russell, signified 'the breadth of its interests, the wealth of its industries, the amazing spirit of progress' animating the locality.[1]

Absent from this stirring portrait remained the people of South Shields. Famed for sending forth coal, ships and other commodities to a voracious world, the town's changing fortunes remained inseparable from relays of conquering invaders, proselytizing missionaries, merchants, traders, artisans and labourers who traversed its 'sea-girt Lawe' over two millennia, shaping landscape, culture, economy and society.[2] The geographical advantages attracting Romans and Danes favoured the town in more prosaic endeavours. Outlet of the Tyne through which the region's wealth flowed to distant shores, South Shields enjoyed longstanding commercial links with European Continental markets and goods via the North Sea, the Baltic, the Mediterranean and beyond.

The local economy relied on extraction and export, primarily of coal, but also related products such as salt, glass and chemicals. Ships to transport the coal demanded Baltic timber and other imports. Related work from stevedoring, and sailmaking to tavernkeeping provided work for local people. It also attracted migrants from elsewhere in Britain, its colonies, Europe and further afield. The town thus benefited from regional, national and global linkages formed not only by trade and commerce, but human brawn and ingenuity. From earliest times, economic development remained inseparable from movements of people, wealth and knowledge. South Shields' fortuitous location at the river's mouth made it the sailor's first port of call and point of disembarkation. This geographical and economic situation attracted a cosmopolitan population connected with and shaped by the sea and the wider world.

This may seem surprising. The people and societies of Northeast England have been characterized as remote, closed and 'clannish', 'a race apart', reflected in the local saying, 'aal tegither, like the folks o'sheels'.[3] Patronizing stereotypes of Geordies, as Tynesiders are called, depict them as 'more isolated, more independent, more self-centred, more provincial' than other Britons.[4] Geordies have been caricatured as an exaggerated version of insular, defensive provincialism ascribed to Britons in general.[5] Yet the history of South Shields reveals local populations remained fluid and diverse, replenished and reconfigured by migration from overseas as well as elsewhere in Britain. Migrants drawn to South Shields helped reshape a unique but continually changing local culture. This flow of people generated conflict and contention only in certain relations and historical contexts.

## Migrants and invaders

Exchanges of people, goods and cultural practices between South Shields and the European Continent, the Mediterranean, the Arab lands and North Africa long antedate the industrial era. Post-Ice Age human inhabitants likely arrived from present-day Denmark millennia ago, traversing the swampy islands and lagoons surviving from an earlier land bridge.[6] Roman times found the surrounding region populated by the Brigantes, led by their queen Cartimandua. The fort, likely erected between 124 and 128 to support Hadrian's Wall, drew soldiers from across the empire: Cohors V Gallorum, the fifth cohort of Gauls, likely arrived between 209 and 213. In the early fifth century, *c.* 411, Tigris lightermen, soldiers from present-day Iraq, were reportedly garrisoned at a fort called Arbeia, most likely that in South Shields.[7] The adjacent civilian settlement attracted traders, artisans and merchants from throughout the ancient world. Burial monuments for Victor the Moor, servant of Asturian trooper Numerianus, and for Regina, the wife of Palmyran merchant Barates, attest this bustling seaport's wealth and cosmopolitanism. Barates' poignant bilingual lament for the British Catuvellaunian freedwoman Regina shows Britain's apparently recent melding of populations and cultures began millennia ago.[8]

With migration came cultural exchange. Consistent with their assimilationist imperial strategies, but also attesting local cultures' potency, the Romans appropriated local dieties including Dea Brigantea. Roman troops imported religions such as Mithraism, while Roman-British cults developed around indigenous gods such as Mars Alator. Silvanus Cocidius, the huntsman or guardian of the frontier, for example, came to be venerated 'in the Roman fashion' using stone altars and Latin.[9] Traces of this ancient occupation mark the modern landscape: until the 1890s housewives in the vicinity of the Lawe obtained their potable water from a Roman well. The Roman road later called the Wrekendyke, wrought, or made dyke, connected the Lawe with Newcastle and Chester-le-Street along a route still used.[10]

The surviving Iron Age settlement, Caer Urfa, trading by sea with Ireland and the Baltic, remained connected to the wider world through flows of people and goods. Angles arriving in the sixth century from near Schleswig occupied the heights, Shields Heugh, giving the Lawe the name it bears today, meaning a conical eminence. Iron Age Christianity inherited Roman integrative functions, drawing personnel, goods and ideas to northern Britain from throughout Christendom. The Irish monk St Aidan founded Northumbria's first Christian church at South Shields, presided over by the Dieran Princess Hild (614–680), possibly at the site of the present church of St Hilda near Shields Marketplace.[11] The sea linked seventh-century Northumbrians to the Mediterranean, while Northumbrian scriptoria produced texts exported to Christians in Germany, Pictland and Ireland.[12] Norsemen followed in their turn.[13] Small in number, the invaders left strong cultural and linguistic imprints, not least through apparent intermarriage with locals.[14] With relics of Roman occupation and the Anglian kingdom of Northumbria, medieval castles and fortifications mark the landscape, betraying the region's long history as a disputed borderland but also a confluence of peoples. With the Norman conquest, demands, exactions and depredations emanating from London cross-cut the North's Scottish and Scandinavian ties.[15] Subsequent overseas migrants arrived not as invaders but often with state sanction. Contributing to commercial and industrial development, they knit South Shields into regional and global flows of people, wealth and goods.

## Industry before industrialization

Unlike Liverpool, Manchester, Bristol and other west coast ports, shaped by the eighteenth-century Industrial Revolution and the Atlantic system fuelling it, Northeastern industrialization partook of more ancient connections to Scandinavia, the Baltic and the Continent. Although the town's most spectacular growth followed 1850, the Northeast enjoyed international trading relationships dating from the Middle Ages. It also pioneered a geographical division of labour and a mobile workforce recruited from far and near, features often thought peculiarly modern.[16] The rise and fall of its early industries bore hallmarks of more recent times: imported labour, often skilled, applied to abundant local raw materials, coupled with dependence on distant and unreliable markets vulnerable to competition, technological change and geopolitical events.

South Shields' industrial development took shape within a web of local, regional, national and global relationships, political as well as commercial. The Northeast relied on a combination of agriculture, farming, fishing, commerce and extractive industry that linked it to national and international flows of wealth and population.[17] Early export industry may have given South Shields the name it bears today: by one account, the town grew up around 'the land by the water-side, formerly inhabited by a few fishermen', who called their shelters, 'sheels' or 'sheals'.[18] Longstanding commercial activity included fisheries first recorded in 1093, shipbuilding in 1109 and trade with the Norwegians in 1213. Mention of the coble, a Pictish boat of stitched skin used for fishing and for loading coal onto seagoing collier boats, dated from 1228.[19]

Located conveniently at the river's mouth, South Shields prospered due to rivalry between the Bishops of Durham, landlords of South Shields who shared its revenues, and the Freemen of Newcastle, 8 miles upstream, who held the royal monopoly of river trade. As early as 1256 the Prior of Durham was convicted of founding a town which catered to 'sailors and strangers', to the detriment of Newcastle's revenues. The Freemen demanded repeatedly that the King prohibit South Shields from having a market, complaining in 1279 of a town 'where no town ought to be', whose vibrant commerce evaded the King's tolls. Distance from London and the countervailing and proximate power of the

Prince Bishops of the Durham Palatinate, however, limited the potency of royal sanction, and the town continued to develop.[20] The town's wealth and notoriety thus remained inseparable from its strategic and contentious engagement in regional, national and international trade and manufacturing, mobilizing in turn mariners, merchants, artisans and others.

Salt panning, dating from at least 1448–49, became the first manufacturing industry to enmesh South Shields in volatile interregional and international trading relations. Originally for preserving fish, salt production benefited from local supplies of cheap, inferior coal, sea water, and efficient water transport for both fuel and product. The Tyne became the most important sea salt manufactory in the Kingdom by the seventeenth century. Linkages through this trade fanned out across the North Sea and Baltic throughout Europe to the Mediterranean. In the eighteenth century South Shields provided 15 per cent of Britain's salt, of which London consumed 40 per cent. By then Shields salt panning was already declining, presaging the fate of subsequent local industries whose vigour rose and fell with distant and ephemeral markets.[21]

From the 1730s the overcapitalized industry, like many after it, faltered due to geopolitical events, competition and technological change. Danish and Norwegian protectionism and war disrupted the Baltic trade, while new salt duties aggravated competition from the Firth of Forth and the Hampshire coast. Polish mines and French works encroached on Continental markets. British consumers began switching to Cheshire rock salt, cheaper and more palatable, after its discovery in 1670. Glass, soap and other emerging local industries competed with salt for hitherto cheap 'small coal'.[22] Like the shades of the Romans before it, the once internationally famed industry lingered vestigially in local place names such as Pan Bank.[23]

Shields glass production too owed much to overseas trade and migration, specifically, imported artisanal techniques applied to local raw materials including potash, and limestone arriving as ballast. Even before the nineteenth century, migrants played key roles in Northeastern industry, as craftsmen and investors. As early as the seventh century, Abbot Benedict Biscop had recruited artisans from Gaul to teach the monks at Jarrow glassmaking, and in the mid-1600s Huguenot refugees from Lorraine practised the craft in the Northeast. Centuries later, local descendants of the De Hennezels (Henzel or Henzy), the De Thietrys (Tytory) and the DuThisacs (Tyzack) remained. South Shields' first glassworks appeared in 1650. In 1737 Newcastle entrepreneur Isaac

Cookson, shifting capital from the failing salt industry, founded Messrs Cookson Crown and Plate Glass works, trading with Hamburg, Danzig, Rotterdam, Copenhagen, Lisbon, Edinburgh, New York and Rhode Island. South Shields became Tyneside's glassmaking centre, and glass the Tyne's most important export after coal, supplying the east coast, the North Sea, the Baltic and later the Americas.[24] By the early twentieth century, Belgian competition reduced this once vibrant industry to one firm, Moores.[25] Still, glass in its turn stimulated other local industries, including alkali, essential not only for glass but for printing as well as soaps, bleaches and dyes for textile manufacture. By 1858, South Shields boasted the largest plant in Britain, employing 1500 men. At its peak the industry employed 10,000 workers in the Tyne, producing nearly half of national output, and supplanting glass as the Tyne's second export. From 1875 the Solvay process shifted the industry to Cheshire, and by 1891 South Shields' industry languished.[26]

With glass and alkali, wooden shipbuilding recouped local saltmakers' waning fortunes. Robert Wallis, the first Shields shipbuilder to flout Newcastle's monopoly, opened a yard in 1720 still occupied by his descendants in the mid-nineteenth century. Between 1789 and 1815, wartime demand made South Shields the Tyne's major builder of wooden ships. This stimulated local industries such as roperies, sailmakers, anchor and cable forges, block and mastmakers.[27]

South Shields thus began the nineteenth century with four major industries: salt panning, glass, chemicals and wooden shipbuilding. All benefited from and drew on increasingly far-flung labour, entrepreneurship, raw materials and markets. Yet by the mid-century all were overtaken by the heavy industries characterizing local development. The bridge between the old and new industries, and the engine of regional development, was coal.[28]

## Coal

Although South Shields' first coal mine, Simon Temple's Templetown Pit, appeared only in 1810, the town's history and fortunes bore the impress of the colliers moored in its harbour and the sailors and other migrants who converged there.[29] Coal formed the backbone of the Northeastern economy, mined and exported from the twelfth century to within living memory. Until late in the nineteenth century, the bulk of coal shipped from the south bank of the Tyne was laded in South Shields harbour.[30] The only major coalfield on the east coast, the Great Northern Coal field, a geological feature, underlay much of Durham and

Northumberland, extending eastwards under the sea.[31] The town and region grew and changed with coal and its integration into national and international markets. Fuel of salt, glass and other local manufactories, and major cargo of Tyne built ships, coal directly or indirectly spurred massive migration to, from and through South Shields.

From the fourteenth century, coal shipped to Zeeland, France, Flanders, Scotland and the Baltic paid for imports including Baltic timber, pitch and bitumen, Swedish iron, salt, cork and wainscot. This trade attracted in turn merchants from the Hanseatic ports as well as Lucca, Florence, Lübeck, Cologne and Brabant. As deforestation depleted wood and peat as sources of domestic and industrial fuel, coal proved integral to late Tudor industrialization. On it depended not only salt and glass but lime-burning, smithying, metal working, malting and brewing, soap, candles, starch, food processing, sugar and textile processes, smelting, alum, brick, tile, saltpeter, gunpowder, and copperas, or ferrous sulphate.[32] Britain's oldest industrial region, the Northeast burgeoned with demand from London, which absorbed an increasing share of its coal between 1550 and 1750. Newcastle coal exports to London rose fourfold between 1590 and 1640, doubling again by 1750 to something like 800,000 tons. Northeastern coal fuelled London's phenomenal demographic and economic growth. London in turn drove the nation, enabling Britain to outstrip industrial rivals.[33]

Tyneside 'sea coal' enjoyed a competitive advantage in an age of slow and cumbersome overland travel. Until 1720, Northeastern coal mines lay entirely within 5 miles of the riverside and mainly upriver of Newcastle. Coal extracted from shallow outcrops or even washed up on the seashore was carried to the riverside by packhorse and wheelbarrow, later in horsedrawn carts and wagons, along wooden tracks called waggonways, later made of iron rails. At the river it was transferred to small, manoeuvrable keelboats which carried it downriver to large 100 ton seagoing wooden colliers. In 1615 400 such colliers plied the two-week coastal journey between the Tyne and London, 600 by 1703, supplying 70 per cent of London's coal, and by 1830 96 per cent.[34]

Coal stimulated nearly every other regional industry, including toolmaking, railmaking, keel and shipbuilding, iron and engineering works, indirectly employing builders, cartwrights, ropers, candlers, nailers and smiths. This in turn attracted seventeenth-century migrants, including keelmen from Scotland and the borders, German swordmakers recruited from Solingen by Ambrose Crowley's Iron works at Winlaton and Swalwell, and Liege craftsmen Crowley imported to Sunderland. The trade likewise drew Shields seafarers to foreign parts: locals jested that to the Shields mariner the four-quarters of the globe comprised 'Roosha, Proosha, Memel, and Sheels'.[35]

South Shields' advantage lay in its position at the mouth of a decreasingly navigable river, coupled with colliers' increasing capacity. As early as 1735 'the Village of Sheals' had become 'the Station of the Sea-coal Fleets', while as late as the mid-nineteenth century Newcastle, the port of record, remained inaccessible to collier brigs. These square-rigged sailing ships, some as large as 600 tons, had to wait in Shields harbour for keelboats carrying coal from upriver. Although J.M.W. Turner portrayed the process in his 1835 *Keelmen Heaving in Coals by Moonlight*, by that time many staithes, long wharves or quays extending into deep water, had been equipped with mechanical drops or 'spouts'. These enabled coal to be loaded directly from the waggonways onto ships.[36] Sir George Head in summer 1835 conveyed the spectacular sights and sounds of the Stanhope and Tyne Railway Company's coal spouts, marvelling at 'enormous mechanical power in action ... creaking and groaning of timber, the stress on the machinery, the grating of the brake, the rattling of the huge links, the clash of the hammer against iron bolts, and the thundering crash of the coal falling through the bottom of the waggon into the hold of the vessel'.[37] South Shields acquired several local pits in the nineteenth century: Templetown in 1810, Hilda Pit in 1825, Harton Pit in the 1840s, Boldon Colliery in 1869 and Whitburn Colliery in 1879.[38] Eventually railheads from North Durham pits converged on the staithes at Tyne Dock, built at Shields opposite Jarrow Slake in 1859. By 1894, Tyne Dock shipped 5.6 million tons of coal, the largest volume in the world.[39]

Tyneside coal and related shipbuilding and heavy engineering peaked between the 1880s and the First World War, decades when these industries contributed most to British prosperity. In 1882, the Tyne ports shipped more coal exports, 8,303,843 tons, than any other in the Kingdom.[40] Coal and coke exports rose again 250 per cent between 1881 and 1911, peaking in 1913 at 20,299,955 tons. As late as the 1920s the bulk of South Tyneside coal continued to be shipped from Tyne Dock, in roughly the same location as the old waggonways.[41] Industry in turn exerted powerful labour demands, transforming local social formation, politics and the landscape itself.

## A thriving seaport

Since the Middle Ages the town of South Shields had consisted of a single 'Low Street', with tributary streets and alleys, hugging the river for over a mile from the Lawe top to Jarrow Slake. A new market square and a Georgian Town Hall surmounted the bluff from 1770, but the low street remained the town's commercial artery into the nineteenth century. Here shipchandlers, provisioners, shops and taverns competed day and night for visiting mariners' trade, while the river bank opposite was lined with 'shipyards, dry docks, ballast quays, raft or timber yards, sail and rigging lofts'. By 1811, factories and with them jobs massed along the Tyne: between 1801 and 1811 the town's population rose by almost half, from 11,011 to 15,165. In 1827, following a half-century of industrial development, *White's Directory* characterized South Shields as a 'thriving sea-port' which had undergone rapid transformation in population, size and wealth. The town then boasted a dozen shipyards and another dozen dry docks, several roperies and two collieries producing a type of coal London consumers knew as Hilda Walls-End. The village of Westoe approximately 1 mile south of the town, once a manor farm, had become a garden suburb, tripling in size after 1801 to approximately 17,000. By 1834, both Newcastle and Shields had sprawled along the river banks, narrowing the distance between them to 9 miles. East Jarrow, facing the tidal pool Jarrow Slake, where the seventh-century Saxon King Egfrith allegedly anchored 1000 ships, by the 1830s boasted more prosaic features: an alkali works, a shipbuilding yard, an iron foundry and a forge.[42]

On the eve of its incorporation in 1850, the town included all of South Shields and parts of Westoe. Much of this area, except for Westoe Village and East Jarrow, remained farmland. Yet the 14 coal staithes or spouts belonging to the town shipped over a million tons of coal per year, the produce of 44 regional collieries. Locals owned 110,000 tons of ships, most of them wooden vessels. Industries lined the riverside, including 15 major ironworks, 14 shipbuilding yards, four glassworks accounting for one-ninth of British output, four major chemical and soda works and another producing oil, paint and varnish. Other substantial firms produced locomotive engines and pottery. The town also boasted six timber yards, three large ballast wharves, two public railways and a colliery, as well as docks and slipways sufficient to accommodate 23 ships needing repair.[43]

Unlike W. Clark Russell a half-century later, Sir George Head in 1835 found the Tyne repellent rather than inspiring, its 'banks on either side, the whole distance from Newcastle ... studded with chimneys [which] vomit into the air a dense mass of smoke and impurities'. To Head, the products of industry seemed to overwhelm 'nature herself' with 'one black, huge cloud' of 'noxious particles and effluvia'.[44] Commissioner

D.B. Reid, MD, concurred, finding working-class districts in 1845 'very much blackened with smoke, and bare, from a total absence of trees in the neighbourhood' denuded by acid rain. The population of 28,974, nearly double that of 1811, comprised 'partly that of a sea-port, partly of a manufacturing town, and partly of a mining population'. Sailors worked mainly in the coal trade, which also employed many ashore.[45] Such observers identified early the paradox that increased wealth and productivity enriched the few through the labour and at the apparent expense of the many.

It remains impossible, indeed, to understand South Shields' industrial development without its political context. The town's fortunes and those of its people were shaped not only by the natural gifts of river, sea and coal but also by longstanding economic relations and rivalries.

South Shields prospered in part because until the 1840s the Tyne, neglected by its conservators, the Corporation of Newcastle, remained shallow and choked with obstructions, impossible for ships over 300 or 400 tons to navigate. A sandbar obstructed the mouth, and low tide drained some parts of the main channel to mere inches of water, exposing over 800 acres of sandbanks. 'Old ladies', local wags told Russell in the 1880s, 'used to be able to tuck up their dresses and wade across the river'. No docks existed until 1827, and even Shields harbour, a natural basin once accommodating 2000 sailing ships, had lost 10 feet in depth since the 1780s, in part due to dumping of ballast.[46] Colliers above a certain size became unable to navigate the shallows, weighing anchor in the shelter of the harbour to await the keels which still transported coal from upriver staithes. This situation aggravated longstanding competition and conflict between Newcastle and South Shields over the lucrative port trade.

On 22 March 1600 through the 'Great Charter', Elizabeth had reaffirmed Newcastle's supremacy over the river, 'unless the ship be of such capacity, or for any reasonable cause, it cannot conveniently arrive at Newcastle'. This caveat suggests doubts about the river's navigability, which continued to deteriorate. The Corporation of Newcastle complained repeatedly of ships dumping ballast at South Shields, creating a wharf for illicit landing.[47] Coal shipowners and masters, conversely, complained to Parliament in 1765 that the Freemen of Newcastle resisted investing to render the river navigable.[48] The outcome of this political stalemate left South Shields the place where foreign-going ships discharged cargo, and passengers and crew joined and left ships. This history may explain why Shields even more than Newcastle continued to host diverse populations of sailors and others arriving by sea.[49]

Only political reform removed the deadlock between Newcastle and Shields, enabling the modernization of industrial infrastructure. Gateshead, Tynemouth and South Shields received parliamentary representation after 1832, while the Municipal Corporations Act, 1835, permitted the towns to incorporate. South Shields became an independent port in 1848, incorporated by charter in 1850, despite opposition from local firms, some absentee-owned. Finally, the River Tyne Improvement Act, 1850, placed jurisdiction over the harbour in the hands of a commission representing all four riverside towns: Newcastle, Gateshead, North Shields and South Shields.[50] Consequently, piers to protect the harbour were erected at South Shields and Tynemouth, the river banks were stabilized, the river dredged, and the channel straightened and deepened, permitting large vessels to travel upriver 3 miles beyond Newcastle.[51] Other improvements included new bridges, docks and deep water quays, coal and shipping staithes.[52] Regional power struggles thus shaped the town's involvement in global industry.

## The wealth of its industries

With Tyne Improvement, as it was called, South Shields and the Tyne boomed. In the process, South Shields became interdependent with and shaped by sites across Britain and the globe, including Britain's formal and informal empire. Annual coal exports quadrupled from 5.25 million tons after mid-century to 21.5 million tons in 1923, while revenues grew from £19,300 in 1851 to £73,700 in 1860, and £261,200 in 1881.[53] Shipbuilding absorbed nearly 30 per cent of British steel production, creating an iron boom from the 1860s that stimulated Tyne and Tees metal trades, shipbuilding and engineering. By century's end, only vestiges remained of such major industries as salt, supplanted by interdependent heavy industries that drove South Shields and the Tyne into and through the 'second' Industrial Revolution. From 1850 to 1950 these included the coal-carrying coasting trade, iron and steel, shipbuilding and marine engineering, and ship repair. The region's disproportionate stake in this handful of industries, part of an intensifying world-scale division of labour, rendered localities such as South Shields vulnerable to fluctuations in global demand far beyond their control.[54]

Tyne shipping and shipbuilding, for instance, produced ephemeral benefits for local people. Both arose for the purpose of transporting coal, yet as late as 1740 South Shields possessed only four shipowners and four ships. Coal exports alone filled 600 colliers a year in Shields harbour, but the ships were not locally owned. Naval warfare between 1776 and 1815, however, increased local ownership by 1834 to fully one-third of the 928 ships and 194,712 of tonnage registered in Newcastle. By 1860, with 336 vessels worth over half a million pounds, South Shields shipping came third after Newcastle and North Shields in volume, tonnage and value within the Tyne, so remaining until the Great War.[55] In 1882, the Tyne ports in turn came second only to London in number of vessels, second only to Liverpool in tonnage.[56] Local control proved short-lived, however. Mid-century Tyne shipowners predominated in investors of modest means, such as widows and tradesmen, but in 1864, three local firms merged to form the Tyne Shipping Company. Thereafter, professional shipowners and wealthy coalowners overtook small shareholders, producing vertical integration in the coal industry and monopolism in shipping, which ultimately passed from local control.[57]

South Shields' major contribution to shipbuilding proved similarly contradictory. The industry likewise developed from the need for ships to carry coal, but also articulated with armaments, engineering and iron.[58] In 1826 George Rennoldson founded the town's first marine engineering works in Wapping Street, followed by Thomas Dunn Marshall, using Wallis' old yard. In 1839 Marshall built the Tyne's first iron vessel, the passenger steamer *Star*. This transition from wooden to iron shipbuilding initiated a new era for the town and the region.[59] By the late nineteenth century, Britain produced 80 per cent of the world's ships, 40 per cent of these in the Northeast. Palmer at Jarrow and Armstrong at Elswick, Newcastle, built warships for the world. Swan Hunter Wigham Richardson built passenger liners and the Smith Dock Company built tugs, trawlers and drifters.[60] The industry, the largest in the Tyne, proved susceptible to euphoric booms followed by brutal depressions, the most violent between the First World War and the peace that followed.[61]

Within this mammoth industry, South Shields inhabited a niche. No South Shields firm produced battleships or oil tankers.[62] Only Readhead's boasted a sufficiently large operation to rank among the country's 31 important shipbuilders, producing relatively modest vessels nonetheless.[63] Still, by 1847, over two miles of river frontage boasted docks and slips sufficient for repairing 21 laid-up vessels, 11 shipyards for wooden shipbuilding and two for iron.[64] By 1858, of 44 shipbuilding and ship-repairing companies in the Tyne, 14, almost a third, were located in South Shields. They included Marshall's iron building yard, producing mainly steam tugs, which he also developed, as well as engines for Sunderland shipbuilders. After Marshall's son relocated operations north of the river to Howden, two of his managers, John Readhead and John Softley, established a shipyard in South Shields in 1865. There they built collier brigs and other small craft, some for the Baltic trade. Bankrupted by the depression of 1874, Readhead, an engineer, recapitalized, expanding operations in 1881 and again in 1905, into Shields' largest shipbuilding firm. Engineering firm J.P. Rennoldson & Sons expanded into shipbuilding in 1890, specializing in tugboats, including the *SS Titan*, 'the most powerful tug afloat', built for the Suez Canal Company in 1898. Another South Shields' firm, J.P. Eltringham & Co., produced mainly marine boilers but also some ships and, with Rennoldon's and Marshall's, helped make the Tyne steam-tug producer for the world: 'Shields built tugs became known the world over for the staunchness of their build and the excellence of their engines.'[65] As the scale of mid-century ships outstripped existing infrastructure, Shields firms stabilized otherwise volatile employment by specializing in the more prosaic function of ship maintenance and repair.[66] The thousands of workers these industries demanded massively expanded and transformed South Shields' population between 1841 and the First World War, connecting the town with the wider world not only through the flow of goods and wealth but also people.

## A swelling tide

South Shields became enmeshed with a protean global system not simply through the vast impersonal structural processes unleashed by industry, empire building and war, but through thousands of individual choices and mundane movements. Together, these remade South Shields and the Northeast repeatedly over the centuries. The town's population tripled between 1563 and 1674, as coal shipping expanded. Regional population grew 161.77 per cent between 1674 and 1801 with the clustering of commercial services, shipbuilding, glassmaking, pottery, iron production and related industries based on cheap local coal.[67] Through these entwined processes, the town and the Northeast became appendages of the global system. For over a century, the industrial system extracted wealth without commensurate compensation from a succession of migrant labour forces from Britain, Ireland, Europe and other parts overseas, including the colonized world.

From the 1840s through the 1870s, a 'swelling tide of in-migrants' arrived in the Northeast, part of a massive and unprecedented global population shift.[68] Between 1851 and 1891, coal and related industries made Durham the fastest-growing county in Britain. Irish migrants arrived to work in iron and steel works, coke oven plants and mines, with miners from South Wales, Staffordshire, Cornwall and Derbyshire. Migration produced urbanization.[69] By 1851 over one-third of Britain's population lived in the 70 'large towns' of over 20,000, their growth rate twice the national average.[70] South Shields numbered among them, with 28,974 people in 1851. The town's population doubled between 1801 and 1841, from 11,011 to 23,072, doubled again by the 1871 to 45,336, and again by 1901 to 97,263.[71] Between 1851 and 1911 the percentage employed in heavy industry also doubled to 25 per cent, with large increases in shipbuilding, engineering and the metal trades. The town's chemical works and shipyards became the 'melting pot of the United Kingdom', attracting migrants from Yorkshire, Staffordshire, Lancashire, Norfolk, Derbyshire, Cornwall, Ireland and Scotland.[72] Irish migrants filled jobs in alkali works, no doubt due to the nasty, hazardous working conditions. Irish migration flowed to Durham and Northumberland at twice the national average throughout the nineteenth century. Although peaking nationally in 1861, substantial Irish migration to South Shields continued through the 1880s.[73] As late as 1911, South Shields had the fifth largest proportion of Scottish-born residents in the country: Newcastle and Tynemouth ranked second and third, respectively. Further, a trickle from Europe and beyond began in the mid-century, accelerating with the close of one century and the dawn of another. They outnumbered the Irish by 1911.[74] South Shields' population peaked at 122,000 in 1921, after which deindustrialization spurred net emigration for the balance of the century.

This diverse workforce encountered a harsh and volatile labour market not only due to the global enmeshment of its major industries, but also due to resistance from local employers and elites. Locally as nationally, the number and proportion of foreign-born sailors increased steadily after the 1849 repeal of the Navigation Act which had restricted 75 per cent of shipboard jobs to British subjects. An influx of Europeans, North and South Americans and others nearly trebled the percentage of foreign nationals aboard British ships. They increased from 7.92 per cent in 1855 to 21.14 per cent in 1900. By century's end, Swedes, Danes and Norwegians together constituted one-third of these.[75] South Shields filled up with sailors, both resident and non-resident, British and not. Tyne colliers alone employed 12,000 sailors in 1850, 4000 of them from South Shields. In 1841 these 4000 accounted for one-third of the adult male workforce, while an additional 1000 shipyard labourers, 700 shipwrights, 500 dock labourers, 200 sailmakers and ship chandlers, and arguably a proportion of the town's 200 public houses and 150 prostitutes, depended indirectly on the maritime industry. By 1891 mariners still made up over one-fifth of the town's workforce. A further 6.4 per cent laboured in the town's shipyards, while many of the remainder provided services to these workers.[76] South Shields became one of Britain's two major tramp shipping ports, where foreign and colonized sailors gained a foothold by working in the technologically backward, unreliable and poorest paid branch of the industry.[77]

Maritime labour proved disproportionately lethal due to chronic undermanning and overloading, and poorly paid as employers sought to outcompete railways for coal haulage. Shipwrecks and accidents exacted even higher death tolls among merchant seamen than miners. Between 1830 and 1870, fully 5–7 per cent of all ships registered in the Tyne sank; in the four years 1832 through 1835, 682 men or approximately 5 per cent of the maritime workforce drowned in collier wrecks.[78] As early as 1832 local Poor Law Guardians lamented the large number of widows on relief, 'ever... the case in Maritime Districts from accidents of death... happening at sea'.[79] Between 1851 and 1914 the job came to be seen as undesirable, a 'residual occupation'.[80] In the same years it drew an increasingly cosmopolitan seafaring population to South Shields. Shieldsmen in turn ranged far: Hodgson reported that 'I'll see you at the cross' became 'the farewell of Shields seamen in the Hooghly, the Canton River, or the Plate'.[81]

While shipboard divisions of labour have been analysed elsewhere, early twentieth-century crew lists show how men of diverse origins converged on South Shields, drawn by the maritime industry that bound the town to national and global economic rhythms.[82] Consider the *SS Newburn*, owned and registered in Newcastle. After a voyage that began in Newport in January 1907 and called at Naples in January, Novorossiisk, a Black Sea port, in February and Bremen in March, the ship paid off, releasing its crew in South Shields, on 29 March 1907. Of its 25 men, all six stokers originated in Greece and were born in Ithaca or Samos. The two stewards and the cook, even lower in the shipboard occupational hierarchy, came from Canton and Hong Kong. Yet these men, like the rest of the crew, reported residence in Britain. The Chinese lived at the same address, 57 Upper North Street, Liverpool, and the Greeks at various addresses in Bute Street in Cardiff's docklands. Although most of the remaining crew reported British birthplaces ranging from Dublin and Dundee to Gateshead and South Shields, two Able Seamen, the carpenter and the boatswain claimed birth in Norway, Copenhagen, Finland and Sweden. When the ship continued on to

Cardiff, Sulina, Alexandria, Antwerp and Barry, the stokers, all but two of them different men, remained Greeks. The catering crew again came from China, and several crewmen from Europe, including Milan and Switzerland.[83] The division of labour aboard this ship illustrated how global processes of migration fed industrial development, while particular industries and the workforce they attracted shaped the peopling and character of localities.

The town's other major occupations offered no more security than seafaring. Shipbuilding platers, drillers, riveters, caulkers, shipwrights, joiners, plumbers, painters, blacksmiths, fitters, electricians, riggers, upholsterers and other skilled as well as unskilled workmen reported twice daily for 'turns' with the same or different employers. As in any such casual occupation, chronic underemployment resulted, and between 1899 and 1914 outright unemployment ranged between 2.5 per cent and 23.2 per cent.[84] Until 1872, County Durham's coalminers remained subject to an annual bond tying them in debt peonage to a single employer. Despite formidable union and political organization thereafter, the work remained perilous and backbreaking, punctuated by lethal accidents, explosions and labour strife. The paternalism of Durham's fusion of Church, state and coalowners aggravated the industry's susceptibility to national and global market shifts, to which wages were tied.[85] Working conditions in the chemical industry likewise remained notoriously brutal, and dock work casual.[86] The town's major occupational groups, maritime, shipyard, chemical and mine workers, thus remained throughout the industrial boom insecurely and casually employed and poorly remunerated.[87] That skilled and often unionized workmen, so-called labour aristocrats, could remain so vulnerable speaks to the nature of the system. Profitability rested on low wages and the maintenance of a 'reserve army' of unemployed. Employers fostered divisions within this reserve army by recruiting strike breakers from the Orkneys, the Shetlands and Scotland in the keelmen's strike of 1831, and from Staffordshire, Nottinghamshire, Derbyshire, Cornwall and South Wales as well as Ireland in the 1840s.[88] Irish migration came to be viewed by some as 'a terrible racial invasion', harbinger of depressed wages and working conditions. 'Racial tension' and 'Anglo-Irish race riots' resulted.[89] Migrants thus proved integral to local, national and global productivity and prosperity at the same time as their presence assisted employers in minimizing workers' share in this prosperity.

With hindsight, the region's success appears fragile and transitory, narrowed to coal, shipbuilding and heavy engineering, dependent on extractive industries and export markets vulnerable to international competition and to global shifts beyond local control. Export and investment, on which Tyneside's and indeed most industrial economies increasingly relied, proved inherently unstable. Substantial unemployment became normative, even in prosperous years, while Northeastern industries' vertical integration produced chain reactions, imploding the local economy in recurrent crises. Reliance on these industries exposed Tynesiders to violent trade cycles and market fluctuations that ruined individual companies. Each drop in the market expelled emigrants from industries such as iron and steel, occurring in 1858, 1862, 1868, 1879, 1886, 1894, 1904 and 1909. This in turn produced labour conflict. As the country's export base shifted from textiles to heavy industry, severe unemployment, paradoxically, intensified in Tyneside as in other regions experiencing the 'second' Industrial Revolution.[90]

As early as 1851 fully one-quarter of working-class households lived in poverty and two-thirds in overcrowded housing. Reports by local Medical Officers of Health show that even during the late nineteenth-century boom years, working people bore the brunt of violent business cycles and consistent severe deprivation. Of 270 deaths among adult males in 1875, only 10 were attributed to 'old age': of the remainder, 133, or fully 49 per cent practised just 6 occupations, including 47 seamen, 24 labourers, 19 shipwrights, 17 pitmen, 15 chemical workers and 11 master mariners. Disproportionate infant mortality and tuberculosis, correlating with depressed trade, likewise dogged South Shields into the mid-twentieth century. The local elite including landlords and the water company actively obstructed amelioration.[91] Instead of local reinvestment or redistribution, the riches South Shields' industries produced were systematically expropriated to London and beyond, draining wealth from Northeastern workers, migrant and native alike.[92]

In the late 1920s investigator Henry Mess enumerated several measures of social deprivation from which Tyneside suffered almost uniquely in Britain. Within the region Gateshead and South Shields, the largest towns on the south bank, fared worst. Rates of tuberculosis and infant mortality stood unmatched anywhere in the Kingdom but the most impoverished London boroughs. Related overcrowding, attributable to low wages, was exacerbated by a normative house size substantially smaller than elsewhere in Britain. 'The Tyneside we deplore', Mess emphasized, 'was the product of a long period of prosperity.'[93] This local social formation characterized by working-class immiseration took shape not only within global markets but within local power relations.

## Woven together in their destinies

Some scholars have counted South Shields among 'company towns' such as Jarrow, Wallsend, West Hartlepool or Barrow-in-Furness. In Shields like these other localities, employers such as Readhead and Rennoldson reinforced their workplace labour control through political control of local government. Unlike Jarrow, Hebburn, Elswick or Wallsend, however, dominated by single firms, South Shields' shipbuilding industry remained decentralized and diversified, relying on several niches including small steamships of around 50 tons, tugboats, and ship maintenance and repair, operated by several companies.[94] Likewise, no single firm controlled local politics: rather an oligarchy composed of shipowners, shipbuilders and other local elite: into the twentieth century, the same men appeared as mayors, members of the town council, poor law guardians and other civic leaders.

In the eighteenth century, effective municipal government comprised a 'select vestry' of 24 men including Isaac Cookson, shipbuilders Thomas and John Wallis, Nicholas Fairles and Simon Temple, owner of Templetown colliery. The town's first civic organization, the 'Lawe Newsroom', formed on 20 February 1788, consisting largely of shipowners. In the 1830s shipowners used their influence to restrict the electoral borough to South Shields and Westoe. By excluding Jarrow, Monkton and Heworth, they controlled the seat until 1903.[95] Local MPs included rope manufacturer Robert Ingham, shipbuilding scion John Twizel Wawn and James Mather, son of a shipowner.[96] Robert Wallis served twice as mayor in the 1860s, and John Readhead, president of the local Conservative Association, became an Alderman and Mayor twice (1893–94), among other offices. Members of the Rennoldson dynasty filled numerous local offices including Guardian, Education Committee, Alderman and Mayor (1891–92), while Richard Shortridge the glassmaker served as a senior magistrate.[97] Still, as early as 1850 and consistently thereafter, migrants from overseas appeared in the electoral rolls, decades before substantial working-class representation, which awaited the electoral reforms of the 1880s. The Jewish community alone contributed several magistrates and other municipal officials to the growing town.[98]

Local industries' dependence on government contracts and distant markets and consumers further blunted the intensity of Victorian class conflict, for employers credibly claimed to lack control over crucial aspects of labour conditions. Slackness of trade could be represented as the fault of the state or of international competition.

When local jobs depended on state funding of investment goods such as railroads, battleships and other infrastructure locally as well as overseas, or on fluctuating global demand for local commodities, employers could appear as much victims as their workers.[99] In the latter sense the local economy depended 'on the subordination of other economies' including colonial ones both formal and informal, forming, arguably, an appendage of Britain's military-industrial complex.[100] Even during the town's prosperity many industrial resources remained out of local control. The Dean and Chapter of Durham, later the Ecclesiastical Commissioners, continued as the town's major landlord. Landowners such as Lords Londonderry and Durham retained ownership of subsoil coal. Major industries founded by non-resident entrepreneurs such as the Cooksons and Brandlings passed by the twentieth century into the hands of distant companies and banks. Finally, the region depended on exports rather than local consumption and on a narrow, volatile and increasingly competitive global market.[101] This lack of local control or accountability increasingly characterizes industrial societies whose major industries become oriented to global markets, rendering South Shields paradigmatic for understanding ongoing processes of globalization.[102] However repugnant some of their tactics, the local elite exercised minimal control.

The people of South Shields thus remained, to borrow Mess' phrase, 'woven together inextricably in their destinies' not only with one another and the industries that drew them to the Tyne, but also with unseen producers, consumers and industries across the globe.[103] When Tyneside industries faltered at the turn of the twentieth century, the people of South Shields found themselves at the mercy of distant forces, states, banks and industrialists.

Britain's relative industrial decline originated in the *fin de siècle*, affecting Tyneside with particular ferocity by the 1920s. The regional economy rested on three of Britain's four 'ailing giants', declining staple export industries including coal, merchant shipping, shipbuilding and textiles. All faced international competition, compounded by technological obsolescence, economic protectionism, disarmament and slack trade due to interwar economic instability.[104] Shipping remained the single most depressed of all Britain's depressed staple industries throughout the interwar years.[105] The dramatic contraction of shipping in turn reduced demand for Tyneside's other major industries: shipbuilding, ship repairing, marine engineering, iron, steel and coal. Reduced international trade rendered the region's historically advantageous proximity to overseas markets nugatory, while it remained geographically distant from expanding domestic demand in the south. Global war demonstrated coal's vulnerability as the German, Baltic and Russian markets, accounting for 80 per cent of output, became inaccessible.[106] Coalminers' unemployment stemmed from mechanization and mismanagement at home as well as depressed demand due to diminution of trade and foreign protectionism.[107] The 1920s and 1930s saw only further constriction as European coal produced in younger mines with newer equipment supplied Continental markets. The gradual but inexorable shift to oil, electricity and water power aggravated coal's distress.[108]

By 1900 foreign competition had also eroded British shipbuilders' market share, which fell to 60 per cent between 1900 and 1914. As late as 1906 Tyneside's production alone equalled that of the entire US industry, exceeded Germany's and remained triple that of Holland and ten times that of Japan. The logical and historical consequence: an early twentieth-century crisis of oversupply. Reprieved by wartime demand, local firms endured a slump with the outbreak of peace, exacerbated by foreign competition. London-based bankers who now controlled capital proved reluctant to invest.[109] Yet as late as the 1920s shipbuilding and ship repair remained the Northeast's largest single industry. By 1925 only four shipbuilders survived in South Shields of 20 in the Tyne: J. Readhead & Sons with four slips, Charles Rennoldson & Sons Ltd, also with four, J.P. Rennoldson & Sons with three slips, and Brigham and Cowan Ltd, who had purchased Hepple's in 1919, with two slips. Additionally, 11 dry docks remained, owned by the Tyne Dock Engineering Company, John Readhead & Sons, Middle Docks and Engineering Company, and Brigham and Cowan. In 1930 the Tyne, with 15 surviving firms and a total of 96 boat slips, still produced more tonnage than the entire German industry.[110] Postwar assaults on labour including wage cutting, speed up and understaffing produced astonishing levels of unemployment even before the global depression of the 1930s.[111]

Chronic unemployment produced by Northeastern reliance on export and investment industries intensified after the war. Structural unemployment appeared intractable, never lower than the 26 per cent it reached in 1929, it peaked at 61 per cent in 1923 and 70 per cent in 1931.[112] A Ministry of Labour investigation in 1934 concluded that the global industries underwriting Tyneside's long boom could never return to pre-1914 levels. The very landscape reflected this, with 'so many abandoned pits, closed shipyards, derelict buildings and unemployed men' as well as 'dreary and forbidding rubbish heaps'.[113]

## A steady exodus

The turn of the twentieth century, when overseas migrants became visible nationally, thus coincided with the onset of regional depopulation and dire unemployment. Although South Shields continued to grow until the 1920s, the population of the Northeast as a whole peaked around 1880, and began to diminish through net out-migration, spurred by industrial malaise.[114] This population movement reflected the aggregation of numberless individual responses to economic slackening. Perceptible only in retrospect, decisions to migrate responded to relative industrial growth rates in the South which began to exceed those in the North from 1891.[115]

From the late nineteenth century onwards, overseas migrants fleeing dislocations in their own places of origin thus arrived in a local economic milieu from which even the limited opportunities of the boom years were ebbing. They replaced native-born emigrants escaping local industrial stagnation and accompanying distress.[116] Peaking in 1921 at 122,400, South Shields' population steadily diminished for the balance of the twentieth century. Between 1921 and 1931 the region lost 148,496 people, all but 19,000 of them in 'a steady exodus from the area which has taken place since the time of the General Strike', whose 1926 defeat perhaps deepened working people's sense of futility.[117] The arrival of Jewish, Scandinavian, Arab and other settlers before and during the First World War thus coincided with a moment of acute economic and cultural crisis.

## The folk of Shields and the world

The globalization of South Shields' population over the course of several centuries holds lessons for British and world history. From earliest times South Shields became interdependent with the wider world through flows of wealth, goods and, not least, people. Migration manifested an ongoing response to capitalist expansion. South Shields arguably exemplified many industrial boom towns worldwide, drawing migrants from near and far into unstable industries and new social milieux. Individual encounter and integration proved contingent on local configurations of class, gender and power that shifted repeatedly between 1841 and 1939. Paradoxically, the town's increasing integration into regional, national and global systems removed control from local hands, leaving migrants and natives alike vulnerable to decisions and processes beyond their control. The town's rise and decline thus typified the volatile trajectory of boom and bust common to numerous localities in the toils of global market forces. Investigating the social and cultural processes emerging from this historical context illustrates how geopolitics have impinged on individuals in the most intimate areas of their lives, from workshop to dinner table to connubial bed. The chapters that follow reconstruct and consider relations between migrants and natives within this context, showing how cultures of inclusion and exclusion have taken shape through local, global and imperial processes.

# 2

# A Stable and Homogeneous Population? Overseas Migrants in South Shields, 1841–1901

> We have a class of croakers in Shields, as mad as the mere Irish, who bawl out Shields for Shieldsmen! scarcely knowing what they say. Why, take from our population all those whose grandfathers and grandmothers were born elsewhere, and you would not have many scores left.
>
> W. Brockie, *Family Names of the Folks of Shields Traced to their Origins, with Brief Notices of Distinguished Persons, to which is Appended a Dissertation on the Origin of the Britannic Race* (South Shields: T.F. Brockie & Co., 1857), 1

Echoing contemporaries of folklorist William Brockie, antagonists of recent migrants frequently contrast a racially and culturally pure and static British past to a disrupted and unstable present and future.[1] The reasons for this counterfactual discourse merit exploration in their own right.[2] Yet its persistence demands investigating the part overseas migrants took in nineteenth-century localities such as South Shields. Alarm about small numbers of post-colonial or other migrants invites comparison with previous ones. Examining Victorian migrants' numbers, class and gender composition, settlement patterns, cultural practices and relations with native Britons repudiates views that recent migrants have threatened a hitherto stable and homogeneous population and culture.

Scholars have focused, rightly, on short-distance 'mundane movements' characterizing most British and European migration. Others have produced studies of internal migrants such as the Irish.[3] Still, dismissing migrants from outside the British Isles as numerically, thus culturally, negligible in the making of British society leaves unchallenged views of recent migrants as unprecedentedly destabilizing, based on linguistic, confessional or cultural differences or ephemeral 'values'.[4] The next three chapters will reconstruct where nineteenth-century overseas migrants originated; how many lived in South Shields and where; their occupational, class and other characteristics; whether and how they maintained and reconstructed kin and cultural networks and institutions; and how they lived, worked and married with natives of South Shields and other Britons.

This evidence reveals a diverse array of people originating overseas lived in South Shields from the time records became available. Absent comparable studies of other British towns, aggregate data show South Shields typical rather than anomalous in containing a significant and growing number and proportion of people from abroad. Like migrants from elsewhere in Britain, they proved highly mobile. Like long-distance migrants generally, they proved mostly young men. Unlike the Irish, they lived and worked with native-born Britons, not only in the same occupations and neighbourhoods but in the same households and families. Their mobility in Britain and globally repudiates the view of British culture and society as homogeneous and monocultural. Migrants from Europe and the colonized world participated in the making of local culture and British society, providing labour, skills, capital and services to key industries producing Britain's industrial boom.

## Mundane migration?

Documenting population fluidity may seem redundant. Britain's diverse and dynamic industrial working class has long been recognized for pioneering an increasingly mobile and global proletariat.[5] Far from disruptive, long-distance migration proved a normal part of life among pre-industrial professionals, artisans, merchants and unskilled workers.[6] They repeatedly adjusted their migratory patterns in response to commercial and industrial development, state formation and state impositions.

Ubiquitous in pre-industrial Europe, migrants faced encroachment from the sixteenth century onwards by states seeking to control valuable labour and exclude political radicals.[7] British settlement legislation in 1662, 1714, 1740 and 1744 purged internal migrants from relief rolls and criminalized them as vagrants, discouraging long-distance migration in favour of seasonal and circular movements, or emigration to the Caribbean, Virginia and New England. In 1662 the Halmote Court of the Dean and Chapter of Durham made South Shields householders financially liable for any lodger or sub-tenant who subsequently became dependent on parish relief, while Shields ferry boats were forbidden to transport paupers to the town. Threats to remove the destitute deterred plebeian migrants specifically, leaving the affluent untouched. Apparent localization of migration resulted, confining eighteenth-century long-distance movement to four major groups: Scots and Irish, Roma, petty chapmen, pedlars and travelling entertainers, and soldiers and sailors.[8] By the eighteenth century, few in the Northeast reported birth outside their parish of residence. Yet given developing industrialization, migration ought to have continued apace: faced with punitive state measures, migrants may simply have suppressed distant birthplaces, yielding a documentary record underplaying the extent of mobility.[9]

Countervailing evidence suggests substantial population fluidity through the centuries, a cultural practice sensitive to economic cycles and available work. Artisanal unions responded to late seventeenth-century economic instability with the 'tramping system' whereby unemployed or striking members searched for work from town to town, travelling by 'Shanks's pony' (on foot) supported by a succession of union houses of call. Prescribed tramping circuits covered hundreds or even thousands of miles, cutting across imputed parochialism as well as regional migration systems constituted by circular and cyclical mundane movements.[10]

By the nineteenth century, workmen in such substantial trades as boatmen, navvies, gas-stokers, chimney-sweeps, building tradesmen and agricultural labourers tramped regularly seeking work. So did hucksters and pedlars, maltsters, gypsies and travellers, Irish veterans, and old soldiers and sailors, the latter perhaps accounting for one-fifth of homeless people. Seasonal migrants followed both short and sprawling routes: tens of thousands of Scots and Irish harvested crops in England. The latter worked as railway navvies in the 1830s and 1840s. The Irish replaced Welsh and French hop harvesters, yielding to urban women and children by the century's end. Irish labourers planted potatoes at home, then worked in England from May through August, often for the same employer from year to year, returning to Ireland for the harvest. Like Italian and Asian labourers, the Irish sometimes worked in gangs hired out by a headman who collected their wages. British artisans and other workers moved back and forth across the Atlantic, and from sedentary to migratory occupations during the life course, or even seasonally.[11]

As agriculture declined through the nineteenth century, the annual journey to seasonal employment became a relentless search for any work at all, rendering migration permanent. Circular movement intensified and peaked between 1850 and 1914, while chain migration, in which emigrants joined distant kin and compatriots, accelerated. These patterns became common to Britain and the Continent. Intensified commodification of land and labour as well as deliberate state policies of expropriation, nation building and persecution expelled unprecedented numbers into the global labour force.[12] As industrialization spiralled outwards from Britain to Europe, the Atlantic and beyond, artisans bearing technical knowledge traversed the globe, from Lancashire to Massachusetts, from Holland and France to Ohio, from Italy to Brazil to Pennsylvania, and back again.[13] Empire building, formal and informal, incorporated increasingly far-flung labour into European economic circuits. Labour systems overlapped and merged, linking Europe and the Atlantic with the Mediterranean, the Indian Ocean, Southeast Asia and the Pacific. Demand for raw materials generated massive exchanges of population, as over a million indentured Indians, Chinese and Pacific Islanders travelled to labour on plantations, mines and railways in the Caribbean, South and East Africa and Southeast Asia. Tens of millions more migrated independently, often in debt bondage: four million to Malaya alone. Hundreds of thousands of Chinese, Koreans, Japanese and Filipinos dispersed to Hawaii, Canada, the United States and Peru.[14] Britain's merchant navy too recruited tens of thousands of colonized mariners in Africa, India and the Caribbean as well as China and elsewhere, often bound by oppressive 'Lascar' or other labour contracts. Many such men might be abandoned or jump ship in British and European ports.[15]

However global in scope and scale, migration occurred within personal social and cultural formations, including family systems, local networks and regional solidarities. Kin or other collectivities might decide who could be spared or excluded: often the young, single and childless. Migrants followed chains of kin, co-villagers and compatriots to unfamiliar lands.[16] In this way, millions of mundane movements produced systemic population redistribution to growing labour markets such as England's Northeast.[17]

These global movements have been overshadowed by a scholarly focus on agrarian proletarianization and displacement that produced massive internal migration in Britain and Europe. County Durham, like other industrializing regions, saw unprecedented population concentrations, mainly due to mundane movements from rural hinterlands and adjacent counties. Yet long-distance migration proved significant in the 1830s and again between 1851 and 1881. The largest share between 1851 and 1911 came from Yorkshire, ranging between 26 per cent and

43 per cent. But the next largest groups came from Ireland, 7 to 23 per cent, and Scotland, 9 to 12 per cent, both exceeding numbers from nearby Cumberland and Lancashire.[18]

Political boundaries imperfectly marked cultural difference, in any case. Given longstanding industrial integration in the Tyne valley, migrants from urban and estuarial Northumberland crossed a political boundary but no great cultural one, while those from rural County Durham might enter a new and bewildering urban world without leaving the county of their birth.[19] Tommy Turnbull likened his family's 20 mile move from the village of Witton Gilbert, known to its inhabitants as Jilbert, to 'emigrating to Australia...we'd hardly ever see our relations...At Harton they called my father a "hillbilly" because he came from Jilbert, and he called them "sand-dancers" because Shields was on the coast.'[20] Likewise, passage from Ireland to the North of England took far less time and money than moving from South to North.[21] Increasing numbers migrated to and through South Shields from the Continent, the colonies and beyond in the course of the nineteenth and twentieth centuries.

As Table 2.1 shows, at every census people originating overseas lived in South Shields, and their number and proportion increased steadily throughout the nineteenth century. Between 1841 and 1871, this population doubled every ten years, from 32 to 63, 142 and 283, growing substantially thereafter, to 1550 by 1901. As a proportion of the town's population, those born abroad increased more than tenfold, from 0.14 per cent to 1.6 per cent by 1901. Including British-born descendants, customary recently, would boost these figures substantially.[22] The steady rise in number and proportion shows South Shields' overseas-born population grew with the town.

Table 2.1 also shows this growth corresponded to the rhythms of local industrial development. While South Shields' overseas migrant population at 1.38 per cent did not approach the national average of 0.2 per cent in 1841, it grew faster, exceeding the national average by 1901. In 1851 such migrants proved few compared to those in West coast towns already booming due to Atlantic trade and related textile production producing the 'first' Industrial Revolution. Liverpool had 1.4 per cent or seven times the proportion of people originating abroad as South Shields, with 0.2 per cent, Bristol 0.9 per cent, or 4.5 times, Manchester 0.6 per cent, or triple, and Birmingham 0.5 per cent, or 2.5 times as many. By 1871, when South Shields' overseas population had risen to 0.6 per cent, Liverpool still had 1.9 per cent, over three times as many, Manchester and Bristol 1.2 per cent apiece, or twice as many, and

*Table 2.1* South Shields residents born overseas compared to national figures, 1841–1901

| | South Shields | | | | England and Wales | | | | |
|---|---|---|---|---|---|---|---|---|---|
| | **Households** | **Persons** | **%** | **Town population** | **Foreign** | **%** | **Colonies** | **%** | **Foreign and colonies** |
| 1841 | 21 | 32 | 0.14 | 23,072 | 39,244 | 0.2 | 1088 | 0 | 0.207 |
| 1851 | 45 | 63 | 0.2 | 28,974 | 61,708 | 0.34 | 33,688 | 0.18 | 0.52 |
| 1861 | 91 | 142 | 0.4 | 35,239 | 101,832 | 0.51 | 51,572 | 0.26 | 0.77 |
| 1871 | 212 | 283 | 0.6 | 45,336 | 139,445 | 0.61 | 70,812 | 0.3 | 0.91 |
| 1881 | 352 | 490 | 0.86 | 56,875 | 174,372 | 0.67 | 94,399 | 0.36 | 1.03 |
| 1891 | 599 | 927 | 1.18 | 78,391 | 233,008 | 0.8 | 111,672 | 0.38 | 1.18 |
| 1901 | 956 | 1550 | 1.6 | 97,263 | 339,436 | 1.04 | 136,092 | 0.4 | 1.44 |

*Source*: England and Wales from *1841 Census Report: Enumeration Abstract I* PP1843 [496] XXII, 459; *1931 Preliminary Census Report: Tables* (London: HMSO, 1931) III Table I, 'England and Wales: Population 1801–1931', 1; *1931 General Census Report* (London: HMSO, 1950), Table LXX 'Birthplaces of the Population… 1851–1931', 169. G.B. Hodgson (1996 [1903]) *The Borough of South Shields: From the Earliest Period to the Close of the Nineteenth Century* (South Shields: South Tyneside Libraries), 179. Percentages for foreign-born from *1911 Census General Report with Appendices* PP1917/18 [Cd.8491] XXV, 217, expressed in persons per thousand in the original: those for colonial subjects figured by the author.

Birmingham slightly more with 0.7 per cent.[23] By 1891, however, South Shields like Manchester had 18 foreign nationals for every one thousand residents: only Cardiff, with 21 per thousand, and London, with 23 per thousand, had more.[24] By 1911, foreign nationals outnumbered the Irish locally by two to one, 1.6 per cent versus 0.8 per cent, while colonized people accounted for a further 0.2 per cent, one-quarter the size of the Irish population.[25] This influx correlated with local industrial development, particularly South Shields' emergence as Britain's second tramp shipping port after Cardiff. Still, as Table 2.1 shows, these percentages remained comparable to those elsewhere in Britain, exceeding the national average, 1.44 per cent, only in 1901, and then only slightly, at 1.6 per cent.

Given their size, neglect or dismissal of these populations in South Shields and Britain appears quite unjustified. These numbers compare to significant migrant populations in other places. Foreigners in the German Reich, for example, peaked in 1910 at 1.25 million or 1.9 per cent.[26] In France, foreign nationals amounted to 1 per cent in 1872.[27] More telling, between 1881 and 1933, the percentage of Jews in Germany's population actually fell, from 1.08 per cent to 0.76 per cent.[28] This shows numbers considerably smaller than 1.6 per cent occasioned concern, and scholarship. Colonial subjects in Britain are finally receiving due scholarly attention, but Continental migrants remain neglected, despite outnumbering them by 2:1 to 3:1 in South Shields and nationally by 2:1. Roughly equivalent proportions of these populations in other British towns suggest findings for South Shields may carry some general applicability.

Answering qualitative questions about cultural impacts or social relations demands analysing the size, origins and other characteristics of South Shields' migrant population. The manageable size of mid-century manuscript censuses permits intensive analysis, establishing patterns that persisted throughout the century.[29]

## Somewhere on the Continent

As sources of information about everyday life and social relations, the decennial or ten-year censuses of the nineteenth century leave much to be desired, especially compared with richer materials available for some European locales.[30] Censuses occurring once per decade ill capture working lives characterized by seasonal or circular migration and other short-term mobility.[31] Scholars estimate periodic censuses massively undercount migration, detecting only the most stable and probably affluent. Of 232,098 arrivals between 1880 and 1900, for example, the town of Bochum netted 10,807, while an estimated 719,903 arrivals and departures in the Ruhr 1848–1904 yielded a net growth of only 97,836. Prussia sustained a population loss of 190,000 from a gross 'population exchange' of 1.5–3 million in the decade 1895–1905.[32] Census evidence thus understates the number of migrants passing through South Shields in the century before 1939. Further, the nineteenth-century censuses were colour-blind: although approximately one-quarter to one-third of migrants came from the colonized world, nothing indicated their racial assignment.[33] This silence may indicate racial categories' relative unimportance to mid-nineteenth-century states as well as census-takers.[34] Despite these and other much lamented deficiencies, censuses, like other sources examined here, contain a wealth of evidence not yet mined effectively. They enable preliminary reconstruction of relations between South Shields' migrant and native populations in the decades after 1841.

Census categories presuppose, shape and contextualize the allegedly objective data filling them, and the British censuses reflect this.[35] Britain's first house-to-house census occurred in 1841: earlier ones, in 1801, 1811, 1821 and 1831, relied on aggregate figures submitted by the overseers of the poor and parish clergy.[36] In 1841 and after, however, each householder received a form or schedule to fill in. An enumerator recruited from among local 'Commissioners, Enumerators, Schoolmasters and Other Persons' collected individual household schedules and copied the data into a Census Enumerator's Book (CEB). Schedules were destroyed, but these CEBs, now microfilmed, remain available to researchers.[37]

The legibility and paleography of the CEBs present substantial challenges. Householders and enumerators made free with both orthography and geography: birthplaces recorded included 'Ipswich, Norwich', 'East Indies, Barbadoes' and 'Harburg, somewhere on the Continent'.[38] Enumerators filled in missing information by interviewing householders, resulting in fanciful rendering of many non-British surnames, such as Oiler for Heuler.[39] This procedure left much in doubt, yet the law provided hefty fines, ranging from 40 shillings to 5 pounds in 1841, for individuals 'refusing to answer, or questioning [the enumerator's] authority to require an Answer, or giving an Answer which he suspects to be false'.[40]

The 1841 census differed not only from previous censuses but also from those from 1851 forward, which specified individuals' birthplaces and their relationships to household heads.[41] In 1841, birthplaces appeared only vaguely, illustrating assumptions structuring the mental geography of census officials, enumerators and their informants.

Enumerators asked two questions about places of origin: 'Whether born in same county' in which enumerated; and 'Whether born in Scotland, Ireland, or Foreign Parts'. An answer of 'no' or 'N' to the first question implied birth outside the county of enumeration but in England and Wales. In the second column, 'S' indicated Scottish birth, 'I' Irish and 'F' 'foreign parts', that is, all other places.

Implying a deterritorialized definition of Britishness, explicit instructions confined attribution of birth in 'foreign parts' to 'those who are subjects of some foreign state and not... British subjects who happen to have been born abroad'. This simultaneously erased the colonial-born and returned emigrants' children, yielding the suspiciously low total of 1088 in Table 2.1.[42] Acknowledging as British those 'who happen to have been born abroad' reflected the centripetal as well as centrifugal movements British and European expansion generated. Some enumerators nonetheless labelled foreign-born individuals 'BS' for British subjects, while others placed the letter 'W' in the column intended for Ireland, Scotland and Foreign parts, indicating Wales' ambiguous status in some minds. These and other departures from prescribed form, like the prescriptions themselves, betray competing and inconsistent mental maps of Britain and the world beyond, hardly evidence of a consensual, homogeneous or unambiguously bounded nation.

In sum, the census of 1841 does not tell who among the population of South Shields was actually born in the town, and if not, where else. Birthplaces were expressed as one of five categories: (Y) born in County Durham, whether in South Shields or elsewhere; (N) born outside of County Durham but in England or Wales; or born in Scotland (S), Ireland (I) or Foreign Parts (F).[43] Still, despite their defects and silences, the CEBs yield significant information about overseas migrants to and even from South Shields.

This analysis will focus on migrants from outside the British Isles. Constraints of space and time have compelled the regrettable omission of Irish, Scots and Welsh as well as other internal migrants. Such comparison could only prove fruitful.[44] By rights internal migrants, colonial subjects were not considered foreigners in nineteenth-century enumerations. As they have been recently, however, it seems useful to attempt to establish the extent of their presence, with that of others born abroad.[45] Hence, the admittedly clumsy term 'overseas' migrants.

## Patterns of migration and settlement, 1841

The small numbers of overseas-born individuals enumerated in the 1841 census render statistical analysis absurd, yet presage patterns amplified as numbers increased throughout the century. Of a population of 23,000, as Table 2.2 shows, only 32 persons reported birth overseas, and only 21 households contained them, a ratio of 0.13.[46] Still, some preliminary but useful observations present themselves.

The striking age and sex composition of this population reflected the structural processes drawing men to work in Tyneside. Fifteen male heads of household made up nearly half of the 32 overseas-born residents, heading three-quarters of 21 households containing members born overseas. Since long-distance migrants tended to be men, particularly younger men, and industrial areas such as Tyneside attracted more men than women, this comes as no surprise.[47] Table 2.2 shows that households whose heads proved the sole member originating overseas ('overseas head') made up the largest category in 1841, accounting for 52 per cent of households, all but one male-headed. An additional three households with an overseas-born head and dependents also from abroad ('overseas families') appeared in 1841, making up 14 per cent of the total. Finally, two lone men appeared in the miscellaneous category for an additional 9 per cent. Twelve of these 15 male householders, almost half of 32 persons, proved the sole household member born overseas, their wives and children British-born.[48] Thomas Rayland, Frederick Coates and George Watley had married local women and six others English or Welsh women.[49] Richard Hagens and boatman John Coppin, both 60, remained single, perhaps widowed. John Birmingham had four children with assorted birthplaces and an elderly woman, Ester Ray, 70, possibly a relative, in the household, but reported no wife on census night. Hannah Thompson, the sole woman householder born abroad, lived with a British-born daughter and grandson, suggesting she, like Birmingham, may have been widowed.[50]

Only three households contained overseas-born members in addition to the head ('overseas families'). These included millwright Jacob Shure, glassmaker Christian Hang and performer Joseph Testor.[51] Shure, Hang and Testor had apparently married and fathered children in their places of origin or some third place before coming to Britain, in a process scholars call family migration. Throughout the century, as Table 2.2 shows, only a minority of migrants, never more than 18 per cent, brought dependents with them from abroad. Instead, like Barates the Syrian, they married and founded families in Britain, becoming integrated into local society and culture while contributing to it.

Throughout the century, however, Britons headed a significant proportion of households with overseas-born members, ranging between 24 per cent and 52 per cent ('British headed'). In 1841 three of these

Table 2.2 Composition of households containing members born overseas

| Household type | 1841 hh | % | 1851 hh | % | 1861 hh | % | 1871 hh | % | 1881 hh | % | 1891 hh | % | 1901 hh | % |
|---|---|---|---|---|---|---|---|---|---|---|---|---|---|---|
| Overseas headed | 11 | 52 | 14 | 31 | 21 | 23 | 72 | 34 | 148 | 42 | 250 | 42 | 418 | 44 |
| Overseas families | 3 | 14 | 6 | 13 | 19 | 21 | 35 | 16.5 | 57 | 16 | 108 | 18 | 163 | 17 |
| British headed | 5 | 24 | 22 | 49 | 47 | 52 | 92 | 43 | 120 | 34 | 184 | 30 | 298 | 31 |
| Miscellaneous | 2 | 9.5 | 3 | 7 | 4 | 4 | 13 | 6 | 27 | 7.6 | 57 | 9.5 | 77 | 8 |
| Total households | 21 | | 45 | – | 91 | – | 212 | – | 352 | – | 599 | – | 956 | – |

*Note*: The miscellaneous category included institutions such as the gaol and workhouse, households with no identified head, and households containing one member.

were women, including Mary Stephenson, an 'Independent woman', possibly widowed, who housed four children sharing her surname; the youngest, John, born overseas.[52] Annie Mackay, a wine merchant, reported her apparent son Christopher, 15, born abroad.[53] Of the others, Jane Arrowsmith, aged 18 and of no reported occupation, lodged two unnamed men originating abroad, and the aged Presbyterian Reverend Charles Toshach and his wife Sarah lodged overseas-born William and John Arrowsmith, aged eight and six, as well as Mary and Charles Arrowsmith, apparently their locally born elder siblings, aged 11 and 10. Perhaps these were grandchildren but these records do not say.[54] Stray children of overseas birth appearing in local households throughout the century suggest that for missionaries, businessmen or widowed seafarers, a port such as South Shields may have proven an accessible location to visit children placed with relatives or other caretakers. It may also indicate informal adoption.[55] Of those originating abroad in 1841 as later, most thus resided not in homogeneous migrant households, much less isolated enclaves, but with native Britons, most often kin.

In 1841 and after, migrants practised a variety of occupations, many demanding a degree of skill or modest capital. Reflecting the make-up of the local workforce, seafaring proved the largest single occupation among the overseas migrants of 1841, accounting for 5 of 16 occupied adults, all men.[56] Two more men, Thomas Rayland and John Coppin, both in their 60s, reported themselves boatmen, for a total of seven of 16 occupied adults (44 per cent) in the maritime industry. After mariners, two labourers and two millwrights brought the working-class portion of this population to 11 of 16 householders (69 per cent). Postman Peter Hull and skilled artisans Silvester Whaley, clockmaker, and glassmaker Christian Hang occupied the skilled artisanal and service stratum (19 per cent). Joseph Testor, performer, and Charles Pelternay, equestrian, the latter at a possible temporary address in the Market Place, skewed the sample in the direction of trades not otherwise substantial in the town, and likely itinerant. While many migrants thus proved mariners, many others brought welcomed skills and capital, contributing to South Shields' industrial development.

This was the make-up of South Shields in 1841. The population originating abroad remained sparse, over half adult men. Women and children from overseas proved few, as most migrant men, 10 of 16, had married British women, four of them (40 per cent) Shieldswomen. Of their 31 children, 24 or three-quarters had been born in Britain. Replicating the town's general class compression, no household in 1841 kept as many as two servants, necessary to free wives and daughters from routine housework for genuine upper-class leisure.[57]

Two households in addition to Reverend Toshach's proved sufficiently affluent to appear in City Directories, which listed less than 10 per cent of local households in 1827.[58] Wine and spirit merchants Mackay appeared under the proprietorship of Alexander Mackay. Between 1828–29 and 1834 the business passed to Annie, possibly his widow, who still held it in 1846, although by 1848 she had apparently retired, assuming the rentier status of 'shipowner'.[59] Christopher Mackay, possibly Annie's overseas-born dependent, appeared in 1846, a solicitor in Chapter Row, and in 1848 a 'master extraordinary in Chancery'.[60] Clockmaker Silvester Whaley also appeared, listed as Wherley, Silvester, in 65 King Street.[61] Although ephemeral in the documentary record, Wherley was apparently well-enough known and remembered by contemporaries, for in the 1850s Brockie recalled, 'A German, named Wehrli, settled some time ago in Shields as an importer of clocks, and the good people here not being able to pronounce or spell his name, altered it to Whirley or Wherely, which he complacently accepted and put on his signboard in King-Street.'[62] While most migrants in 1841 occupied humbler strata of the town's generally working-class population, the relative prominence of these overseas-born merchants shows migrants were not relegated to a marginalized underclass in Victorian South Shields. Throughout the century, they proved slightly more skilled and affluent than natives.

All of this suggests that overseas migrants to South Shields proved typical rather than atypical of long-distance migrants to industrial towns across Europe. Only 3 of 21 households contained overseas-born kin apart from the household head, reflecting younger and single men's greater likelihood of moving long distances.[63] The skills and capital they brought with them corroborate the observation that transnational migration created a 'brain drain' and a skill drain of sending societies' 'most mobile, active and enterprising' members, a form of economic aid to receiving societies.[64]

Since this was the first census enumerating individuals, how long people had lived in South Shields remains opaque in most cases. The presence of locally born Mary Moray, 25-year-old daughter of William Moray, and Susannah Joseph, 17, daughter of Peter Joseph, suggested their overseas-born fathers had resided in County Durham since the 1820s and 1830s, respectively.[65] Other families had ranged far: children's birthplaces in households headed by Annie Mackay, Mary Stephenson and John Birmingham marked the indirect paths they had followed to and sometimes from South Shields. Even Peter Josephs and William

Moray may not have remained in South Shields throughout their daughters' lives. Information about co-resident children, most of whom left home by their late teens, can thus yield inclusive but not exclusive measures of local longevity.[66]

The diversity and mobility of South Shields' population was not exceptional, but rather characteristic of nineteenth-century working people. Broader scholarship indicates longstanding residents such as Peter Joseph and William Moray proved exceptional, and peripatetic families such as Birmingham, Mackay and Stephenson typical. A respected scholar characterized conclusions drawn from evidence about stable residents alone as 'worthless' in illuminating the lives of the majority.[67] Data for 1841 show that even before the industrial boom drawing migrants to South Shields, local society hardly remained closed or homogeneous. Individuals and families from Europe and the colonized world lived in the town, and some, such as Grace Mather and Sylvester Wherley, became prominent. Compelling evidence of the fluid and changeable nature of local populations emerges in the effort to locate the overseas-born of 1841 in 1851.

## Persistence, disappearance and self-naturalization

Affirming rates of mobility common to Europe and other industrial societies, South Shields' population originating abroad not only expanded in the intervening decade, but was all but entirely replaced. Of 32 overseas-born individuals present in 1841, only three remained in 1851: John Coppin, now destitute and in the workhouse at age 70; Peter Hull, 76, still residing with his wife Hannah and daughter Sarah, and Peter Joseph, 95, and his wife Susannah.[68] Of them, two were married, held in South Shields by family ties; the third, with no kin to fall back on, ended in the workhouse. All were advanced in age, affirming scholars' view of migration as a young man's endeavour.

Fuller information in 1851 yields a more detailed picture of these three men, and what their persistence in South Shields might mean. First, their birthplaces no longer remained a mystery: Coppin proved a native of Switzerland, Hull of Norway and Peter Joseph of Nantucket, roughly reproducing the proportions from the old and new worlds for the balance of the century.[69] Peter Hull remained a post office messenger, while Coppin, reduced to the workhouse and Joseph to parochial relief, reported their occupations as 'mariner', an unlikely step up from boatman in Coppin's case. Peter and Susannah Joseph still resided in Wellington Street near the old docks, while Peter, Hannah and Sarah

Hull, the latter now a teacher at age 13, had moved from Queen Street near the Market Place to nearby Salem Street. Coppin had left his residence in Comical Corner for the Union Workhouse in German Street.

Coppin, Hull and Joseph shared additional characteristics distinguishing them from many of the 29 people who disappeared in the preceding ten years: as males they retained their surnames lifelong; two of the three were married, giving them reasons to settle in South Shields and making their households easier to identify due to the presence of other family members; and all three were elderly, their travelling days over.[70] The vast bulk of those originating overseas in 1841, the most mobile and occupationally marginal, had departed South Shields by 1851, whether via Shanks' pony or the grave.[71] Those remaining proved male, aged and in two of three cases married.

Three individuals of 32 amounts to roughly a rate of 9 per cent for a 10-year period, remarkably low compared to rates for British industrial populations later in the century, but comparable to those in American towns and cities.[72] Population in mid-century Britain proved notoriously fluid, with numerous workers 'on the tramp'.[73] Most of the overseas-born performers, labourers, artisans and mariners, for whom mobility remained a condition of employment, disappeared from South Shields between 1841 and 1851.[74] This likely reflected the greater propensity of those who migrate once to move again, biasing the record to more stable, affluent individuals. This axiomatic 'mover-stayer dichotomy', with high rates of mobility generally, characterized industrializing societies from Britain and Europe to Asia, Africa and North America.[75] This may account for the disappearance of artisans such as Christian Hang or the brothers Shure. In successive censuses, South Shields' overseas population exhibited progressively higher rates of intercensal persistence, consistent with scholars' observation of industrial working-class populations' stabilization or 'thickening' by the century's end.[76] Still, the extraordinary mobility of this small sample of overseas migrants suggests more work might profitably be done in measuring their persistence rates against those of internal migrants.

Even migrants who had departed left traces on the town. Between 1841 and 1851, in addition to three surviving individuals, the households of several others remained without the overseas-born head. Mariner William Moray's widow Sarah, 67, now a tripe merchant, and their daughter Mary, 29, continued to live in West Holborn as in 1841.[77] Born in Bristol and South Shields, respectively, neither woman would appear in aggregate tallies of overseas migrants, despite prior decades of life in a household headed by someone from abroad. Likewise, Frederick Coates' widow Elizabeth resided next door to her married daughter Elizabeth and son-in-law Alexander Wilson, co-resident in 1841.[78] The descendants of overseas migrants thus lived on in South Shields, blending imperceptibly, as Brockie suggested, into the local population, their influence on local culture and society hidden from the documentary record.[79]

Finally, two individuals reporting birth overseas in 1841 underwent an apparent change of natality by 1851. William Arrowsmith, 17, the right age to be Charles Toshach's lodger of 1841, reported birth in Jarrow.[80] Most spectacular in this regard, Chief or Chiefton Smith proved the sole individual found in 1841, 1851 and 1861, residing throughout, remarkably, in the same location, Wawn Court. This unfashionable riverside address also accommodated his wife Mary and assorted children and relatives. Chief Smith reported himself born overseas in 1841, but in South Shields in 1851. In 1861 he once again claimed birth abroad, specifically France.[81] Claiming French birth jibed with his occupation, alternatively as a labourer and 'glasman' [*sic*], the latter common in South Shields as glass manufacturers imported French artisans to establish their production processes.[82]

Whether individuals changed their minds about their birthplaces out of fear, expediency, whim or levity remains opaque. The first British census of 1801 aimed explicitly to assess manpower for the Napoleonic Wars. Families decades later may have misreported ages and birthplaces to protect husbands or sons from conscription or naval impressment, afflicting South Shields until 1841.[83] Fears of taxation also surrounded several early censuses. Local birth, conversely, protected the destitute from removal.[84] More useful than attempting to establish the truth of William Arrowsmith's or Chiefton Smith's birth might prove the humbling recognition that the documentary record conceals as much as it discloses about human experience and motivation: others possibly hid distant birthplaces.[85] Whether circumspection, guile or playfulness motivated such changes of testimony, they confront scholars with fundamental limitations in pursuing the past. Much of this confirms the biases scholars attribute to the sources themselves. These cases enable insight into multiple experiences by differing historical actors, or even by the same one at different times. They also reaffirm Brockie's conviction that South Shields, like the British nation, comprised 'representatives... of every race of which British history has left any record'.[86]

Examining the whole overseas-born population of South Shields in 1851 shows this. The overwhelming majority recent arrivals, they continued to reflect surprisingly disparate origins. By 1851, migration had substantially augmented the Northeast's population: County Durham figured among a handful of urbanized areas with over 500 persons per square mile. South Shields had grown from 23,072 in 1841 to 28,974, a rise of 25.5 per cent. This placed it among England's 70 'large towns' of over 20,000, by then containing one-third of Britain's population. In the same decade the number of South Shields residents born abroad nearly doubled, from 32 to 63, distributed among 45 households, more than double those in 1841, now amounting to 0.2 per cent of the town's population, and outstripping the town's overall growth by 2:1.[87] In County Durham this figure was 0.3 per cent, representing 1273 of the county's 411,679 residents. Nationally, 100,755 of Britain's population of 20,959,477, or 0.52 per cent originated overseas, as shown in Table 2.1.[88] South Shields contained 63 of 1273 or 4.9 per cent of County Durham's foreign-born population, but 7 per cent of the County's population overall. The proportion of the town's population born abroad thus exceeded neither national nor county-wide averages, and cannot be thought anomalously large. Given mid-century mobility rates, moreover, these 63 people likely represented only a fraction of those passing through in the intervening decade.

The make-up of this population had changed, however. In 1841, two-thirds of household heads remained the sole member born overseas, but Table 2.2 shows that by 1851 this proportion had diminished to less than a third ('overseas headed'), 14. The larger number and proportion of residents born abroad appeared in dependents found in 23 British-headed households (British headed), perhaps due to reporting precise birthplaces rather than assigning British nationality as in 1841. In addition to Peter Hull and Peter Joseph, 16 overseas-born men headed households. Nine of them had only British wives and children and no dependents born abroad like themselves. Five of these came from the European Continent: Frenchmen Robert Henry Hazard, a cooper, and William McDonald, a glassmaker, Norwegian publican Henry Henderson, and mariners Nicholas Johnson, a Dane, and John Pearson, a Swede.[89] The balance came from British overseas possessions, including Canadian blacksmith Henry Knowles, shipwright John Brown of Quebec, retail dealer John August Noel from Kingston, Jamaica, and blacksmith John Williamson from the East Indies.[90] Between 1841 and 1851, family migration had thus increased at the expense of lone migrants.

Six households containing children, siblings or other adults had moved en bloc from Europe. Families such as that of Prussians John and Margaret Reack and their small son John were completed in Europe before moving to Tyneside. The entire family of general dealer Isaac and Blume Jacobs too apparently migrated together from Poland, including grown children Hyman, Henry and Sarah. Glassmaker Louis Amede, 34, his wife Mary, also 34, his brother Joseph, 20, and his son Louis, 11, all came from France, like previous glassmakers.[91] Dependent adult men and women born overseas had increased proportionally.

Many such households revealed evidence of indirect or 'step-wise' migration, consisting of multiple short moves, as well as of intermarriage that crossed national boundaries.[92] Such patterns are not of mere antiquarian interest, but suggest the ways industrial structures might shape personal lives, breaking down or solidifying occupational with cultural or linguistic endogamy. French glass flattener Napoleon Gaible had a Belgian wife, Augusta, and the couple shared their home with Augusta's brother Bartholomew Don and a third Belgian glassmaker, Peter Deward. They also accommodated Fanny Hindhaugh, a visitor from France. Belgian glassblower Emile Bouillet, 28, and his wife Elen, 23, from Birmingham, had their eldest child, Joseph, three, in France, and their second, Elic (Elise?) in Belgium. Only their infant son Ernest had been born in Britain, in nearby Sunderland.[93] A fourth glassmaker, French-born William McDonald, married an Englishwoman. The cluster of French and Belgian glassmakers suggests either recruitment by a local glassmaking firm or chain migration, in which individuals or couples moved to South Shields, perhaps after intermediate stops in Belgium, to join kin or compatriots already established there.

Migrant women's appearance throughout the century offers a useful corrective to the emphasis on lone men as archetypal migrants. Women originating overseas headed three households in 1851, including German widow Elizabeth Hoyler with her two small daughters Catharine, seven, and Christiana, five, and American-born widow Eleanor Gray, 64, living with her grown son James.[94] Wine and spirit merchant Grace Mather, 48, wife of local reformer and Abolitionist shipbroker James Mather, and daughter of Jamaican slaveholders, headed a household containing her brother-in-law and two servants.[95] Two other women, both with small children, American Matilda Sharp, 30, and Norwegian Ann Lackey, 33, described themselves as married or as mariners' wives, suggesting a living husband of unspecified origin.[96]

Returns for 1851 permit a precise account of migrants' places of origin, establishing patterns persisting throughout the century. Of a total of 63 in 1851, as Table 2.3 shows, exactly two-thirds, 42, came from the European Continent, residing in 25 households. One-third, 21, came

*Table 2.3* Origin of overseas-born residents of South Shields

| From the European Continent | 1851 | 1861 | From the (ex)-colonized world | 1851 | 1861 |
|---|---|---|---|---|---|
| France | 12 | 6 | Canada | 5 | 11 |
| German lands | 9 | 55 | West Indies | 4 | 3 |
| Poland | 5 | 3 | Jamaica | 4 | |
| Belgium | 5 | 2 | The United States | 3 | 6 |
| Denmark | 1 | 6 | America | 2 | 3 |
| Sweden | 1 | 5 | India | 2 | |
| Norway | 4 | 5 | East Indies | 1 | 5 |
| The Netherlands | | 4 | North America | | 2 |
| Italy | 1 | 3 | Australia | | 2 |
| Switzerland | 1 | 2 | Gibraltar | | 2 |
| Greece | 1 | | Madeira | | 2 |
| Portugal | 1 | 2 | | | |
| Spain | 1 | 2 | | | |
| Russia | | 10 | | | |
| Austria | | 1 | Subtotal colonies | 21 | 36 |
| Subtotal Europe | 42 | 106 | Grand total | 63 | 142 |

*Note:* Although Poland was not a nation-state in the nineteenth century, it is reported here as in the CEBs. Similarly, somewhat hazy distinctions among Canada, the United States and 'America' are reproduced.

from the Colonies or former colonies including the East and West Indies, Canada and the United States. These figures prompt several observations. First, all but 2 of 20 households containing colonial-born members housed only one, while this obtained in only 17 of the 25 households containing European members. Four of the former appear as youth lodging with native British relatives, suggesting transatlantic kinship networks within which young people might be sent 'home' to Britain temporarily or permanently.[97] Admittedly, three such 'children' were Thomas Delevoy, 19, a groom in the Russell Street household of surgeon James Eddowes, Mary Beeson, 19, and Mary Elizabeth Phillips, 18, all from the West Indies.[98] In contrast to lone colonial subjects, Europeans appeared more likely to move as families.[99] With the sole exception of George Gibson, an apparent grandson reported as a visitor, all children born in Europe remained with their parents, whether British or European, while Mary Beeson was the only colonial-born child living with a parent.[100] Among Continental migrants, women and children outnumbered adult men slightly (22:20 or 52 per cent versus 48 per cent), while among colonials these proportions were inverted: women and children amounted to only 10 of 21 (10:11 or 48 per cent versus 52 per cent). In 1851, therefore, migrants from the colonies tended to be professionals or children rather than working men and their families like Continental migrants. These numbers remain too small to make a strong case, but subsequent censuses continued to reveal divergent migration patterns for colonial as opposed to Continental migrants.

Migrants' diversity of origin shown in Table 2.3 not only challenges assumptions about British homogeneity but also problematizes scholars' bias towards studying visible migrant communities. This customary approach may exclude the majority of migrants who lived outside such enclaves. Except for mid-century French and Belgian glassmakers and the Jewish and German communities appearing later in the century, South Shields' migrant population proved disparate in origin and grew more so with each decade. The majority, significantly, did not inhabit clearly identifiable 'ethnocultural' communities, although less prominent networks appeared. The unexpected composition of South Shields' migrant population demands re-envisioning Britain's people, not as a collection of discrete and mutually exclusive communities, but as heterogeneous and interpermeated, continually remade through work, marriage, kinship and relentless mobility.

## Movers and stayers, 1851–61

Comparing households in 1851 with those persisting until 1861 affirms wives' and families' importance in keeping men rooted in South Shields. One-fifth of unattached men present in 1851, two of ten, remained in 1861, while a total of 11 families of 45, over one-quarter, survived in some form, a persistence rate more than twice that between 1841 and 1851. Of 18 households headed by overseas-born men in 1851, four, those of Henry Knowles, John and Margaret Reack, Robert Henry Hazard and Chiefton Smith, survived in 1861.[101] In addition, Stephen Lloyd, a lone lodger in 1851, had married and settled, and 'W.N.', an 81-year-old mariner from Gibraltar who may have been William Nesbitt, passed census night in the workhouse.[102] Households headed by Grace Mather, Eleanor Gray and Jane Hardy, the latter now widowed, also survived.[103] Most colourful appeared the case of German-born Elizabeth Hoyler and her daughters Catharine and Christiana. By 1861 coalminer Peter Hughes, Elizabeth's lodger in 1851, had captured the landlady's affections, assuming the role of husband and household head. Catharine, now 17, had become a servant in a nearby household in Slake Row Cottages.[104] Like Peter Josephs and William Moray before them, individuals remaining between 1851 and 1861 appeared held there by family ties. The sole apparent exception, if indeed he was William Nesbitt, seems, like John Coppin, to 'prove the rule', as his lack of kin may have forced his recourse to relief.

Confounding views of migrants and natives as discrete and bounded populations, several households previously consisting entirely of native Britons had acquired members born abroad by 1861. John and Jane Lillico, although locally born, had apparently moved to 'Canada West', there producing a son, James. Whether or not fortune smiled on them, Jane returned to South Shields in time for the birth of their daughter, Troth, barely 20 months later. She reported herself a widow at the time of the census four months after that.[105] Abraham Muncy of Halifax, Nova Scotia, first appearing in 1861, married local widow Jane Groat, present in 1851 but married to another mariner. Her four locally born children remained in Muncy's household in 1861.[106] Master mariner John Wright had apparently lost his wife Margaret, a Shieldswoman, between 1851 and 1861, acquiring a young Chinese-born wife, Mary. Richard Howse, a bachelor schoolteacher residing with in-laws in 1851, had by 1861 married and set up housekeeping with Hamburg-born Emily, producing four children. Between 1851 and 1861, Eleanor Harper lost her husband but acquired two Australian-born great-grandchildren, Elizabeth, three, and Richard, one.[107] These changes illustrate how newcomers became incorporated into local families and households, while natives might become migrants.

In the same decade, the town's population originating abroad more than doubled, from 63 to 142, residing in 91 households as opposed to 45. Overseas-born householders doubled, from 20 to 40: those heading otherwise British households grew 50 per cent, from 14 to 21. Whole families increased faster than migrants as a whole, and lone migrant men heading otherwise British households increased more slowly. The shift from lone migrant men marrying and settling in South Shields to the increasing arrival of whole families may reflect circular mobility yielding to unidirectional and finite migration, driven by economic and political upheaval in Europe.

Viewed in the national context, such figures prove far from disproportionate. Ninety-one households making up 142 overseas-born people amounted to 0.4 per cent of the town's population of 35,239, smaller than the proportion, 0.77 per cent, in England and Wales.[108] Table 2.3 shows their places of origin reflected patterns established between 1841 and 1851, differing only in the increasing concentration of Germans. The overwhelming majority of 84,090 'subjects of foreign states' then in Britain consisted of 73,434 Europeans, clustered in a handful of cities. London led with 30,057 in 1851 and 48,390 in 1861, Liverpool had upwards of 4000, Manchester and Salford 2035 in 1851 rising to 3086 by 1861, and Birmingham, Hull, and Brighton approximately 1000 apiece. No other British locality had as many as that.[109] South Shields' overseas-born population, 63 in 1851 and 142 in 1861, proved neither the largest nor anomalous within Victorian Britain, nor even within County Durham.[110] That South Shields, with modest proportions of overseas migrants, proved yet so diverse, demands further research into the composition of other British localities, reconsidering assumptions about their essential homogeneity.[111] Numbers and places of origin alone explain little about how migrants fare in localities however. Much hinges on the character of receiving societies as well as migrants' resources, skills and social networks. The position migrants occupied in South Shields' labour market bore this out.

## Migrants and labour markets

Hostility to migrants has often been attributed to employers' manipulation, exemplified by importation of Irish and other strike breakers. In France and the United States, native workers apparently monopolized skilled and lucrative work, leaving migrants with unskilled service occupations such as transport, administration, commerce and domestic labour.[112] Nineteenth-century Britain proved more complicated: migrants' experience varied by birthplace. Longer-distance migrants tended be older, to have planned the move carefully, and to arrive with more skills and capital than natives, while short-distance migrants had fewer such resources, proving less able to compete with local workers. This in turn influenced decisions to stay or move on. If migrants from distant places brought more skills and wealth to South Shields than mundane movers, this may explain various migrants' reception and integration in Victorian South Shields.[113]

Table 2.4 shows overseas migrants did prove affluent relative to the town's native population, bringing skills and capital to developing industry and commerce.[114] The vast bulk of occupied migrants in 1851 as in 1841 proved to be skilled workmen with a sprinkling of professionals and businesspeople. Measuring the overseas-born against the town's whole workforce reveals a higher proportion in stratum III, skilled working class, and far fewer in the bottom sections IV and V, the semi-skilled and unskilled. In addition to the continuing prevalence of mariners, ten in 1851, French and Belgian glassworkers accounted for the next largest occupational cluster of seven. The most stable householders reflected

*Table 2.4* Overseas migrants compared to South Shields' population by occupational class

| | | South Shields' population 1851 (%) | Migrants 1841 number (%) | Migrants 1851 number (%) |
|---|---|---|---|---|
| I | Professional | 3 | 0 | 1 (3) |
| II | Small master/shop | 18 | 2 (12) | 6 (17) |
| III | Craft | 23 | 11 (65) | 26 (74) |
| IV | Semi-skilled | 40 | 2 (12) | 0 |
| V | Labourer/pauper | 17 | 2 (12) | 2 (6) |

*Source*: Figures for South Shields from J. Foster (1979 [1974]) *Class Struggle and the Industrial Revolution: Early Industrial Capitalism in Three English Towns* (London: Methuen), 76. Figures in Table 2.5 show an emerging geographical division of labour. While nearly all European migrants in 1851 proved working class, several of those from the colonies were business-people or professionals. Only two of six in class II came from Europe: Italian William Gadola, an interpreter, and Henry Henderson, a Norwegian publican.[115] The sole individual in class V, conversely, hawker Hyman Isaacs, came from Poland.[116] This shows economic migration might take several forms: the privilege British diaspora exercised in colonial contexts coupled with residual family networks in Britain perhaps enabled them to amass wealth and compete more effectively with native Britons than European migrants could.

the make-up of South Shields' labour market, consisting of a generous leaven of three mariners, four glassmakers, two blacksmiths, a cooper, a shipwright, a retail dealer, a general dealer and a publican. All fell into occupational class III except for the publican in class II.

By 1861, a significant influx of Prussians and other Germans supplanted colonial subjects in dominating class II. The sole individual in class I, Grace Mather, came from Jamaica.[117] The overwhelming bulk of men in class III, 50 of 62, proved mariners, dwarfing all other occupations. This reflected the 1849 repeal of the Navigation Act that had restricted maritime employment to British subjects, coupled with Tyne improvement. Of 48 apparently unattached men in 1861, the vast bulk, 39, proved mariners, with a residuum of two glaziers, a mechanic, a labourer, a shoemaker, an interpreter and a grocer's traveller. All but ten were in their 20s and 30s. Most, regardless of occupation, hailed from the Baltic and North Sea, 27 in all (56 per cent), and 10 from America.[118] Overseas migrants engaged in nearly every major trade by 1871, although in highly variable proportions. Among men, only pilots, a notoriously closed occupation, excluded foreigners altogether.[119]

This reflected national patterns in which French, Germans and Italians, the three largest Continental groups in 1861, occupied distinct

*Table 2.5* Occupied overseas migrants from Europe versus the colonies, 1851 and 1861

| Class | | 1851 | | 1861 | |
|---|---|---|---|---|---|
| | | Colonies | Europe | Colonies | Europe |
| I | Professional | 1 | | 1 | |
| II | Small master/shop | 4 | 2 | | 16 |
| III | Craft | 7 | 19 | 19 | 43 |
| IV | Semi-skilled | | | 1 | 4 |
| V | Labourer/pauper | | 2 | | 6 |
| Total | | 12 | 23 | 21 | 69 |

*Note*: The Armstrong-Booth occupational classification scheme is explained in Armstrong, 'Use of Information about Occupation', 191–310, esp. 215–23, derived from *Census 1951: England and Wales General Report* (HMSO 1958), Appendix C: 'Constitution of the Socio-Economic Groups and Social Classes', 214–20; also see K. Schürer and H. Diederiks (eds) (1993) *The Use of Occupations in Historical Analysis* (Göttingen: St Katherinen); A. Miles (1999) *Social Mobility in Nineteenth- and Early Twentieth-Century England* (New York: St Martin's), 191–2.

occupational niches in classes II and III, prominent among them musicians, artists, artisans, teachers, servants, skilled workers and merchants. Foreign-born merchant seamen numbered 15,561, 'Chiefly from Norway, Denmark, Sweden and Germany, descendants of the same races as invaded England.' In the northern counties including County Durham, Europeans clustered similarly in a handful of occupations, including 4310 merchant seamen, over a quarter of them Norwegian, 103 commercial clerks, mainly from northwest Europe, 77 musicians, 47 of them German and 30 Italian, 64 plumbers, painters and glaziers, and 51 shipbrokers or agents.[120] The population of South Shields thus exemplified national patterns, given unique shape by local and global industrial structures.

Throughout the century, migrants continued to contribute skills and capital to the local economy. Whereas the population of the town preponderated in semi-skilled class IV, Table 2.6 shows overseas migrants remained disproportionately in classes II and III: skilled workmen, small employers and lower professionals, in common with other long-distance migrants.[121] Simultaneously, their proportion in the maritime industry remained substantial, swamping other occupations throughout the century.[122] Seafaring remained the town's largest single occupation in 1861, with 2279 of 11,769 occupied men, or 19 per cent, but accounting for 50 of 90 occupied men from overseas.[123] These data demand more

*Table 2.6* Migrants by occupational class 1841–1901

| | **1841** | **%** | **1851** | **%** | **1861** | **%** | **1871** | **%** | **1881** | **%** | **1891** | **%** | **1901** | **%** |
|---|---|---|---|---|---|---|---|---|---|---|---|---|---|---|
| I | 0 | – | 1 | 3 | 1 | 1 | 3 | 1.6 | 3 | 0.1 | 4 | 0.6 | 15 | 1.4 |
| II | 2 | 12 | 6 | 17 | 16 | 18 | 46 | 25 | 66 | 19 | 71 | 11 | 134 | 13 |
| III | 11 | 65 | 26 | 74 | 62 | 69 | 109 | 60 | 231 | 66 | 457 | 70 | 673 | 63.6 |
| IV | 2 | 12 | 0 | – | 5 | 5.5 | 9 | 5 | 31 | 9 | 69 | 11 | 119 | 11 |
| V | 2 | 12 | 2 | 6 | 6 | 6.6 | 14 | 8 | 21 | 6 | 48 | 7 | 117 | 11 |
| Total | 17 | – | 35 | – | 90 | – | 181 | – | 352 | – | 649 | – | 1058 | – |

sustained analysis than time and space permit: this would be repaid by a better understanding of migrants' contributions to local economic development.

Still, analysis shows migrants from abroad, in their generally modest means and compressed class structure, proved more similar than different from the townspeople at large.[124] Consistent with broader scholarship, however, overseas migrants, like other long-distance migrants, appear to have escaped the fate of the Irish. While some experienced upward mobility after settling in South Shields, most appear to have arrived in the town bearing skills or modest capital that relieved them of competing with the least skilled local workers for the most vulnerable employment.[125] These resources, conversely, contributed to local economic development, providing skills, services and capital to local industries such as glassmaking and especially merchant shipping.

Relative affluence in turn supported political participation out of proportion to migrants' numbers. In 1850, when all but 3 per cent or 914 of the town's population remained unenfranchised, Norwegian postman Peter Hull, Polish shopkeeper Isaac Jacob, Jamaican retailer Augustus Noel and Norwegian publican Henry Henderson, amounting to 6.3 per cent of migrants, exercised the vote. By 1857 their numbers included Jacob's sons Henry and Hyman, French glassmaker Napoleon Gaible and others.[126] Like Manchester Jewry, overseas migrants in South Shields took part in the making of Victorian South Shields. Entering local labour markets at mid-century, while urban populations and class itself remained fluid, such migrants helped build the town economically and politically.

## The world in South Shields

Accounting for all overseas migrants to South Shields reveals unexpected diversity in their origins and paths. This breadth and variety has been missed by studies focusing solely on the experiences of highly organized and visible 'ethnocultural' communities. Such communities did coalesce in South Shields and will be explored. Reconstructing the whole migrant population, however, demands broadening the focus of migration studies from relations between distinct and implicitly bounded groups, migrant and native alike. Instead, migrants and migration must be re-envisioned within a global and ever-shifting panorama of people, ideas and cultural influences.

While conclusive arguments await investigation of other British towns, these results cannot sustain a view of South Shields as statistically or otherwise peculiar in its broad array of foreign-born residents, within County Durham or nationally. Rather, the town exhibited demographic and cultural diversity increasingly common in Britain and the world. Close analysis of early censuses discloses trends intensifying through the end of the century. As early as 1841, before the mass migrations associated with the industrial period, the town knew an array of sojourners and settlers from across the globe. Overseas-born residents of South Shields proved even more mobile than British internal migrants, yielding massive turnover between censuses, a characteristic common to industrializing societies the world over. Men who migrated alone constituted the overwhelming majority, outnumbering those accompanied by family members by over 4:1 in 1841, 3:1 in 1881, 2:1 in 1851, 1871 and 1891, and 2.6:1 in 1901. Such men did not remain alone, however, as many, and in some years most, married and founded families in Britain. Mariners made up a substantial proportion. Colonial or ex-colonial subjects amounted to about one-third of migrants in the nineteenth-century censuses, the balance drawn from Europe. The preponderance of northern Europeans, suggests the North Sea and Baltic littoral must be understood as a zone of contact criss-crossed by webs of migrants, overshadowing the Atlantic as a source of local cultural influence.

While scholars have focused on prominent Continental migrants, Europeans in South Shields came from the humbler, middling strata: shopkeepers and artisans, more financially secure than most Shields natives but insufficiently affluent to compete with the town's elite.[127] Throughout the century, merchants such as Sylvester Wherley the clockmaker established themselves and prospered locally, sometimes into multiple generations. Given the labour market's harshness, even for skilled workers, migrants' high mobility can be no surprise. Those with less skill or capital, or those in mobile occupations such as performers or labourers, proved even more so. This applied particularly to mariners increasingly deskilled as steamships supplanted sailing vessels. This analysis suggests the Irish, systematically deprived of skill and capital by centuries of colonial domination, proved anomalously vulnerable compared to other long-distance migrants. In turn, the Irish experience has informed unfounded assumptions that other long-distance migrants met similar obstacles.

Unexpectedly, in 1841 and throughout the century a large proportion of overseas-born individuals resided in families and households headed by native Britons. This not only reflected British working people's global travels, but further problematizes the view of Britons and their culture as static and homogeneous, parochial and defensive. Blending of existing South Shields' families and households such as Jane Groat and her brood with overseas-born newcomers such as Abraham Muncy, coupled with evidence about return migrants such as the Lillicos, affirms the multivectoral character of migration and cultural change. Migration, even across seas and oceans, proved far from a unidirectional process, nor was Tyneside, as a centre of industry, simply a venue through which lone foreigners drifted rootlessly in and out. This emerges with closer examination of the personal, kin, compatriot and occupational networks that drew particular migrants to South Shields and held them there.

# 3
# Migrants' Networks and Local People

Pork butcher John Birkett and his wife Wilhelmina Magdalena, from Württemberg in southwest Germany, moved from Sunderland to South Shields in the 1870s. They set up shop at 63 Thrift Street near the riverside, assisted by two Württemberger domestic servants, Magdalena's brother Rick Katzenberger and Mieka Shoff. In 1891, Magdalena, now widowed, remained in business with Rick's help, and the household continued to import compatriots, including boarder Annette Zimmerman. By 1901 Magdalena, apparently retired, reported her occupation as a boot club woman, but Frederick and his wife Rosine now operated their own butcher shop in Rutland Street near Tyne Dock, employing two young shop assistants from Germany.[1] As the Birkett-Katzenberger household's evolution illustrated, networks built on origin, occupation and kinship structured South Shields' migrant communities. Some, like Germans and Jews, resembled 'model subcultures' found in the United States.[2] Yet most migrants more resembled master shoemaker Frederick Jensen, from Brunswick in north central Germany. Jensen appeared in 1871 with his Australian wife, Lena. The couple had ranged widely, with children born in Sheffield, Ireland, Cardiff and Hartlepool.[3] No evidence suggests Frederick and Lena partook in South Shields' tight-knit German colony despite Frederick's German origin. By 1881, they had moved on.

As these divergent examples illustrate, migrants converged in South Shields from every corner of the globe, but principally northern Europe. Where they lived and worked once there, whether they prospered, and who they loved and married proved equally varied. Some, such as the Birketts, arrived as families rich in kin and other resources, while others came alone. Some found spouses in the old country via family and personal networks, while others married locally or, like Frederick Jensen, en route. Some founded institutions around which vibrant and longstanding communities coalesced, while others inhabited networks barely discernable a century later. The vast majority, like Frederick and Lena Jensen, disappeared after a brief stay, leaving little trace. A very few placed a foot on the ladder of local political power.

These patterns proved neither accidental nor of mere antiquarian interest. They reflected transformations in migrants' places of origin that compelled them to new lands, and the resources they brought with them. They also took shape through demands for skills and services in South Shields and elsewhere. Finally, they followed ancient patterns of commerce and mobility increasingly articulated with global and imperial ones. Whether people settled in South Shields or sojourned fleetingly, they remained embedded simultaneously in regional and global networks as well as local and national ones. Analysing this population in all its variety enables a richer understanding of migrants' multifarious participation in shaping British society.

## Migrant ghettos?

Migration scholars have generally examined visible enclaves resembling archetypal American Chinatowns and Little Italies.[4] Postwar studies of British neighbourhoods such as Cardiff's Tiger Bay, Bristol St Paul's and Stepney may have fostered the impression that colonized or other overseas migrants lived exclusively in such areas, apparently ghettoized.[5] European scholars resist universalizing patterns derived from American milieux fraught with intense xenophobia and labour market segmentation.[6] Still, similar enclavement, characterizing Irish and some Jewish communities in Britain, appeared among Belgians in Roubaix, Flemings in Halluin and Neapolitan fishermen in Marseilles, the latter subdivided further by village of origin. Poles in France and Germany also clustered.[7] Yet most migrants to South Shields departed from this pattern. Scholarly focus on conspicuous communities has missed the ebb and flow of the majority.

Examining Victorian South Shields begins to fill a gap in historians' knowledge about migration to Britain, which leaps from the moral panic against the pauperized Irish in the 1840s to the anti-Semitic xenophobia of the 1890s.[8] The intervening period and other populations remain under-researched. Germans formed the largest group of overseas migrants in Britain between 1841 and 1891, yet no study exists of any German settlement.[9] Nor has any town's whole migrant population been analysed to reconstruct not only prominent communities but less visible individuals and their networks. In the absence of conflict, relations between migrants and native Britons also remain virtually unexamined. Yet discrete communities were not transplanted intact from distant places, but took shape in new lands dialectically, through class, socioeconomic status and other historical processes. These might erode or reinforce imported cultural practices, creating new identities.[10] Resulting variations may be typologized heuristically into *migrations de maintien* and *migrations de rupture*. A migrant undergoing *migration de rupture,* a permanent breach with the place of origin, 'invests intensely in the new homeland'. The *migrant de maintien,* in contrast, maintains old country culture through communication and exchange with those left behind.[11] This model presents a false dichotomy. Many migrants did not foresee permanent alienation, long cultivating 'the myth of return', while for some such as refugees the rupture proved involuntary.[12] Still, it offers ways to understand variation among and within groups in maintaining cultural practices in Britain. *Migration de maintien* appeared most intense in South Shields among Germans and Jews. The tightest knit formed 'kinship colonies', importing relatives and compatriots such as Rick Katzenberger.[13] Other migrants, particularly the lone men who preponderated, betrayed little effort to maintain old country cultural forms. Analysis will show that most migrants inhabited a continuum between these poles.

Migrants in Victorian South Shields enjoyed varying degrees of cohesion, altering over time. The most visible communities stood out due to numerical size, family migration, extended households, institution building and endogamy, that is, marriage within the group. Only Germans and Jews met these criteria. Most similar to migrant communities studied elsewhere, many Germans' and Jews' migration proved unidirectional and finite, built on relays of imported compatriots the Birkett household exemplified. Possessing modest capital or skills, and kin whose labour they could mobilize, both built longstanding communities and vibrant institutions in the town. Not all who came to South Shields, however, intended to settle or did. Migrants of diverse origins took part in and drew on more diffuse and less visible kin and compatriot networks differing in degree but not in kind from those sustaining Germans and Jews. Traces of these networks emerge for others, less prosperous and more transient, including Italians, Spaniards and the town's many Scandinavians. Predominantly although not exclusively seafarers, their marriage and settlement locally may have proven unforeseen or fortuitous.

Analysing the whole migrant population further reveals most, whether Jewish, Danish or Chilean, lived in households with locally born people, and if not, next door to them. Overseas migrants did not form ghettos in Victorian South Shields. Whatever cultural and linguistic differences overseas origin implied, they proved insufficient to create social or spatial segregation. Rather, integration into local society varied not simply according to cultural differences, but migrants' wealth, skills, occupations, marital and kin strategies, and other variables.

Questions of spatial integration, cohabitation and exogamy, or intermarriage, prove salient because scholars have interpreted segregation and endogamy as evidence of discrimination and embittered intergroup relations.[14] Liverpool's legacy of Protestant against Catholic sectarian conflict allegedly produced polarization between locals and migrants, Irish and even Welsh, who became geographically segregated in the town. Evidence for absence of tension between Jews and Irish Catholics, conversely, has been sought in their co-residence in the same urban space, Glasgow's storied Gorbals.[15] Since scholars emphasize segregation and enclavement to argue for incompatibility, its apparent absence among overseas migrants to South Shields merits exploring. Overseas migrants' integration into local society showed not only in their gradual spatial dispersal through the town, but in the overwhelming proportion of households in which migrants and natives cohabited. Their sprawling occupational, kin and social networks articulated with and were secured by those of native-born Britons with whom they lived, worked and married.

This proves surprising, as spatial segregation along occupational, confessional and cultural lines prevailed, notoriously, in mid-century South Shields. D.B. Reid, reporting for the Royal Commission on the State of Large Towns, reported pilots, glassmakers, alkali labourers and pitmen resided near their work. Sailors he found 'chiefly confined to the streets bordering the river', particularly Wapping and Shadwell. Tradesmen and shopkeepers resided in the 'principal streets', no doubt because many lived in or above their shops, and the wealthy, especially shipowners, in the new upper town and the leafy village of Westoe. Only shipwrights, keelmen, trimmers, scullermen and labourers resided throughout.[16] Occupational clustering reflected the need not only to live in walking distance of work but also to maintain the social networks giving access to steady employment.[17] Housing segregation, implying discrimination and hostility, mutually reinforced endogamy in the case of the largest long-distance migrant group, the Irish. In 1851, artisans and labourers, English and Irish people, lived in distinct neighbourhoods, and their sons and daughters intermarried far less than in comparable towns.[18]

Brockie reported historic discrimination against Scots as well.[19] Half a century later, as Tommy Turnbull recalled,

> Shields was divided into villages, and where you lived depended on what you did for a living. The likes of doctors, lawyers and businessmen lived in Westoe. Shipping people lived on the Lawe Top, seamen near the market, and dockers and railwaymen near Tyne Dock. Pitmen lived in Boldon Lane and Whiteleas... any Shields miner could tell which of the four Shields pits, Harton, St. Hilda, Boldon or Whitburn, a man came from, as soon as he opened his mouth.[20]

Such segregation, structured by the labour market, arguably fostered corporate loyalties to specific trades and industries, inhibiting class solidarities.[21]

Overseas migrants' apparent advantage over Irish workers stemmed in part from the diverse skills and resources they, like many long-distance migrants, brought to the local economy. Their historical and cultural positionality also differed. Colonization, class and the vagaries of local politics reinforced or trumped confessional or other cultural differences.[22] In contrast to Irish subordination, Victorian South Shields, if measured by intermarriage, 'who married whom' and spatial proximity, 'who lived next to whom', appeared relatively open to overseas migrants.[23]

## Who lived next to whom?

Throughout the century, migrants from overseas appeared spatially distributed according to occupation, suggesting class and trade outweighed cultural differences. In 1841, mariners and boatmen resided in the waterside districts, Coates and Coppin in Comical Corner, Wilson in Shadwell Street, and Joseph and Rayland in or near Wellington Street. Moray and Watley lived at some distance upriver, in West Holborn and Corstorphine Town. In contrast, Hull the postman, Whaley the clockmaker, Hang the glassmaker, Testor the performer and Pelternay the equestrian resided in commercial streets in or near the Market Place. Patterns of residence thus corresponded with proximity to work rather than ghettoization as outsiders (Map 3.1).

Work structured residence patterns in 1851 also. Eleven mariners, still the largest single occupation, lived at the waterside, in Wapping

*Map 3.1* Spatial distribution of migrant households in 1841

and Shadwell Streets, Comical Corner and Hospital Quay, and further south in East Holborn. Two apparent clusters appeared in 1851, Prussian seafarer Henry Sales lodged at 23 Albion Street, near John Reack and his family, also Prussian, who lived at number 24, while French and Belgian glassmakers Emile Bouillet and Louis Amede and their families resided in Cuthbert Street. A third French and Belgian glassmaking household appeared in Dean Street near the Market Place, with artisans such as blacksmiths John Williamson and Henry Knowles. If migrants gathered

*Map 3.2* Spatial distribution of migrant households in 1851 (Not shown: households in Harton, East Jarrow, Jarrow)

in enclaves defined by birthplace, this proved barely discernable in 1851, nor did enclavement develop later. Maps 3.2 through 3.7 show overseas migrants dispersed steadily as South Shields grew.

## Who lived with whom?

Migrants not only lived throughout the town, but few resided entirely with other migrants. The vast majority had spouses, children or other household members born in Britain, fostering integration and cultural

*Map 3.3* Spatial distribution of migrant households in 1861 (Not shown: households in Tyne Dock, East Jarrow)

exchange at the most intimate level. While almost universally married, only a minority of householders originating overseas had wives also from abroad. Even fewer had children born there, in many cases the eldest only. As shown in Table 2.2, the proportion of overseas-born householders living with even one dependent also originating overseas ('families') never rose much above one-fifth and generally amounted to far less.[24] An even smaller number of such households, ranging between 3 per cent and 9 per cent contained no one born in Britain. Many

*Map 3.4* Spatial distribution of migrant households in 1871 (Not shown: households in Tyne Dock, East Jarrow, Harton, Boldon, Whitburn, Marsden, Undercliffe Hall)

of these consisted of couples only. Only a handful, seven in 1891, fit the stereotype of a migrant family moving en bloc from abroad, such as glazier Moses Henry, his wife Rebeca and their four sons aged 12–22, who moved to South Shields from Russia after the birth of their youngest. Some such families, like Benedikte Thorkeldsen and her children Theodora, five, and Laureus, three, remained sufficiently young that more children might be born and schooled in Britain.[25] Most couples originating abroad, indeed, had British-born children. Andreas and Ida Corneliason, for example, had a son, Conrad, 19, born in Norway

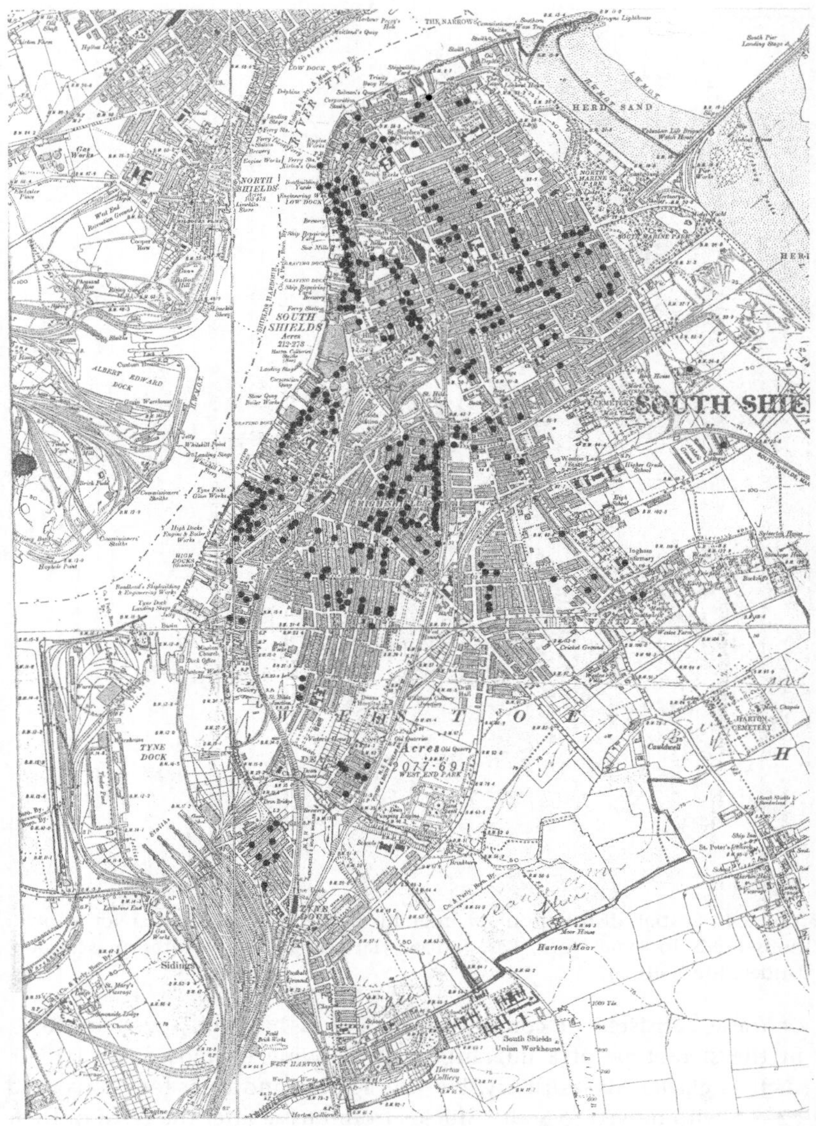


*Map 3.5* Spatial distribution of migrant households in 1881

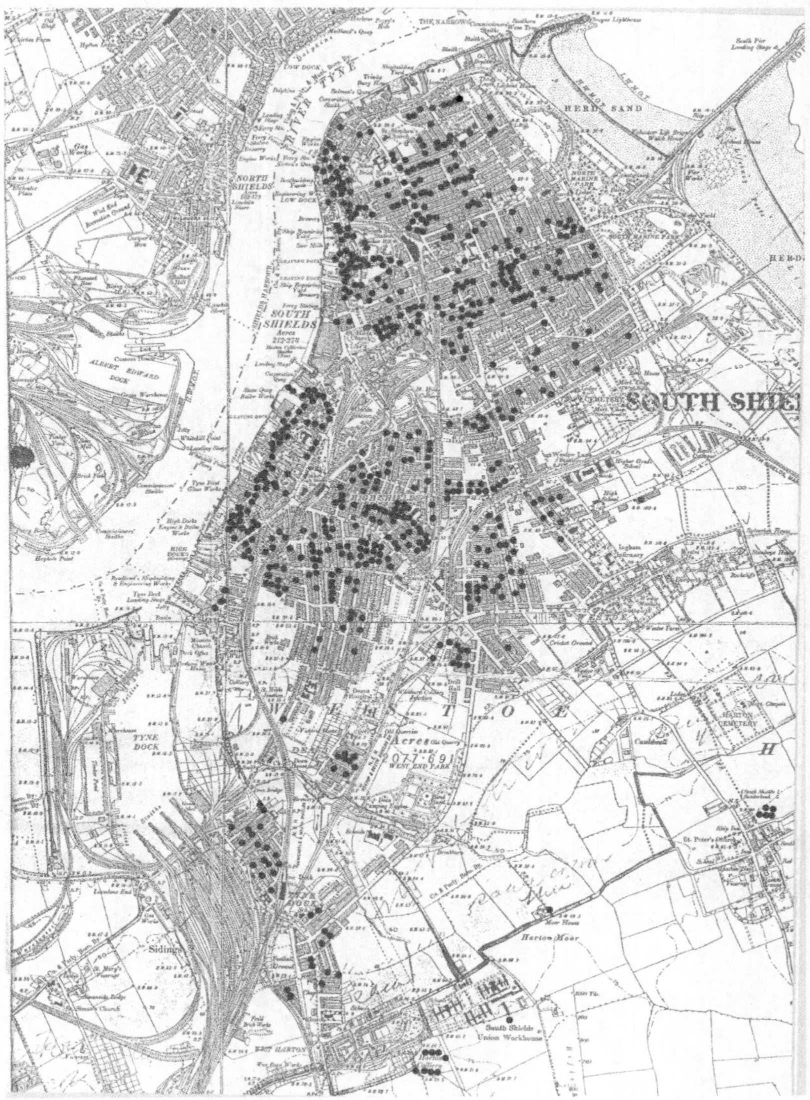


*Map 3.6* Spatial distribution of migrant households in 1891 (Not shown: households in West Boldon, Boldon Colliery, East Boldon, Whitburn, Marsden Colliery, East Jarrow)

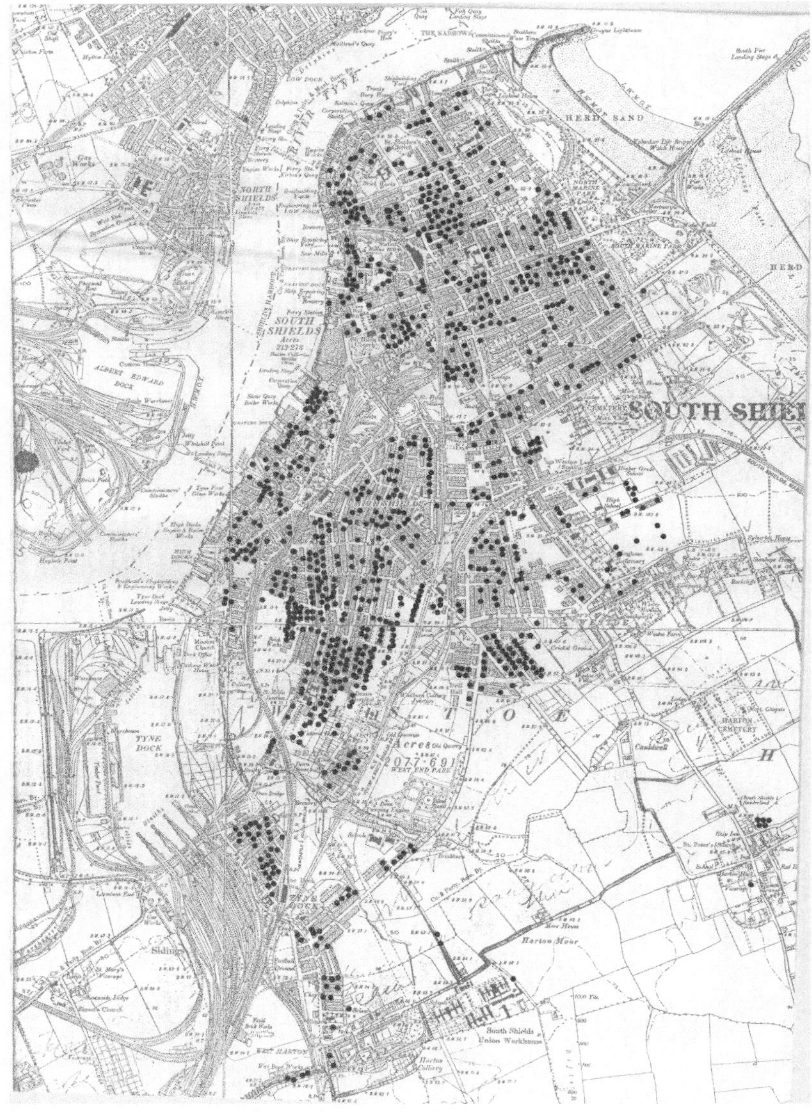


*Map 3.7* Spatial distribution of migrant households in 1901 (Not shown: households in East Jarrow, Boldon, East Boldon, Whitburn, Marsden, and Souter Point)

like his parents, but Ida, five, and Charles, three, born in South Shields.[26] Children, regardless of birthplace, rendered their families vulnerable to indirect discipline and cultural influence from South Shields schools and other authorities, hardly evidence of a migrant population isolated from local society.[27]

These families embodied the disarrangement of borders and cultural syncretism global migration encouraged. Few consisted entirely of people born in the same place, such as steamship stoker Fredrik Sveden, his wife Hannah, their infant son Ernest and their boarder Ludvig Hokanson, all Swedes.[28] Instead, like Frederick and Lena Jensen, many proved internally diverse. Family members often originated in multiple countries: Belgian glassblower Emile Bouillet and his English wife Elen had a son, Joseph, in France, a daughter, Felice, in Belgium a year later, and had lived in Sunderland only three months before, where their son Ernest was born.[29] Others had ranged widely, even globally, before arriving in South Shields. Children's far-flung birthplaces not only revealed couples' indirect routes to South Shields, but their prior cosmopolitanism and exposure to multiple cultural milieux. Global mobility itself militated against forming closed, homogeneous cultures and communities in Britain.

## Global migrants, local families

The vast majority of migrants did not leave their birthplaces married, however, much less heads of families. Most married in Britain and others en route. South Shields, like heavy industrial centres throughout Europe, attracted young male migrants able to travel long distances unencumbered.[30] Men thus preponderated in overseas-born populations, nationally as locally. Bachelors arrived alone but rapidly acquired British-born spouses, children or other kin, and often lodgers, boarders, visitors, servants and apprentices. Hardly a household in South Shields containing people originating abroad did not also contain someone born in Britain. The bulk of overseas migrants at every census except 1861 proved men who brought no dependents with them from abroad. The majority had married British women, indicating they likely arrived single.[31] In 1871, for example, of 107 householders originating abroad, 64 lived with British-born wives. Of 135 British-born children in their households, 95 (70 per cent), had been born in South Shields. Figures proved similar for other years. Most children not born locally originated elsewhere in County Durham or Northumberland, such as Birketts' eldest daughter, born in Sunderland. In 1881, 148 of 203, or 73 per cent of overseas-born householders proved the sole household members from abroad (Table 2.2 'overseas headed'). Vastly more migrants had British-born wives (119) and children (345) than overseas-born ones, while kin such as parents, in-laws, siblings, stepchildren or nieces and nephews made up about one-third (31) of remaining British-born members. Except for 31 servants and 26 lodgers and boarders in migrant households, all British-born dependents lived there due to apparent kin relations with the head. These proportions held in other years.

Almost universally, then, migrants formed the most intimate relationships with British people across the boundaries of national and geographical origin. Contact between migrants and natives occurred primarily within kin relations formed through exogamous marriages, and secondarily through co-residence with lodgers or other secular relations. Rather than homogeneous migrant enclaves, the censuses overwhelmingly reveal co-residence between migrants and natives, with corresponding implications for cultural exchange. Few households consisted entirely of migrants, nor did significant spatial clustering or ghettoization appear. This suggests that centres of heavy industry such as South Shields, in attracting mainly unattached male migrants, fostered cultural syncretism through exogamous marriages with local women. These marriages and other relations flowing from them helped integrate globally mobile migrants into local society, with commensurate implications for British culture.

## Origins

Migrants' numbers and origins reflected industrialization, political upheaval, government policies and demographics in sending societies; historical links with and geographical proximity to the Northeast; skills and resources migrants brought with them; and the relative appeal of alternative destinations. As Table 3.1 shows, the French outnumbered all other migrants to South Shields in 1851, but Germans overtook them by 1861, remaining the largest group locally through the century. France enjoyed relative economic stability throughout the century, discouraging emigration except to Algeria. German like British industrialization, conversely, displaced rural artisans, small proprietors, tradesmen and labourers. Resultant economic dislocation and political strife prompted German states to relax prohibitions on emigration, followed in turn by the Swiss cantons, the Low Countries, and finally

*Table 3.1* Birthplaces of overseas-born residents of South Shields, 1851–1901

| | **1851** | **1861** | **1871** | **1881** | **1891** | **1901** |
|---|---|---|---|---|---|---|
| France | 12 | 6 | 12 | 22 | 25 | 21 |
| Prussia | 4 | 30 | 34 | – | – | – |
| Germany | 3 | 21 | 47 | 115 | 181 | 252 |
| Hamburg | 2 | 4 | 7 | – | – | – |
| Poland | 5 | 3 | 4 | 17 | 14 | 15 |
| Belgium | 5 | 2 | 7 | 5 | 15 | 13 |
| Norway | 4 | 5 | 13 | 54 | 122 | 227 |
| Denmark | 1 | 6 | 13 | 38 | 73 | 99 |
| Sweden | 1 | 5 | 33 | 62 | 176 | 244 |
| Switzerland | 1 | 2 | 2 | 2 | 1 | 4 |
| Italy | 1 | 3 | – | 2 | 16 | 21 |
| Greece | 1 | – | – | 5 | 9 | 9 |
| Portugal | 1 | 2 | 2 | 2 | 2 | 6 |
| Spain | 1 | 2 | 2 | 1 | 2 | 16 |
| Russia | – | 10 | 5 | 9 | 25 | 123 |
| The Netherlands | – | 4 | 10 | 14 | 16 | 19 |
| Austria | – | 1 | 1 | 3 | 8 | 14 |
| Finland | – | – | 2 | 13 | 22 | 49 |
| Turkey | – | – | 3 | 5 | 8 | 9 |
| Romania | – | – | – | – | 2 | – |
| Europe Total | 42 | 106 | 197 | 369 | 713 | 1141 |
| Latin America/West Indies | 8 | 3 | 15 | 14 | 27 | 46 |
| Canada | 5 | 11 | 17 | 25 | 37 | 38 |
| The United States | 3 | 6 | 8 | 14 | 42 | 105 |
| America | 2 | 3 | 4 | 23 | 21 | 50 |
| North America | – | 2 | 10 | 2 | 3 | 2 |
| Heligoland | – | – | 1 | 4 | 6 | 7 |
| Mediterranean Islands | – | 2 | 4 | 9 | 17 | 26 |
| Madeira | – | 2 | – | – | – | – |
| Africa | – | – | 2 | 3 | 9 | 30 |
| Madagascar | – | – | – | 1 | – | – |
| East Indies | 3 | 5 | 19 | 11 | 31 | 44 |
| Australia | – | 2 | 6 | 10 | 12 | 48 |
| New Zealand | – | – | – | 1 | 5 | 7 |
| China | – | – | – | 3 | 4 | 3 |
| Aden | – | – | – | – | – | 1 |
| Afghanistan | – | – | – | – | – | 1 |
| Unknown | – | – | – | – | – | 1 |
| Colonies Total | 21 | 36 | 86 | 120 | 214 | 409 |
| Grand Total | 63 | 142 | 283 | 489 | 927 | 1550 |

Mediterranean and Eastern European states. The last abolished serfdom only at mid-century. German migrants followed ancient seaborne connections to South Shields. After German unification in 1871, political repression and accelerated industrialization swelled emigrants' ranks. Waves of eastern and southern Europeans followed. By century's end, Eastern European Jews overtook Germans in number nationally although not locally. Corresponding processes disarranged colonized societies, mobilizing migrants into the global proletariat.[32] By 1901 the British mercantile marine recruited tens of thousands of men in Asia, Africa and the Caribbean, thousands of whom settled in British ports, including South Shields.[33] Local migrant populations, shown in Table 3.1, reflected this history, predominating in people from the North Sea and Baltic littoral, and secondarily elsewhere in Europe, with smaller numbers from colonies and former colonies such as the United States. In turn, this affected their visibility and organization in South Shields.

## Little Germanies?

Germans and Jews proved conspicuous in South Shields for several interrelated reasons. Their close-knit communities differed in numerical size, gender and age composition and resources from the bulk of long-distance migrants. Headed by artisans or shopkeepers, their households often appeared relatively affluent, not only compared to lone migrants but to most local people. Bringing skills, capital and the human capital of conjugal and extended kin from abroad, networks of these households formed the core of South Shields' most visible and well-organized migrant settlements. Their prosperity, however modest, enabled them to import additional household members and to establish trades and businesses in South Shields. This wealth in turn underwrote religious congregations and other institutions.

Both communities coalesced from deterritorialized Continental networks. In industrial South Shields, Germans formed the most close-knit, built around occupational, kin and confessional networks. They practised distinct trades and maintained ties with their birthplaces, reflected in ongoing co-residence, marital endogamy and importation of relatives, apprentices and servants from the old country.[34] This hardly rendered them a closed community, however, for in the process Germans forged kin and personal networks linking German provinces such as Mecklenberg, Württemburg and Prussia with Northeastern towns including South Shields, Jarrow, Sunderland and Newcastle. The Jewish community too maintained transnational networks of co-religionists from Germany, Russia, Poland, Holland and Austria, linking places of origin with regional locales including South Shields, North Shields, Sunderland, Newcastle and beyond. Finally, Scandinavians formed a pool of mobile men and women who intermarried across national lines, likely encouraged by linguistic affinities such as Germans and Jews shared. By 1901 Norwegians had developed local institutions. South Shields' German and Jewish communities' visibility stemmed superficially from their large numbers relative to most other groups in the town, shown in Table 3.1. Jews, including nearly all Russians and Poles, but also Germans and others, made up the second largest and most organized community. By century's end, Scandinavians too boasted substantial numbers. Germans, Jews and Scandinavians exemplified cultural practices such as chain migration, marital endogamy and compatriot co-residence shared by the more mobile majority.

Size alone, however, cannot account for the form these communities took. Germans and Jews stood out from the proletarianized majority because wives, children and other household members accompanied them from abroad. Kinship itself proved a resource, giving access to family capital and facilitating migration through family networks. Co-resident kin might assist in the family business. Housing and work with already established relatives or co-villagers, conversely, eased young people's migration, offering greater security than lone men enjoyed. Multiply overlapping bonds of mutual obligation created by exchanges of apprentices, pooling of capital and co-residence knit these communities together. These characteristics rendered the German and Jewish communities recognizable and similar to migrant enclaves scholars have normally examined, suggesting overlooked similarities between Britain and acknowledged countries of migration.[35] German and Jewish populations nonetheless differed from stereotypical migrant settlements in their internal diversity of origin, a degree of overlap, spatial dispersal within the town and continuing links not only to specific places of origin but throughout the lands surrounding the North Sea and Baltic.

German links with the Northeast spanned the millennia from the Beaker people to the Angles, Saxons and Jutes to the medieval Hanseatic League or Hansa, whose outposts from 1281 included Newcastle, to sixteenth-century Protestant refugees and seventeenth-century

Ashkenazi Jews. Eighteenth- and nineteenth-century political repression and economic upheaval swelled the influx. While the bulk of 4,800,000 German emigrants finished in America, part of an unprecedented world-historical exodus from Europe between 1815 and 1930, smaller numbers went to Britain. By 1871, 32,823 Germans accounted for over one-third of the 89,829 Europeans in Britain. By 1911 they numbered 53,324.[36] Outside London, settlements formed in Bradford (3721), Liverpool (1326), Manchester (1318), Hull (654), Leeds (325) and Salford (201) with significant concentrations in Belfast, Dundee and Nottingham. Secured by religious institutions and political clubs, Germans also enjoyed integration into these localities. Nottingham and Belfast elected German mayors, and J.B. Priestly averred that in his Bradford childhood, 'A Londoner was a stranger sight than a German.'[37] Still, apart from a few prominent individuals such as Karl Marx and Ludwig Mond, German migrants to Britain remain neglected, especially those outside London.[38]

Germans in South Shields numbered 252 in 1901, offering the opportunity to analyse one substantial settlement in detail, the first for any in Britain. This reveals the emergence of a 'kinship colony' within a diverse migrant population. This colony's visibility and coherence both contrasts with and sheds light on more submerged and loose-knit networks and relations sustaining the majority of Germans as well as other migrants, from Spaniards to Jamaicans. It also reveals many local migrants remained outside formal institutions such as the German Evangelical congregation, an institution, conversely, imbedded in regional and global connections. This challenges views of migration as a unidirectional and finite process and of migrant communities as closed, homogeneous enclaves.

Who counted as German itself remains problematical, ill coinciding spatially or temporally with shifting political boundaries. Nineteenth-century cultural affiliations remained unstable, as likely to coalesce around regional or provincial as national identities, and subject to the economic and political upheaval that propelled migrants to Britain. The German nation remained deterritorialized for much of the nineteenth century, rendering identities multiple and fluid. Dispersed German settlement in Central and Eastern Europe created the nineteenth-century German Question unresolved by 'unification' in 1871. Culturally and linguistically German diasporas, as disparate as similar, remained outside the newly created German Reich, not only in Austria but Switzerland, Russia and elsewhere.[39] Non-German minorities, conversely, remained inside nominally German lands. While scholars invoke the tautological category 'German speaker ... originating in German Europe', it appears necessary to accept at face value the birthplaces historical informants reported.[40] These reflected formal and not necessarily personal identities, much less the internal cultural variety of the sprawling German lands. This work proceeds conservatively, counting only individuals reporting birthplaces in the German states or Austria.

The results are reported in Table 3.2, which shows substantial numbers of Germans did not arrive in South Shields until the 1860s, and that sex ratios proved much less lopsided than among most other migrants, although growing more so by 1901. In 1861 Germans represented nearly two-fifths (38 per cent) of all overseas-born people in the town. As late as 1901 they accounted for more than one-sixth (17 per cent). Although receiving states preferred unskilled, dispensable and malleable labour, those in South Shields typified long-distance migrants; displaced artisans and tradesmen. Nationally as locally, many concentrated in occupations such as clerical, domestic service, waiting and textiles, sometimes actively recruited by employers seeking apprentices or trainees and offering meagre wages. Others, however, including pork butchers, sugar-bakers, language teachers, musicians and hairdressers, brought skills the native population lacked.[41] In addition, with Swedes, Danes and Norwegians, they made up a large proportion of local seafarers.[42]

*Table 3.2* Germans and Austrians compared to whole overseas-born population, 1841–1901

| | Persons | | | | Households | |
|---|---|---|---|---|---|---|
| | **Men** | **Women** | **Germans** | **% of all migrants** | **German households** | **% of migrant households** |
| 1841 | 1 | 0 | 1 | 3 | 1 | 4.76 |
| 1851 | 4 | 5 | 9 | 14 | 7 | 15.5 |
| 1861 | 33 | 23 | 56 | 39 | 35 | 38 |
| 1871 | 54 | 35 | 89 | 31 | 59 | 28 |
| 1881 | 74 | 44 | 118 | 24 | 83 | 24 |
| 1891 | 126 | 63 | 189 | 20 | 131 | 22 |
| 1901 | 183 | 83 | 266 | 17 | 165 | 17 |

*Note*: Percentages reflect proportion of Germans to whole overseas-born population.

To what extent Germans in South Shields constituted a community demands interrogation. If endogamy, co-residence and associational life measure community, little evidence of this appeared before the 1870s and 1880s. Instead, Germans at mid-century, like most other migrants, appeared integrated into local society through marriage and co-residence with native Britons. No autonomous institutions appeared. The visible German community organized around the Evangelical mission did not exist, even nascently, until the last decades of the century. Nor did longstanding German residents such as butchers George and Catherine Brauninger and Thomas Rogers, present from 1861 and 1871 respectively, appear involved with the mission after its establishment. South Shields' German population hardly made up one homogeneous community, but rather took different forms over time. Migrants from specific regions and localities practised particular occupations in South Shields and Britain; they observed different faiths or none; and their households and families took varied forms depending on historical contexts in Germany and Britain, globally and locally.

Mid-century German migrants predominated in women and children, transient as pre-industrial mundane movers. Only one person in the 1841 census proved identifiable as German, and then only because of William Brockie's laconic report about the clockmaker Wehrli. The census of 1841 shows clockmaker Silvester Whaley with his locally born wife Sarah and small children Silvester and Thomas, residing in Long Row near the riverside.[43] By 1851 Wherley or Whaley had apparently moved on, replaced by nine Germans, three of them sailors and the rest women and children. Three survived later in the century: Hamburg native Jane Hardy, wife of locally born master mariner Robert Hardy, and the widow Elizabeth Hoyler, a native of Frankfurt am Main, with her young daughters Catharine and Christiana, the elder also German born. Jane Hardy, now also widowed, appeared in 1861 and 1871 living with her son John, daughter Jane and young grandsons John and William.[44] That women and children outnumbered men at mid-century suggests gendered patterns of long-distance migration before industrialization differed from later ones, meriting greater scholarly attention.

Distinct migrant chains appeared only from 1861, suggesting overseas migrants like others experienced 'thickening' after mid-century. A handful appeared in successive censuses, the most stable and prosperous forming the nuclei of the town's German and Jewish communities. Unlike previous Germans, they formed families, often extended ones, continuing to import compatriots. They also practised trades requiring skill and capital, enabling them to establish longstanding businesses in South Shields. They included confectioners Martin Measer and Benjamin and Janet Lewis, and the first of numerous butchers: George and Catherine Brauninger, John and Barbara Schroth, George Frederick, Alfred Sonenwolk and Sigfrid Velingley.[45] Others appear to have been Jewish, including interpreter Meyer Loewinsohn, boarding housekeeper Rachel Levy and Joel Gaskell, a licensed hawker and jeweller.[46] Continuing a centuries-old pattern, the preponderance, 30 of 56, reported birth in Prussia and secondarily places accessible to the North Sea and the Baltic such as Memel and Hamburg.[47] Yet a significant minority, all butchers, hailed from southern Germany, including the Brauningers from Bavaria, Velingley from Baden and the Schroths from Württemberg.

Germans, Jewish or not, clustered initially with Scandinavian sailors in the maritime districts.[48] In Wapping Street, for example, appeared the shops or residences of pork butchers Schroth at number 32, and Velingley at number 79, as well as general dealer Moses Marks of Prussia at 88 Wapping Street. Another Moses Marks, a glazier from Poland, did business in nearby Kirton's Quay.[49] Hawker Samuel Levy and his family lived in the tenemented Old Hall, West Holborn, unaware or unconcerned that the house was reputedly haunted.[50] General dealer Mark Woolman and pawnbroker Henry Jackson, both from Prussia, did business at 76 and 101 West Holborn, respectively. Further downriver, at 51 East Holborn, appeared pork butcher George Frederick.[51] The town's dock areas, like the Lower East Side of New York or London's East End, possibly proved accessible and familiar to new arrivals who recently disembarked there. The maritime industry provided a ready market for goods and services, perhaps encouraging businessmen to set up there. Discrimination may also have kept them in the riverside areas, but not for long. Germans' clustering proved peculiar to 1861, not observed in earlier or later censuses.

Perhaps due to their prosperity, or possibly the stabilization of late Victorian working-class populations, six German households and families new in 1861 remained for decades, although exhibiting no apparent relations with one another.[52] Bavarian pork butchers George and Catherine Brauninger, with a growing houseful of children, and in 1871 George's sister, survived in the same premises at 15 Cuthbert Street until 1891, where Catherine, now widowed, conducted business, assisted by several grown children. By 1901 Catherine reported herself a schoolmistress and her sons were running the business. Their apparent descendants survived in the town until after the First World War.[53] Prussian Henry Gillert, a coal trimmer, survived in 1871, baker Martin Measer, also Prussian, until 1881, and Charles Hanson of Danzig, sometime seafarer, until 1901, each acquiring locally born wives and families.[54] Prussian Mary Levy, wife of Russian-born Samuel, appeared in each census between 1861 and 1891, latterly as a widowed second-hand clothes dealer still heading a household in Thrift Street containing several adult children.[55] Paulina Gompertz, also of Prussia, and wife of Dutch clothier Aaron Simon Gompertz, first appeared in 1861, likewise presiding over a burgeoning brood of children and other relatives over several decades.[56] These children and other kin, like those of Brauninger, Levy and Measer, assisted in the family business, likely enhancing their families' stability and longevity not only in South Shields but often in the same premises. Local Germans' character thus changed in mid-century from substantially transient to stable, yet betraying little evidence of institution building.

By 1871, when the German Reich forcibly incorporated formerly independent lands into a Prussian-dominated confederation, many in South Shields reported birth simply in Germany. This drop in apparent Prussians may not reflect on population diversity. Some, such as Henry Gillert, Prussian-born in 1861, but German in 1871, merely exchanged provincial for imperial identity. Of those specifying, 24 of 92 still hailed from the Baltic and North Sea region, including Frederick Jensen of Brunswick and Charles Hanson of Danzig.[57] In addition to Prussians, a handful of Hanoverians clustered in Wapping Street and Thames Street. They included glass dealer William Sachse, his wife Dorothe and their son Charles, who established an independent household in Half Moon Quay in 1881.[58] Provincial clustering suggests that despite political unification, German imperial identity remained less salient to many than provincial loyalties.[59] Throughout the century, South Shields' German population thus remained diverse by occupation and regional origin, yet exhibited distinct patterns. Significant numbers appeared Jewish. Although most came from northern Germany, concentrations from specific trades including pork butchers and clockmakers arrived from the south, principally Baden, Württemberg and Bavaria, possibly repelled by the campaign against the Catholic Church in the Kulturkampf, 1872–79, the anti-Socialist laws of 1878, or more diffuse objections to 'Prussianism' that motivated southern German emigrants from the newly formed Reich.[60]

From 1871, divergence appeared between lone men who may have made little effort to maintain kin or other ties in Britain, as in *migration de rupture,* and those such as the Mansons who reconstituted communities in South Shields, as in *migration de maintien.* Compatriots and co-religionists joined pioneers such as the Brauningers, Levys and Gompertzes, constituting discernable networks. Thrift Street outfitter and lodging housekeeper Charles Carlberg, for instance, pillar of the South Shields German Church, first appeared in 1871, removing by 1881 to open cocoa rooms in West Holborn that provided employment for three local people by 1891.[61] Those migrating as families continued intermittently housing extended kin, compatriots and co-religionists. Mariner Frederick Manson and his wife Maria, from Memel, had one child in 1871, but ten years later a houseful, including three daughters and Maria's mother and brother from Memel, the latter a draper's apprentice. All but Maria's brother remained in 1901.[62] John and Barbara Schroth brought with them two children and a nephew, Alfred Sonenwolk, John's assistant. Family migration perhaps corresponded with maintenance because unlike lone proletarians, kin had a collective stake in capital to which all contributed and required access. Those who migrated alone, such as Thomas Rogers, Carlberg and Hanson, in contrast, married local women and, apart from Carlberg, maintained no visible old country networks.[63]

## Social mobility?

Skills and capital not only stabilized German migrants but enabled several German and Jewish households to undergo modest upward mobility. Mainly merchants and tradesmen, they included German pork butchers George and Catherine Brauninger, Samuel and Mary Levy, Moses Marks and Martin Measer. Originally from Prussia, Measer progressed from a baker's confectioner to a baker between 1861 and 1881.[64] Samuel and Mary Levy, from Warsaw and Prussia, raised eight children over 20 years, while Samuel, originally a hawker, became first an outfitter and then a general dealer.[65] Moses Marks and his wife Line first appeared in South Shields in 1861, with three children born in North Shields and two, aged four and two, in South Shields. Moses too changed jobs, becoming a tobacconist in 1871 and a picture frame maker in 1881.[66] Persistence correlated imperfectly with advancement however: Thomas Rogers, a butcher in 1871, appeared downwardly mobile, reporting himself a labourer in 1881 and 1891.[67] This caveat notwithstanding, persistence alone suggests a measure of local economic success compared to the majority who left before a decade's time. This longevity appeared attributable to the skills and resources migrants brought with them, not only stabilizing their own livelihoods, but enriching local society.

Table 3.3 affirms this, showing Germans, like other overseas migrants, prospered relative to the town's whole population. The bulk practised skilled trades or operated shops, insulating them from competition for unskilled labour encumbering the Irish. By 1901, the community boasted six substantial merchants, enhancing its visible affluence. These merchants' emergence coincided with deskilling within the maritime workforce, proliferating class divisions not only among Germans but,

*Table 3.3* Germans and Austrians in South Shields by occupational class, 1841–1901

| | 1841 | 1851 | 1861 | 1871 | 1881 | 1891 | 1901 |
|---|---|---|---|---|---|---|---|
| **Class II** | | | | | | | |
| Butcher | | | 3 | 8 | 8 | 21 | 25 |
| Clothier/outfitter/draper | | | 2 | 9 | 7 | 7 | 1 |
| Watchmaker | 1 | | | | 3 | 5 | 3 |
| Construction trades (proprietor) | | | | 3 | 6 | 2 | |
| Baker/confectioner | | | 2 | 1 | 1 | | 1 |
| Clerical/professional | | | 1 | 2 | 2 | 8 | 4 |
| Grocer | | | | | 1 | 1 | |
| Boarding housekeeper | | | 1 | 1 | 2 | 3 | 4 |
| Tobacconist | | | | 1 | | | |
| Pawnbroker | | | 1 | 1 | | | |
| Merchant | | | | | | | 6 |
| **Class III** | | | | | | | |
| Mariner | | 3 | 8 | 14 | 28 | 55 | 50 |
| Glazier | | | 3 | 2 | 1 | 1 | 1 |
| Musician/performer | | | | | 9 | 7 | 6 |
| Waiter/service | | | | 2 | 1 | 4 | 14 |
| Skilled trade | | | 3 | 1 | 3 | 5 | 13 |
| Shoemaker | | | 1 | 1 | 1 | 1 | 2 |
| Musical repairer | | | | 1 | | 1 | 1 |
| **Class IV** | | | | | | | |
| Domestic servant | | | 2 | 2 | 4 | 10 | 11 |
| Coalminer | | | 3 | | | | 2 |
| Unskilled maritime | | | | | | | 14 |
| **Class V** | | | | | | | |
| Dealer/hawker | | | 5 | 3 | 4 | 4 | 1 |
| Labourer | | | 2 | 2 | 4 | 11 | 23 |
| Total | 1 | 3 | 37 | 54 | 85 | 146 | 182 |

as the town's largest occupation, among the local population generally. Mariners still made up the largest single group of working men among Germans as other migrants, amounting to three-quarters of employed Germans in 1851, and over a third in 1881 (28/85), 1891 (55/146) and 1901 (64/182). Germans in South Shields did not, therefore, make up a unitary, homogeneous community. Those from southern Germany formed the nucleus of the kinship colony that founded the Evangelical mission, while others, including most northerners, resembled other long-distance migrants in their apparent cosmopolitanism and lack of accompanying kin.

## Kinship colonies

South Shields' largest migrant community, indeed, proved least representative of overseas migrants as a whole. German pork butchers apparently mixed less with Britons through marriage, co-residence or work relations, instead building their community by importing compatriots. Such kinship colonies, also found among transatlantic migrants from rural Norway to rural Wisconsin, diverged from cosmopolitan proletarianized single men such as those who migrated from Norway's coasts to American cities.[68] Yet scholars have focused on such colonies as the most visible form of long-distance migration. Business and domestic relations blended in their households so that servants, shop assistants, employees and relatives lived together, resembling pre-industrial patriarchal households rather than nuclear families with conjugal kin strongly distinguished from other kin and non-kin. South Shields' colony established its most conspicuous migrant institution, South Shields Evangelical Church and Seamen's Mission. Despite excluding most Germans in the town, the Evangelical congregation hardly proved closed or parochial however. Through the mission it served far-flung mariners of several nationalities while drawing support from regional and international as well as local resources.

Its first extended household, that of George and Catherine Brauninger described above, appeared in 1861, accommodating Caroline Noimun and her children, and in 1871 George's sister Catherine, described as a servant.[69] By 1871 George Dietrich had arrived, and by 1881 John and Magdalena Birkett, John and Mary Cook, and Emmanuel and Elisabeth Bruninger.[70] In 1891 the Hertrich, Hub and Dietz households joined them. Württembergers Hub and Hertrich became stalwarts of the German congregation. In 1891, German master pork butcher Henry Hub housed not only his brother Andreas, a shopman, but also apprentice

Karl Stir and two domestic servants including his sister Margaret, all from Germany.[71] Frederick Kauft, described as a butcher's assistant, resided with fellow German and butcher George Brokett.[72] Several reproduced a protoindustrial practice in which teenaged children worked as farmhands, apprentices and servants in neighbours' households. John Hertrich's apprentice Carl Hub, 15, may have been related to Henry Hub, while Barbara Kenzer, 16, niece of Charles and Susannah Steel, was described as a general servant, and John Dietz's nephew Frederick, 16, as a pork butcher's assistant.[73] Several other German pork butchers housed compatriot employees.[74] Chain migration continued in 1901 in the households of pork butchers Frederick and Wilhelmina Seitz, Frederick and Mary Seitz, locally born John Dietrich, whose wife Annie came from Germany, and Barbara Sieber, who employed four German-born servants.[75] Family migration indicated relative prosperity; conversely, additional household members enabled families to maximize opportunity in South Shields.

Kinship relations reinforced vocational and provincial ones in other German households, such as that of watchmaker Andrew Shankle, who housed his 17-year-old niece Henning, also from Baden.[76] Additional chain migration networks appear half-submerged in the record. Clockmaker Silvester Whaley disappeared after 1841, but in 1881 Cornelius Wherly, a watchmaker from Baden, lived with the family of his cousin, clock and watchmaker Frederick Wiehl, also from Baden and a commercial traveller on behalf of the Baden Clock Company.[77] By 1891 Germans accounted for fully half of extended migrant households. They contained 7 of 14 householders, 4 of them pork butchers John Dietz, Charles Steel, George Krafft and Henry Hub, and 8 of 16 extended kin.[78] As these close-knit relations illustrate, Germans' significance stemmed from more than sheer numbers. Kin, capital and skill reinforced their prosperity and visibility.

Whatever attracted the first south Germans to South Shields, they apparently initiated a chain of migrants, not only to South Shields but nearby Jarrow. This showed most dramatically in the records of German applicants for naturalization between 1889 and 1934. This group included numerous German pork butchers originating in a small corner of southwestern Germany. Götz, the first naturalized, and a resident of Jarrow, came from the Grand Duchy of Baden in southwest Germany, but the rest, whether from Jarrow or South Shields, reported birth in the neighbouring Duchy of Württemburg, which haemorrhaged nineteenth-century emigrants in recurrent subsistence crises.[79] Most came from a cluster of towns within 20 miles of one another, including Künzelsau, Schwäbisch Hall, Mosbach and Chrispenhofen.[80] Church records also reveal substantial marital endogamy. Finally, the community stood out due to several families' prominence in the German Evangelical Church and Seamen's Mission. This institution bound Germans in Tyneside into a web of global and regional relationships.

## South Shields German Church

South Shields' German Evangelical congregation and mission stood at the intersection of regional networks linking South Shields and Jarrow to Sunderland and Newcastle, and international connections to the Church consistory in Prussia as well as parishioners' homelands in Mecklenberg and Württemberg. Ill fitting the image of a parochial institution serving a closed ethnocultural community, the mission drew support from disparate regional actors including clerics, German officials and maritime employers, linking townspeople with seafarers of many lands. Pastor Harms, based originally in Sunderland, walked 10 miles to Tyneside in the 1870s to establish its first congregation in a building lent by the Wesleyans in Saville Street, North Shields.[81] The mission soon relocated to South Shields, the larger and more dynamic meeting place for seafolk and settled townspeople. There, Charles Carlberg, a Mecklenberger from northern Germany and a former mariner and boarding housekeeper, not only offered space in his Thrift Street coffeehouse gratis, but also took personal initiative in gathering seafarers and German townspeople to services.[82] In 1879 several English shipowners, no doubt appreciating the mission's services to their crews, provided the means to hire Philip Hornung, a young ex-teacher also from Mecklenberg, as its first missionary. Hornung and his Peruvian wife Luise remained in 1891.[83] In 1880, the German consul, with several Newcastle shipowners, provided financial support to extend the mission's work to the upper Tyne. Under the aegis of a newly formed *'Deutsche Evangelische Gesellschaft für die Tyne Distrikt'* a reading room was rented for religious services.[84] Membership remained open to all Germans in Tyneside from South Shields to North Shields, Jarrow and Tynemouth.[85] In the 1890s an assistant priest was dedicated to pastoral duties for mariners.[86] Hardly an institution imported by migrants from Germany, the mission may instead have attracted the most devout to South Shields. Most members, including Hub and Hertrich, arrived only after 1881. Some time around 1907 the Berlin Consistory of the Evangelical State Church of Prussia granted the congregation incorporation (*Anschluss*) or autonomy, and Pastor F. Singer (1907–14), a Württemberger like most members, arrived to see them through complete independence from Sunderland when Pastor Harms retired in 1912.[87]

Although the congregation appears to have stabilized with the arrival of the Württemberger kinship colony, its amenities for seafarers continued to draw support from officials and others in Tyneside and beyond. Between 1906 and 1909, for instance, a London benefactress, Mrs Lewis, financed a new seamen's home and chapel.[88] The mission's chairman, the German Consul, resided in Newcastle, as did Vice-Chairman R.O.G. Lüdtke, Honorary Secretary-Treasurer J.A. Meyer and two committee members, Rev. J. Roeber and W. Walther. Two others, G. Balbach and E. Bittermann, lived in North Shields. Only Reverend F. Singer and one committee member, J. Hub, lived in South Shields. Local men, however, remained responsible for the Institute and Sailors' Home in Coronation Street.[89] By 1913, the eve of world war, the South Shields German Evangelical Mission, the largest in the world, enjoyed transnational and regional institutional support while ministering to globally mobile seafarers.[90]

Like Arab boarding housekeepers a generation later, the German mission sustained the maritime industry, performing secular as well as spiritual services for mobile seafarers. In 1913 missioners paid 2701 visits to sailors aboard ships in the Tyne and at Blyth on the Northumberland coast, distributing literature and promoting Temperance. The words of a professed atheist, 'I am always glad... to receive a visit from the mission, although I have no religious belief', suggested pastoral visits nourished spiritual and cultural yearnings beyond doctrinal ones. Staff also paid 225 visits to men in hospital in 1913, Missionary W. Kortmann writing monthly to the parents of one severely ill mariner. Thanks for services to ill seafarers came from as far away as South America.[91] Although local congregants hailed largely from Mecklenberg and Württemberg, a postcard from the Imperial German Consulate in Newcastle attested that F. Singer acted as an intermediary in establishing the birthplace of deceased Schleswiger mariner Hans Heinrich Henningsen.[92] The mission served German-speaking seafarers of nationalities as disparate as the Dutch, Baltic Russians and Scandinavians, many of whom spoke no English. Missioners acted as interpreters in local hospitals and obtained Danish and Norwegian language reading matter 'to relieve [patients'] unbearable monotony'. The mission reading room received 6911 documented visitors in 1913, and 1638 persons spent a total of 11,549 nights in the Home. Despite these impressive numbers, the

Home apparently possessed a core constituency, often 'obliged to turn away men, even old friends due to full capacity'. Residents collected 19s 6d for a 'regular' hospitalized in a distant port.[93] The mission thus provided for impressive numbers of transient mariners, anchored by a small resident congregation organized around social and occupational networks of Mecklenbergers and Württemberger pork butchers, and common allegiance to the Evangelical Church based in Prussia. The Württemberger kinship colony in turn remained linked with their south German homeland through replenishing relays of kin, with the Church in Prussia, with other Northeasterners through religious affiliation, and with thousands of sojourning seafarers from the North Sea, the Baltic and beyond, whether German, Scandinavian, Protestant or unbeliever. Analysis of the South Shields Mission shows that even an institution closely identified with a single migrant colony almost unavoidably enjoyed multiple transnational as well as regional and local connections and impacts.

Despite this global reach, however, the congregation excluded many local Germans. By the most generous definition, counting as 'active' not only holders of Church offices but any household appearing even once in 35 years (1904–39) in the Church's marriage, baptism, confirmation or burial records, the German congregation numbered 52 households, including the Hausvater of the Seamen's Home.[94] Selective by religion, region, occupation and class, this most visible institutional evidence of German community encompassed barely 40 per cent in 1891 and less than a third in 1901 of the scores of Germans living in the town.

What of the majority of Tyneside Germans excluded by rather than included within these sprawling networks? Perceptible even in records a century old, the exclusivity of this prosperous community as well as their apparent sponsorship by regional industrialists may have proven an irritant in ways other migrants, even other Germans, did not. Visible out of all proportion to their numbers, these pork butchers bore the brunt of local anti-German violence during the First World War. In contrast, most local Germans remained outside networks of either pork butchers or Evangelicals, most obviously those in South Shields' multinational Jewish community. Before examining South Shields Jewry, it may be useful to consider how other Germans' religious affiliations affected relations with other migrants and South Shields natives.

Records of St Bede's Roman Catholic Church show Germans among other overseas migrants participated in the predominantly Irish congregation, one marked as subordinate by origin and confession. Catholicism's purported universalism may have lent itself to German

Catholics' integration with co-religionists, migrant and native. Germans marrying or baptizing children at St Bede's, or witnessing for others, included Martin Wherly and Maria Wiehl, who witnessed the wedding of Franz Sleege of Danzig with Rosine Lorentz, daughter of Charles Lorentz, on 21 May 1879, and George and Catherine Brauninger, whose daughter Catherine married William Devlin on 7 January 1884.[95] Italians and Spaniards too reinforced cultural, kin and compatriot networks by witnessing and participating in one another's christenings and other religious rituals at St Bede's.[96] The Church also proved a locus where new relationships took shape spanning origin and culture, notably when Mahomet and Rosetta Mukbul, pillars of South Shields' Arab community, christened their daughters Maria and Nora Eileen at St Bede's.[97] Families such as the Brauningers, Wiehls and Wehrlys, in attending St Bede's along with other Catholics, including Italian, Spanish, Portuguese and other migrants, perhaps became better or differently integrated into local society than the more visible and cohesive German Evangelicals.[98] The majority of South Shields' Germans thus remained outside the vibrant Evangelical congregation, most without religious affiliation, some integrated with native Britons and other migrants in existing Christian congregations, Protestant and Catholic, and others pioneering South Shields' Jewish community.

## Jewish community?

The coercive and divisive nature of German imperialism and nation building complicated affiliation for many Germans, not least the substantial Jewish population converging in South Shields in the middle and late-nineteenth century. Jewishness remained an equally or more complex identity even than Germanness, not only deterritorialized but multinational. The diverse origins and experiences of British Jewry, migrants and natives, Dutch, German, Russian, and others, Sephardi and Ashkenazi, rich and poor, Londoner and provincial, observant and secular, meant Jews in Victorian Britain inhabited multiple worlds simultaneously, confounding even the question of who was a Jew.[99]

Britain's Jewish leadership remained dominated by descendants of the Sephardim readmitted to Britain in 1655 during the secular Protectorate of Oliver Cromwell. From the seventeenth century, however, Ashkenazim of German, Dutch and Polish origins increasingly settled in provincial towns such as Manchester and Birmingham.[100] The nineteenth century saw the paradoxical process of Jewish 'emancipation' and rising nationalist persecution, while industrialization disproportionately impoverished this artisanal people. Dramatic political eruptions such as the failed revolutions of 1848 propelled some, but most Jewish emigrants harboured more prosaic motivations; land-hunger and poverty. While Jews in Britain numbered some 60,000 in 1880, between the first Tsarist pogrom in 1881 and 1905 perhaps 100,000 Russian Polish Jews arrived in Britain. By 1914, the Jewish population reached 300,000, approximately one-third of them Russian Polish in origin and another 20,000 German, Austrian or Romanian.[101] Scholars know little about modern Jewish communities outside such major centres as London, Manchester and Leeds.[102] Analysing South Shields' Jewish population offers the opportunity to redress this neglect, showing South Shields Jews, like Germans, inhabited local, regional and transnational networks simultaneously.

Jews arrived in South Shields at mid-century, embarking from Hamburg, Danzig and Rotterdam for the Northeast coast. The census of 1851 reported no Jewish place of worship in South Shields, and only one local family, Isaac and Blume Jacobs and their adult children Hyman, Henry and Sarah.[103] By 1861, however, a significant Jewish population of diverse national origins appeared, shown in Table 3.4, mixing, like French and Belgian glassworkers in 1851, not only in the same riverside neighbourhoods but also in the same households. Of 91 migrant households in 1861, as many as 15, or 1 in 6, may have been Jewish. All but one of these, Rachel Levy's Hamburg Hotel, was headed by a male originating abroad. They concentrated in a few occupations, including merchants such as shipchandlers and outfitters serving the maritime industry, general dealers, skilled workmen such as glaziers and confectioners, and unskilled trades such as hawking.[104] Even more than other migrants, no doubt based on historical experience, they deployed entrepreneurship to insulate themselves from labour market discrimination.[105] Nearly all arrived with resources to establish businesses, or, failing that, possessed skills such as glazing. Prussians, the largest single group, accounted for 11 of 15 apparently Jewish households in 1861, several originating in Margonin and Posen. Two of three Russians, both Polish, one of 12 other Germans and one of two Dutch households accounted for the others.

Diversity of origins and practices, coupled with a high degree of assimilation, complicates the question of who was a Jew and by what criteria; voluntary affiliation reflected in communal participation, or an identity imposed by outsiders. Like race, another category of recent historiographical interest, religion remained unrecorded in the CEBs.[106] The researcher must rely on the method pioneered for studying Manchester

*Table 3.4* Putative Jewish households (hh) and persons (per) by place of origin and as percentage of overseas-born (ov)

| | hh | per | Prussia | Poland | Russia | Holland | Germany | Austria | Jamaica | % ov per | % ov hh |
|---|---|---|---|---|---|---|---|---|---|---|---|
| 1851 | 1 | 5 | | 5 | | | | | | 8 | 2.2 |
| 1861 | 15 | 30 | 20 | 2 | 6 | 1 | 1 | | | 21 | 16 |
| 1871 | 14 | 31 | 16 | 4 | 3 | 2 | 6 | | | 11 | 6.6 |
| 1881[a] | 25 | 40 | 5 | 11 | 10 | 4 | 8 | 2 | | 8 | 7 |
| 1891 | 26 | 53 | 3 | 13 | 17 | 5 | 12 | 2 | 1 | 6 | 4.3 |
| 1901 | 57 | 132 | | 19 | 87 | 2 | 17 | 7 | | 8.5 | 6 |

*Note*: [a] Water damage to a section of the 1881 census schedules renders this a likely undercount.

Jewry, a combined test of common names and occupations.[107] This certainly yields an undercount, and reveals nothing about personal commitment to Judaism or communal life.[108] Table 3.4 shows the population so identified continued to grow throughout the century, from 30 persons in 1861 to 132 in 1901. In 1861 South Shields' Jewish population accounted for over one-fifth (30/142) of total overseas-born people, and 8.5 per cent (132/1550) as late as 1901. Since northern German states such as Prussia actually imposed fewer disabilities on Jews than southern ones, the northerners preponderant in mid-century South Shields, apparent in Table 3.4, likely migrated to the Northeast coast due to geographical proximity rather than anti-Semitism alone.[109] Table 3.4 shows that by 1881 Russians and Poles already outnumbered Prussians and Germans in the town's Jewish population, antedating the influxes stimulated by Tsarist pogroms in 1881 and 1903. The dislocations of Continental industrialization and modernization, albeit inseparable in practice from persecution, apparently propelled Jews to South Shields as elsewhere in Britain.[110]

Jews like other Germans more frequently migrated to South Shields as families than individuals, thus the incidence of overseas-born wives and other women in both populations.[111] Jewish family migration has been attributed to their refugee status, but in South Shields the practice antedated the 1880s and appeared among Dutch and Prussian as well as Russian Jewish migrants. The multinational character of this settlement also reflected a longstanding Jewish survival strategy.[112] Russian outfitter Samuel Levy's wife Mary was Prussian, and Russian Samuel Finn, a bachelor in 1871, married Dutch-born Alida. Although Polish draper Wolfe Shelman's wife Minnie was born in Russia her father, Moses Render, came from Poland, and Shelman's nephew, also visiting on census night, from Russia.[113] The Jewish population also grew through chain migration. Of eight households containing apparent non-kin in 1861, those of Edward Taylor, Henry Karroskey and Moses Marks lodged compatriots from Russia and Prussia, while Polish outfitter Isaac Friend and Dutch outfitter Simon Arons housed apparent co-religionists; hawker Shnider Baker of Germany and glazier Thipel Tyber from Margonin. Arons and Marks had large and in the latter case extended families as well as lodgers.[114] Family migration, transnational ties and chain migration thus enriched the Jewish like the German community, militating against forming a closed community.

As the German Evangelical Church represented a subset of Germans, the Jewish congregation overlapped imperfectly with all Jews in the town. The earliest Jewish residents did not necessarily take active part.

Of its founders, Aaron Simon Gompertz and Samuel Levy appeared in 1861 and Henry Kossick in 1871. Other prominent members included Lazarus Joseph, who first appeared in 1881, and Joseph Pearlman, who arrived via Sunderland in 1891. As the German community appeared a satellite of Sunderland, so South Shields' Jewish congregation focused initially towards North Shields.[115] Clothiers and outfitters Aaron and Paulina Gompertz, from Amsterdam and Prussia respectively, started their family in North Shields in the 1850s, moving to South Shields shortly after, where they had at least eight additional children, owning several shops by 1899.[116] Polish outfitters and clothiers Isaac and Rachel Cohen arrived in South Shields, the birthplace of their son Asher, no later than 1866, yet kept an older niece and later her brother born in North Shields.[117] Observant Jews like Evangelical Germans may not have comprised all local Jews, yet maintained regional ties.

From the 1870s, however, the community in South Shields began to acquire critical personnel: Hebrew teacher Lewis Sager arrived from Poland via Manchester in the 1870s with his wife Lean and daughter Polly, who married locally born Moses Marks, while Rabbi Philip Phillipstein presided over a synagogue on Heugh Street in 1873.[118] Rabbi Joseph Rosenbaum of Russia lodged in 1891 with Israel Rosen and his family[119] Selig Neumann, a kosher butcher, arrived from Russia via Sunderland in approximately 1895, setting up shop at 42 and 40 Derby Street, and Rabbi Abraham Rosenberg, his wife and a niece came from Russia by 1901.[120] The congregation occupied a series of premises in Palatine Street, the Mill Dam, Sunny Terrace and Charlotte Square, before acquiring a house in Ogle Terrace opposite the new Town Hall in 1914. Indicating South Shields Jewry's integration into local society as well as British Jewry, attendance at the 1932 dedication of a new purpose-built synagogue at 14 Ogle Terrace included, in addition to the Chief Rabbi, the Mayor of South Shields, the local Member of Parliament, representatives of local government and Northeastern Jewry, as well as Alderman G.H. Levy. As late as the 1980s the Jewish congregation remained one of seven surviving in Tyneside.[121]

Jews, Germans or other overseas migrants suffered no apparent ghettoization, isolation or ostracism in Victorian South Shields. Unlike the Irish at mid-century, limited in their choices of residence due to vulnerability within the labour market, migrants from abroad filled occupational and commercial niches that dispersed them throughout Victorian South Shields. Neither German nor Jewish merchants made up a migrant service sector, but rather served the townspeople at large, in numbers unsustainable by compatriots or co-religionists alone. Seven guests in

Rachel Levy's Hamburg Hotel included only one fellow migrant, Jacob Cohen, for example, while an unnamed informant recalled with relish the delectable pork sandwiches purveyed by 'Hubbs, at the corner of Laygate Lane'.[122] As years passed, some migrants and their descendants became prominent locally. In addition to Alderman Levy, the Jewish community contributed one Freeman, two Magistrates and a Councillor to local government, while George Birkett of the Ironfounders' society, son of George and Wilhelmina, chaired a mass meeting of labour in 1918.[123] Many migrants also became naturalized, discussed below, drawing on networks that included co-religionists but also many other Shields residents.

Even when overtaken in number by Scandinavians and other migrants late in the century, Jews and Germans shared visibility out of proportion to their size. This stemmed from their kin, occupational and confessional networks and their relative affluence, capital and skill, individually and collectively. Stable communities and institutions distinguished them from the majority of migrants who moved on. In turn, these resources enabled them to contribute religious and commercial infrastructures to industrial South Shields. Ironically, these shared advantages making conspicuous communities of Jews and Germans rendered them vulnerable when overtaken by world-historical events. Both communities disappeared from twentieth-century South Shields, Germans in a dramatic paroxysm of wartime violence and Jews more gradually, as children and grandchildren joined the exodus of the young, skilled and educated from Depression-era Tyneside.

## Loose-knit networks

Apparent Jewish kin and confessional networks, like the occupational ones of French and Belgian glaziers or German pork butchers, proved easily detected. Similar albeit more diffuse affinities structured by kinship, origin, confession and vocation bound other migrants with compatriots and native Britons. Those who arrived in South Shields from myriad origins survived with the aid of kin, co-villagers and compatriots who offered lodging, jobs and support, as well as co-workers and others whose occupational solidarities transcended national boundaries. As Table 3.1 shows, Swedes and Norwegians constituted the largest and growing national groups after Germans, making up an increasing proportion of the maritime workforce, and boasting a Swedish union delegate, Robert Lawson, by 1901.[124] A more proletarianized group with fewer resources, Scandinavians nonetheless co-resided, practised chain migration and intermarried across lines of Swedish, Danish and Norwegian nationality. By 1901 they also enjoyed a Norwegian newspaper edited by Emil Odgaard and Johan Eriksen; a Church of Norway missioner Anton Theodorsen, a Scandinavian Temperance Sailors' Home at 64 and 66 Eldon Street in High Shields operated by Norwegian Julius Hansen and his family and housing Norwegian seafarers exclusively on census night; and a Royal Swedish and Norwegian vice-consul, Gustaf Wachmeister. Another Norwegian missionary of unspecified denomination, Ingmar Egenson, resided at 60 Heugh Street with his wife and child.[125] Households containing extended kin appeared relatively affluent, headed by merchants or professionals. Danish provision dealer Hans Kemp, for example, employed as assistants his Danish nephew, Seton Sonnichsen, and a Norwegian youth, Daniel Granby.[126] Norwegian draper's traveller Erhard Baker accommodated his sister-in-law, dressmaker Josephine Dalstrom, who perhaps assisted in the family business.[127] Scandinavians' networks and practices, like those of less numerous groups such as Italians, thus differed more in degree than in kind from those of more prominent and affluent groups.[128]

Other evidence bears out scholars' observation that kin provided support that minimized the trauma of migration, whether for overseas or internal migrants.[129] By 1891, overseas-headed households contained two extended kin for every three children originating abroad. While one-third of wives reported birthplaces elsewhere than the householder's, all but one relative came from the same place. This remarkably high ratio indicates ties to compatriots, possibly kin, remained strong, even when men sought wives from outside the group. Naturalization applicants also revealed numerous kin connections. Mariner Otto Anderson lived with his brother from his 1902 arrival in South Shields until his marriage, and Giovanni Valentini reported that during a visit to Italy his business was carried on by a brother in North Shields.[130] Numerous migrants also lodged with compatriots: Nicholas Nelson entertained as a visitor on census night 1881 fellow Norwegian Christiana Lodin. Five households contained visitors in 1891, three of them from the householder's birthplace. One of these, Jens Yessen, 28, shared both Danish nationality and seafaring vocation with his host Hans Rasmussen. Fritz Truwert, a Russian subject born in Ösel, Lifland, stayed with a Russian boarding housekeeper at 52 Corstorphine Town 'for some years'—between 1903 and 1908, to be precise.[131] Such networks extended to other British locales. When in Cardiff, Danish mariner Hans Madsen lived at 29 Patrick Street, the boarding house of another

Scandinavian, Mads Poulsen.[132] Intergenerational endogamy also drew on migrants' networks: Antonio Bianchi married London-born Mary, whose father, Gaetano Taroni, like Antonio himself, came from Italy. Their elder children's names, Lorenzo, Giovanni, Gaetano, Theresa and Margarita, reflected cultural continuities.[133] These examples show less numerous and more proletarianized migrants such as Italians and Scandinavians drew on similar networks to Germans and Jews.

Given their modest numbers shown in Table 3.1, and their spatial dispersal, reconstructing colonial subjects' networks through evidence of endogamy, chain migration and other practices proves difficult. Consistent with evidence from 1841 through 1861, a greater proportion proved either lone householders or dependents of return migrants, discussed in the next chapter. A handful of households showed evidence of colonial-born members in addition to the head. Examples from 1901 included Charles Williams, a seagoing steward and his British wife, who offered housing to fellow Jamaican William Butler, a ship's cook; and Gibraltar-born Alfred Ryan and his locally born wife who housed Alfred's brothers Leopold and Ernest, also from Gibraltar.[134] Through such daily choices migrants reconstructed overlapping networks of kin and compatriots, intense among Germans and Jews, dispersed among Finns and Jamaicans, spanning South Shields, Cardiff and elsewhere in Britain as well as their places of origin.

## Occupational networks

Even relations seemingly founded strictly on business reflected channels of information and possible personal connections. Among apparently lone migrants, business or vocation often mixed with personal relations and common origin, bringing apparently unrelated individuals together under a roof.[135] Most unattached overseas migrants lodged with families, whether British or migrants, rather than in commercial premises. Those cohabiting with other migrants, if not linked to their hosts by kinship, often shared origin or occupation. In 1881, for example, many lodgers plied the same trade as the householder: Swedish mariner Olof Carlson and his Danish wife Andrea, for instance, housed three Norwegian mariners, Tollip Hanson Saglan, Mikal Jeremesson and Henrik Beer Johnson, while Finnish ship's carpenter Adam Nordberg and his wife Louisa accommodated Neil Branstum, a Swedish mariner.[136] Greek shipbroker George Vanakiotte and his family housed Constantinos Pappalus, a Greek ship's captain.[137] Others simply took in a lodger or two to make ends meet. So appeared Norwegian ship's carpenter L. Erikson, who accommodated Norwegian musician John Carelson and Danish hawker Martin Erlandson.[138] Even apparently secular relations thus partook of personal and compatriot networks like those structuring more visible communities.

Only a handful operated large-scale commercial establishments, and these like other migrant businesses served a disparate clientele, principally mariners, British or otherwise, making up the town's single largest labour force. Bombay-born refreshment housekeeper William Walters housed four seafarers, including two Swedes and a Frenchman. Fred Peterson, a Danish outfitter, housed assorted boarders from Martinique, Denmark, Finland, America, Australia and Shrewsbury.[139] In 1891, 98 apparently unattached men originating abroad boarded or lodged with overseas-born householders. These householders formed two distinct groups: 12 kept one or two men, often sharing their origin or occupation, and 13 commercial establishments accommodated large numbers of residents of mixed origins, nearly all sailors. All of the commercial establishments clustered in South Shields' maritime district, consisting by 1891 of East Holborn, Laygate and West Holborn. The four largest together housed half or 49 of 98 lodgers. Even in these commercial premises, in part because of their size, one or more residents proved compatriots of the proprietor. All residing in the commercial establishments and all but a handful in the smaller ones were sailors. These patterns held in 1901, when of 23 non-commercial landlords, 16 shared the nationality of at least one lodger, while of 14 commercial enterprises, 13 lodged at least one man sharing the landlord's nationality. Apparent kin, trade, compatriot and confessional connections between householders and lodgers, whether in private households or commercial establishments, thus integrated overseas migrants into local society in similar ways to other migrants in Britain's nineteenth-century industrial towns. Simultaneously, they provided critical services to the global workforce of the town's major industry.

## A man of colour

Birthplace reveals nothing about racial assignment, however, nor did this evidence yield any other such indications. Since 'race' remains fundamentally fictive, efforts to identify people of colour in these records risk reinforcing spurious racial discourses. The language of racial difference was deployed against a variety of migrant populations in the Northeast, starting with the Scots and Irish in pre-industrial centuries, while 'Northern' identity itself has been deprecated through racializing, infantilizing, exoticizing and Othering discourses.[140]

The people of Tyneside remained innocent neither of Victorian racial debates nor of people of colour. From at least the 1840s, Abolitionist activists including Frederick Douglass, African-American and Australian Aboriginal cricket teams, and performers such as the Original African Opera Troupe circulated through Tyneside. Racial discrimination by magistrates and racist discourse reproduced through the press kept racial issues before the public, as did an interracial seamen's strike in 1866, and a radical Abolitionist and anti-racist newspaper, the *Newcastle Daily Chronicle*.[141] Yet the very ambiguity and contextuality of race obscures colonized people in the historical record. Most Afro-Caribbean people and many Africans had European names, and many migrants Anglicized theirs upon arrival in Britain.[142] For Anglo-Indians, travel to Britain itself constituted part of a 'whitening' process.[143] Thus the racial assignment of hundreds originating in the colonies and the Americas remains inaccessible through the CEBs.

The first identifiable person of colour appeared in 1881, exposed by the race-conscious management of the Ingham Infirmary, the local subscription clinic. In 1879, young Dr Rajaonah, house surgeon at the Darlington Hospital, applied for the post of senior house surgeon. Although clearly the best of three finalists for a position plagued by high turnover, Dr Rajaonah, recipient of numerous honours and prizes at Edinburgh University, came under special scrutiny due to 'the fact of his not being an Englishman', but rather from Madagascar.[144] Alerted by the committee's inquiries in Darlington, 'about the appearance of Dr Rajaonah', and, 'advised by his friends at Darlington that the fact of his being a man of colour would probably be the reason', Dr Rajaonah requested a meeting with the committee. 'After some conversation with him', and a letter from his pastor attesting his 'unbroken fellowship' with the Congregational Church, the committee unanimously recommended Dr Rajaonah to the Governors.[145] Dr Rajaonah worked in South Shields from May 1879 to May 1882, departing for 'an important appointment under the government of Madagascar'.[146] Whether the late nineteenth-century intensification of racism accompanying British recourse to formal empire building rendered Dr Rajaonah's origins newly problematical, these records cannot tell.[147] A second identifiable person of colour appeared in the census of 1891: Asad Ali Khan, an 18-year-old Indian scholar in the household of schoolmaster John Barker, and a third, Michael Swallow, through the dubious distinction of being charged with manslaughter after a drunken altercation.[148] While sailors of all lands trod the streets of Victorian South Shields, the presence of Dr Rajaonah, who ministered to thousands of patients in three years spent in South Shields, as well as the less public figures of Asad Ali Khan and the unfortunate Michael Swallow, confirm colonized people of all ranks lived and worked there, decades before South Shields' visible Arab community took shape.

## Woven together

The substantial numbers of migrants arriving from abroad between the Irish in the 1840s and the Jews in the 1880s have received scant scholarly attention. This neglect has skewed the historical record, depicting overseas migrants as catalysts for conflict, and British people as fundamentally intolerant of cultural differences. Firm conclusions await investigation of other British towns, but South Shields' residential patterns and domestic arrangements call into question assumptions about migrants' inevitable ghettoization and disadvantage. Instead, overseas migrants formed communities and institutions built from networks of kin, confession and calling intersecting multiply with those of native Britons. Throughout the century most shared households with native Britons, including wives, children and other kin, becoming integrated into local society and culture in workplace, lodging house and domestic circle. The CEBs reveal a high degree of co-residence between migrants and natives, few homogeneous migrant households, no evidence of spatial segregation and little residential clustering.

If, as in South Shields, conspicuous 'ethnocultural communities' comprised a minority of migrants, scholars' almost exclusive focus on them may require rethinking. If such communities have been identified only when conflict erupted, views of migrants as inevitably disruptive may be based on exceptional rather than representative cases. South Shields' migrant population remained as protean as other long-distance migrants, undergoing constant metamorphosis through seven decades. A handful of the most stable constituted the core around which German, Jewish, Scandinavian and other networks coalesced. Ironically, those most successfully established in South Shields also maintained the most vibrant compatriot networks and institutions, often garnering support from local elites. Even these, however, maintained far-flung transnational and regional connections, hardly operating as closed communities.

Close analysis shows most migrants maintained compatriot networks. Co-villagers and kin served as initial points of contact with and initiation into the complexities of urban life, providing temporary housing, help in finding work and aid in crises. They shared cultural practices found among British migrants from rural areas to industrializing towns such as Preston, where kin assisted migrants in adjusting to town life.[149] Germans and Jews proved stabler than seafaring proletarians due to relative affluence, networks and resources, not cultural differences from other migrants or greater affinities with native Britons.

Rather than relying on compatriots for custom, migrants brought businesses and skills to South Shields that serviced a growing town composed of migrants and natives alike. Like Manchester Jewry, migrants from Europe and the colonies took part in the making of Victorian South Shields. Bringing talent and capital to the developing industrial economy, they filled niches such as pork butchery and provided skills and services to local industries. Their sons and daughters contributed to cultural, political and economic life. Migrant householders, in private homes or operating commercial boarding houses, performed the dual function of facilitating compatriots' chain migration while providing housing and other amenities for the burgeoning maritime industry. While German, Jewish and Scandinavian networks grew up with the town, they remained fluid and permeable. Numerous overseas-born householders married, fathered, housed and employed native Britons as well as compatriots and other overseas migrants. In turn, native Britons integrated overseas migrants, illustrated by local householders' relations with overseas-born family, lodgers and other dependents.

# 4
# Moving, Staying, Coming, Going: Migrants and Remigrants in Provincial Britain

William and Jane Garbutt returned to South Shields in the 1840s with two young children, Loredda, six, and Alfred, nine, born during a stay in France. The family disappeared by 1861, perhaps overseas, but by 1871 Loretta had returned, married John Matthew Selby, a labourer like her father, and had three young children. A middle-aged matron in 1891, Laura or Loretta raised seven children, while her husband had obtained the less arduous job of goods checker.[1] In the meantime, coalminer William Anderson and his wife Elizabeth returned to Tyneside with four sons born during a sojourn in Australia during the 1850s and 1860s: John, 17, Robert, 13, Stephen, 11, and William, 10. By 1891 John, now 27 and a housepainter, had founded a family of his own, while Robert, 23, had married a local woman, becoming a greengrocer. Stephen and William, now grown, had become a butcher and a clothier's assistant, continuing to live with their widowed father at 47 Eldon Street, down the street from John's family and not far from Robert's in nearby Palmerston Street. The residential clustering this family exemplified has contributed to the English working-class's reputation for parochialism, homogeneity and insularity.[2]

Globally mobile families such as the Garbutts and Andersons cast doubt on this view. Between 1841 and 1901, hundreds of children, as well as wives, extended kin, employees, visitors and others originating overseas lived in households headed by native Britons. Lone male migrants lodging with apparent strangers accounted for many of these, but the make-up of other households proved far less predictable. The local birth of some family members might deceive one into viewing such families as unworldly, provincial, rooted in place. Yet the presence of Loredda and Alfred Garbutt or John, Robert, Stephen and William

Anderson betrayed far-flung travels and exposure to multifarious cultural influences. The Garbutt and Anderson families' emigration and return to South Shields complicates models of unidirectional, finite migration as well as assumptions that migrants and natives can be easily distinguished. The town's migrant and native population remained fluid and permeable, not only over space and time but also in kin and cultural affiliation. The hundreds of returned sojourners in Victorian South Shields problematize views of British society and especially provincial society as closed and defensive, and of overseas migrants as few and far between, limited in impact because isolated from ordinary Britons.

British emigration enjoys a substantial literature, but scholars have devoted little attention to return migrants, despite calls for more.[3] Yet decades of scholarship has documented coming and going on a global scale. Most migrants intended to return to their places of origin, rendering the popular dichotomy between temporary and permanent migration or 'immigration' fallacious. Return migration rates between Britain and the United States ranged from 16–55 per cent for English migrants, 7–55 per cent for the Welsh, 14–46 per cent for Scots and 10–42 per cent for the Irish. Comparable rates obtained among Poles, Serbs, Croats, Slovenes, Greeks, Italians, Magyars and Slovaks. Even Jews, many fleeing persecution, returned at a rate of 20 per cent.[4] Yet scholarship on remigration to Britain remains thin.[5] Evidence of these comings and goings can be found in the many South Shields households headed by natives such as William Garbutt, William Anderson or John Selby, but containing wives, children and other dependents originating abroad.

## Global families

Throughout the century, such households remained comparable in number and structure to those headed by overseas migrants. Table 4.1 shows British-headed households accounted for 24–52 per cent of those containing people originating abroad, and approximately one-third, 27–46 per cent, of such people.[6] Unrelated lodgers constituted a slight majority of these in 1851 and 1861, but from 1871 onwards most overseas-born dependents proved wives, children or other kin of the householder, confounding views of migrants and natives as discrete and bounded populations. In 1841, five households contained seven members born abroad. Although their relationship to the British householder remains unknown, shared surnames suggested kin relationships among some.[7] In later years, better evidence showed numerous British men had acquired wives from Europe, the colonies and beyond. In addition, as

*Table 4.1* British-headed households with dependents born overseas

| | 1841 | 1851 | 1861 | 1871 | 1881 | 1891 | 1901 |
|---|---|---|---|---|---|---|---|
| Number of households | 5 | 22 | 47 | 92 | 120 | 184 | 298 |
| % of all households with members born overseas | 24 | 49 | 52 | 43 | 34 | 30 | 31 |
| Persons born overseas in British households | 7 | 23 | 65 | 107 | 150 | 254 | 452 |
| % of all persons born overseas | 32 | 36.5 | 46 | 38 | 34 | 27 | 29 |
| Wives | – | 3 | 10 | 14 | 21 | 46 | 75 |
| Children | – | 5 | 13 | 34 | 45 | 65 | 102 |
| Kin | – | 3 | 3 | 14 | 15 | 24 | 44 |
| % dependents related to householder | – | 41 | 47 | 55 | 52 | 53 | 56 |
| Unrelated lodgers, etc. | – | 12 | 39 | 45 | 69 | 119 | 231 |
| % unrelated to householder | – | 59 | 53 | 45 | 48 | 47 | 44 |

*Table 4.2* Children of internationally mobile parents, 1851–1901

| | 1851 | 1861 | 1871 | 1881 | 1891 | 1901 |
|---|---|---|---|---|---|---|
| Europe | 4 | 5 | 16 | 10 | 18 | 18 |
| Americas[a] | | 5 | 8 | 21 | 30 | 50 |
| Colonies | 1 | 2 | 10 | 14 | 17 | 34 |
| Total | 5 | 13 | 34 | 45 | 65 | 102 |

*Note*: [a]Vague use of the description 'America' in these records necessitated combining North and South America with the Caribbean, even though some territories remained colonized.

shown in Table 4.2, many children born abroad proved those of returned British emigrants rather than parents also originating overseas.

Children's birthplaces shown in Table 4.2 traced the indirect paths families followed to and from South Shields.[8] In 1851, two locally born couples and two locally born widows had a total of three children born in France, one in Lisbon, Portugal, and another in the West Indies, evidence of long-distance migration patterns similar to and continuous with the circular mobility characterizing more mundane movements. Alice Beeson, born in Tynemouth, bore a daughter, Mary, in the West Indies and another, Eliza, in Kent, their ages, 19 and 16, marking with some precision the family's return to Britain in the early to mid-1830s. Widow Bridget Carl, a lodging housekeeper, bore her first child in her native Ireland and her 4-year-old daughter Mary Anne in France before moving to Sunderland where her son Peter was born.[9] Householders also originating overseas had more children born abroad than British householders in 1841 and 1851, but the proportions reversed dramatically thereafter. While 17 children born abroad lived in South Shields in 1861, only one, Rebeck Taylor, four, daughter of Edward and Rahel Taylor, shared her parents' overseas origin.[10] The others proved children, grandchildren and a niece of native British householders.[11]

British people had children overseas for various reasons, most obviously the householder's occupation. Labourers' seasonal migration to France or the United States apparently accounted for some such as the Garbutts. During the 'Hungry Forties', ironfounders, engineers, millwrights, machine makers and bricksetters emigrated to Europe, North America and Australia, often returning disappointed.[12] Others may have numbered among skilled workmen despatched by firms such as Palmer's and Armstrong's to assist in founding shipyards in such places as Italy and Russia.[13] Many South Shields parents did practise mobile occupations: wine merchant Annie Mackay and her daughter Ann, 12, originated in County Durham, but Annie's son Christopher, 15, was born abroad, tracing the circular path Annie's business demanded.[14] Two mariners had children born in Canada, a steamboat owner, William Clasper, had a daughter, Mary Ann, born in Russia, and an enginemen, Robert Fairley, a son born in Spain.[15] Two lodging housekeepers, one a retired engineer, had children in Italy, Bombay and Canada.[16] Of 18 such householders in 1871, four were master mariners with children born in Shanghai, Constantinople, Calcutta, Valparaiso and the Falklands.[17] In addition, James Garrett, a Chelsea pensioner, had a daughter Margaret, nine, born in the East Indies, and Sidney Hawkes, a barrister, five Belgian-born children.[18] A smattering of missionaries also appear.[19] A minority of men had married while abroad: Robert Bowes, a furnaceman, had a wife and four children born in America, and master mariner George Olditch, a Swedish wife and son.[20]

Other parents reported an array of more pedestrian occupations, children's birthplaces revealing improbable travels. Joseph Raven, a Leicester brickmaker, had a 14-year-old daughter, Alice, born in Ballarat, Australia, and William Alderson, a glassmaker from rural County Durham, a son, John William, ten, born in Holland.[21] This evidence illustrates the propensity of British families from all walks of life, even with small children, to try their fortunes abroad, hardly a characteristic of a closed and parochial society.

Global circulation survived late into the century, a cultural practice neither peculiar to mid-century flux, nor to idiosyncratic employment. Occupations continued to range across the social classes, from dock labourer Thomas Cavnagh, a widower residing at Cat Leap Stairs, whose 15-year-old daughter, Calcutta-born Susannah, kept house for the family, to David Ross, MD, whose daughter Isabella was born in Dutch Guiana.[22] Professionals such as John Gillie, an examiner in navigation, and assurance agents, John Palmer and Henry Fox, had ventured as far as China, Cawnpore and Montreal, begetting daughters Grace, 18, Elizabeth, 13, and Mary, 5.[23] Labourers continued to range widely, from France to Calcutta, while a brassfounder and a furnaceman had seven American-born children between them. For some families South Shields represented the end of a journey beginning in Scotland, London, Ireland or some remote corner of England. Others, particularly widows such as Elizabeth Felstead or brass- and ironfounder Robert Atkinson, had returned home, the child they brought with them a memento of sojourns beyond the seas, marked, in Elizabeth's case, perhaps, by tragedy.[24]

Just as Tyneside sent forth coal and ships to the world, by the late nineteenth century its skilled workmen travelled the globe, facilitating industrialization in then-developing countries in Continental Europe, the Americas and the colonies. Apart from two mariners with children born in Belgium and the Mediterranean, and six labourers, half returned from Malta, remigrants in 1891 and 1901 represented an array of mostly skilled trades. This reflected the attenuation of the market for unskilled itinerant labour by century's end.[25] Returned migrants included coalminers and colliery workers, a ship caulker, a boilermaker, a shoemaker, two grocers, a brass and ironfounder, a quarryman, a blacksmith, a platelayer, an iron and steel roller, a joiner/undertaker and a foreman in a chemical works. They formed part of a broader skilled labour force who ranged across the industrializing world.[26]

Of the children themselves, only one survived in South Shields between 1851 and 1901: Thomas Storey, six in 1851, born in Lisbon to South Shields natives William, an enginewright, and his wife Catherine. Thomas became mariner, residing with his widowed mother, a charwoman, in 1871 and 1881, as she provided for a family of lodgers. In 1891 and 1901 Thomas remained, a bachelor shipyard labourer apparently supporting his elderly mother.[27] Other remigrant children such as Selina Richardson, born in Calcutta to a master mariner and his wife, also lived on in South Shields for decades, ministering, like Thomas Storey, to her widowed mother in the family home.[28] While such children apparently blended or settled into local society, others moved on to destinations unknown. Their presence, enduring or fleeting, shows assumptions about the parochialism of British society generally and the Northeast in particular cannot withstand scrutiny.

## Closed communities?

World travellers residing in the nearby coalmining villages of Harton, Whitburn, Marsden and Boldon equally problematize pit villages' depiction as isolated, homogeneous, clannish and backward.[29] Their presence, in turn, repudiates the dismissal of South Shields' diversity as the peculiarity of a port population. Antedating the release of the miners' bond in 1872, these villages boasted a population comparably cosmopolitan to that of urban South Shields. Irish shoemaker Thomas Craig, residing in Boldon Village in 1871, had a son Henry, nine, born in the West Indies, while Edith Harrison, 12, residing in Whitburn, came from Bangalore. Jamaican-born Isabel Good, ten, also lived in Boldon with her widowed grandmother and great-grandmother.[30] These cases reflected a general although not perfect bifurcation in pit villages between children born in the colonies and ex-colonies such as America, and adults who more often came from Europe.

Table 4.3 shows that by century's end, 1891, the four colliery villages contained 49 people from overseas, distributed among 42 households. In addition to householders from France, Germany, Italy, Denmark, Australia and America, eight originating in Britain had children born during sojourns in America. These included five coalminers, a commercial traveller, a labourer and one reporting no occupation. Wives, widows, in-laws and parents more often than children hailed from the Continent: Germany, France and Italy, or further afield such as Turkey and India. Thomas Temple, lighthousekeeper at Souter Point, had a wife

*Table 4.3* Origin of 1891 colliery populations from abroad

| | | | |
|---|---|---|---|
| America | 18 | Italy | 1 |
| Germany/Prussia | 7 | Finland | 1 |
| India | 6 | Canada | 1 |
| Australia | 4 | Denmark | 1 |
| Madagascar | 3 | Turkey | 1 |
| France | 2 | Belgium | 1 |
| Heligoland | 2 | Sweden | 1 |
| | | Total | 49 |

and eldest son born in Heligoland, while the wife of Arthur Chiswell, a Whitburn cleric, came from India, and three of their four children from Madagascar, perhaps born during missionary service. Colliery villages in 1891 accommodated coalminers from India and America lodging with other miners, and two Australians, a joiner and a sailor, also living with local families.[31] Only Margaret Poole, an Indian-born woman of independent means, resided in the less intimate venue of a lodging house in Front Street, Whitburn.[32] This evidence cannot support pit villages' portrayal as closed communities, suggesting that even localities commonly thought provincial and insular apparently experienced significant circulation of long-distance migrants, a question meriting further research.

These unexpected patterns reveal traces of return migration, a freely acknowledged but little studied phenomenon in global migration history. Emigrants from Italy, China and the Caribbean have been widely known to return and often retire to their places of origin, but scholars know little about return migrants to the British Isles.[33] The peregrinations evident among South Shields' working people undermine distinctions among migrants, emigrants and immigrants, affirming that much migration proved neither unidirectional nor finite.[34] It seems fair to suppose households with children were not the most mobile section of the population.[35] Where such travels can be reconstructed through children's birthplaces or other evidence, they show that censuses document merely the most visible traces of massive movement. The data at hand show this mobility might well prove global as well as mundane. Analysing remigration throughout the century suggests that while governments and even labour spokesmen found emigration a panacea, it might prove otherwise for individuals.[36] It further undermines views of nineteenth-century emigration as unidirectional, thus of plebeian and working-class Britons as isolated, unsophisticated and innocent of the world and its inhabitants.[37]

This evidence raises more than answers the question of remigrants' cultural impact. Other scholars have found substantial importation of, for example, Indian food, clothing and other artifacts by returned memsahibs.[38] The diversity found in Boldon, Marsden, Harton and Whitburn may explain why local coalmining argot contained Norwegian, Belgian and Dutch terms. James Kirkup recalled a childhood street game he later observed in France, Spain, Germany, Sweden and Denmark.[39] Recondite census data reflect years spent abroad more subtly, in the names children bore back to Britain, such as Loretta Garbutt, born in France, and Fedila McLenahan, named for her mother, both of them natives of Bilbao.[40] Not only such children but their

British-born parents with life experience overseas participated in and shaped Victorian South Shields in the alleged heyday of a parochial and static working class.

## Extended kin

Examining only globally peripatetic nuclear families would however misrepresent the composition of South Shields households. British householders like those from abroad also gave homes to significant numbers of extended kin and other dependents originating overseas.[41] At mid-century, most came from the colonies, but later from across the globe. In 1851, three households otherwise consisting of locals included more distant kin from abroad. Eulalia Thompson, three, birthplace Ram Ganges, India, and her Newcastle-born sister Margaret lived with their native grandparents, brewer Robert Kidd and his wife Hannah.[42] Margaret and John Phillips, 21 and 24, born in the West Indies, resided with their aunt Elizabeth Mitchelson and her seven small children. Mary Elizabeth Phillips, 18, birthplace Jamaica, lived with her widowed grandmother Elizabeth Phillips.[43] That all in 1851 and again in 1861 originated in British colonies suggests that kin networks on which British people relied for childcare, to ease migration and for other everyday purposes, extended from local to global scale.[44]

Table 4.4 shows 14 extended kin originating abroad lived with British householders in 1871, 15 in 1881, 24 in 1891 and 44 in 1901. These included parents, in-laws, siblings, grandchildren, nieces and nephews, their origins ranging from Europe to the Americas to Africa, India and China. Two sets of siblings again show migrant and native families analytically inextricable: Swedish pedlar Carl Wikstrum and his younger sister, dressmaker Jane Williams, born in Yorkshire, and Sarah and Ann Trotter, the former a grocer born in America, and the latter and younger in Morpeth, Northumberland.[45] Betraying the increasing diversity and mobility of British society, later decades found unrelated migrants from Europe and elsewhere living with local families, hardly evidence of homogeneity or hostility to newcomers.

*Table 4.4* Overseas-born extended kin in British-headed households

| 1851 | 1861 | 1871 | 1881 | 1891 | 1901 |
|---|---|---|---|---|---|
| 3 | 3 | 14 | 15 | 24 | 44 |

## Lodgers

In addition to relatives, dozens of local households also accommodated apparently unrelated dependents originating abroad. Mainly male lodgers and boarders, they differed from servants, apprentices or other non-kin in migrant-headed households, who were often bound by sentiment or a common stake in household enterprise. In addition, small numbers of lone women originating overseas mostly resided with employers as domestic servants, including Norwegian Martha Johnson, 19, a servant in the Black Swan in Thrift Street in 1871.[46] Most lodgers, however, shared characteristics with other long-distance migrants; young, single men with no apparent local ties.

## Occupational networks

Many such men, like lodgers in migrant households, found accommodation through occupational networks. Most of those housing them did not operate commercial establishments but provided room and often board in a family context, blurring boundaries between public and private as well as those between personal and cash relations. Examining these households may help illuminate what proportion of South Shields' migrant population fit the stereotype of a floating population of rootless social marginals.

Just as occupational and cultural affinities bound landlords and lodgers with common overseas origins, work relations apparently linked native landlords with migrant lodgers.[47] Labour cultures in many trades cut across national and linguistic barriers. Shipboard culture necessarily incorporated a multinational workforce, albeit subject to increasing racial segregation as the century waned.[48] Tommy Turnbull, on the one hand stressing Shields miners' provincialism, commented to his nephew Joe Robinson, 'pitmen and pitfolk are always the same wherever you go'.[49] Scholars argue that workers' geographical circulation helped generalize expectations about wages and working conditions, creating a culture of militancy among a globalized proletariat.[50] The relentless mobility this project documents arguably broke down barriers, fostering cultural exchange evident in the internationalization of pit talk. The same skills that advantaged long-distance migrants in the labour market appear in turn to have gained them access to housing and through it personal relationships with native Britons.

Mariners throughout the century obtained lodging through similar personal and occupational networks to other workers, repudiating later depictions of seafarers as marginal and disreputable.[51] In 1851 five mariners of ten lodged with householders sharing their occupations. These included Henry Inglis, 18, a seamen's apprentice from Hamburg residing at 9 Comical Corner with James Blackburn, late seaman pauper; Stephen Lloyd of St Johns, British America, also lodging with another mariner; Joseph Levecque, also from Canada, in a seamen's lodging house in Shadwell Street; Henry Sales of Prussia, living with shipwright George McMain and his family; and William Nesbitt, 69, from Spain, visiting the family of mariner William Slatter.[52] Such relations no doubt originated in the cash nexus: families rented rooms because they needed the money. Still, that half of mariners lodged with a fellow mariner suggests they obtained information and referrals through occupational networks.

Similar relation appear to have structured living arrangements in trades other than seafaring. Archibald Lillie of Melbourne, Australia, labourer in a chemical works, lodged in 1871 in Wind Mill Hill with the family of James Rowthorne, a warehouseman at the works; Barbadian Adolphus Sandeford, 14, lodged with the family of another young boilermaker, Christopher Smith, 15.[53] In 1881, five men apparently found British landlords via occupational networks or affinities, and in 1891 seven lodgers or boarders, two of them coalminers living in Boldon, practised the same trade as the householder. Personal and occupational networks thus continued to bring lodgers and landlords together across barriers of language and origin.[54]

Another form of occupational connection appeared when employers housed employees, reminiscent of pre-industrial household forms. In 1851, D. Ramsay, rector of St Bede's Roman Catholic Church, resided in the rectory with his assistant, Francis Kuwle of Holland, while German George Mott Russell, journeyman pork butcher, lived in the household of King Street pork butcher George Loarmount.[55] Similar arrangements survived in 1871, including James Edmond, a young doctor from Bengal who assisted GP James Williamson, residing with his family.[56] These examples suggest migrants who arrived in South Shields from overseas with skills thereby gained access to occupational networks that facilitated finding housing in the first instance, and through it integration into local society.

If kin or occupational links between migrants and local people explain their cohabitation, more surprising may be the number of local householders with no apparent connection still offering housing to overseas migrants. Their primary motivation no doubt stemmed from the money to be made. Yet taking in boarders, unlike other methods of raising cash, muddled hegemonic distinctions between the private and public spheres, the cash nexus and labours of love. That so many Shieldsmen and women thus opened their homes suggests factors such as the town's dependence on the sea may have overridden or rendered irrelevant cultural differences.

## Making ends meet

Scholars disagree whether keeping lodgers, common to one-third of Tyneside households in the late nineteenth century, exacerbated the region's notorious overcrowding or indicated extra room and the status derived from extra income.[57] Widows and large families frequently accommodated migrants, suggesting the desire for supplementary income rather than extra house space motivated local people. Co-residence, even with loved ones, remains no guarantee of harmonious relations. Still, overseas migrants' cohabitation with British families apparently implied personal relations, mutual support and acculturation.

Census categories lodgers, boarders and visitors proved fluid in practice. Lodgers, like boarders, often ate at the family table. Landladies and other family members performed 'surrogate family activities' such as washing, many of which carried maternal, familial and even sexual overtones. Some lodgers reciprocated, in one case finding an apprenticeship for a landlord's son. For widows or other vulnerable householders, lodgers' contribution might prove critical to survival. The ambiguity of providing personal service for pay, like the apparent breach of the private family sphere, lent itself to personal relationships beyond mere cash transactions. The eventual marriage of Elizabeth Hoyler and Peter Hughes exemplified this.[58] Surely not all such relationships ended so happily. The stereotyped financially exploitative 'wheedling landlady' or crimp, who stripped mariners of their pay in exchange for overpriced services, dated from the seventeenth century.[59] Still, the presence of overseas-born migrants in an increasing number and proportion of local homes throughout the century must modify any view of British society as culturally static, closed and homogeneous, and of British working people as intolerant and inward-looking.

Table 4.5 shows except for 1861 and 1901, more overseas migrants lived in private homes than commercial establishments, enjoying quasi-familial intimacy with an array of modestly situated Shieldsmen and women.[60] Most British households lodging apparently unrelated migrants accommodated small numbers. Only a minority operated

*Table 4.5* Lodgers originating overseas in British households

| | 1851 | 1861 | 1871 | 1881 | 1891 | 1901 |
|---|---|---|---|---|---|---|
| Total households lodging migrants | 12 | 24 | 34 | 30 | 72 | 97 |
| Total migrant lodgers | 12 | 40 | 36 | 64 | 94 | 180 |
| Private homes housing migrants | 9 | 14 | 21 | 18 | 49 | 56 |
| Commercial establishments housing migrants | 3 | 10 | 13 | 12 | 23 | 41 |
| Migrant lodgers in private homes | 9 | 19 | 21 | 37 | 64 | 60 |
| Migrant lodgers in commercial boarding houses | 3 | 21 | 15 | 27 | 30 | 120 |

large-scale boarding houses as a business proposition. Most apparently housed lodgers in their homes for extra income or simply to make ends meet. Lone lodgers or visitors unrelated to other household members numbered 12 in 1851, all mobile by reason of occupation. In addition to five mariners, William Gadola, 64, an interpreter from northern Italy, lodged with blacksmith Henry Watson's family, and David Aitkin, 45, a professor of languages from Jamaica, with the family of colliery worker Charles Harrison.[61] Sarah Dunn, a widowed charwoman with three children to feed, had three lodgers including comedian Harry Nadforth, 50, born in Greece, and his wife.[62] Most lone lodgers, such as Joel Paulding, 31, a compositor from the United States lodging with an elderly widow, Margaret Davison, might be expected to move on, and apart from mariner Stephen Lloyd and possibly William Nesbit, no trace of any of them appeared again.[63] Yet even these individuals may not have been as rootless as they seemed: Henry Sales lodged next door to fellow Prussians John and Margaret Reack in Albion Street. Sales may have found housing with their neighbour through the Reacks, or chosen to live near them due to cultural and linguistic affinities.[64]

These patterns held in ensuing decades. Many householders apparently took in a lodger or boarder to eke out the proceeds of a working-class occupation. Most commonly, local families housed one or two lodgers or boarders, such as laundress Ellen Ratcliff, who with her adult daughter lodged two seamen 'visitors' including Daniel Wilson, a Swede, in their home in Studley Stairs. Shoemaker Robert Gillespy incorporated 17-year-old East Indian seaman Manill (Manuel?) Daymane into a household containing his wife and four children. Not all boarders were connected with the maritime industry. Widow Margaret Atkinson lodged Italian-born mechanic Robert Kerr and George Walker, an enginewright from Kent. Several widows such as Mary Ann Chadwick, sole support of four daughters, headed such households. Men in marginal or unskilled occupations and taxed with many children, such as Scottish dairyman Hugh Graham, also did so. Along with a wife and four young daughters, Graham housed Polish slipper-maker Harris Jacobs.[65]

In addition, by 1881, modest operations, often run by widows, housed up to four lodgers, including public houses such as the Havelock Arms near the Market Place. Comparing figures in Table 4.6 with the total number of overseas-born mariners shows as late as 1891, even most mariners, the archetypal 'floating population', continued to lodge with families, either their own or a British one. Sailors of many lands mixed freely, not only in the streets and pubs of maritime districts, but apparently in the homes of local people. Only a minority of mariners resorted to large-scale commercial boarding houses, increasingly segregated from the community.

Mid-century evidence permits little effective distinction between professional boarding housekeepers and householders who merely took in a lodger or boarder as an income supplement. Rather, a continuum appears between private domestic situations and commercial enterprises. As Table 4.5 shows, of 12 British households with unrelated overseas-born dependents in 1851, only three appeared to be operating commercial premises. Located in the oldest riverside districts, they included Thrift Street publican Robert Dish, Wapping Street eating housekeeper Margaret Thompson and Shadwell Street lodging housekeeper Elizabeth Wood. Even these housed only two or three apiece on census night.[66] This changed towards century's end. As Table 4.5 shows, by 1891, 72 Shields households housed 94 overseas-born lodgers and boarders, nearly all men. Of them, 23 appear run on business lines but more than twice that many, 49, not. Thirty of the

*Table 4.6* Mariners in private homes versus commercial lodging houses

| | 1851 | 1861 | 1871 | 1881 | 1891 | 1901 |
|---|---|---|---|---|---|---|
| Mariners in homes | 3 | 14 | 9 | 28 | 46 | 34 |
| Mariners in commercial houses | 2 | 21 | 9 | 17 | 15 | 107 |
| Total | 5 | 35 | 18 | 45 | 61 | 141 |

94 boarders, less than a third, stayed in commercial houses, the remaining 64 in family homes. Two-thirds of overseas-born sojourners thus lived essentially with British families. Even most lodgers and boarders without apparent personal ties to those with whom they resided thus remained far from isolated from local society, or it from them.

## Lodging commercialized

The proportion and scale of commercial lodging houses nonetheless expanded as years passed, and they became concentrated in the increasingly dilapidated and disreputable dockside areas. As early as 1861, some British landlords clearly operated large-scale businesses, such as John Lawler's public house in Long Row, which boarded nine mariners including three Swedes, a Dane, a Prussian and Henry Seaman of Hamburg. John McManus in 99 Wapping Street likewise accommodated ten mariners, including five Americans.[67] Still, of 13 British households with one or two lodgers, only one appears a business; the others involved widows or large families likely needing extra income. Of eight houses lodging three to ten in 1861, most stood near the riverside, obviously professionals inviting a maritime clientele. These included Scottish mariner William Scrunger, who lodged six mariners including a Frenchman and a Norwegian in premises in Wapping Street.[68] Many such enterprises still proved modest in scale, allowing for significant contact between lodgers and proprietors.

By 1881, however, large houses proliferated in districts including West Holborn, Long Row and Thrift Street. Joiner Patrick Clark, for example, accommodated 20 men of various occupations, including a troupe of five German musicians, in a house in Salt Well Lane near the Market.[69] Hawkers Alexander Levitt and Iman Arias from Austria and Poland, respectively, lived among 24 British-born men in a boarding house in 41 Thrift Street.[70] The large scale of such businesses diminished the likelihood of intimacy between proprietor and lodgers, while their confinement to the riverside segregated residents from other local people. Among 121 mariners, large commercial premises accommodated 27, or approximately one-quarter, of those originating overseas. Yet Table 4.6 shows these 27 men still accounted for only 17 of 45 mariners, or 38 per cent. Further, they made up only 27 of 64 such lodgers overall, as shown in Table 4.5, or 42 per cent, a majority in neither case.

Between 1851 and 1901 hundreds of South Shields residents thus opened their homes to workingmen from beyond the seas. Men of diverse origins, including British ones, mingled in these lodgings, with little evidence of segregation or self-segregation. Only municipal intervention at century's end began to segregate mariners from local society.

## On the beach

Backbone of the local economy, mariners formed a substantial proportion of overseas migrants throughout the century. As shown in Table 4.7, they accounted for between 40 per cent and 55 per cent of those reporting an occupation at every census except 1851. In 1858, approximately 15,000 sailors resided more or less permanently in South Shields, while another 40,000 passed through the port each year. Perhaps more visible than other migrants as many spent the winter months 'on the beach', that is, workless and in port, mariners also burgeoned with the town's overseas-born population as the mercantile marine expanded and industrialized, drawing its workforce from increasingly disparate locales.[71]

Foreign nationals increased as a proportion of British merchant sailors after the 1849 repeal of the Navigation Acts, which had mandated British crews for British ships. Political and economic upheaval on land and sea displaced Europeans and others, some of whom sought work in the world's largest mercantile marine. Maritime districts from across the Atlantic world sent sailors to South Shields, including Hamburg, Kingston, Lisbon, Nantucket, Nova Scotia and other Canadian ports, forming a dense web of migration routes. Smaller numbers from Africa and Asia appeared in South Shields as the industry recruited colonized personnel. Tyneside, the Baltic, the Caribbean, the North Atlantic and beyond may be understood not merely as one continuous and inclusive zone of migration but as a zone of contact, a borderland or frontier not just between different peoples, but between the cultures of land and sea. As the industry expanded throughout the century, many ports in Britain, a maritime society, no doubt partook of this process.[72]

*Table 4.7* Mariners as a percentage of employed migrants

| | **1841** | **1851** | **1861** | **1871** | **1881** | **1891** | **1901** |
|---|---|---|---|---|---|---|---|
| Migrants reporting occupations | 17 | 35 | 90 | 181 | 352 | 649 | 1058 |
| Mariners among them | 7 | 10 | 50 | 75 | 159 | 347 | 503 |
| Mariners as percentage of those employed | 41 | 28.5 | 55.5 | 41 | 45 | 53 | 47.5 |

Seafaring proved a transitional occupation for some. Several arriving in South Shields as lone mariners shifted from seafaring to jobs ashore between 1861 and 1881. John Brown of Hamburg became a painter, Charles Hanson of Danzig held a series of jobs including tailoring while fathering five children, and Charles Musgrave of Halifax, Nova Scotia, became a chemical labourer.[73] How households altered in the intervening decades revealed as much as their persistence. Examining the 35 households surviving between 1871 and 1881 shows of 12 mariners only 8, or two-thirds, remained in the trade ten years later. Heinrich Vasey's switch to labouring on the railway and Frederick Hanson's to iron drilling, while a step down from the status and perhaps pay of maritime labour, may have been compensated by the satisfactions of living with their locally acquired wives.[74] For others the shift to work ashore involved a degree of upward mobility. George Johnson had become a wine and spirit merchant by 1881, and William Brown a lodging housekeeper.[75] Examining these long-term residents reveals much could change in 20 years, even for people who remained in the town. For a significant proportion, seafaring proved a temporary stage of working life, a transition from sojourner to resident, from mariner to landlubber, lone stranger to patriarch of a local family.

For those who remained mariners, the work and with it their status deteriorated as the century waned. Most land-based migrants in South Shields continued to come from the skilled or small proprietary classes III and II. In contrast, from 1881 onwards, mariners became increasingly deskilled by industrialization. Labour specialization accompanying the shift from sailing to steamships created a small elite composed of marine engineers and others, placing four men in class II in 1901, while a growing minority came to occupy the semi-skilled stratum class IV. Deskilled stokers, coaltrimmers, donkeymen, firemen and greasers made up 35 of 347 (10 per cent) of mariners from abroad in 1891 and 73 of 503 (14.5 per cent) in 1901.[76] These changes coincided with the recruitment of increasing numbers of foreign and colonial seamen, shown in Table 4.8, enabling employers to depress wages and working conditions in the process of technological change.[77] Mariners' increasing numbers, their mobility and their proletarianization became consequential for relations between migrants and natives in twentieth-century South Shields.

In the same decades, the state intervened to segregate mariners from local society. Although seamen's boarding houses provided services sustaining the maritime industry, the authorities historically viewed them askance on class and gender bases.[78] This hostility increasingly became

*Table 4.8* Origin of mariners residing in South Shields, 1841–1901

| | 1841 | 1851 | 1861 | 1871 | 1881 | 1891 | 1901 |
|---|---|---|---|---|---|---|---|
| Prussia | | 2 | 5 | 8 | 4 | | 2 |
| Other Germany | | 1 | 2 | 6 | 22 | 49 | 67 |
| Denmark | | 1 | 6 | 6 | 17 | 45 | 51 |
| Sweden | | 1 | 4 | 19 | 30 | 101 | 128 |
| Norway | | | 5 | 9 | 27 | 73 | 101 |
| Holland | | | 3 | 5 | 2 | 3 | 6 |
| France | | | 2 | 2 | 8 | 5 | 5 |
| Switzerland | | 1 | 2 | | | | |
| Austria | | | 1 | | 1 | 3 | 3 |
| Finland | | | | 1 | 9 | 10 | 22 |
| Russia | | | 1 | 1 | 2 | 5 | 15 |
| Greece | | | | | 1 | 3 | 6 |
| Spain | | 1 | | | | | 3 |
| Italy | | | | | | 1 | 2 |
| Belgium | | | | 2 | 1 | | 1 |
| Portugal | | | 1 | 1 | 1 | | 3 |
| Turkey/ Constantinople | | | | | | 1 | 2 |
| Latin America/ West Indies | | | | 2 | 7 | 11 | 24 |
| Canada | | 2 | 5 | 5 | 8 | 7 | 8 |
| The United States | | | 6 | 2 | 7 | 11 | 11 |
| America | | 1 | 2 | 1 | 4 | 4 | 10 |
| Heligoland | | | 1 | 1 | 4 | 4 | 2 |
| Malta | | | | | 3 | 4 | 5 |
| Gibraltar | | | 1 | | 1 | | 5 |
| Madeira | | | 2 | 1 | | | 1 |
| Africa | | | | | | | 3 |
| East Indies | | | 1 | 1 | | 3 | 5 |
| Australia | | | | 1 | | 1 | 7 |
| New Zealand | | | | | | 2 | 1 |
| China | | | | 1 | | | 4 |
| 'Foreigner' | | | | | | 1 | |
| Total | 7 (nationality unknown) | 10 | 50 | 75 | 159 | 347 | 503 |

inflected with xenophobia and racism as the workforce grew more diverse and militant. To protect mariners ashore, a group notoriously vulnerable to 'crimps' charging extortionate rents and worse, from 1887 'all persons and bodies keeping houses in which seamen are lodged' must submit to licensing and inspection on pain of a hefty 20-pound fine. Licensed houses must keep a register recording each guest, his nationality, age, last and next ship and port. Lodging housekeepers could lose their licenses for condoning 'drunkenness, gambling, or immoral or fraudulent practices' or for failing to 'remove ... persons of known immoral character' or harbouring reputed thieves or prostitutes. Local controls simultaneously affirmed rank and status, as ship masters, mates and engineers remained free to live in common accommodation, avoiding invasive surveillance.[79]

Still, because small scale, casual landlords and relatives remained exempt from regulation; as late as 1891, two-thirds of unattached mariners, or 46 of 61 shown in Table 4.6, continued to live with families rather than segregated in dockside establishments. This suggests efforts to detach townspeople from the maritime workforce proved ineffective initially. As Table 4.6 shows, however, these proportions reversed dramatically between 1891 and 1901, when only 34 of 141 unattached mariners originating overseas continued living in private homes. The balance, 107 men, had been confined to large commercial boarding houses near the river or the Market Place. Between 1891 and 1901, several Temperance Hotels and other large institutions emerged, housing sometimes a dozen men. These coincided with the virtual disappearance of occupational affinities between lodgers and hosts generally. Of 34 men lodging in private homes in 1901, only seven mariners and three others, a dock labourer, a shipyard worker and a collier in Boldon, lived with a fellow worker. The cash nexus appeared paramount in the frequency of widows housing the balance. Long a locality where land and sea folk met and mingled, South Shields became in the wake of local and national state formation a site of unprecedented barriers to co-residence, and by implication other forms of social relations. Polarization between mobile, unattached seafarers and those settled in the town mirrored a broader bifurcation among workers as the century waned. While respectable working men had tramped in the 1840s, by the *fin de siècle* working-class industrial populations stabilized, leaving mobile men disproportionately young and increasingly disreputable.[80]

The 107 mariners in large dedicated boarding houses still represented barely a fifth, 21 per cent, of 503 local mariners originating overseas. Most continued to live with family in the town. Elite efforts to stigmatize and control mobile workers in general and mariners in particular apparently enjoyed little purchase with local people. For the folk of Shields, boundaries between the cultures of town and sea, Britain and the world, were drawn not by place of origin but by the presence or absence of kin, trade affinities or other personal relations.

## Provincial and parochial?

Literature on the English abroad has focused largely on a relative elite including tourists, missionaries and civil servants.[81] Analysing South Shields reveals global mobility and cosmopolitanism characterized humbler Britons: most obviously mariners, but also people from nearly every walk of life. A challenge to imputed working-class parochialism and defensiveness may be found in the substantial numbers of individuals living in local families who originated abroad, from Kingston to Constantinople, Lisbon to Singapore. Hundreds of South Shields households contained both native and overseas-born members related by blood, confounding distinctions between migrants and natives. Arguably, this dispersed and less cohesive overseas-born population, composed of spouses, children and other kin residing in households headed by native Britons who had travelled the world, contributed as much to shaping multicultural South Shields as the tight-knit and visible networks of Germans, Jews and other migrants.

Scholars initially found remigrants' impact on their places of origin nugatory or conservative. The most prosperous and stable, thus visible, succeeded in amassing sufficient capital to enter the petty proprietary class. Subsequent research turned to humbler return migrants making up the global working class as well as the majority of South Shields' world travellers. Results suggest that they built a common culture, internationalizing expectations about wages, working conditions, militancy and solidarity. European officials apparently thought so, deploring the 'democratic spirit' infecting return migrants and threatening to spread.[82] Along with a democratic spirit, Tyneside's global emigrants also appear to have shown openness to other people and cultures, reflected in marriages with women they met abroad, children named for people they met there and words of languages they acquired, found useful and incorporated into local argot.

The ease with which overseas migrants throughout the century obtained bed and board with South Shields families repudiates their characterization as rootless social marginals and that of Victorian working people as inhospitable to newcomers. Throughout the century the vast majority of overseas migrants lived in households with British-born people, hardly isolated from the broader society and culture. The same skills that advantaged long-distance migrants in the labour market gave them access to occupational networks facilitating co-residence and social interaction with native Britons. Resultant personal relationships were likely better developed than the record can disclose, particularly in view of the clues revealed by more intensively documented relationships on which naturalization rested. Victorian South Shields became a crucible of transcultural class and social formation not due to the formation of migrant enclaves, but to co-residence of migrants and natives, return of emigrants, often with family members acquired abroad, and exogamous marriages. Relations between migrants and natives rendered the town a 'transboundary social formation' within which hegemonic national state boundaries proved secondary to everyday relationships formed by kinship, work and marriage.[83]

# 5
# Gentlemen of the Highest Character: Negotiating Inclusion with the People of South Shields

Between 1879 and 1939, hundreds of the untold thousands of overseas migrants who passed through or settled in South Shields applied for and received naturalization as British subjects. Hundreds of local people stepped forward to support them, making public their friendships with foreign-born migrants. Their testimony rendered visible only a fraction of the relationships and social networks that developed between migrants and natives in industrial South Shields. Examining these well-documented cases illuminates the sorts of relationships integrating overseas migrants into local society, whether or not they ultimately pursued naturalization. It reveals how migrant networks described in previous chapters articulated with those of native-born Britons, belying the comforting but spurious projection of recent xenophobia onto past people. The 1897 petition of Swedish mariner Andrew Anderson 'to obtain the rights and capacities of a natural born British Subject' exemplified the grounds on which migrants pursued naturalization: 'a desire to continue and improve his said calling so as to obtain an honorable [*sic*] independence from such calling to provide for his after years and sustenance and because your memorialist having resided within Great Britain for so many years and having become very much attached to the manners and customs thereof desires to be and remain a resident therein for the remainder of his life'.[1] In spite of the world-scale upheavals that brought him to Britain, Andrew Anderson's professed motives remained profoundly personal, mediated by class, gender and locality. Independence and honour expressed deeply classed and gendered definitions of manliness.[2] Attachment to 'manners and customs' bound him firmly to locale, in Tyneside, arguably, a distinctive regional identity in tension with hegemonic Britishness.[3] Testimony by naturalization applicants and their native referees shows naturalization was a multivectoral process. Not simply an objective, legal and secular contract between an individual and the state, it involved personal, subjective and collective processes in which migrants' native-born friends and neighbours proved decisive in formalizing claims to belong established through routine practices of daily life.

Analysing the permeability and openness of local social formation provides an antidote to prevalent emphases on popular nationalism, xenophobia and racism. A rich literature has explored the construction of discursive categories and the intensive policing of borders and boundaries necessary to sustain social hierarchies.[4] These include the imagined boundary of the nation. Abundant scholarship documents elite and state efforts to construct and impose hegemonic definitions of national identity, including nationality itself, but effective measures of their success in enlisting ordinary people into these nation-building projects remain elusive.[5] Scholars know little about how and whether such people experienced, participated in or identified with national agendas as elites envisioned them.[6] Some argue nationalism presupposed some 'prior unity of territory, language or culture', implying a correspondence between 'culture' and 'customary practice'. Others respond that ordinary people had no stake in nationalism. 'Becoming national' in their view, involved 'delocalization of feelings of belonging'.[7] Only historical investigation can determine whether formal definitions of the nation reflected or conflicted with local custom and culture in industrial South Shields. Analysing naturalization cases reveals the material barriers and discursive categories of national inclusion and exclusion proved permeable, mutable and unstable. In industrial South Shields, they also proved vulnerable to structural shifts as well as individual choices.

This evidence demands reconsidering views of British people and society as inherently xenophobic. Historians have interpreted the abundant documentation generated by episodes of conflict and violence as evidence of submerged but pervasive 'anxiety toward minorities' latent in British social relations.[8] Analysing naturalization cases qualifies this monolithic characterization by recovering countervailing customs of integration and inclusion practised by a significant section of Victorian society. It further shows how these customs and practices of inclusion were repeatedly reshaped in asymmetrical and not unproblematical dialogue with changing state agendas.

Petitions for naturalization originating in late nineteenth- and early twentieth-century South Shields also offer a glimpse into how overseas migrants articulated and negotiated the transition between their original identities and their embrace of British nationality, reconciling global mobility with local relationships and affiliations. Analysing them sheds light not only on these hundreds of migrants, but their social networks composed of neighbours, friends, spouses, employers, business and religious contacts, landlords as well as the customary practices integrating them into local society. For each was embedded in a web of relationships formal and informal, on which he or more rarely she drew to formalize their relationships with state and society. Their stories show that for the people of South Shields the meanings and purposes of naturalization formed in dialogue between local people and the state. This dialectic contained significant instabilities and discrepancies between local and state agendas.

To what degree Andrew Anderson's petition expressed individual subjectivity remains debatable. What Britishness meant to Anderson or other migrants proves unclear because the process itself restricted individuals' expression in formulaic ways. Language in the petitions as well the opportunity for naturalization itself increasingly reflected state expectations and demands. Broad shifts in the timing and volume of naturalizations, shown in Table 5.1, like migrants' origins and professed motives, reflected the world-historical European and global transformations of the nineteenth and twentieth centuries. They also responded to British state interventions in pursuit of geopolitical agendas such as industrial primacy and war. Individuals' incorporation thus occurred in dialogue between local custom and culture and the global ambitions of industry and state.

As Table 5.1 shows, applicants proved overwhelmingly male throughout this period. Of 755 cases between 1879 and 1939, only 27, less than 4 per cent, concerned women, and 19 of these clustered in the years 1914–19, for reasons explored elsewhere.[9] Several factors contributed to men's preponderance. Although women predominated among nineteenth-century migrants, they tended to move shorter distances. Those crossing national boundaries into Victorian South Shields proved overwhelmingly male.[10] Equally important, however, appeared women's legal *coverture*, their inability to act publicly on their own behalf independent of husbands or fathers. Lacking basic civil personhood, including the right to own property, to represent themselves in court or to vote, most women might have found national status and its prerogatives irrelevant. The records themselves reflect this in the invisibility and often namelessness of hundreds of women and children whose nationality altered with that of heads of household between 1879 and 1939.

*Table 5.1* Pace and volume of naturalizations in South Tyneside[a]

| Dates | Men | | Women | South Shields | Jarrow | Hebburn | E. Boldon | Total |
|---|---|---|---|---|---|---|---|---|
| 1800–1902 | 51 | | | 47 | 4 | | | 51 |
| 1903–14 | 23 | + 211 expedited mariners | | 232 | 2 | | | 234 |
| 1915–24 | 35 | | 19 | 50 | 3 | 1 | | 54 |
| 1925–30 | 13 | | 4 | 17 | | | | 17 |
| 1931–35 | 101 | | 2 | 101 | 1 | | 1 | 103 |
| 1936–37 | 137 | | 1 | 136 | 2 | | | 138 |
| 1937 | 78 | | | 76 | 2 | | | 78 |
| 1938 | 51 | | | 50 | 1 | | | 51 |
| 1939 | 28 | | 1 | 29 | | | | 29 |
| Total | 517 | 211 | 27 | 738 | 15 | 1 | 1 | 755 |

*Note*: [a]Other South Tyneside towns are included both to enhance the pool and to allow for comparisons.

Beyond wildly disproportionate sex ratios, Table 5.1 shows dramatic variation in the volume of naturalization over time, due to shifts in British state policies, notably expedited admission for mariners between 1903 and 1915, and hounding of Arab mariners in the 1930s, both discussed below. Discontinuities in applicants' numbers and origins shown in Table 5.2 reflect their response to these changing regulatory regimes and the geopolitical upheavals of the nineteenth and twentieth centuries. These propelled migrants from successive geographical territories into the global labour force, and eventually to South Shields.[11] Pulses of naturalization applicants, first from western and northern Europe, later the Baltic, and finally the Gulf of Aden, parallelled trends within the larger migrant population, displaced by market penetration, political instability, empire building and persecution.

Colonized and Continental migrants arrived in Britain in the process of intense competition for empire that reconfigured national borders, imposing new identities. While Britain, France and other industrializing nations expanded beyond Europe, creating countervailing streams of migrants from Asia, Africa and the Americas, wars of conquest and redivision redrew Continental boundaries. The eighteenth-century partition of Poland erased the ancient kingdom to feed the territorial aspirations of the Hohenzollern, Romanov and Habsburg empires.[12] During the Napoleonic Wars, Russia seized Finland from Sweden, and Sweden annexed Norway from Denmark.[13] Between 1864 and 1871, the German Empire took shape at the expense of Denmark, Austria and France, incorporating neighbouring states, through conquest and coercion, under Prussian domination.[14] Pursued in the name of national unity but achieved through force, Continental empire building mirrored the violent processes simultaneously expanding the overseas empires of Britain, France, Italy and Belgium, and indeed the Spanish, Portuguese and Dutch before them.[15] State-sponsored nation building exhibited imperialistic disregard for indigenous institutions and loyalties.[16] As Italy and Germany took shape through warfare, German language and culture were imposed, if imperfectly, in the Habsburg lands and later Prussia. Russification campaigns in the Romanov Empire and Turkification in the Ottoman followed.[17]

Nominally dynastic projects, Russian and German empire building, like that of other European powers, remained inextricable from the drive to industrialize.[18] Hegemonic nation building, integral to economic and political modernization, displaced petty gentry, peasants, teachers, clergy and intellectuals, and proletarianized artisans.[19] Simultaneously, in spite of or perhaps because of nineteenth-century

*Table 5.2* Naturalizations in South Shields by place of origin

| Origin | 1879–1902 Men | 1903–14 Men | 1903–14 Expedited mariners | 1915–24 Men | 1915–24 Women | 1925–30 Men | 1925–30 Women | 1931–35 Men | 1931–35 Women | 1936–39 Men | 1936–39 Women |
|---|---|---|---|---|---|---|---|---|---|---|---|
| Russian | 8 | 6 | 16 | 14 | – | 1 | – | 16 | – | 7 | – |
| German | 15 | 10 | 27 | – | 13 | – | 1 | 2 | – | 1 | – |
| The Netherlands | 2 | – | 3 | – | – | 1 | – | 1 | – | 3 | – |
| Denmark | 5 | – | 37 | 2 | 1 | 2 | – | 7 | – | 4 | – |
| Sweden | 17 | 4 | 72 | 5 | 2 | 2 | 1 | 16 | – | 14 | – |
| Norway | 2 | – | 43 | 5 | 1 | 1 | 1 | 11 | – | 14 | – |
| Sweden/ Norway | 2 | – | – | – | – | – | – | – | – | – | – |
| Austria | – | 2 | 3 |  | 1 | – | – | – | – | – | – |
| Portugal | – | – | 1 |  | – | – | – | – | – | – | – |
| Italy | – | – | 2 | 1 | – | – | – | – | 1 | – | – |
| Spain | – | 1 | 2 | 1 | – | – | – | 2 | – | 1 | – |
| Estonia | – | – | – | – | – | 4 | 1 | 11 | – | 8 | – |
| Greece | – | – | 2 | – | – | – | – | 2 | – | 2 | – |
| Brazil | – | – | 1 | – | – | – | – |  | – | – | – |
| The United States | – | – | – | 2 | – | – | – | 3 | – | – | – |
| No nationality | – | – | – | 2 | – | 1 | – | 3 | – | 4 | – |
| France | – | – | – | 1 | – | – | – | – | – | 1 | – |
| Ottoman | – | – | 1 | – | – | – | – | – | – | 2 | – |
| Latvia | – | – | – | 1 | – | 1 | – | 11 | – | 6 | 1 |
| Chile | – | – | – | 1 | – | – | – | – | – | – | – |
| Belgium | – | – | – | – | 1 | – | – | – | – | – | – |

*Table 5.2* (Continued)

| Origin | 1879–1902 Men | 1903–14 Men | 1903–14 Expedited mariners | 1915–24 Men | 1915–24 Women | 1925–30 Men | 1925–30 Women | 1931–35 Men | 1931–35 Women | 1936–39 Men | 1936–39 Women |
|---|---|---|---|---|---|---|---|---|---|---|---|
| Uncertain | – | – | – | – | – | – | – | – |  | 2 | – |
| Yemen | – | – | – | – | – | – | – | – | – | 119 | – |
| Arabia | – | – | – | – | – | – | – | 8 | – | 98 | – |
| Romania | – | – | 1 | – | – | – | – | – | – | – | – |
| Lithuania | – | – | – | – | – | – | – | – | 1 | – | – |
| Poland | – | – | – | – | – | – | – | 2 | – | – | – |
| Egypt | – | – | – | – | – | – | – | – | – | 1 | 1 |
| Luxemburg | – | – | – | – | – | – | – | 1 | – | – | – |
| Japan | – | – | – | – | – | – | – | – | – | 1 | – |
| Finland | – | – | – | – | – | – | – | 4 | – | 4 | – |
| Switzerland | – | – | – | – | – | – | – | 1 | – | – | – |
| Argentina | – | – | – | – | – | – | – | – | – | 1 | – |
| Indian States | – | – | – | – | – | – | – | – | – | 1 | – |
| Total | 51 | 23 | 211 | 35 | 19 | 13 | 4 | 101 | 2 | 294 | 2 |

'emancipation', Europe's Jews faced renewed persecution.[20] Large portions of the non-European world came under British formal and informal domination in the same years, rendering South Shields' growing non-European population too an effect of empire building. These economic and political destabilizations expelled diverse populations into the global labour market, stimulating unprecedented migration. Scholars estimate 60–70 million transatlantic 'comings and goings' occurred between 1850 and 1925.[21] Hundreds of thousands migrated to Britain, many passing through or settling in South Shields.

Northern Europeans preponderated among those naturalized in nineteenth-century South Shields, roughly reflecting proportions in the town's whole migrant population. They originated disproportionately from among subject and marginalized populations of encroaching Continental empires. Five of the first eight Russian subjects reported birth in the Baltic lands, including the Kingdom or province of Poland, and Kovno, now in Lithuania.[22] With a sixth originating in Grodno, now Hrodna in Belarus, and a seventh in Archangel, they also appeared Jewish, judging by names of family members and occupations, doubly threatened in the increasingly hostile climate of imperial Russia.[23]

A similar pattern emerged among natives of the German lands. Political subordination to Prussia intensified the economic and political dispossession of peasants, artisans, shopkeepers and journeymen, groups corresponding to the pork butchers and master mariners accounting for 12 of 15 Germans naturalized before 1903.[24] Of these, four originated in Schleswig, a culturally and historically Danish Duchy forcibly annexed by Prussia in 1866 and incorporated five years later into the German Empire. Each of these Schleswigers explicitly qualified his relationship to Germany. Carl Christian Bruhn and Engelbrecht Degn identified their parents as subjects of Denmark, while Peter Sonnichsen had become a naturalized Danish subject in 1875.[25] The most adamant rejection of imperial subjection came from John Christoph Peterson, who reported that he had definitively severed this connection, although British law permitted naturalized subjects to retain their original nationality in their native lands:

> as I received my Certificate of naturalization i saw a Clause in wich it said that i would not be Deamed a British Subject with in the limits of the state of which i was a subject previous . . . unless I seece to be a Subject of that State. now Sir as soon as i saw this Clause, i wrote to the athority in Flensburg [Schleswig] to ask them to withdraw my name from the Books. as i thought when i took the oath of

> Allians i wald not belong to two Contrys. i ricived a letter from the athority of Flensburg. to say that i allrady acording with the act of June 1 1870. that after 10 years absent from the Contry, i forfit all rights and preveleges. of a German Subject. Therefor i now Claim no other nation then England as my home. and as such will be loyal and faithful to Englands Queens and Krown. hens. pleace would i now be acknowleged as a British Subject.[26]

Other Germans emphasized provincial origins in Baden, Württemberg, Saxony and Hamburg. Samuel Finn likewise asked for reassurance that he would be treated as a British subject on business trips to his native Russia.[27] Like Finns, Lithuanians, Estonians and Latvians who disaffiliated from Russia after the First World War, those seeking formal incorporation into the British nation in the Victorian period apparently wished to shed imperial subjection in their places of origin.

Geopolitical factors alone cannot explain, however, why some chose to consummate their passage to Britain by seeking naturalization, nor what this meant to them and the people of South Shields. The hundreds of case records reveal discursive forms of self-disclosure heavily mediated by engagement with the British state. They expose dialogue between individual and collective agendas and shifting national and global imperatives.

## An honourable independence

Taking men's professed reasons at face value would neglect how state policies and agendas simultaneously limited as they conveyed individuals' choices and aspirations. Procedures for applying for naturalization altered several times between 1850 and the 1930s, and with them the characteristics of those selected for inclusion. Over the years the British state prescribed a variety of application procedures: early petitions were handwritten, later ones normally submitted on pre-printed forms. Yet even handwritten responses such as Andrew Anderson's appear copied almost verbatim from a boilerplate obscuring as much as revealing individual agendas. Language in naturalization petitions conformed to apparent state expectations. Men's professed motivations hardly proved spontaneous, but rather influenced by past applicants' collective experience of which reasons had proven acceptable. State discourses thus shaped applicants' overtures at every point.

Until 1844, naturalization remained an elite prerogative requiring an Act of Parliament and fees starting at one hundred pounds.[28] Until 1825,

*Table 5.3* Naturalizations by occupation, 1879–1902

| | | | |
|---|---|---|---|
| Master mariners | 29 | Boot and shoe dealer | 1 |
| Pork butchers | 4 | Boarding housekeeper | 1 |
| Pawnbrokers | 3 | Coal agent | 1 |
| Mariners | 3 | Caulker | 1 |
| Drapers | 2 | Clerk | 1 |
| Marine engineers | 2 | General dealer | 1 |
| Clothier/outfitter | 1 | Licensed victualler | 1 |

it involved taking the sacrament, and until 1844 a Christian oath, effectively barring Jews among others.[29] Legislation in 1844 and 1870 made naturalization more accessible, but it remained expensive and cumbersome, after 1880 requiring a fee of 5 pounds, more than a month's wages for a skilled man in work.[30] The occupations and relative affluence of the 51 Victorian applicants, as well as their professed reasons for seeking naturalization, reflected these constraints. The first successful case from South Shields, that of Samuel Finn, occurred only in 1879, years after it became legally available.[31] Most naturalized before 1903 proved skilled tradesmen or small businessmen (Table 5.3). After 1903, discussed below, relaxed terms of eligibility yielded a more diverse and less pecunious population including labourers, women and hundreds of proletarianized seafarers, especially between 1903 and 1914 and again in the late 1930s.

The bureaucratic process of obtaining naturalization repays scrutiny, illuminating relations between states, local governments, police, industrialists and ordinary people. It shows their priorities altered repeatedly between the 1870s and the 1930s. The basic sequence of events throughout the period was this: an individual prepared a 'Memorial', a sworn petition containing personal information, to the Home Secretary.[32] Gustaf Anton Petterson's neatly transcribed Memorial typified many nineteenth-century petitions. These might be filled in by paid agents or in an unknown hand, perhaps that of a wife, girlfriend, workmate or, well-known among colonized men, a boarding housekeeper. Many men submitted forms directly to the Home Office, but frequently agents or solicitors based in Tyneside or London handled part of this process. In addition, each applicant must furnish signed and witnessed affidavits from four referees guaranteeing his moral probity as well as the bona fides of statements in the Memorial. Often a fifth referee attested to his residency before a magistrate.[33] As a group of referees deposed in 1912, 'from our respective acquaintance with the manners, habits and mode of life of the said Edward Benson, we do confidently vouch for his loyalty and respectability and verily believe that a Certificate of Naturalization may with safety and propriety be granted to him.'[34] Upon receipt the Home Office Aliens Department forwarded these declarations to local officials, initially the mayor, later police. The latter must investigate the 'respectability' of applicants and referees alike, and the veracity of signatures and sworn statements. If all was in order, local authorities returned the Memorial with their report to the Home Office, who issued the man or his agents a Certificate of Naturalization. This contained a loyalty oath to be sworn and witnessed. The applicant kept the original certificate, while the official who administered the oath returned a duplicate to the Home Office for registration. A man's Certificate of Naturalization remained ineffective until the oath of allegiance was witnessed. Thereafter he was expected to keep the document on his person.[35]

Beyond these purely bureaucratic requirements lay other hurdles. The Home Office might return a form for what they admitted was 'a mere triviality' lest correspondents 'get careless if they are not kept up to the mark'.[36] Men at sea, especially those without wives, normally had little choice but to rely on lawyers or others ashore whose reliability varied: Alexander Sundstream's case was delayed from April to November 1897 'through neglect and embezzlement of the stamp money by my agent at Shields'.[37] Even an honest broker might lose the paperwork: James W. Browne, solicitor for Michael Friedrich Rupp, attributed a long delay to 'inadvertence. The papers disappeared in my office... until a few days ago when they were discovered wrapped up with another bundle.'[38] The Registrar-General of Shipping and Seamen might delay a man's record of sea service, essential to expedite mariners' petitions, until other documents went out of date.[39] The Aliens Department themselves misplaced Ludvig Rasmussen's papers in their office between May and November 1898, and in 1909 posted the wrong man's papers to Cardiff.[40] They might retain a seaman's discharges, his records of prior employment, long enough to imperil the man's livelihood: Henry Adolphus zur Nedden's solicitors remonstrated, 'applicant cannot go to sea without them'.[41] In 1894 Andrew Anderson's agents responded with exasperation to the Home Office's complaint that the man's 'prolonged absences' had 'caused the postponement' of their decision: 'We have... repeatedly pointed out that he went [on] long sea voyages and was a very short time at home between them... he was in Shields a few hours only on the last occasion of his being in England.' Their client had already endured 'inconvenience, annoyance, and expense... Is it necessary that he should lose a voyage?'[42] Men might be simply overwhelmed by the complexity of the process: Robert Severin Gabrielson, deprived of his job in 1917 due to a wartime prohibition on aliens, 'appears to have been under the impression that by filling up a form of application in 1908, he had done all that was necessary to make him a British subject'.[43]

Even without mishaps, the process proved no mere formality but involved evaluating a man's fitness in dialogue among local and national officials and the people of South Shields. Reliance on local police to investigate implicitly criminalized the process, disturbing some applicants. It also gave the chief constable substantial although not decisive influence over Home Office decisions. In effect, by the twentieth century, the chief constable was well placed to harm the prospects of individuals of whom he disapproved. This position William Scott, chief constable between 1902 and the late 1920s, embraced with evident relish.[44]

Colourful cases exposed the limits of local authorities' discretion, discrepancies between local and national definitions of respectability, and the critical role women and gender relations played in securing the latter.[45] In 1908, Norwegian mariner John Andrew Rodsett was denied naturalization, even under the lax terms then prevailing for mariners. This rebuff stemmed from his cohabitation with a Mrs Kirkham, 'having enticed the latter away from her husband'. Rodsett also had several convictions for drunkenness, assault and other violent crimes. In 1914, however, Rodsett successfully renewed his case, having abandoned Mrs Kirkham and their two young children in North Shields to marry another woman. While Chief Constable Scott deemed Rodsett now 'very respectable', Home Office personnel considered the man's conduct 'greatly to his discredit', granting his petition nonetheless.[46] In contrast, Scott objected to another mariner because 'The applicant when staying in South Shields has been associating with prostitutes.' Home Office personnel dismissed his concern, commenting, 'it is strange that the Police of a sea-port town should have made a point of mentioning such association in the case of a single young sailor. The H[illeg] has not yet made chastity a requirement.' Yet the sealed envelope remaining in the man's file a century later showed the oath was never administered.[47] Political as well as moral proclivities figured in Scott's assessments, betrayed in his endorsement in 1923 of Martin Putnin, a Latvian seaman, stating he was 'of excellent character...not identified with any political organisation'.[48]

Respectability did prove compatible with other forms of masculine misconduct, such as drunkenness and brawling.[49] Mariners Max Auffinger and Karl Gottfried August Parlow and coalminer Henry August

Anderson all passed muster in spite of police records and small fines for petty crimes. Of the last, employed by the Harton Coal Company, police reported, 'with this exception his character has been good and he is respectable'. Auffinger too 'otherwise... appears to have a good character'.[50] The cash basis on which respectability rested became clear in the comment that mariner Anton Andreasen, among others, was 'very respectable' because residing in a house he 'regularly rented'.[51] Edward Benson's respectability, indeed, derived from other men's drinking: endorsing his case in 1912, the chief constable cited his liquor licenses for the Alum House Ham Inn and the Staithes House Inn in Holborn, for which previous 'inquiry was made regarding his character'.[52]

In general, however, state approval remained contingent on prior relationships, not only with the state but also within the locality. Put plainly, applicants' chances of approval depended not simply on submission to hegemonic state discourses, but developed in dialogue between the state and the people of South Shields.

## Love and money: paths to naturalization

In negotiating their way from foreign to naturalized subjects, overseas migrants drew on relationships already developed with the state and with local people. As the scrutiny and rejection of applicants and their referees illustrated, one route to recognition by the state lay via personal relationships formed locally and socially, such as friendships, business transactions, marriage and parenthood. The other route ran increasingly through relationships forged with industry and the British state. These included obtaining state-sanctioned qualifications such as seamen's certificates, service in the mercantile marine or the military, marriage, a contract with the state as well as the community and, finally, the discourses and practices attending naturalization itself.[53]

Reasons men gave for seeking naturalization reveal the multiple relationships, informal and contractual, preceding and supporting their claims. Carl Christian Bruhn cited bonds already forged within local society and with British industry and the state, including

> a desire to continue and improve and develop his business connection he having married an English wife and having invested capital in real estate and other securities in England and also having been exclusively employed for twenty-five years first in English vessels trading from English ports and his business connection is entirely with England, and also he desires to become possessed of other

freehold property in the United Kingdom of Great Britain and to obtain an honourable independence from such business to provide for his after years and sustenance'.[54]

This somewhat breathless statement illustrated how men drew on established relationships to support bids for naturalization. For Bruhn as for many others, the formal passage to British nationality proved only the most recent in a series of compacts with state and society.

Table 5.4 shows men's most frequent reason for seeking naturalization proved profoundly personal: marriage to a British woman and the welfare of their native-born children. Max Buetow, who had lived in Britain for 20 years, declared 'his connections with the German Empire are severed, and his children being born in this country he wishes them to have the privileges of British subjects'.[55] George Adolf Christensen, deprived of his livelihood in 1909 by restrictions on aliens, sought naturalization, 'that my children may continue to live in this country, where they have been born and educated [and] whose sympathies and interests are wholly British'.[56] The state itself viewed marriage and family as persuasive evidence of a man's attachment to Britain. In the case of Peter Julius Jensen, marriage to a British woman made the difference between the grant of naturalization and its denial: wrote Home Office personnel, 'it is very likely that the applicant who is married keeps a house permanently and is therefore established in the U.K.' Responded another, 'Perhaps therefore we might make an exception in his case.'[57] This shows applicants and the state alike prioritized personal and private relations above all others in establishing claims to belong.

Other frequently cited and accepted reasons involved men's public roles as producers and property holders. Twenty-three men cited business connections or the desire to improve their businesses: Swedish boarding housekeeper and outfitter Edward Olsen reported he had 'by

*Table 5.4* Reasons for seeking naturalization, 1879–1914[a]

| | |
|---|---|
| British-born wives and/or British-born children | 29 |
| Desire to improve an existing business, business connections | 23 |
| Real property or aspirations to property holding | 21 |
| Long service in British ships or British industry | 19 |
| Prior contract with state, e.g. maritime qualifications | 15 |
| Desire to exercise the franchise and/or hold public office | 15 |

*Note*: [a]After 1914 applicants' goals became moot as the process shifted in favour of state agendas.

great exertions succeeded in forming a lucrative connection in his aforesaid business in England', while Austrian jeweller Markus Bortner 'has business premises in this and other towns and wishes to have all the rights of an Englishman'.[58] Twenty-one men justified their petitions through the revered imperative to property holding, only open to aliens after 1870.[59] Christian Nelson harboured 'a desire to acquire and hold shares in a British vessel', while Erich Magnus Ahlstedt declared that 'what savings he has is invested in England'.[60] In a country with a property franchise, men's stake in the nation served as compelling evidence of genuine commitment.

Other men cited their contributions to British prosperity through long service in British ships or British industry: Hans Christian Sophus Thomas Christensen, originally from Copenhagen, reported 'being constantly employed in the British Mercantile Marine, and being engaged in the coasting trade, and having married a British subject and formed friendships in and about South Shields aforesaid'.[61] Paul Arthur Eggert cited employment 'for ten years past in English vessels trading from English ports and his business connections being entirely with England'.[62] Carl August Nordberg had sailed in British ships for 27 years, and Hans Frederick William Rasmussen for 19.[63] In some cases the employer himself apparently exercised compulsion. Carl Bernhard Morck, reportedly 'employed by the same firm, Messrs Ropner and Co. of West Hartlepool since 13 June 1885', sought naturalization in 1898, amid the rising xenophobia accompanying *fin de siècle* imperial rivalry, as 'his said employers ... repeatedly advised him to do so'.[64] In 1901, Swedish master mariner Erich Ahlstedt likewise reported 'a desire to continue his aforesaid avocation as his employers prefer that he should be a naturalized British subject'.[65] Fifteen men supported their claims to British nationality citing maritime qualifications won through Board of Trade examinations, a credentialling process signifying respectability and embourgeoisement.[66] Ten held Master Mariners' Certificates of Competency, while George Segar, who held a First Mate certificate, sought naturalization so he could sit further examinations.[67] Ernest Dabbert, holder of a Master Mariner's certificate of competency since 1880 and commander of a ship for ten years, stated: 'Having married an English woman and holding command of an English vessel by virtue of an English certificate of competency he is desirous of becoming legally recognized as a British subject.'[68]

Such credentials embodied evidence of a man's commitment to Britain, but also a means of obtaining an additional reference, that of the Registrar-General of Shipping and Seamen at the Board of Trade.[69]

Men claiming sea service in support of their petitions must supply evidence, in the first instance Certificates of Discharge containing a record of past voyages. As discharges were not given in some trades, such as the 'weekly boats', of the coasting trade, the Registrar General might be called on to verify or supply a man's work record directly to the Home Office.[70] This procedure could potentially disqualify a man, although not Erick Magnus Ahlstedt, of whom the Registrar-General found, 'nothing recorded in this department adversely affecting his character'.[71] Through such means men leveraged participation in British society to secure their status.

Thirteen men indeed expressed the desire to exercise the franchise or to hold public office.[72] Christian Nelson declared his wish 'that he may vote at Parliamentary and Municipal elections'.[73] Lazarus Josephs sought 'the right to vote and to hold Freeholds and exercise all rights and capacities of a natural born British subject'.[74] Mayor W. Pearson reported applicant Michael Frederick Rupp, a 20-year resident of Jarrow, and 'a large property owner in the town' cherished a 'desire to enter the Town Council'.[75] Niels Jorgen Waldemar Jorgensen and Simon Junala professed intentions to 'join the British naval reserve'.[76]

Several men, finally, reported primarily sentimental reasons for desiring naturalization. Hermann Voss had been 'so long ... engaged in the British Merchant Service that he has become attached to the United Kingdom and its government'.[77] Christopher Nagel 'has made many friends in this country to which he has become attached'.[78] Like Lazarus Josephs, Samuel Finn declared his loyalty to 'Her Most Gracious Majesty the Queen'.[79] For others, naturalization merely formalized their relationship to the only home they knew: Fridjof Jacobson had resided in Britain for 35 of his 37 years, while Charles Bernhard Andersson too had lived there 'since he was a lad'.[80] Anders Christian Andersen had lived in the town since age 13 and attended Stanhope Road school: his parents had lived there as well and his mother was interred there.[81] Mused William S. Daglish, Town Clerk of Jarrow of John Christoph Petersen, 'I cannot say whether he can assign any reason why he prays for a Certificate of Naturalization ... I may add that his wife is an English woman and that the whole of his family were born in Jarrow and he is employed by Messrs. Palmer's Shipbuilding and Iron Company Limited, as a caulker, and he takes a very prominent part in the affairs of the Salem Baptist Church, and to all appearances is a very loyal subject.'[82]

This last example like the first illustrates that many men petitioned on multiple grounds, founded on prior relationships and attachments to the British state, to local people or both.[83] Such qualifications proved profoundly gendered, not only explicitly, as most remained unavailable to women, but implicitly, as men imbued them with the language of mastery, competence, honour and independence.[84] Further, most such motives remained personal, instrumental and local, focused on marriage, family, business and local politics rather than reasons of state, nation or patriotic fervour.

In addition to individual transactions with the state and industry, naturalization depended more fundamentally on informal relations forged through daily contact among the people of South Shields. The demand that candidates produce British-born referees made relations between migrants and the state contingent on prior relationships with neighbours, co-workers and local states. This process revealed much, not only about migrants themselves, but the milieu they inhabited, particularly whether migrants were welcomed or shunned by local people.

## Collusion and surveillance

Some referees embraced the invitation to surveille and police their friends and neighbours on the state's behalf. Respectability to banker John Ridley and John Laurence Hall, JP, implied allegiance to the state or at least the monarch. They declared Samuel Finn 'perfectly loyal in his conduct towards our most gracious Queen and the Government of this Kingdom [prospectively] a loyal and respectable subject'. Referees for master mariner James Meier similarly endorsed him as 'a responsible man…we believe he will be a loyal subject to Her Majesty'.[85] Patrick Smith assured South Shields police that the proximity of his grocery shop to Edward Benson's alehouse afforded 'every opportunity of observing the mode of life of Mr Benson'.[86] The 'chargeman of the squad' of coaltrimmers including applicant Emil Granlund volunteered in 1919, in the overheated atmosphere of the immediate postwar period, that 'had he [Granlund] been the least anti-British' the declarant 'would have been the first man to disclaim him'.[87] Collusion with state agendas may have been more apparent than real, however: significant discrepancies between state and local expectations emerged when they disagreed about what constituted respectability, or when the authorities found native-born referees wanting.[88]

## Gentlemen of the highest character

Local and national authorities vetted not only applicants but also their referees. The process imposed disciplinary mechanisms not only on naturalization candidates but their social circle, prescribing the conduct of personal and professional lives. A referee must be a natural-born British subject and a householder but not the applicant's agent or solicitor. As years passed, the Home Office increasingly demanded, as evidence of intimacy, that referees attest to visiting applicants in their homes, an expectation at odds with working-class custom. A man and his referees must also exhibit that critical but elusive Victorian virtue, respectability.[89] Accordingly, William Morant, chief constable in 1896, reported of a draper, an ironmonger, an engineer, a butcher and a miner, all referees for master mariner Christian Nelson, 'The above named referees are householders, British born subjects, and respectable men.'[90]

These criteria were observed strictly in the nineteenth century: Daniel Lord, for example, despite eminent stability derived from holding a responsible position with the same firm for 18 years, proved unacceptable as a referee for Ludvig Rasmussen because he was not listed as a householder in the Byker Poor Rate rolls.[91] For the most part, however, referees' suitability hinged on their perceived moral character: rejecting William Haynes as a suitable referee for mariner Andrew Anderson, Chief Constable Morant explained, 'Mr Haynes is at present homeless, and of drunken habits. He was summoned before the court on the fifth March 1897 for threatening his daughter.'[92] Chief Constable William Scott later rejected boarding housekeeper James Hanson as a fit referee for Oscar Isaacson. Hanson had a series of petty convictions for brawling as well as breaches of wartime regulations demanding that boarding housekeepers such as Hanson inform the police about alien guests.[93] Magnus Cheyne failed to pass muster because he had never visited Martin Stephan in his home, while James Reside, an engine fitter, fell foul of Chief Constable Scott by consorting with bookmakers.[94]

In 1912 Scott rejected Brockett Lowery as a referee for publican Edward Benson. Separated from his wife and living with his father, Lowery, a deputy overman at Harton Colliery, had forfeited householder status. More seriously, Lowery had a string of convictions in Tynemouth and Sunderland for petty crimes ranging from larceny of beer to arrears of maintenance and threats, perhaps related to his troubled marriage. Producing a fifth referee, Patrick Smith, a 'highly respectable' tradesman, Benson duly received naturalization.[95] In contrast, the chief constable praised referees for Dutch mariner Christian Herder as 'gentlemen of the highest character and respectability'.[96] None other than the Mayor of Jarrow attested to the 'character and respectability' of Michael Friedrich Rupp and his referees.[97] A man's fitness for naturalization thus rested not only on his own conduct and attainments but those of the company he kept. In turn the process of naturalization extended local and central government discipline beyond individual migrants into the community at large. Candidates' personal and local friendships and associations determined whether they achieved formal incorporation into the nation.

## Having lived close beside them all the time

Given the prospect of such rigors, what manner of men and women formed friendships with migrants strong enough to sustain a naturalization bid? Between 1879 and the 1930s, hundreds of South Shields residents from every walk of life did so: adults of all ages and stations, women as well as men, clergy and laity, professionals as well as workingmen and women.[98] Some candidates appealed to authorities such as an employer, family doctor, union representative or teacher. Most, however, drew on neighbours, co-workers, business contacts, co-religionists and relatives, men and women of similar standing to themselves, with whom they interacted in the course of daily life. Referees reported scores of occupations, from well-represented trades such as butchers (33), grocers (31) and master mariners (18) to rare ones such as the isolated medical botanist, the single tallowchandler, or the lone private enquiry agent and furniture dealer.[99] Befriending a migrant, although not the statistical norm in industrial South Shields, was hardly confined to isolated social marginals. It appeared a commonplace thing to do, a customary practice in this maritime society.[100]

Omissions in the data preclude statistical precision, but of 414 referees reporting an occupation, as opposed to 'J.P'. or 'landlady', the vast bulk proved skilled workmen or small shopkeepers, similar to the applicants they supported. Collectively, they enjoyed a slightly more prosperous class position than the general population of the town. Table 5.5 shows more came roughly from class II, largely petty proprietors such as grocers and ironmongers, than from class III, skilled workmen. Very few occupied the ranks of the semi-skilled or unskilled. Examining these referees illuminates the public and private relationships migrants forged in industrial South Shields, integrating them into local social networks whether or not they ultimately pursued naturalization. The content of such relationships, so rarely articulated, emerged in the statements with which men and their referees supported naturalization petitions.[101]

Most visibly, bonds formed among men practising the same trade. Table 5.6 shows nine butchers, more than any other single trade, drew support from fellow butchers, 13 in all. Most proved German pork butchers whose social networks extended between South Shields, Jarrow

*Table 5.5* Social class of referees, 1879–1924[a]

| Social Class | | 1879–1902 | | 1900–24 | |
|---|---|---|---|---|---|
| I | Professional | 24 | 13% | 14 | 6% |
| II | Intermediate | 87 | 48% | 127 | 54% |
| III | Skilled | 68 | 38% | 78 | 33% |
| IV | Semi-skilled | 1 | 0.05% | 6 | 2.5% |
| V | Unskilled | 0 | – | 9 | 4% |
| Total | | 180 | – | 234 | – |

*Note*: [a] Five-point scale derived from W.A. Armstrong (1972) 'The Use of Information about Occupation, in E.A. Wrigley (ed.) *Nineteenth-Century Society: Essays in the Use of Quantitative Methods for the Study of Social Data* (Cambridge: Cambridge University Press), 215–23; and from Appendix C: 'Constitution of the Socio-Economic Groups and Social Classes', *1951 Census General Report* (London: HMSO, 1958), 214–20.

*Table 5.6* Naturalization referees' relationships to applicants, 1879–1924[a]

| | Referees | Applicants |
|---|---|---|
| **Business and professional contacts: total** | 60 | 54 |
| Business transactions (to 1914) | 11 | 11 |
| **Same trade: subtotal** | 29 | 23 |
| Master mariner | 9 | 8 |
| Butcher | 13 | 9 |
| Other | 7 | 5 |
| **Professional relationship: subtotal** | 20 | 20 |
| Family doctor | 3 | 3 |
| Union representative | 5 | 5 |
| Teacher | 3 | 3 |
| Board of Trade officer | 4 | 4 |
| Postman | 2 | 2 |
| Norwegian consulate | 1 | 1 |
| Building Society Secretary | 1 | 1 |
| Vicar | 1 | 1 |
| **Neighbours: total** | 53 | 34 |
| Same street (relationship not specified) | 21 | 16 |
| Residence in same street | 8 | 7 |
| Business in same street | 13 | 7 |
| Business in proximity | 11 | 4 |
| **Work relations: total** | 23 | 16 |
| Shipmates | 7 | 5 |
| Workmates | 6 | 3 |
| Employer or supervisor | 10 | 8 |
| **Personal relations: total** | 48 | 33 |
| Relatives | 5 | 4 |

*Table 5.6* (Continued)

| | Referees | Applicants |
|---|---|---|
| Home visits | 13 | 9 |
| 'Meeting him in company' (nineteenth century) | 3 | 3 |
| Introduced by in-laws | 2 | 2 |
| Introduced by wife | 5 | 2 |
| Landlord/landlady | 6 | 7 |
| Church/synagogue/chapel | 10 | 5 |
| Same lodge | 4 | 1 |
| Total | 184 | 137 |

*Note*: [a] These numbers will not add up, as some individuals drew referees from more than one relationship, while many referees did not specify their relationship to Memorialists.

and southwestern Germany. Between 1889 and 1934, 14 pork butchers were naturalized, nine from South Shields and five from Jarrow. The first three, Ernest Götz (1889), Charles Henry Phaffley (1896) and Michael Friedrich Rupp (1898) resided in Jarrow: Phaffley and Rupp were supported by John Mcnab, a butcher in 1889 styling himself a gentleman in 1898, and Thomas Wright Massey, an ironmonger in 1889 and a tobacconist in 1898. Frederick Keith and Johann Heinrich Hertrich too shared a referee, fellow butcher Matthew deRedder. This evidence shows personal relationships built out from native into migrant networks: fellowship among skilled tradesmen transcended local particularism, offering *entrée* to migrants from distant lands, mutually enforcing occupational solidarities and compatriot networks. It also renders visible the geographically broader and multiply layered networks truncated by this analysis confined to one town.[102] That the first three naturalized lived in Jarrow suggests social intimacy in this much smaller town facilitated migrants forming relationships with natives. This inverts assumptions about the cosmopolitanism of larger towns and the small-minded parochialism of provincial England.

Master mariners too enjoyed a high degree of support from their fellows, seven endorsed by another master mariner, and Carl Christian Bruhn by two. The prominence of these two trades suggests how older forms of fraternal solidarity might be harnessed and rearticulated with modern state building.[103] Five more men drew on fellow practitioners of their profession, including marine engineer Emeterio Bilbao, innkeeper Edward Benson, outfitters Abraham Levy and Aaron Gompertz, and technical chemist George Edwin Anderson. Although striking, occupational brotherhoods still proved less significant numerically than daily interactions in street and neighbourhood: in most cases a majority of referees came from outside a man's trade.

Other workplace contacts also sustained friendships, shown in Table 5.6. In the nineteenth century, even simple commercial transactions with a tailor or furniture dealer sufficed to legitimate a relationship. Innkeeper William Sketheway reported 'having from time to time during the last five years and upwards bought furniture of' Isaac Pearlman,[104] while John Edmund Bilbrough had traded in coal with Pearlman's brother Joseph.[105] Auctioneer Alexander Flint and Jacob Chapman, proprietor of market stalls, became friends with Samuel Schenker 'by working the Markets—the applicant having been a dealer in linoleum and floor-cloths'.[106] Eight men called on employers or supervisors: John Firbank supported master mariner Edward Harmann Korn who 'served his time in my vessel the "Hilda", in the Merchant Service'. John Edward Bowser, a prominent Newcastle shipowner, and his partner Charles William Ormston had employed master mariner Charles Kragh for seven years as a mate and then a captain.[107] Frederick James Boyd, Emeterio Bilbao's 'superior officer' on the *SS Stonehenge*, reported Bilbao 'one of the best men he has ever known'.[108] Five mariners called on a total of seven shipmates, and three men on six workmates.[109] John Isaac Magub declared he and Carl August Nordberg had been 'shipmates ... three times'.[110] J. William Wood McAlister spoke for John Christoph Petersen, a co-worker at Palmer's shipyard.[111] All four of Emil Granlund's referees, coal trimmers like himself, worked with him in the same squad.[112]

Men also mobilized professional relationships: three their family doctors, three Charles Bellam or Frank Cahill, local representatives of the National Sailors' and Firemen's Union (NSFU), and two William Burdon, Secretary of the Institute of Engineers, the marine engineer's union.[113] Thomas Young, a surgeon, declared that Andrew Anderson 'and his family have been attended by me ... as their medical man during the last eight years'.[114] Leslie Pearlman called on his schoolmaster William Thomas, Andrew Anderson on his teacher H.B. Duncan, who 'prepared applicant for his extra examinations in seamanship', and George Edwin Anderson on Peter Phillips Bedson, his former chemistry professor at Armstrong College. The Reverend Horace Sydney Sylvester Jackson, Vicar of St Jude's, also knew George Edwin Anderson as a regular churchgoer and resident of the parish.[115] Ottar Motzfeld relied on a British-born contact in the Norwegian Consulate, and mariners Charles Wahlquist, Isak Olson, John Sprogas and Johan Gustaf Wiberg on Board of Trade Officers, who routinely certified seamen's eligibility for work.

Durable relationships also formed between lodgers and householders. Seven men relied on landlords, landladies or rent collectors, particularly useful to document residency. Mrs Jane Eales, a lodging housekeeper, vouched for both Carl Bernhard Morck and Charles Wahlquist, and a Mrs Grieves for Christian Nelson.[116] Felix Sarah supported Hermann Christian Voss, who had lodged with Sarah intermittently for the previous 11 years. Voss also 'served as mate in the vessel commanded by Sarah and they have sailed together for several years'.[117] William Harvey Bailey based his 'particular knowledge' about Reynold Erickson from 'collecting his rent weekly...in fact he has seen him weekly for ten years'.[118]

Five men mobilized relationships formed in the institutional settings of Church, chapel, synagogue and fraternal organization. John George Lawson supported Christian Herder based on 'twelve years as a churchgoing companion, an intimate friend, and on visiting terms'.[119] Three of Julius Klotz's referees, a carpenter, a builder and a steelworker, found common ground in the Baptist Chapel, of which Klotz, who had resided in Britain for over 40 years, served as Secretary.[120] John Frederick Erickson also met coal agent Alfred Thompson Storey in chapel, while Samuel Schenker and Moses Netz mobilized a total of five co-religionists. The chief constable observed that Netz and his referees, 'Messrs Levy, Kossick, and Jackson...are of the Jewish persuasion'.[121] Other friendships may have originated in such institutions, remaining submerged in the record: while two members of the South Shields Town Council, licensed victuallers Christian Henry Marsh and John Wilson, attested of seamen's outfitter Erik Erickson that they 'met him almost daily', the chief constable revealed that Erickson and his referees were 'all...members of one lodge'.[122] Yet most relationships appear to have taken shape outside such formal institutions.

Many men, indeed, professed longstanding and intimate relations that crossed the divide between work and leisure, public and personal life. The bland formulation 'frequently meeting him in company when ashore and having had business transactions with him' obscured the complexity and durability of relationships grounded in daily practice.[123] Agent William Suckling, for example, lived adjacent to marine engineer Alexander Sundstream between May 1887 and May 1895, attesting to 'daily intercourse' with Sundstream 'both on board vessels on which he has been engaged and at the houses in which he has resided'.[124] Of Peter Trapp, a licensed victualler, referees declared, 'being in business adjoining the applicant they have all seen him daily, and also knew him when he was following a seafaring life'. One of them 'in business for many years in this district... had many opportunities of seeing the applicant when he was sailing out of this port, and since he has taken up business he sees him almost daily, and has business transactions with him'.[125] John George Robinson derived his knowledge of George Edwin Anderson from 'having been postman on the walk for 17 years and knowing his father well'.[126] Herbert Dixon reported that Marten Luther Rasmussen resided nearby and both men worked for the River Tyne Commission.[127] Daily interactions thus forged multiple bonds between migrants and natives.

Revealing the potency of spatial proximity in integrating migrants, men who resided or did business in the same street or locality proved by far the most numerous. Table 5.6 shows 16 men presented a total of 21 referees with addresses in the same street. A further nine referees specified that they resided nearby, while 13 referees had businesses there. Eleven more owned businesses in close proximity. Coal agent James William Southern based his support on 'my being a tradesman seeing the said Augustus Lundean carrying on his business at 31 Hudson St. Tyne Dock South Shields aforesaid almost daily'.[128] Matthew DeRedder, 'a shopkeeper in the same locality' as butcher Frederick Keith, reported 'attending the Markets, and meeting him almost daily'.[129] Referees 'in business near' Abraham Levy 'see and speak to him daily, and have done so for a number of years'.[130] Confectioner Giovanni Valentini drew support from an auctioneer, an estate agent, a builder, a joiner and a plumber, all 'in business in close proximity to the applicant and see him daily'.[131] John William Kirby conducted 'business myself in the vicinity of' Johann Andreas Hub's butcher shop and home.[132] Pork butcher Christopher Nagel and his referees 'each have businesses of long standing in the same locality, and see each other daily'. One of them, John Wann, owned the building where 'the applicant resides and carries on his business'.[133] Thomas Oliver Stewart, a butcher, vouched for George Adolf Christenson and his family's eight years of residence in Jarrow, 'having lived close beside them all the time'.[134]

In contrast, only 13 referees, for nine men, reported primarily social relationships, based on home visits as the state prescribed: William Stoker, a shipping agent, attested a 'close personal acquaintance' with Carl Christian Bruhn, 'having visited him at regular and frequent intervals at his residences'.[135] Archibald Anderson declared that 'for eleven years prior to 1897 he resided neighbours with' Lorentz Larsson, and 'frequently visited him at his residence there'.[136] John Alder and his referees 'see each other almost weekly... on very friendly terms' and 'visit each other at their homes'.[137] Even such personal relationships evidently developed out of workaday, public ones: Frederick George Henderson, former chief chemist of the Walker and Wallsend Gas Company, reported that George Edwin Anderson 'held a responsible position as my chief assistant, and was solely in charge of a ... plant; He visits my house frequently as a personal friend and confidante.'[138] Five merchants in business near John Christian Egner's butcher shop in Eldon Street 'gained there [*sic*] acquaintance as neighbours, and later as personal friends'. One of these began by 'supplying him with mineral waters' but 'kept up the acquaintance by visiting him at his house'. Thomas Whittaker, a schoolmate of Leslie Pearlman, continued the relationship afterwards.[139] Robert Jude, a newsagent and stationer, reported that Max Buetow 'has been in the habit of frequently visiting me at my place of business and I have frequently visited ... at his various residences'.[140] Although William Simpson and John Sprogas first met at sea, their friendship dated from 1907 'when he came to reside at my house': Sprogas' landlady was Simpson's mother-in-law.

For in addition to friendships, men mobilized the kinship ties that had already incorporated them into local families. Four men called on relatives to support their petitions, three on brothers-in-law, and Martin Putnin and Markus Bortner on men they had met initially through their in-laws. John Henderson was related to Samuel Danielson by marriage.[141] Charles Wahlquist's referee Lindsay Forster may have been related to his wife Jane Riddle Forster Wahlquist, a hypothesis given weight by the fact that they all lived in the same house. George Edwin Anderson was 'a college chum' of plasterer John Turner's son.[142] James Walter Scott, an ironmonger, met Paul Arthur Eggert through Eggert's intended before they married.[143] Reported joiner Thomas Paul: 'I am brother-in-law to the Memorialist', Swedish mariner John Albert Klebert, 'and have always been on intimate terms with him'.[144]

Integration was helped not only by relative affluence but the stability the state demanded. Referees for a number of men declared friendships of over 20 years, and two of Auguste Edward Desire Magnan's referees had known him 35 and 44 years.[145] Affidavits for Christian Nelson affirmed only the previous five years, but Chief Constable Morant reported his referees had known Nelson for far longer.[146] The chief constable of Jarrow reported the same of Michael Freidrich Rupp.[147] Several men, indeed, had lived since childhood in South Shields. Henry Levy, born in Richmond, Virginia in 1889, moved to Britain two years later with his parents but remained a subject of the Russian Empire until naturalized in 1913. Alexander Galloway, a family doctor living in the same street as Levy, now a Cambridge undergraduate, 'has watched the growth of the applicant since he was a child'.[148] Although born in Italy in 1866 and married there in 1893, Giovanni Valentini had lived in Britain since age 14.[149] Even the authorities themselves claimed personal knowledge gained from the routines of work and neighbourhood. Owen McCormack, a South Shields' police inspector, had known Moses Netz for 15 years due to 'personal visits paid to me to obtain a pedlar's license every year', and because 'for the last three years and nine months he has resided in the same street opposite to my house' in Challoner Grove.[150] Formal integration thus rested on informal processes common to overseas migrants generally, including business and professional transactions, spatial proximity, co-residence and intermarriage.

In addition to scores of townspeople who acted as referees, an infrastructure of legal services also supported migrants' claims to British nationality. At least 28 law firms in South Shields, Jarrow, Sunderland, Newcastle and London assisted in processing naturalization claims. Local firms such as Young & Green, Grunhut & Gill and Hannay & Hannay submitted paperwork and corresponded with the Home Office on petitioners' behalf. Several firms in London also took part, notably, Messrs Waterlow Brothers & Layton, who assisted with at least 27 cases from South Shields between 1884 and 1922.[151] Their involvement offers further evidence of native Britons' participation in incorporating migrants into British society.

Naturalization thus appears merely to have formalized integration long established through the informal routines and practices of daily life. Migrants' relations with friends, kin, neighbours and co-workers reveal British nationality not simply as a hegemonic imposition obliterating local identities and affiliations. Nor did it reflect an unproblematical and consensual unity of custom and culture with state agendas. Instead, migrants' incorporation occurred in asymmetrical dialogue between local and national, migrants and natives, state and society. Migrants pursued British nationality for profoundly personal and instrumental reasons: to secure families and livelihoods. Men who spent most of their lives in Britain yet remained technical aliens exposed most starkly the tensions between local custom and culture and the requirements of increasingly exclusive state-driven nation building.

## Everyday customs of inclusion

Analysing the process of naturalization affords intimate insight into how migrant networks in industrial South Shields extended into the native-born community and took root there, through work and leisure, chapel, Church and synagogue, neighbourhood, marriage and kinship. Not all such informal relationships eventuated in formal incorporation.[152] Examining state-sanctioned processes illuminates the less formal relationships integrating the bulk of individuals who did not pursue naturalization. The men discussed here doubtless formed a relatively privileged, thus somewhat unrepresentative, section of South Shields' migrant population. Stayers rather than movers, unlike the majority they had remained in South Shields, prospering sufficiently to aspire to the expensive and cumbersome process of naturalization. Relative affluence may have made them more welcome, at least to 'gentlemen of the highest character', than pauper strangers excluded from localized 'communities of obligation'.[153] Yet these migrants and their referees, judging by occupation, residential distribution and other variables, appear little different from the broader population of the town. The bulk practised skilled trades or tended shops, with a sprinkling of professionals such as chemist George Edwin Anderson and labourers such as John Christoph Petersen, 'by profession a caulker'.[154]

In constructing a case for naturalization a man might draw on prior contractual relationships with the state as well as his informal, personal social networks. Further, these two routes proved dialectically interdependent: a man's ability to conclude a formal bid for naturalization depended on his previous formation of local personal relationships. This showed in the weight the state placed on applicants' marriages to British wives, and the demand for four native-born referees who might be friends, relatives, neighbours or business associates. Effectively, the state depended on local people to vett applicants in spite of their divergent agendas. Fitness to become a British subject rested in turn on informal acceptance into local networks as a precondition for the formality of naturalization. Migrants' journey from abroad to incorporation into British society therefore proved not simply an individual process, but a social one that took shape informally for most applicants before they sought to formalize it.

Given this evidence, local and provincial custom and culture appear more open and permeable than bounded and unitary, the British people more accommodating than intolerant and xenophobic. Between 1879 and 1924, hundreds of respectable British men and women, dozens of firms of solicitors, local officials such as mayors and municipal officials, chief constables and local police, participated in incorporating hundreds of foreign-born men and two foreign-born women into British nationality. They did so through a cumbersome and highly public process in which referees voluntarily subjected themselves to the scrutiny of states local and national, and all concerned were called on formally to stake positions. Neither insubstantial in number nor socially marginal, the gatekeepers and border benders of industrial South Shields enacted a contradictory duality: on the one hand, they participated in forms of nation building heavily mediated by state agendas, yet, paradoxically, as disputes about men's respectability revealed, they influenced and contested the meaning of British nationality in dialogue between the agendas of the central state and local values and practices with autonomous trajectories.

This analysis also sheds light on practices of male sociability, gender and class solidarities that knit migrant and native alike into local social networks. Scholars have shown how poor women created social and cultural institutions and practices such as neighbourliness, involving frequent sharing, borrowing and barter, that functioned as critical survival mechanisms rooted in the daily life of street and locality.[155] The foregoing shows that merchants and tradesmen who inhabited these localities partook in similar cultural processes, through workaday transactions such as delivering mail or purchasing mineral water. These likewise forged personal bonds through which migrants became incorporated into localities. Male sociability may have taken its most visible forms in pub and club, but appears nourished by more mundane practices such as business transactions and daily routines, from the purchase of a carpet to the furling of a blind. Migrants became integrated into local society through residence and participation in the daily life of street, neighbourhood and workplace. Hundreds of friendships between native men and women and foreign-born residents of South Shields so documented exposed the everyday and informal relations binding migrant with native whether they sought naturalization or not. Only via such daily and local relationships could migrants secure their status with the central state. Yet shifting relations between migrants and an increasingly interventionist state dislocated such arrangements in ensuing decades.

# 6
# His Wife Must Surely Know: Women and Migrants' Integration

On 19 January 1898, Carmen Zugasti married Emeterio Bilbao, a marine engineer from San Nicolas, Bilbao. The couple had four children between 1899 and 1904 while living in Desierto Erandio, Viscaya province. In 1901 Emeterio Bilbao began sailing in British ships, in 1906 moving his family to Newport, Monmouthshire where Carmen bore two more children, Emeterio in 1906 and Jose in 1910. On 21 July 1912 Carmen died in Newport, and her family dispersed rapidly. The children returned to Spain, while her widowed husband passed the bulk of nine subsequent years on the *SS Stonehenge*, plying between the Continent and various British ports. Bilbao proved so mobile that police in Swansea, London and South Shields had difficulty interviewing him regarding his naturalization petition, as he 'is seldom in these districts'. In 1921, Bilbao sought naturalization upon deciding to remarry a British woman, retrieve his younger children and reconstitute his family: 'in the event of his marriage the children will take up their abode at his home wherever it may be'.[1]

The psychic dimension of this love and loss remained unspoken, betrayed only because the man's own statements contradicted the documentary record. Emeterio Bilbao declared that 'the wife of your Memorialist died ... since which date your Memorialist has lived on board the *S.S. Stonehenge*', representing himself as essentially homeless since Carmen's death. Yet the Chief Constable of South Shields reported that Bilbao received his mail and resided when in port at 98 Commercial Road, the boarding house and bakery of Mrs Mary Zarraga, whose husband Enrique also came from Erandio.[2] For a man such as Emeterio Bilbao, sojourns ashore in lodgings, even with a compatriot, offered meagre emotional sustenance compared to the wife and family he lost and then, when the opportunity arose, recovered.

As Emeterio Bilbao's story illustrates, local and migrant women played a variety of vital roles, integrating migrants into local families and networks, as well as stabilizing culturally distinct German, Jewish and other migrant communities. Landladies who welcomed migrants into their homes, native women who married migrant men and women who arrived from overseas with their families all proved critical in shaping the character of local society. Without them the town's maritime and other industries could not have functioned.

As men have comprised the bulk of long-distance migrants, women's role in such migration has received scant historical attention.[3] Analysing native and migrant women's contributions to South Shields' multicultural milieu demonstrates their centrality to newcomers' survival and integration. Women's assistance not only proved vital to migrants themselves, but sustained industry while aiding the state in tracking and controlling migrants' labour and movements.[4]

## Landladies

Migrants disembarking in South Shields first encountered women of the town as landladies of lodgings, to whom many formed remarkably strong attachments. Numerous men followed particular landladies from one address to another over years. Swedish mariner Nils Peter Johanson, for example, lodged repeatedly with the same landlady at three different addresses in South Shields, 88 Cleveland Street, 14 Empress Street and 3 Gowlands Street, between June 1900 and June 1906.[5] Latvian mariner John Sprogas lodged with his first and only landlady, Mrs Julia Brown, at four different addresses in South Shields over 13 years.[6] For an unattached mariner with few other relationships, a landlady might prove his sole sustained human contact ashore. When Newport Police proved unable to trace Portuguese ship's cook Felisberto Pestana, a former landlady, Mrs Whiston of 49 George Street, saved his case by assuring the Chief Constable that he was former lodger, 'well known to her [as] a very respectable, honest, and sober young man, and can speak English well'. Her word carried weight with Detective William Tanner, who commented that Mrs Whiston 'is well known to the Police as a respectable woman and what she has stated can be relied on'.[7] At times the connection proved even more tenuous: although Peter Julius Jensen's landlady Mrs Palmgren had died, her sister Mrs Annie Tyler affirmed that Jensen had lodged with Mrs Palmgren 'about the times stated'.[8] Even those who deplored landladies as part of a parasitical seaport service sector designed to part the hapless mariner from his pay also acknowledged that they provided essential services and stability to peripatetic seafarers.[9]

Migrants' acculturation might begin in the domestic and quasi-familial relations between landladies and lodgers.[10] Boarding house-keeper Mrs Robb professed to know ship's fireman Anastasios Andriotis well as 'a very decent, respectable man, sober, and industrious', adding that her son had helped obtain books whereby Andriotis became fluent in English.[11] Ship's carpenter Fritz Truwert and his wife Mary Ann named their firstborn son Fred Waddel after their landlady Mrs Waddel, suggesting strong affection and perhaps kin relations.[12] The volatile bundling of age disparity, unsupervised gender relations, cash exchange and personal service in relations between lodgers and landladies bothered Victorian observers, as it confounded public and private, domestic, maternal and sometimes covertly sexual functions.[13] Relations between migrant lodgers and native landladies often did segue into the most common, or at least best-documented role native women played in migrants' experience, that of wife.

## Why not exogamy?

Given longstanding maritime connections across the North Sea and the Baltic, and the town's location on Britain's cultural and geographical periphery, marriages between local people and overseas migrants may require little explanation. South Shields drew its prosperity from industries embedded in and vulnerable to the world market, and from the migrants who converged to make them profitable. Attendant human and economic relationships sprawled across national boundaries.

Local sex ratios may also have encouraged exogamy. In South Shields, as in most industrializing societies, a predominantly male population of long-distance migrants encountered a native population with a slight surplus of women. Figures in Table 6.1 show women outnumbered men in South Shields throughout the period in question, except for 1871, 1891 and 1931. In 1881, men and women resided in County Durham in roughly equal proportion, but among British natives women outnumbered men by a ratio of 113 women for every 100 men.[14] Males' population figures may have been inflated however: they customarily included ships' crews not actually present on census night, much less resident in the town.[15] By the twentieth century, moreover, this apparent surplus of women may have been no more severe than in other British locales.[16] Henry Mess characterized women as a relatively 'scarce commodity' due to the convergence of mostly male migrants

*Table 6.1* Sex ratios in South Shields, 1841–1931

| | Males | Females | Surplus women |
|---|---|---|---|
| 1801 | 4,452 | 6,559 | 2,107 |
| 1811 | 7,072 | 8,093 | 1,021 |
| 1821 | 7,158 | 9,345 | 2,187 |
| 1831 | 8,036 | 10,720 | 2,684 |
| 1841 | 10,524 | 12,548 | 2,024 |
| 1851 | 14,089 | 14,885 | 796 |
| 1861 | 17,427 | 17,812 | 385 |
| 1871 | 22,750 | 22,586 | −164 |
| 1881 | 28,373 | 28,502 | 129 |
| 1891 | 39,381 | 39,010 | −371 |
| 1901 | 48,358 | 48,905 | 547 |
| 1911 | 53,286 | 55,361 | 2,075 |
| 1921 | 57,580 | 59,055 | 1,475 |
| 1931 | 54,805 | 53,380 | −1,425 |

*Sources*: George B. Hodgson (1996 [1903]) *The Borough of South Shields: From the Earliest Period to the Close of the Nineteenth Century* (South Shields: South Tyneside Libraries), 6–7; *1911 Census: Administrative Areas PP1912–1913* [Cd.6258] CXI Table 10, 125; *1921 Census of England and Wales: County Durham* (London: HMSO, 1923), Table 2, 2; *1931 Census of England and Wales: County Durham Pt .II* (London: HMSO, 1937) Table E, 23.

on the shipyards and collieries of industrial Tyneside.[17] Still, since women like men almost universally married as a survival strategy, and Tyneside marriage rates exceeded national averages, a relative shortage of native men may have encouraged local women's liaisons with migrants.[18]

Statistics are not destiny however: intermarriage between migrants and natives partook of and perpetuated longstanding cultural practices of social permeability. Residence, occupation, proximity and mobility presented opportunities for and obstacles to intimacy. Evidence about individual lives shows marriages between migrants and natives occurred in social and structural contexts shaped by South Shields' centuries of communication with the North Sea, the Baltic, the Mediterranean and beyond.

## Marriage integrated migrants

Intermarriage between long-distance migrants and natives has most often occurred between migrant men and native women.[19] In South Shields, the earliest such marriage recorded occurred between Barates of Palmyra and Regina, a native British Catuvallaunian, during the Roman occupation.[20] Historically, exchanges of women such as daughters and sisters have cemented political alliances.[21] Marriage into an established or powerful local family might give a newcomer access to kin networks, property and political connections.[22] Attempting to quantify these advantages seems futile, but abundant anecdotal evidence attests to local women's role as points of entry and gatekeepers into British society. Although most assumed this role informally, their personal choices proved critical to migrants' relations with the state and society.

In industrial South Shields, numerous unions occurred between migrant lodgers and native landladies or other household members.[23] Danish able seaman Kristian Lindemann lodged at two different addresses with a Mrs Wright, who became his mother-in-law when he married her daughter Anna Mary.[24] Russian able seaman Ivar Eklund originally lodged at 124 Chichester Road: after he married a daughter of the household, Wilimina Richardson, the couple continued residing with Wilimina's parents.[25] Like Peter Hughes, Massimo Moiraghi, a mariner, married his landlady Mrs A. Hunt in August 1910, adopting her several children.[26] Such marriages reflected the appeal of a familiar and proximate woman for men encumbered in the marriage market by linguistic and other cultural barriers, compounded by seafarers' frequent absences. It also echoed pre-industrial nuptial practices, in which marriages united and were witnessed and guaranteed by kin and social networks rather than individuals.[27] At the very least, marriage between a migrant and his landlady or her daughter assured both bride and groom of the character of his or her intended in an otherwise risky marriage market.[28]

Once married, migrants continued to call on wives' relatives for various forms of assistance. For five years, Russian AB Edmund Morreno aka Francis van Kursacoff and his wife Polly Louisa continued living with her parents, where Morreno had lodged previously.[29] Ship's carpenter Ernest Feldman and his wife Johanna shared a household with her mother at 51 Westoe Road.[30] Latvian marine officer Martin Putnin and his wife lived with an apparent relative bearing Mrs Elizabeth Wigg Putnin's maiden name, Henderson. Master mariner Henry Henderson acted as a referee for Putnin's naturalization petition, as did James Inkster, whom Putnin met through his father-in-law.[31] Relationships developing between lodgers and landladies thus led to marriage and other forms of integration, while a man marrying a local woman thereby acquired social and kin networks as well as a wife.

## Women anchored seafaring men

In ports such as South Shields, even more than inland towns, women provided mobile mariners such as Emeterio Bilbao a sense of continuity and psychic anchorage.[32] Wives often formed the critical link between a man's peripatetic life on the sea and society ashore. Danish ship's carpenter Benthien Nielsen for years resided between voyages in a series of seamen's boarding houses, including the Sailor's Home, Leith, the Sailor's Home, North Shields, and finally the boarding house of a Mr Toward in West Holborn, South Shields. There he met and married Margaret Brown, his landlord's granddaughter, enabling him finally to establish his own household at 15 Edith Street in March 1903.[33] Master mariner Carl Bernhard Morck, lodging in South Shields while his wife and four children lived with grandparents at Enebak, Norway, 'desires to bring his wife and family to establish his home' in Britain.[34] Losing their wives apparently prompted several other men to reassess their relationships with local society and the state. Swedish ship's cook Peter Lind responded to his wife Mary's death on 17 August 1912 by swearing out a Memorial for naturalization only a week later, on 24 August 1912, securing and affirming his attachment to Britain.[35] Ship's fireman Fothel Ali likewise pursued naturalization after his wife Yeshia's death in 1940, an event apparently severing his last substantial link with his native Yemen.[36] Less tragically, when mariner Gillis Schelin's wife Bertha left South Shields for a 12-month visit to Sweden, her absence left Gillis with no home but his ship.[37] In addition to providing emotional stability, living wives also performed numerous vital functions for migrant husbands, especially those at sea.

## Gatekeepers

Naturalization petitions provide a rich source of information about women's centrality, revealing migrants depended on wives and other women to mediate relations with the central state and local society. The state in turn depended on local women essentially to vett male migrants' fitness for naturalization. Only a handful of women acted as referees, but women nonetheless played critical and even decisive roles in determining men's success in attaining formal incorporation.[38] In the nineteenth century, the mere existence of an unnamed wife, especially a British one, strengthened a man's case. In the twentieth century, as application processes grew more exhaustive, women were increasingly called on to participate actively, providing and relaying information, and appealing to the authorities on men's behalf.

The state treated marriage to a local woman as compelling and persuasive evidence of a man's legitimate and bona fide commitment to the country. In their eyes, founding a family in Britain enhanced the likelihood a man would stay permanently. In 1863, the Home Office refused naturalization to Edward Mogensen, a Dane living in North Shields, on the ground that he remained unmarried: 'The distinction is drawn between unmarried seamen and those who are married and have an established residence in this country occupied by their families during their absence at sea.'[39] Of 51 men naturalized in South Shields between 1879 and 1902, only two, Peter Sonnichsen, 24, a German shipchandlers's clerk, and Johan Gustaf Wiberg, 32, a Swedish master mariner, remained unmarried.[40]

In the twentieth century, marriage continued to enhance men's chances of obtaining naturalization. Petitions by Karl Makevit, a Swedish ship's carpenter, failed in 1904 and again in 1906 because as a single man he appeared too unsettled, lacking sufficient ties with the community. In 1904, for example, 'The Chief Constable of Bristol has been unable to trace him, nor ... obtain any information with regard to his character and respectability, nor his intention to reside permanently in the United Kingdom.' As Makevit lived on board ship when in port 'The Police have been unable to find anyone who knows him.' Only in 1907, after he married an Englishwoman, Elizabeth 'Tulip' Makevit, producing a daughter, Jane Ellen, the authorities relented, after Tulip furnished information during her husband's absence at sea.[41] For Austrian mariner Antoni Kerrick, marriage to a British woman made the difference between the grant of naturalization and its denial: The Home Office overlooked discrepancies in his record as 'the report is otherwise favourable and the applicant has married' Miss Sally Bismith, born at Newport of a British mother and an Austrian father.[42]

The Home Office frankly bent the rules for men married to British wives: regarding Carl Heinrich Frederick Möhle, a German ship's steward with 'a wife of British origin ... we have accepted rather less than five months shore residence and rather less than three months in the case of mariners married and occupying houses or rooms regularly rented by them'.[43] Anshelm Hermann Strom, a Russian ship's carpenter who had lived ashore for only four months of the previous five years, proved acceptable because 'He is, however, married to an English wife and rents a house.'[44] In 1906, the Home Office commented that 'if an alien has (as often) married an English wife, it gives him considerably more claim.'[45]

In contrast, the Home Office suspected the intentions of Russian able seaman John Wannag as he planned to marry Agusta Snider, who lived in Hamburg. They acceded when Wannag explained that the couple intended to live in South Shields.[46]

An unstable marriage, conversely, could call a man's character into question. Although rejected applications remain inaccessible, several successful ones show the authorities took a wife's conduct explicitly into account when assessing her husband. Christian Jensen, although separated from his wife for two years 'through some accusation he made against' her was still judged 'of good character and respectable', perhaps because Jensen had lived in the neighbourhood for 22 years, working ashore as well as at sea. His children's naturalization, however, remained in jeopardy.[47] The 'drunken habits' of Greek ship's carpenter Robert Petirs' wife exonerated him from suspicion raised by the couple's separation, while second mate Christian Roemeling's wife was dismissed as 'a drunkard ... recently imprisoned for three months for neglecting her children'. Roemeling was held blameless as 'his occupation would prevent him from exercising a close surveillance over her'.[48] These cases reveal minute scrutiny of migrants' personal lives, particularly of their wives and marriages. They also betray marriages' vulnerability to wives' isolation during men's prolonged absences at sea, during voyages that might last years.[49] Still, not only did a wife, especially a British one, legitimate a man's case in official eyes, but wives, daughters, landladies and other women actively facilitated migrants' livelihoods as well as their relations with industry and the state.

## Deputy husbands and business agents

Evidence about migrants' wives belies Tyneside women's lingering albeit spurious reputation as economically and socially marginalized 'domestic victims'.[50] Repudiating Victorian ideologies of women's unworldliness and dependence, scholars have documented the autonomous action afforded New England women who functioned as 'deputy husbands', licensed to transgress purely domestic roles to carry out absent householders' agendas.[51] Maritime culture demanded women assume such responsibilities on an ongoing basis. Whalers' wives acted as 'business agents' for men at sea, while seventeenth- and eighteenth-century wives of chronically unpaid British mariners coped with state fiscal irresponsibility through a strenuous economy of makeshift including substantial public roles: market activity, litigation, collective protest and lobbying.[52] In the twentieth century, Liverpudlian wives of Chinese mariners, like other working-class wives, survived through pawning, credit, taking in lodgers and laundry, charring, sewing and even restaurant work.[53] Abundant scholarship documents women's integral role in sustaining the fishing industry, but less appears known about merchant seamen's wives.[54] Native women married to migrants arguably exercised greater authority and autonomy even than other mariners' wives, as they normally possessed more local cultural capital than their husbands, including language competency and personal connections. Norwegian mariner N.K. Eilertsen's wife Annie, for example, headed their household, as the furnishings and the tenancy remained hers since before the marriage: 'Houses have been rented in the name of the wife... the rent being paid out of the applicant's earnings.'[55]

Not all such women proved British. A substantial number originating overseas reported their occupations as 'mariners' wives': one apiece in 1851 and 1861, nine in 1871 and 12 in 1881. Representing their status and work thus, seafarers' wives defied the convention that a woman with a living husband normally downplayed her labour. Those listing themselves as householders in their husbands' absence reflected the practical reality that a mariner's wife shouldered extraordinary responsibility in his absence, entailing autonomy and perhaps empowerment.[56] Such responsibilities, of course, included filling in the census schedule. Reporting her occupation as 'wife' also reflected such a woman's privilege relative to a widow who, without a male breadwinner, must find some other way to make ends meet in an unpromising labour market. Elizabeth Hughes specified her occupation as 'miner's widow', perhaps for similar reasons, including the arduous round-the-clock labour miners' womenfolk performed to maintain this overwhelmingly male workforce at employers' disposal.[57] This suggests that while most wives in Victorian South Shields submerged their work in accord with prevalent norms, many mariners' wives retained explicit work identities, reflecting their integral role in sustaining household and industry.

Wives' critical role in sustaining men at sea, and in turn maritime society, emerged in naturalization processes. Many assisted with the paperwork, and several drew on their own personal relationships in the locality to find referees for husbands' petitions. In his absence, master mariner Charles Kragh's wife Dorothy, for example, forwarded the correct names of his parents to the Home Office, and supplied information to police.[58] The wife of Carl Christian Bruhn verified his references during his absence at sea.[59] Louise Anderson wrote to her husband Andrew's solicitors from Dunkerque, where she had travelled to meet her husband when his ship docked, to say he would arrive in England in a few days'

*Table 6.2* Men naturalized: routine versus expedited mariners/married versus single

| | **Routine cases** | | | **Expedited mariners** | | | | |
|---|---|---|---|---|---|---|---|---|
| | **Total** | **Married** | **Single** | **Total** | **Married** | **Single** | **Widowed** | **Total** |
| 1879–1902 | 51 | 49 | 2 | | | | | |
| 1903–14 | 23 | 21 | 2 | 211 | 141 | 64 | 6 | 234 |
| 1915–24 | 35 | 27 | 8 | | | | | |
| 1925–30 | 13 | 11 | 2 | | | | | |
| 1931–35 | 101 | 64 | 36[a] | | | | | |
| 1936–39[b] | 294 | 87 | 207 | | | | | |

Notes: [a] One unknown. [b] Numbers were inflated 1903–14 and 1936–39, explained below.

time. It thus appears Louise Anderson took responsibility for her husband's correspondence, perhaps due to her greater facility with local language and culture, even when he was in port and presumably could have done it himself.[60]

Between 1903 and 1914, expedited naturalization became available to mariners, contingent on proof of continuous service in the British mercantile marine. As Table 6.2 shows, while the process continued to advantage married men even among mariners, 141 married versus 64 single, it created a loophole through which dozens of single men attained British nationality. Ostensibly premised on a man's relationships with the state and industry rather than family or community, this simplified application process demanded, paradoxically, that women assume even more central roles in many transactions. Wives, after all, remained ashore while many men became virtually unreachable at sea. Peter Johnson's wife, for example, was contacted to identify his signature, while Danish ship's fireman Peter Larson's wife verified the signatures on his petition.[61] Carl Andreas Knudsen's wife contracted his business with the police while Knudsen, a Norwegian ship's master, remained at sea. Second mate Frithiof Gustafson received naturalization after his wife assured the authorities of 'his intention to reside permanently within the United Kingdom'.[62]

The central government themselves encouraged local police to treat wives as intermediaries for men at sea. When South Shields' Mercantile Marine Office superintendant informed the Home Office that 'it is not known when' Hilmar Kristofferson 'will return to the U.K', they retorted, 'But his wife must surely know. Ask her.'[63] The Home Office themselves asked William Hesse's wife 'to enquire of her husband the port next visited in the U.K' so that they could issue time-sensitive documents.[64] Such offices could only be rendered with men's cooperation, of course. Charlotte Anderson, wife of Alexander Anderson, although able to authenticate her husband's signature, 'cannot definitely state how long her husband would be away, but would inform him upon his return, to call at the Central Police Station'.[65] Martin Putnin's solicitors complained, indeed, that the arrival of police at her home had 'upset our client's wife, who is in a rather poor state of health', having recently given birth.[66] Marriage thus advantaged migrants in forging relations with the state. The state in turn relied on wives, through the marriage market, effectively to screen likely candidates for incorporation into British society. Once married, wives assisted in completing men's formal political inclusion.

Wives' kin and social networks also reinforced men's access to and credibility with the British state. Referees supporting George Segar's naturalization in 1921 reported meeting him at the 'home of his wife before their marriage', in other words, through his future wife Hannah.[67] John Frederick Erickson's wife Mary Ann rather than he apparently negotiated his naturalization, relying heavily on her own contacts and connections: his referees included two brothers-in-law, John Martin Carney and John Hutchinson, and Mary Ann's nephew William Carney.[68] Swedish ship's steward Herman Julius Hermanson benefited because the investigating 'officer has known his present wife and her parents for some years as respectable people'.[69] An undertaker, a butcher and a joiner supporting Enrique Zarraga, a rivetter employed by Smith's Dock Company, did business 'in close proximity' to his wife Mary's bakery and boarding house, sometime home of Emeterio Bilbao[70] For some women, centrality in initiating and integrating husbands into local society may have garnered power and authority within their marriages and also within migrant networks. This might partially offset disadvantages they faced due to their husbands' legal disabilities and lack of such connections.[71] Enhanced authority may even have made marriage to a migrant an appealing alternative to the male dominance of native Geordie culture, which archetypally ignored or minimized women's contributions in favour of masculine brawn and sinew.[72]

Women other than wives, such as daughters, sisters and landladies, also assisted migrants with numerous practical matters. Herman Julius Hermanson proved more fortunate than Emeterio Bilbao: he had an aunt residing at 11 Cleveland Street, South Shields, who cared for his children between his first wife's death and his remarriage in 1904, enabling him to live with them when ashore.[73] In Matthew Pearson's absence, his daughter identified his signature as a referee for Louis Korner, while Carl Nordberg's sister verified his signature.[74] Jeweller Marcus Bortner, although single, appeared stabler to the authorities than a lone man because he shared rented lodgings with his sister.[75] Margaret or Maggie, a housemaid in a Thrift Street boarding house, wrote letters for her employer and future brother-in-law, Nassar Abdula.[76] In 1930, as unemployment devastated dockland communities, landladies Mrs Clara Bellanato of 84 Alex Road in Newport Docks and Mrs Mohamed Ahmed, wife of a Cardiff boarding housekeeper, contacted the Colonial Office, the latter seeking assistance with the upkeep of 79 destitute boarders.[77]

The foregoing suggests that local women functioned as gatekeepers into local society and culture. They served not simply as sexualized bodies, of which little explicit evidence survives, but as cultural and practical interlocutors and negotiators.[78] This evidence attests to women's centrality in sustaining not just individual men but industry and state agendas. In spite of their critical role, however, women remained shadowy figures, often nameless unless called upon to verify a signature or relay a message for a husband at sea.

Women also prove difficult to trace because most changed their names with marriage.[79] Only a handful of cases reveal what became of migrants' daughters. Some remained part of compatriot networks after marriage. Catherine Diehl, born in Chesterfield, Derbyshire, but the daughter of stonemason Casper Diehl from Frankfurt am Main, married German master mariner Frederick Koster.[80] Others married into the native population, as did Edith Alexandra Johnson, locally born daughter of Swedish marine donkeyman Augustus Johnson and his Norwegian wife Tomina Christina. When Edith Johnson married native Briton Jesse Dodd, the couple moved into the house next door to her parents at 137 H.S. Edwards Street. A common working-class residential practice, proximity kept them involved with her parents and perhaps the compatriot community.[81] In 1921 Jesse Dodd served as a referee for his father-in-law's naturalization case.[82] This alone rendered Edith, who from all documentary evidence blended imperceptibly into South Shields' local population, visible as a descendant of migrants. Still other migrants' daughters married exogamously to other migrants. Elizabeth Erickson and Andrea Olefine Swan, daughters of Norwegian fathers and English mothers, and Annie Malanson, daughter of a French Canadian, in turn married men from Germany, Sweden and Denmark.[83] Wilhelmina Ali's distinctive given name suggests she too may have had German parents, or migrated herself, perhaps rendering her open to marrying another migrant, Ali Abdul.[84] Other suggestive cases include Alvera Ali, wife of Ahmed Ali, found in Tyne Dock Ward in 1930, Wilhelmina Deen, wife of Mea Kain Deen, living at 15 Cornwallis Square, Holborn Ward, in 1939, and Wilhelmina Musleh, wife of Yemeni Mahomed Musleh.[85] Daughters' marriages to migrants who were not their parents' compatriots suggests exogamy more likely partook of local cultural practices of integration than of defensive, inward-looking migrant enclavement. Native women of migrant parentage thus embodied bridges between migrants and natives. They not only facilitated additional migrants' incorporation into local society, but, as agents of cultural fusion and transformation, confounded facile distinctions between migrants and natives on which xenophobia and other forms of national exclusivity have fed.

## Migrant women and community cohesion

While local women, as landladies, wives or other relatives, eased migrants' integration into local society, women in the German, Jewish and other migrant communities, so often migrants themselves, helped sustain these groups' distinctiveness. Almost no historical scholarship examines women in pre-1948 British migrant communities.[86] In other historical contexts, however, equal sex ratios, denoting substantial family migration, occurred primarily among prosperous and religious communities.[87] Large numbers of women born overseas correlated with the development of German, Jewish and Scandinavian communal institutions in South Shields. This suggests such women proved critical to the survival and stabilization of migrant networks that remained culturally, albeit not geographically, distinct within local society.[88]

Table 6.3 shows Germans, including Prussians, accounted for the largest number of endogamous migrant couples appearing in the census between 1861 and 1891, overtaken in 1901 by Russians. Swedes, Norwegians and Danes together outnumbered both from 1891. Among 48 couples in 1891 originating in the same place, several patterns emerge. Twenty-two, fully 45.8 per cent or nearly half, of endogamous couples were German or Prussian, among them eight pork butchers.[89] A further nine endogamous couples were Swedish (19 per cent), six Norwegian (12.5 per cent), six Danish (12.5 per cent) and two apiece Russian and Polish (4 per cent). Two-fifths (43 per cent) of the householders proved sailors, nearly all Scandinavians, while those from Central Europe, apart from pork butchers, practised an array of skilled or retail trades as glaziers, musicians and the like, many apparently Jewish.

*Table 6.3* Husband and wife of same origin (second column 'J' indicates number of these possibly Jewish)

| | **1851** | **J** | **1861** | **J** | **1871** | **J** | **1881** | **J** | **1891** | **J** | **1901** | **J** |
|---|---|---|---|---|---|---|---|---|---|---|---|---|
| France | 1 | – | – | – | – | – | – | – | – | – | – | – |
| West Indies | 1 | – | – | – | – | – | – | – | – | – | – | – |
| Poland | 1 | 1 | 1 | 1 | 1 | 1 | 2 | 2 | 2 | 2 | 3 | 3 |
| Prussia | 1 | – | 7 | 4 | 7 | 4 | 4 | 1 | – | – | 1 | – |
| Other Germany | – | – | 4 | – | 8 | – | 12 | – | 20 | 1 | 21 | 2 |
| Russia | – | – | 2 | 1 | – | – | 2 | 2 | 2 | 2 | 24 | 20 |
| Sweden | – | – | – | – | 1 | – | 4 | – | 9 | – | 13 | 1 |
| Denmark | – | – | – | – | 1 | – | 1 | – | 6 | – | 1 | – |
| Canada | – | – | – | – | 1 | – | 1 | – | – | – | – | – |
| Australia | – | – | – | – | 1 | – | | – | – | – | – | – |
| The United States | – | – | – | – | – | – | 1 | – | – | – | 1 | – |
| Norway | – | – | – | – | – | – | 2 | – | 6 | – | 19 | – |
| Finland | – | – | – | – | – | – | 1 | – | 1 | – | 3 | – |
| Italy | – | – | – | – | – | – | | – | 1 | – | 1 | – |
| Austria | – | – | – | – | – | – | | – | 1 | – | 1 | 1 |
| Total | 4 | 1 | 14 | 6 | 20 | 5 | 30 | 5 | 48 | 5 | 88 | 27 |

Concentrations of endogamous couples might appear simply an effect of these groups' larger numbers in the migrant population. As discussed in Chapter 3, however, Germans and Jews proved more likely to have migrated as families precisely because they possessed skills and modest capital. This in turn enabled them to prosper in South Shields by mobilizing the labour of wives, children and other kin. Most Scandinavians, in contrast, arrived as mariners, although some amassed sufficient capital to operate boarding houses or other businesses.

Table 6.4 shows migrant women married to migrant men of different origins apparently found their husbands either through Jewish networks (21 of 80 or 26 per cent) or in the course of mariners' travels (36 of 80 or 45 per cent), especially in the Baltic and North Sea (26 of 80 or 32.5 per cent). Most appeared either Jews from Central and Eastern Europe or Holland, or the husband was a mariner, most often Scandinavian.[90] Jewish confessional networks included a transregional marriage market that functioned to enhance community cohesion, as Jews shared a nominally common culture regardless of birthplace. Examples included Harris and Mathilda Alprovich, from Poland and Prussia, respectively.[91] Among non-Jewish mixed couples, two-thirds or 28 proved of mixed Scandinavian origin, suggesting Scandinavians like Jews and Germans shared a deterritorialized collective identity.

*Table 6.4* Couples both originating overseas but in different places, 1851–1901

| | Couples | Jewish | One Scandinavian | Mixed: both Scandinavian | Mariner husband: Scandinavian | Mariner husband: other |
|---|---|---|---|---|---|---|
| 1851 | 1 | | – | – | – | – |
| 1861 | 2 | 2 | – | – | – | – |
| 1871 | 9 | 3 | 2 | 1 | – | – |
| 1881 | 15 | 5 | 1 | 6 | 4 | 2 |
| 1891 | 23 | 5 | 4 | 9 | 10 | 3 |
| 1901 | 30 | 6 | 7 | 12 | 12 | 5 |
| Total | 80 | 21 | 14 | 28 | 26 | 10 |

These arrived later in the century than Jews, but soon made up a plurality. Examples included Hans and Caroline Harild, from Denmark and Sweden, respectively.[92] Germans made up much of the remainder. Most mixed or exogamous couples thus shared Jewish or Scandinavian cultural affinities despite apparently disparate origins. These reinforced migrant networks and institutions in South Shields.[93] Migrant women, whether in endogamous or exogamous marriages, thus lent cultural continuity and coherence to their families and communities in ways less available to the majority of migrant men who married British women.

## Migrant women's economic contributions

Defying the stereotype that women in the Northeast did not work for wages, the German and Jewish population also contained a number of prominent businesswomen, including hotelier Rachel Levy in 1861, pork butchers' wives Barbara Schroth, Catherine Frederick and Catherine Brauninger, and clothes dealer Mary Levy. Brauninger and Levy eventually carried on their deceased husbands' businesses, as described in Chapter 3.[94] Responding to the same forces propelling their families into the global labour market, many migrant women had already entered commercial activity in their places of origin. Eastern European Jewish women, in particular, prepared for lives of responsibility in commerce and industry should they marry scholars.[95] Germans, including Austrians, Prussians and natives of Hamburg, predominated among migrant women reporting workforce participation, as shown in Table 6.5. Like Levy, Brauninger and Birkett, they also appeared in more substantial and professional jobs, as retailers and musicians. Women from elsewhere tended to practise marginal and sex-typed trades such

*Table 6.5* Women reporting occupations (excluding servants)

| Birthplaces | 1851 | 1861 | 1871 | 1881 | 1891 | 1901 |
|---|---|---|---|---|---|---|
| West Indies | 2 | 1 | – | – | – | – |
| Germany/Austria | – | 1 | 5 | 6 | 5 | 10 |
| North America | – | – | 2 | 1 | 4 | 7 |
| Sweden | – | – | 1 | 1 | 2 | 3 |
| Poland | – | – | – | 1 | – | – |
| Russia | – | – | – | 1 | – | 3 |
| Constantinople | – | – | – | – | 1 | – |
| Norway | – | – | – | – | 1 | 2 |
| Malta | – | – | – | – | 1 | – |
| India | – | – | – | – | 2 | 2 |
| Genoa | – | – | – | – | 1 | – |
| Belgium | – | – | – | – | – | 2 |
| Denmark | – | – | – | – | – | 1 |
| Natal | – | – | – | – | – | 1 |
| Total | 2 | 2 | 8 | 10 | 17 | 31 |

as dressmaking and laundering, the resort of widows or other lone women, characterized by low pay, unreliable employment and poor job security.[96] Of 70 women reporting employment other than domestic service in the six successive censuses including 1851 and 1901, German or Austrian women accounted for 21 of 36 retailers or tradeswomen, or 58 per cent, two of five teachers, or 40 per cent, but only 5 of 29 or 17 per cent of dressmakers, laundresses and other marginal occupations. In practising skilled and visible occupations, migrant women differed dramatically from native-born women, among whom work, paid and unpaid, remained notoriously undervalued and under-reported.[97] While British-born wives of householders from abroad outnumbered those originating overseas by 121:38, or 3:1 in 1881, to pick a year, those reporting employment exceeded women from abroad by only 5:4. All of the migrants in 1881 shared their husbands' occupations. Migrants' willingness to acknowledge wives' social labour embodied tacit recognition that the vibrancy of their communities rested on women's skilled labour, and the flow of capital through kin and compatriot networks marital endogamy consolidated.[98] It might equally have reflected fewer inhibitions about public sphere employment, an effect of cultures of origin less permeated by Victorian gender prescriptions. Women in these communities thus contributed disproportionately to local economic development through higher levels of workforce participation in less sex-typed occupations than native women.

Apart from market activity, little direct evidence survives of women's roles within the German, Jewish or other migrant communities. In other historical contexts, migrant or cultural minority women, including Jewish women, remained domestic repositories of language, custom and culture while husbands and children assimilated publicly.[99] Women in South Shields' Jewish, German, Scandinavian and other communities no doubt performed similar roles, accounting for the survival of these culturally distinct communities.

Women's prominence in South Shields' most visible migrant communities contrasts with the absence of visible communal institutions among migrant groups containing fewer women. This may indicate lone men's absorption into native kin and social networks via marriage to local women, although Emeterio Bilbao's gravitation towards the Zarraga household belies any stark dichotomy. While exogamy between migrants and natives facilitated integration into local society, endogamy apparently enhanced the distinctive cohesion and visibility of the German, Jewish and Scandinavian communities.

In contrast, women originating overseas but not residing within migrant households remain enigmatic, their relationship to these close-knit networks largely illegible. Wives usually proved the sole household members from abroad, with British husbands and children. In 1871, 12 women from overseas were married to or dependent kin of British-born householders. Only one, Mary Stephenson, had children also born abroad. Her husband Robert, a Wesleyan minister, had apparently ranged far from his birthplace in nearby Houghton-le-Spring: Mary came from Stockholm, yet her first four children were born in India. In 1881, similarly, only two such couples had dependents also born abroad.[100] As disparate as migrant men, such women hailed from across the globe. In 1881 alone, six claimed birth in Norway, four in Germany, two each in Sweden and Holland, and one each in Barbados, Denmark, Russia, the United States, India, Montreal, Belgium, Burmah and America. Why their husbands took wives abroad remains obscure. In 1871, only 3 of 12 were mariners at the time of enumeration, although those of several French women proved labourers, presumably retracing the well-trod migratory circuit between France and Britain. Other women may have migrated to Britain before, not after their marriages, whether as members of families such as Loretta Garbutt, or on their own.[101] Perhaps some women even met their husbands in some third place, but these records do not say.[102] This raises the still under-researched question of women's long-distance migration.

## Migrant women householders

Asymmetry in number between hundreds of households headed by husbands and fathers originating abroad and the few headed by wives or widows affirms men's prevalence among industrial migrant populations. Still, a few dozen women originating overseas headed households independently, as shown in Table 6.6. Ten did so in 1871, six of them widows, including Elizabeth Hughes, now 47 and widowed for the second time.[103] Women originating abroad headed 23 households in 1891, seven married, 11 widowed and 5 unabashedly single. No married woman reported an occupation, but ten others did. Several single women operated substantial businesses by 1891, suggesting the town's growth may have created opportunities for women's autonomy, in some cases based on hitherto unorthodox domestic arrangements and marginal occupations. Apart from Germans, businesswomen in 1891 included Marie Jeffreson, a Swede, who took in lodgers, Spanish-born Elizabeth Forde, who ran a shop, and American-born Jane Fairles, a fruiterer.[104] Norwegian Inga Olsen, 28, boarded barman William Hodge, 42, perhaps disguising a common law marriage, but one in which she retained nominal control.[105] Most others practised sex-typed occupations. Among them only German-born Anna Brown, a teacher of languages, reported a profession likely to have actually supported her and her widowed mother, Maria.[106] Others included charwoman Carolina Norman from Norway, mother of a five-year-old daughter, and dressmakers Charlotte Newton, born in Calcutta, and Amelia Hagen from Norway.[107] Such occupations as charring and dressmaking yielded a marginal living at best. This shows migrant women lacking resources and support available to those living with family or compatriots remained as vulnerable as native women in local labour markets, perhaps more so.

## Servants

Only a small residuum of women born abroad lived outside family settings, nearly all in other people's homes. Domestic service subjected

*Table 6.6* Women householders originating abroad, 1841–1901

| 1841 | 1851 | 1861 | 1871 | 1881 | 1891 | 1901 |
|---|---|---|---|---|---|---|
| 1 | 4 | 4 | 10 | 5 | 23 | 23 |

them to the worst of patriarchal discipline combined with the relentless work regimen Victorian employers demanded.[108] In 1871 and again in 1881, all nine such women originating abroad but not living with kin reported their occupations as some form of domestic service.[109] All resided with employers. Elysee Chevallier, a 'French governess' employed in 1871 by brewer W. St Allison and his wife Margaret, no doubt lent Continental cachet to their affluent and well-staffed household, Undercliffe Hall, while housemaid Harriett Hay, 21, of Bombay, ornamented the Westoe Village home of Matthew Wood, a substantial brewer.[110] Clearly there was money in beer. Most other servants appear little different from other young women in the town, for whom domestic service loomed large among a narrow and unappealing array of occupational choices.[111] Other domestics served in commercial establishments, for instance, Norwegian Martha Johnson, 19, one of two servants in the Black Swan in Thrift Street.[112] Such relationships could prove durable: licensed victualler Edward Buddle and his wife Elizabeth, proprietors of the Dock Hotel, employed Barbadian nurse Mary Ann Taylor, 35, to look after their five children. By 1881 Elizabeth had remarried another licensed victualler, James Robson, but Mary Ann, now 45, remained in her service. Sadly, Mary Ann's loyalty appears to have availed her little, for by 1891 she had resorted to the workhouse.[113]

Although the town continued to grow, migrant women in service diminished by 1891. Only five servants resided in British-headed households, none in opulent surroundings such as Undercliffe Hall. Alice Longfield, 49, a housekeeper, seemed to be substituting for the dead wife of widowed householder James Palmer while German Annie Kaiser assisted in the enormous extended household of eatinghouse keeper William Curry, and perhaps with the business as well.[114] Possibly, rising xenophobia in the late nineteenth century rendered British householders less open to servants from abroad in 1891 than 1881. More likely, alternative job options in retail, clerical and other *fin de siècle* service occupations drew lone women away from the rigors and humiliations of domestic service.

In all, a small minority of women originating abroad lived apart from their families, and most of these ended up as servants. This corroborates scholars' findings that most women who migrated long distances did so as part of families. In South Shields as elsewhere, the most autonomous women migrants, lacking communal resources available to those moving as part of migrant chains or families, ended up in poorly paid, unskilled and insecure employment.[115] In this sense, lone women, like lone migrant men, became less distinguishable from natives as their ties to places of origin attenuated.

## Anchors and bridges

Male control of women's sexual and generative capacity has historically proven fundamental to social order. Women's sexual agency, particularly in forming exogamous relationships, threatened male prerogative as well as group solidarities and boundaries and the resources and hierarchies they secured.[116] Many scholars approach gender relations across national, confessional, ethnic and racial boundaries from this implicitly patriarchal and statist perspective, depicting them mainly as sources of social conflict.[117] Evidence about South Shields suggests the prevalent focus on conflict has neglected how intermarriage and other relationships between migrant men and native women, rather than disruptive to local society, promoted cultural exchange, integration and incorporation.

Before the Great War, women played critical roles, anchoring rootless men to locality, and bridging migrant and native communities. They eased migrant men's integration into local society and culture by giving access to personal networks and knowledge, and interceding with the state. The British state did not merely tolerate them, but actively encouraged, promoted, rewarded and relied on local women who assisted migrants' incorporation. Germans and Jews, conversely, established and maintained autonomous communities because their settlements contained significant numbers of women from abroad. The interwar Arab community discussed in Chapter 8 differed from either pattern because Arab migrants married native or local women, yet retained their religious and other cultural practices, to which many Arabs' wives assimilated. Women's role and agency in each of these communities thus proved crucial in distinguishing or integrating migrants in industrial South Shields. Further, German and Jewish retailers, hoteliers and tradeswomen contributed disproportionately to South Shields' economic development. Migrant women detached from compatriot networks, whether domestic servants or mariners' wives, occupied a similar vulnerable position to other Shieldswomen. It seems unlikely that, given high rates of market participation and exogamy, either group 'interacted primarily with women of their own background', as in the United States.[118] Instead, like migrant men, these women, particularly prominent businesswomen such as Rachel Levy, appear to have experienced substantial exposure to and integration into native households, families and business networks.

Evidence about South Shields does reinforce the hypothesis that women proved less committed than men to maintaining social boundaries of class or culture, perhaps because they benefited less from the power relations these boundaries reinforced.[119] Local women's apparent openness to marrying migrant men jibed with patterns of cross-class mobility: Britain's nineteenth-century marriage market proved more fluid than its labour market.[120] Exogamous women acted as primary agents of intraclass solidarity, while exogamy and occupational mobility proved mutually reinforcing. Victorian society apparently remained relatively open to women's sexual agency, at least in this respect, growing more rigid with total war and economic and state crises.[121] Analysing Victorian South Shields shows hostility to exogamous couples proved far from universal or constant, remaining contingent on historical context. Rather than suggest, conversely, that endogamy was bad because it exposed South Shields' tight-knit German community to popular hostility during the First World War, one must ask instead why this community lived unmolested in South Shields in the nineteenth century but came under attack in the twentieth century. Answers, however partial, must be sought in the structure of local and global labour markets and economy, and the impact of world war and state intervention.

# 7
# Men of the World: Casualties of Empire Building

Naturalization processes illustrated how relationships with workmates, spouses and kin integrated migrants into local society. The many lives of Robert Shaumann provide a vivid example of such informal incorporation. Originally from the Baltic port of Memel, Robert Shaumann gradually metamorphosed into Robert Sherman, birthplace South Shields, during a lengthy seafaring career. Born in 1848 or 1849 according to various documents, Robert Sherman stood 5 feet 4 1/2 inches tall and had blue eyes and black hair, or 5 feet 5 inches with brown hair. His earliest discharge papers, dating from the 1860s, identified their holder as Robert Schaumann or Heinrich Schaumann, born in Memel, then in Prussia. He sailed several times out of Memel to Dublin, Quebec, Bordeaux, Newcastle, Portsmouth, Swinemunde, Dunkirchen and Birkenhead in the Mersey.[1] From 1870 Robert Schaumann or Schaman began sailing out of British ports, and in the course of 56 subsequent voyages between 1870 and 1913 reported birth in Sweden in 1870–73, Memel in 1873–74, in Germany as Robert Shamman in 1875, in Memel and Sweden in 1876 and in London in 1877–78. During 21 voyages between 1879 and 1889, he was born in Stockholm, Sweden or Memel. Robert Sherman first claimed birth in South Shields in 1890, and more or less permanently assumed this name, which he had been using intermittently since 1877. He also exaggerated his age as 24 in 1870 when he was barely 21 or 22, depending on which document one trusts, if either. Between 1900 and 1912, Robert Sherman, birthplace South Shields, served 20 additional voyages from East coast ports such as Newcastle, London, Middlesborough and of course South Shields, apparently undetected by Mercantile Marine officers in these ports.[2] A Shipping Federation document of 1905 found him at the improbably youthful age of 44, living at 105 Robinson Street in South Shields;

a benefit certificate found him at 94 Victoria Road. In 1913, pensioned off by the Pelton Steamship Company after 'lengthy and faithful service', Robert Sherman lived on the north bank of the river at Willington Quay-on-Tyne.

What moved Robert Schaumann to shift his name, his age, his birthplace from one voyage to the next? Was it the rational calculation of interest, to maximize his employability or evade impressment or conscription? Was it 'peasant cunning', everyday resistance to the exclusions implied in demands for specific birthplaces, ages and names?[3] Was there not an element of whimsy in these random changes of name and birthplace, or of bloody-minded refusal to be contained and disciplined? Or were there multiple Robert Schaumanns, trafficking in discharge papers, as the authorities sometimes alleged? Less than a desperate survival strategy, Robert Sherman's shape-shifting, his 'self-naturalization', partook of evasion and subversion, the timeworn weapons of the weak against states and bureaucracies seeking to name and thereby control.[4] The trick remains, finally, on the researcher who seeks in the documentary record a stable truth with which to comprehend an unruly past. Whatever official records reveal about aggregate patterns of birthplace, migration and settlement must be balanced against this human capacity for creativity, resilience and play, rendering conclusions provisional at best.

Scholars continue debating states' aspirations to control egress and ingress in the nineteenth century, once thought a period of untrammelled migration.[5] Unlike the merchants and artisans forming the core of South Shields' migrant communities, Robert Schaumann, like many passing through between 1841 and 1939, resembled 'political amphibians' inhabiting Continental borderlands. Multilingual and multicultural, such mobile people, exasperating states and officials, assumed alternative identities strategically, maximizing claims to rights and resources.[6] Robert Schaumann and other such shape-shifters passed undetected, suggesting mid-century efforts to control human mobility proved largely ineffective.[7]

Such fluidity has produced a view of mariners as marginal and disreputable, contributing nothing to local societies and cultures. Many sojourners in South Shields indeed belonged to a transitory population enjoying little integration any place ashore. Although numerous migrants became incorporated into local families and networks, others remained limited by the nature of seafaring life and labour. Recognizing this, maritime scholars eschew geographically fixed locations, approaching the sea itself as a primary rather than a residual location, the mariner who traversed it a cosmopolitan 'man of the world ... whose labors linked ... continents and cultures'. To such men, national boundaries and allegiances remained moot.[8] Others depicted mariners in less flattering terms, as deserters and vagrants, 'restless men, part sailor, part tramp, part casual labourer', Scandinavian, German, Australian and American as well as British, 'who wandered from one continent to another'.[9] Unrestricted migration allowed such men of the world to enjoy varied relationships with British and other societies and industries. From the turn of the century onwards, however, state intervention eclipsed personal agendas, rendering the rewards and penalties of nationality explicit. Restriction cut across mariners' customary freedom to get a livelihood relatively unimpeded by national borders or the states imposing them. The last years of Robert Sherman's life saw non-British mariners, then Jews and finally Germans like himself, deprived of their livelihoods, incarcerated, even subject to violence due to national identities imposed without their consent, which many had implicitly rejected by migrating.

This chapter brings new evidence to bear on this process, shifting focus from elite efforts to tailor national identities to geopolitical, economic and imperial agendas to the actions of ordinary people such as Robert Sherman. It analyses how nation building, empire building, global depression and world war gave integration, incorporation and naturalization, formal and informal, new meanings and purposes for migrants and native Britons alike.[10] It shows local people hardly embraced elite defined national identities uncritically. Pressure for national affiliation and allegiance prompted subterfuge and evasion. Ultimately, state-led persecution and exclusion sundered local societies such as South Shields.

Intensified policing of transborder migrants followed short-lived relaxation of restriction from the 1820s. This coincided with Britain's era of free trade imperialism but also with a liberal migration regime across Europe. By the mid-nineteenth century, when Robert Schaumann embarked on his travels, barriers fell in overt efforts to attract labour. Industrial development, market penetration and resultant political instability, as well as state policies of overt exclusion, religious, political and other forms of persecution, warfare and imperial expansion, expelled diverse populations into the global labour market. Nation building, simultaneously a process of 'nation destroying', stimulated voluntary and forced migration, especially of minority and marginalized populations. People displaced by conquest, colonization, enslavement and other forms of political and economic coercion migrated to developing industrial centres such as South Shields, sometimes crossing borders and sometimes not.[11]

## Self-naturalization

Scholars continue debating top-down mechanisms of exclusion and inclusion whereby states defined and constricted nationality, citizenship and rights to enter, stay, depart or return.[12] Social historians, in contrast, pursue 'bottom-up' processes through which individuals such as Robert Sherman decided whether and how to participate in prescribed institutions, thereby shaping their contours. Plebeian folk, denied legal or economic means formally to contract marriages or dissolve them, practised 'self-marriage' and 'self-divorce', collectively sanctioned forms of cohabitation and serial monogamy.[13] Regardless of state-defined national identities, ordinary people likewise defined 'street citizenship', contesting and reshaping social identities.[14] To maximize access to work and other choices, migrants such as Robert Sherman analogously engaged in self-naturalization.

Self-naturalization took many forms, on a continuum from Anglicizing a name to radically recasting a life history. Robert Schaumann's name changes followed historical precedents so ubiquitous they appear customary cultural practice. Medieval Europeans adopted Christian or German colonizers' names, seeking purchase in a newly dominant culture.[15] The most notorious case of enforced assimilation, that accompanying Jewish 'emancipation', involved heavily coercive and contradictory naming politics, as Jews and non-Jews shed 'Jewish-sounding' names.[16] Like Robert Schaumann, Scots seeking the freedom of Newcastle, naval deserters and overseas migrants to the Northeast had been changing or Anglicizing their names for centuries.[17] Mariners evading impressment or conscription changed their names and traded documents routinely.[18] John Anderholm explained, when authorities queried a discrepancy, that 'his proper name is Anderholm... but he took the name of Anderson when he went into British ships'.[19] Some changes occurred involuntarily: the captain of Paul Wilhelm's first ship 'put Paul Williamson on his discharge paper... and he has gone under that name since'.[20] Among others, Frederick Jacobson and his son Fritz were both 'known as' Frederick Jackson, J.A. Bjerkin became Berken, David Jokelsohn became Jacobs and Kristaps Grinfelds became Christopher Greenfield. Yemeni Mohamed Mosley lived in South Shields in the 1930s.[21] However expedient in motive, changing one's name, a socially constituted marker of identity, implied a personal rite of passage towards social integration.[22]

Anglicization might reflect xenophobic pressure or discrimination, or, equally, incorporation into local society. In the 1880s a Shields-based crew dubbed a Norwegian workmate 'Tyne Dock Tom', denoting his status as 'one of us'.[23] Several men in addition to Robert Sherman self-naturalized without apparent detection or penalty. Reynold Erickson, for example, reporting himself a naturalized British subject in the 1891 census and apparently accepted as such by the local enumerator, acquired this status officially only in 1904.[24] Thomas Rogers claimed the same in 1871, yet, like Robert Sherman, he never obtained naturalization formally, leaving his widow a vulnerable alien during the First World War.[25] From the turn of the century, self-naturalization increasingly collided with state imperatives to control and manipulate labour, subjects and citizens in peace and eventually war.

## Self-decolonization

Paper identities carried with them burdens and benefits created by intertwined processes of *fin de siècle* nation building and empire building. Migrants subverted these through self-decolonization. The map of Europe altered dramatically in living memory of nineteenth-century people, as nations and empires were carved from contested ground. Continental territorial empires, some of recent and violent origin, commanded allegiance inconsistently from culturally disparate subject populations. Confected national identities suppressed some affiliations while foregrounding others: within each state and across boundaries, agendas diverged by class, occupation, region, language and other variables. German nation building produced political and class effects: territorial consolidation dispossessed the very artisans and plebeians most likely to migrate and, alternatively, to form anti-imperialist nationalist movements. Baltic nationalisms partook of similar complexities.[26] Imperial states in turn increasingly sought to surveille and regulate citizens as well as subjects to exact military service, taxes and labour, and to enforce desired behaviours.[27] Imposing military service on all Romanov subjects, for example, formed part of a campaign to Russify subject peoples. The 1901 Conscription Manifesto for Finland provoked civil turmoil: statesmen expected it to spur emigration.[28]

For some migrants, national or imperial identity might thus connote encumbrances rather than rewards: moving from the Continent to Britain might signify escape from subject status or simply a shift from one imperial margin to another. Traces of the popular resistance that destabilized and finally destroyed European empires emerged in the evasion and refusal migrants conveyed as they told and revised their stories.[29] Many distanced themselves from imperial power, embracing provincial over imperial identities or professing personal loyalty to monarchs, seeking to escape, if only rhetorically, identities disadvantaging and marginalizing them. Others, like Robert Schaumann, concealed their origins to elude imperial compulsion.

By the early twentieth century, many originating in Russia's Baltic possessions routinely evaded state service by falsifying their identities. John Wannag, a Lithuanian who 'passes himself here as a Norwegian', explained in 1904 that he had sailed under the name Erlick as 'I was advised by my chums' aboardship 'to change my name in case I went back to Russia in any ship... as the Russian Authorities would have impressed me into the Navy'. A Board of Trade official appeared unfazed, recognizing that Wannag sought 'to avoid conscription in Russia'.[30] The most dramatic of many cases, Karl Tomson, naturalized in 1907 as a subject of Norway, revealed his true origins in 1916 as Estonian. In approximately 1896 at the age of 17 Tomson, from the South Baltic island of Tago, contracted rheumatism while serving aboard the Russian schooner *Otto*. Recuperating in a Newport hospital, he determined not to sail on Russian vessels, 'having been badly treated and receiving little pay'. He secured a job aboard a British ship bound for the Black Sea, but the captain nearly rejected him, fearing that 'both he and myself would have trouble with the Russian authorities if I signed on as a Russian. The Shipping master then advised me to sign on as some other nationality', a fiction Tomson maintained until 1916. Commented a Home Office official, 'This is another of the not infrequent cases in which a Russian has sailed under another nationality and has had to stick to the lie.'[31] Like Robert Schaumann, Frederick Nelsen, a Dane, sailed for years with papers claiming birth in South Shields, 'A common practice with alien seamen... who desire to avoid military or naval service in their own country', explained a member of the Home Office staff: '[We] take no notice of the practice.'[32] Rejecting state exactions may not reflect a highly politicized anti-imperial consciousness, yet it proved one of the sincerest forms of disaffiliation from nation-building projects.[33] Its prevalence among imperial subject people suggests evading the burdens of empire carried cultural and political as well as practical implications, an everyday form of 'self-decolonization'.

Men also professed provincial origins subversive of imperial hegemony. Reynold Erickson identified himself in 1904 as a subject of the 'State of Finland', and his parents as subjects of Finland, as did several others.[34] This may have been a point of pride, as the Duchy of

Finland retained substantial administrative autonomy within imperial Russia.[35] More subtle yet proved the case of Edward Apiht. Born in Riga in 1864, Apiht reported his nationality as Swedish, that of his father as Lettish, and his mother as Swedish. Likewise, he identified his wife as German, her father German and her mother 'Lettish and brought up in Riga'. This reflected the complexities of political and cultural allegiance in the Baltic, where historically German ports such as Memel and Danzig perched on the coasts of largely Slavic-speaking hinterlands, and where the sea itself promoted mixing of peoples.[36] This reflected a more general pattern: like colonized people, subject peoples' relationships with European imperial powers grew increasingly contentious as the twentieth century unfolded, aggravated by empire-building projects such as Russification.[37]

Self-decolonization betrayed national identities' fluidity and indeterminacy, but also their utility: politically and culturally amphibious migrants found varied uses for origins and affiliations, finding them open to contestation and interpretation. Local custom and culture in South Shields, commensurately plural, unstable and fluid, hardly lent itself to the rigid and opportunistic reasons of state increasingly encroaching on migrants and natives alike. Several episodes illustrate individuals' inability to avoid implication, even complicity, in European nation building.

## Reasons of state and industry

While states have attempted to manipulate migration for centuries, the turn of the twentieth century witnessed intensified efforts at control.[38] The late nineteenth-century territorialization of 'mutually exclusive bodies of citizens' embodied states' paradoxical response to skyrocketing mobility their policies stimulated. Coinciding with mature capitalism, the Great Depression, 1873–96, and the 'second' Industrial Revolution, state formation widened differentiation between internal and transborder migration. While internal migration remained subject to individual choice, states increasingly constrained transborder migrants, cross-cutting the geographical and occupational mobility of an unprecedentedly global working class.[39] Legislative coercion reified national identities and boundaries, creating the category 'immigrant' as distinct from other migrants.[40] Restricting migration partook of a class project whereby states defined and selected desired migrants only, seeking economic advantage within an increasingly chaotic global system.[41] The poor thus remained unwelcome regardless of nationality, vulnerable to states' developing capacity to police and regulate. Simultaneously inclusive and exclusive, states defined social citizenship around a fictive and bounded organic community, offering entitlements such as the franchise and social provision in exchange for duties such as military service and submission to social regulation.[42] Nationality became increasingly freighted with new meanings, privileges and disabilities. These intertwined processes of nation building and empire building threatened migrants' freedoms and livelihoods.

In Britain this emerged most visibly in the Aliens Act, 1905. The response to an orchestrated campaign by identifiable right-wing anti-Semitic xenophobes, it also marked industrialized nations' recourse to migration restriction.[43] More significant for South Shields, intensified scrutiny and regulation of aliens in the maritime workforce also heralded the new century. Imperial rivalry and consequent xenophobia produced efforts to exclude non-British subjects from obtaining masters' and mates' certificates and pilots' licenses, and the imposition of an English language test on alien mariners. Such measures anticipated armed conflict, ostensibly aiming to prevent 'a foreign master using a British vessel to assist the enemies of this country in time of war'.[44] The Merchant Shipping Act, 1906, gave local Board of Trade superintendents powers to exclude non-British mariners lacking sufficient English language to understand orders.[45] As French citizenship acquired value when the French state attached entitlements to it, the language test and other provisions acted as a negative form of social citizenship, making access to work contingent on British nationality.[46] Anticipating employers' objection to this restriction on their labour pool, the same legislation offered a loophole: alien mariners with four years' service in the British mercantile marine could be naturalized through 'an easy process, without expense'.[47] From 1903, the British state consequently relaxed the costly and cumbersome process hitherto barring all but the most determined and affluent from naturalization. Thwarting the impending language test and other measures, the Board of Trade in London established an expedited route to British nationality for merchant seamen only, many with only tenuous links to any locality ashore.[48]

Previously footloose men of the world then confronted a stark choice to forgo their livelihoods or submit exclusively to British discipline, extraction and control. The trickle of naturalization petitions from prosperous merchants and artisans consequently swelled to a torrent after

*Table 7.1* Largest groups of migrants and mariners in South Shields' population and naturalized

| | Germany | Denmark | Sweden | Norway | Russian | Empire |
|---|---|---|---|---|---|---|
| 1901 census: all migrants | 252 | 99 | 244 | 227 | 123 | – |
| 1901 census: all mariners | 67 | 51 | 128 | 101 | Finns 22 | Other 15 |
| Naturalized 1879–1902 | 15 | 5 | 17 | 4 | – | Other 8 |
| Naturalized 1903–14 | 43 | 36 | 76 | 43 | Finns 8 | Other 13 |

the turn of the century, augmented by thousands of foreign-born sailors compelled to seek British nationality to keep their jobs. Between 1903 and the outbreak of war in August 1914, 211 mariners received naturalization as South Shields residents through this inexpensive and simplified process. In number they dwarfed the 51 men naturalized between 1879 and 1902 as well as the 23 conventional cases between 1903 and 1914. Table 7.1 shows five of the six largest nationalities in the 1901 census.[49] These five nationalities accounted for the bulk of naturalizations between 1903 and 1914, 226 of 234. Over half of Swedes (128/244) and Danes (51/99) and nearly half of Norwegians (101/227) in the 1901 census proved mariners. Likewise, Danes, Norwegians and Swedes, who also made up one of South Shields' major migrant networks, accounted for two-thirds (66 per cent) of naturalizations (155/234) between 1903 and 1914.

To the normal stream of naturalized British subjects was added from 1903 a second whose *entrée* to British nationality bypassed local relationships, custom and culture in favour of a direct contract with the state. The perfunctory 'Prescribed Form of Application' for mariners contrasted with the flowery language in Victorian Memorials. Men submitted these applications directly to the Registrar-General of Shipping and Seamen, who, after corroborating their service, forwarded them to the Home Office. Local Board of Trade officials called Mercantile Marine superintendents returned the completed forms, including oaths, to the Home Office.[50] Whereas previous applicants had paid a substantial sum, often hiring a solicitor, fees were waived for mariners and the Registrar-General acted as their agent: a man incurred the nominal expense of a stamp costing 2 shillings and 6 pence.

The demand for five years' residence in Britain became nugatory in favour of a total of three years' service in British ships. Regarding George Adolf Christensen, for example, the Home Office commented: 'if the applicant has been serving on ships registered at British ports for at least three years out of the last eight and intends to continue in such service, he may be eligible for the grant of a Certificate....'[51]

Officials took a lenient approach to missing or inaccurate information. Of the incomplete application of Martin Weide, Home Office personnel commented, 'Pass. He has paid his 2/6 and the name of his mother is not material.'[52] Hilmar Kristofferson also passed muster although residing 'with his wife and family in Apartments, not as Householders'.[53] Even naval service in foreign vessels, in Martin Masur's case those of his native Germany, could not disqualify him.[54] In effect this category of naturalized British subject attained British nationality bypassing the local relationships prior migrants needed.

Such men differed most from those naturalized under normal conditions in their somewhat lower class status. As Table 7.2 shows, nearly all nineteenth-century applicants belonged to the skilled and petty proprietor classes III and II, among whom seafarers proved master mariners almost exclusively. Most admitted under special provisions between

*Table 7.2* Naturalized mariners' occupational class to 1914

| | 1882–1902 | 1903–10 | 1911–14 |
|---|---|---|---|
| **Class II** | | | |
| Master | – | 7 | 1 |
| Marine engineer | 2 | 7 | 1 |
| Master mariner | 26 | 8 | – |
| Quartermaster | – | 1 | – |
| Boatswain | – | 5 | 7 |
| **Class III** | | | |
| Mariner | 3 | 1 | 1 |
| Mate | – | 16 | 7 |
| AB (Able Seaman) | – | 35 | 33 |
| Cook | – | 6 | 1 |
| Steward | – | 10 | 8 |
| Carpenter | – | 15 | 7 |
| **Class IV** | | | |
| Donkeyman | – | 7 | 6 |
| Fireman | – | 9 | 10 |
| Pumpman | – | 1 | – |

1903 and 1914, in contrast, came from humbler strata of the maritime workforce, including able seamen, mates, stewards, donkeymen and firemen.

For some these provisions proved an affordable opportunity to regularize longstanding residence in Britain: John Poulson, a boy when he arrived in England in 1872, had 'served his apprenticeship in British ships, and... has never served in foreign vessels'.[55] William Henry Henricks, having sailed in British ships for 23 years 'intends making his home when ashore in England in future'.[56] Many reported periods well in excess of the required eight years. These included Massimo Moiraghi, with 17 years' service in British ships, and Johann Heinrich Frederick Kohler, who had served from 1869 to 1913.[57] Like conventional applicants, some such men offered references even though none were demanded, including ship's captain Alfred Jansson, described by shipowner John Bull, his employer, as 'honest, trustworthy, sober, and in every way attentive to his duties'.[58] Personal bonds also emerged in Hans Jensen Brick's decision to delay taking the Oath of Allegiance until his employer, a magistrate, could administer it.[59]

Like conventional applicants, many had wives and families ashore, including Axel Gustafson, who worked on weekly boats, allowing him to spend the intervals between voyages with his wife Ruth in South Shields.[60] Charles Henry Hanson had maintained a wife and four children at 269 South Taylor Street in South Shields for 14 years, although his time ashore amounted only to seven months and 23 days.[61] Alfred Bernard Carlberg, with an English wife and three children aged 20, 18 and 15, had lived at 34 Eldon Street in South Shields for 18 years and served for 30 years in British ships.[62] Many mariners naturalized between 1903 and 1915 thus enjoyed the same deep and longstanding connections with local people as more affluent migrants who gained British nationality via normal channels.

Other men's integration into local society proved more limited, however, stemming partly from the relentless mobility seafaring labour demanded. Attenuation of landward ties showed in numerous men's response to the state's confounding demand for a 'settled place of business', appearing in nineteenth-century Memorials. Responded Carl Bernhard Morck in 1898, 'Your memorialist's settled place of residence is at 60 Elizabeth Street South Shields, but by reason of his employment as a Master Mariner his business is conducted on board the steamships of his employers.'[63] Maritime employment lent itself to the sojourning life, in which the sea itself remained some men's primary affiliation.

## Men of the world

Demanding that mariners account for themselves in a naturalization process simultaneously attaching them unequivocally to Britain rendered visible a group of elusive men of the world, seafarers enjoying minimal connection with South Shields or any community ashore.[64] The invasive process demanded of men seeking conventional naturalization proved a far cry from the ease with which men of dubious reputation and ambiguous identity attained the same status after 1903. Whereas regular applicants' reasons for seeking naturalization came under intense scrutiny, indeed, discursive prescription, mariners' usefulness to state and industry rendered individual agendas moot. Men simply signed a declaration pledging 'it is my intention to continue permanently to reside in the United Kingdom or to serve in British Ships'.[65] Such men need take no part in civic duties or social networks in order to be naturalized as residents of South Shields: their relationship with the state, forged through its major industry, overshadowed or superseded local ties or their absence.

Among those who spent more time on ships than ashore, John Anderholm passed eight years working the weekly boats plying between the Tyne ports and Hamburg. In spite of his marriage to a British woman, Martha Winter Clark, and their two teenaged children Margaret Jane, 18, and John Robert, 16, 'He has only been at home a few days at a time when the ship was discharging and re-loading cargo.' Consequently, like many mariners naturalized between 1903 and 1914, the man proved unable to reconstruct the time he had spent in the town, a period the Home Office estimated might amount to 19 days in five years.[66] Fortunately for Anderholm, he had established a reputation through working aboard the same ship consistently. Frederick Koster, master of the *SS Tynemouth*, himself naturalized in 1904, verified that Anderholm served as his first mate from 14 July 1909 to 25 October 1912: 'I have found him strictly sober, very industrious and always willing and attentive to his duties.' In addition, 'I have also known Mr John Anderson for many years previous to becoming my Chief Officer and have always recognised him as a good alround Man and a good Citizen.' The Mercantile Marine Supervisor at the Board of Trade shipping office in South Shields also affirmed Anderson's 'respectability, having known him for a number of years', and the Registrar-General of Shipping and Seamen furnished a complete record of Anderholm's sea service.[67] Other men proved less well connected.

Many men's residences ashore, indeed, consisted entirely of seamen's boarding houses in various ports, in which they often remained but a few days or weeks. This living arrangement explicitly disqualified nineteenth-century applicants. Carl Oscar Enlund's residence in Britain amounted to barely seven months, but what mattered were his seven years and four months of sea service, a total of 12 voyages in ten ships.[68] William Frederick Theodor Birkedal had lived for no more than eight months ashore in eight years.[69] Although Teodolf Mattison had spent a mere ten months ashore, the Home Office judged it 'perhaps... sufficient', citing a precedent in which 'a Certificate was granted to a mariner who could show only two and one half months.'[70]

The sea itself thus proved many men's primary location, punctuated by brief sojourns in ports of call.[71] Capiton Ketchen, a Romanian ship's carpenter, for example, could not be traced in the records of the Cardiff German Sailors' Home or the Sailors' Institute, but the Registrar-General of Shipping and Seamen furnished a record of 39 consecutive voyages, all but the first 14 on the same ship, the *SS Ferek*.[72] Anders Johan Lagerberg had 'invariably lived on vessels in the harbour' until November 1900, and thereafter in a seamen's lodging house at 186 Palmerston Street, South Shields, 'several times for a few days when his vessel has been in the harbour'.[73] Some men spent so much time on ships and so little ashore that the authorities themselves proved hard pressed to complete the paperwork: August Ferdinand Grönberg's first application in 1910 failed because an absence at sea of 12 months delayed his interview.[74] Gustaf Louis Lindgren's Certificate was forwarded to Dundee and then South Shields before he finally took his oath in Hull.[75] On shore, many such men moved seemingly unobserved through a landscape on which they left little trace. Their minimal impact and human contact often inhibited them from demonstrating they had been in South Shields at all.

## Invisible men

Such transitory figures fit the stereotype of atomized, marginal sojourners. Hans Rudolf Persson reported 24 periods ashore between September 1904 and June 1913, many in seamen's boarding houses in Barry, Cardiff and South Shields. Not surprising given their brevity, the Glamorgan Constabulary proved hard pressed to verify several of these due to errors in dates and addresses, finding one house in Travis Street, not 'Travel Street', as Persson remembered.[76] Of Simon Junala,

South Shields police commented in frustration, 'It cannot be ascertained where this man was between February and September 1902.'[77] Seamen's boarding houses could prove ephemeral: the registers recording men's stays and even the houses themselves might disappear: number 1 Carpenter Street in South Shields 'has been pulled down and the owner is dead'.[78] Landlords might leave the town or even the country: Cardiff police could not trace Ernest Feldman, as 'Peter Stank, who kept 1 Sophia Street... has left this country taking the registers with him'.[79] Other landlords had dispersed to Hamburg or the colonies.[80] At times even the authorities admitted defeat: South Shields police failed to corroborate several residences John Adick Eliasson reported, as 'one of the people has since died, and others have left the town leaving no address, and the applicant has nothing to show that he did live at these addresses'. The Home Office decided to overlook unanswered questions, and Eliasson received a certificate nonetheless.[81] For some such men, constant movement and the anonymity it conferred may have proven an end in itself, an opportunity for self-fashioning, reinvention, subterfuge or simply play.[82] Indeed, such motives emerged in the handful of cases proven in some way irregular—the shape-shifters and tricksters who could not muster even a minimal account of their movements ashore.

## Trickster tales

One such proved Swedish seaman Teodolf Fridolf Mattison. Few recalled him and even fewer could affirm his residence, possibly because 'he has a way of omitting to pay his board.' Mattison's first petition failed when police could not trace him at any of the 12 residences he reported between 1906 and 1910. Number 8 Dean Street did not exist, while the occupiers of numbers 4 and 6, formerly a Temperance hotel, could not remember Mattison. Mrs Zaganowsky, landlady at 20 Nelson's Bank, recalled Mattison rather better, as he had 'left without paying his board, and is still owing it'. A seamen's boarding house in 10 Market Place had on its register a P. Martinson claiming birth in Riga, who had likewise disappeared without paying. A common lodging house in 82 East Holborn kept no register, while the occupants of number 5 Thames Street, the address Mattison claimed when signing on the *SS Aral* in April 1910, knew nothing of him, nor did those at addresses in Govan near Glasgow or Barry Dock in the Bristol Channel.[83] Mattison's second petition succeeded only because several of these landlords, their memories refreshed by recent visits, and perhaps arrears of rent, now verified his claims. Mrs Wilson of 82 East Holborn reported that although he had lodged with her several times, 'she did not know his name until he called on her', suggesting he had used a pseudonym.[84] Despite remaining lacunae and discrepancies in his record, Mattison received naturalization in 1911.[85]

Another enigmatic character, Hilmar John Stenwick, listed nine addresses in South Shields, North Shields, Cardiff and Blyth for the period 2 December 1903 to May 1910. Interspersed between 18 voyages in 12 ships, Stenwick's brief periods ashore, like those of most mariners, ranged in length from a few days to a few months. North Shields police reported the address Stenwick gave at 54 Prudhoe Street non-existent: a seamen's boarding house stood at 51 Prudhoe Street but 'the party who kept it in 1903 and 1904 is now in America'. South Shields police found an H. Stenwick, birthplace Sweden, in the register of a licensed seamen's boarding house at 25 South Eldon Street for the period 3–28 September 1903, while his Continuous Discharge Book showed him as Norwegian. Queried about this discrepancy Stenwick dismissed it as 'a mistake in the Boarding House Register'. Verifying his identity with the landlady, however, proved impossible as 'owing to mental condition' she now lived in the Shetland Isles. Cardiff authorities likewise proved unable to trace Stenwick or his last vessel.[86]

Were such men merely having fun at the authorities' expense, or had they dark secrets to hide? Their appearance in the record at all betrays the net tightening around them in the early twentieth century, as states demanded durable identities stabilized and reified through credentialling.[87]

## Global ties

Such elusive men might maintain far-flung personal relationships invisible to the authorities. A glimpse of these appeared in the story of Knud Hansjorgen Olsen, a man hardly ashore anywhere, for 'being Boatswain of the ship, he was often ordered to keep watch on Board whilst the ship was in port'. When Olsen 'fell down a ships hold at GENOA on or about Christmas, and broke his leg, he was taken to an Infirmary there and has not since been heard of'. Hundreds of miles away, a boarding housekeeper at 42 Green Street, South Shields, reported this silence 'unusual as OLSEN was in the habit of writing to him'.[88] Such personal relationships, albeit tenuous, proved vital and valued: John Wannag had kept track of a former landlord, Mr Mengel, a fellow Russian subject, and knew his current address.[89] The rootlessness they might minimally alleviate resonated in Martin Putnin's statement, 'I have never had settled residence in England but have slept in lodging houses chiefly in South Shields at 400 Eldon Street.'[90] Across seas and borders, such relations could connect even the most transient of men with local people.

Men apparently drew on networks that spanned the seas from their homelands to British shores. In ports they sought out compatriots, emerging most strikingly in their choices of lodging. Between 1900 and 1906, John Leonard Pehrsson resided when ashore in London at the same lodging house in 80 Morant Street, Poplar, run by a Mrs Pehrsson '(but no relation) ... principally patronised by Swedish sailors'. Between 1895 and 1905 Pehrsson also stayed intermittently at 79 East India Dock Road, a boarding house run by a Swede named Holsson, largely accommodating Swedish sailors.[91] Spanish mariner Jose Mendez Busto boarded briefly in 1901 at a house in 18 Dock Street, South Shields, kept by a fellow Spaniard, Peter Domingo Donald, while for 15 years Ernest Heinrich Freidrich Schulz, resided when ashore in the German Sailor's Home.[92] Evidence of compatriot networks most apparent among long-standing Württemberger settlers thus appeared even among the most mobile migrants: invisible bonds linking men and women across vast spaces and time.

Durable compatriot networks betrayed men's reluctance to sever ties to their homes and families across the water. Sojourners often aimed to stabilize subsistence in their original homes through cash remittances, harbouring no intention of settling elsewhere.[93] Deterritorialized families and personal relations emerged in the case of Jacob Strybos, who had lived with his wife in Holland until September 1905, and Massimo Moiraghi, who had broken his residence in Britain by returning to Italy 'at the request of his parents', working in a cycle factory between 30 April 1908 and 27 June 1909.[94] Twenty-two-year-old Christian Hartvig Warrer, who had stayed in South Shields and Hartlepool as well as Nordby, Faro, Denmark, confessed, 'I go home periodically to spend a few weeks with my parents', then apparently thought better of it, crossing out the word 'home' and replacing it with 'to Denmark'.[95] In truth, Christian Warrer, like many mariners, had spent much more of the previous six years at sea in British ships than in Denmark or Britain.[96] Many men's mobility suggests a deliberate strategy to minimize contact with and accountability to any state. *Fin de siècle* border controls and demands for exclusive political allegiance not only threatened their livelihoods but their transborder personal, kin and cultural networks.

## Employers' coercion

Mariners seeking naturalization simply to keep longstanding employment found themselves forced into unforeseen relations with the central state.[97] This coercive context departed starkly from the collective and community-based processes through which individuals sought and attained naturalization in the nineteenth century. Along with the most transient, longstanding Tyneside residents also found their livelihoods menaced by economic nationalism. One such proved George Adolf Christensen, a 43-year-old chargeman labourer with nearly 30 years of sea service and six children to support. Christensen came under duress from an unnamed employer, telling Jarrow police in 1909 that 'he cannot return to work until a Certificate is granted and he is in poor circumstances'.[98] Disabled mariner Harry Johnson sought naturalization in 1910 because his former employer of 18 years, James Knott, owner of the Prince Line and MP for Sunderland, had 'for political reasons promised to employ British Subjects only'. Although Home Office personnel argued 'it is... rather for the shipowner to relax his requirements than for the HO to make an exception', ultimately they relented.[99] The flood of naturalizations in the new century may thus have reflected, perversely, diminishing rather than enhanced feelings of belonging; migrants on the defensive against rising xenophobia. These developments marked a widening breach between local custom and culture that integrated nineteenth-century migrants, and the increasingly instrumental state mechanisms that dislodged and displaced twentieth-century populations: the process of selecting mariners and others for inclusion overtly excluded others.

But was naturalization or self-naturalization, whether formal and state-sanctioned or self-fashioned and community based, a permanent, unidirectional path to integration? Subjected to the stresses of global war, both proved fragile, even reversible. Germans, Jews and other migrants who had resided for decades in South Shields unmolested became vulnerable, not due to local dynamics, but because geopolitical, industrial and imperial rivalries destabilized and poisoned local relationships.

## Global war and local relations

The First World War, culmination of imperial competition and nation building, intensified the 'nationalization of culture' in Britain and elsewhere.[100] State agendas overshadowed the customary rights and human relationships previously defining belonging. Wartime measures in several countries included voluntary or forced repatriation and legislative migration restriction, disrupting labour flows throughout Europe.[101] British policy developed ad hoc, enhancing mechanisms of state intervention and encroachment antedating and surviving the war.[102] Restrictions originating against enemy aliens gradually broadened to encumber and implicate friendly aliens. The Aliens Restriction Act passed 5 August 1914, one day after the declaration of war, authorized a series of increasingly severe measures. Eventually, all aliens entering or leaving Britain must register immediately at the nearest registration office, usually the police station. The Home Secretary acquired power to exclude or deport aliens without appeal.[103] In May 1917 the Tyne, due to its strategic location and industries, became classified as a 'prohibited area' within which residence and movement were restricted.[104] Casualties included the elusive and shape-shifting men of the world inhabiting Britain's maritime industry, as well as stable and longstanding residents.

Several episodes illustrate the paradoxes and contradictions of nation building and empire building intensified by war. Norwegian-born Thomas Harold Henrickson became a naturalized British subject in January 1914 under the special concessions for mariners. He had the misfortune to be in a German port aboard the British steamship *Fleetwood* at the declaration of war, and was promptly interned in the German prisoner of war camp at Ruhleben. From Ruhleben, he appealed in 1916 to the Norwegian Legation in Berlin for assistance in gaining release. The Germans, however, refused to release him as he was also a British subject.[105] Harry Kwist found himself in a similar predicament. Born in Hasenpot near Libau in Courland, Kwist had represented himself for 14 years as German to evade Russian imperial service. He was consequently imprisoned in Britain for three months in 1914 for failing to register as an enemy alien. Released at the intercession of the Russian Consul, Kwist was subsequently conscripted, went to war under British colours with the Third Yorkshire Regiment, and was captured by the Germans in 1918.[106]

From 1914, compliance with aliens regulations themselves became another relationship for migrants to manage with local and central states, mediated by local police. In contrast to prewar applicants whose performance of Britishness secured their naturalization, failure to behave as an alien by observing wartime restrictions could prejudice a man's case.[107] Apparently swayed by wartime xenophobia, William Scott, Chief Constable since 1902, acquired a punitive and officious approach even to friendly aliens. Still, measures in South Shields proved less than draconian initially: in August 1914 police told Joseph Goldman, who sought to register his Russian mother-in-law Masha Lewis, that 'they had no slips, but it would be all right unless his mother-in-law was going to change her residence'. Although penalties for evading wartime regulations prescribed fines of up to one hundred pounds and six months' imprisonment, as late as April 1915 two Norwegian mariners paid 10 shilling fines for failing to return to their ship by the 10 p.m. curfew, and a Swedish sailor, Anders Gabriel Soderquest, faced a similarly nominal fine after he 'came ashore to get a drink', lacking the disembarkation permit now required of alien mariners, 'and lost himself'.[108] The state's changing demands thus did not immediately mould popular subjectivities.

Negotiations and outright refusals to fit prescribed categories, or to collaborate in the state's increasingly intrusive surveillance, emerged as men sought naturalization under duress. Restrictions against aliens rankled some longstanding residents, for instance, J.F. Erickson, a 25-year employee of South Shields shipbuilder Readhead and a 20-year resident of South Shields. Erickson paid a 10-shilling fine in May 1915 for failing to notify his change of residence. For this petty infraction, and despite acknowledging Erickson's 'good character', Chief Constable Scott urged that Erickson's naturalization certificate, pending since August 1914, 'be withheld that this person may remain under the Aliens Restriction Order, that his movements may be under the observation of the Police'.[109] By summer 1916 a further year's delay had produced domestic drama in the Erickson home. On 13 July, Erickson's wife Mary Ann appealed directly to the Home Secretary to expedite the case: 'Mr Walker of the South Shields Police Station said everything was quite in order and he thinks we ought to have had the papers long ago.' Erickson 'is now in bad health and his Doctor has ordered a change of air for him but he does not care to leave this town until he has obtained his naturalisation papers'. Solicitors Grunhut and Gill explained, 'our client... does not care to... be put to the bother of registering, reporting, etc.', yet 'he must get away' during his impending holiday, to ease a cardiac condition. Erickson observed that a number of other Swedes had obtained naturalization while he had been waiting: 'the affair is worrying our client and making his trouble worse'. Erickson finally swore his loyalty oath on 21 August 1916.[110]

Erickson's case illustrated the dilemma aliens faced in wartime Britain: unlike nineteenth-century migrants whose relationships with local people made them more appealing to the state, aliens must enact their difference and separateness from natives of South Shields to attain bona fides. Rootedness in family and community became commensurately devalued. Several other longtime residents found their living imperilled by state and industry prohibitions against employing aliens. In January 1917, Robert Severin Gabrielsen, a 25-year resident of Britain, lost his job as chief engineer of the *SS Wisbech* because wartime policy forbade aliens from ships on Admiralty charter. Gabrielsen's solicitors remonstrated that their client, who had served aboard the *Wisbech* for 15 years, 'could be doing more good by going to sea than by staying ashore at the present time'.[111] Later that year, Palmer's Shipbuilding and Iron Company of Jarrow, on an Admiralty directive, dismissed all employees who were not British subjects, among them Johannes Hüttmann, a Dane by birth, who had worked for them since 1871, over 45 years. Hüttmann had left Denmark permanently in 1862, served on British ships as a sailor and fireman, married a British subject in 1871 and raised three children in Jarrow. Although he had 'a record of very good standing at Palmer's', who professed eagerness to hire him back, at age 72 Hüttmann had few prospects for alternate employment. For Hüttmann, like hundreds of mariners before him, British nationality became merely an instrumental means to preserve his livelihood, a bureaucratic obstacle he had lived without happily for decades.[112]

Palmer's also terminated cabinetmaker Auguste Edward Desire Magnan, a 52-year resident of Jarrow, in November 1917 at government behest. Aged 81 and Parisian by birth, Magnan had married his British wife Elizabeth in 1863, worked for Palmer's since 1865, lived at the same address in Hibernian Road, Jarrow, since the 1870s and had two sons in the British army. Palmer's 'would willingly reinstate him', like Hüttmann, 'if naturalised'. Local police seemed unaware Magnan had been sacked at Admiralty behest, concluding that he was 'turned off... on general principles, not for any personal reason... because the Company feared some trouble with their other employees'. This evasion effectively shifted responsibility for his plight from the Admiralty and the company to his fellow workers. Reluctantly, 'our hands forced', the Home Office decided that Magnan, like Hüttmann, had 'special claims', and authorized his naturalization.[113] Several men who had lived in Britain since childhood also found themselves treated as aliens, among them George Edwin Anderson and Matthew Charles Tubanski.[114] For such men, pressure created by global war and the national state, not the cultural processes of local society, demanded exclusive allegiance on pain of exclusion.[115]

Men who had fled Europe to evade conscription occupied a particularly poignant position.[116] Efforts to induce or bribe resident aliens to enlist included expedited naturalization after three months' military service: professed willingness to serve, conversely, became de rigueur.[117] Russian Jews, who associated czarist conscription with discrimination and forced conversion, confronted contradictory demands to enlist and discrimination when they attempted it.[118] John Alder, who had lived in Britain since childhood and had 'always understood he was a British subject', due to his father's naturalization, applied for naturalization in 1914 saying he would join the army, but instead appealed for reassignment as a War Agricultural Volunteer. This change of heart, compounding prior conflicts over 'lighting of his premises', so displeased Chief Constable Scott that he opposed the man's case, on the pretext of 'the unsettled state of Russian affairs'. This effectively delayed Alder's naturalization until after the war.[119]

Like Alder, brothers Leopold and Leslie Saville had had minor brushes with the Chief Constable. Scott had betrayed no discernable animus against several Jews naturalized between 1902 and 1914, but delayed Leopold's and Leslie's applications, with those of their apparently blameless brothers David and Emmanuel, from August 1914 until August 1916. He released them only to render them eligible for conscription in a time of 'great demand for recruits to join His Majesty's Forces'. When the men then declined to pursue their cases, Scott attempted to have them deported. David Saville, despite serving in France in the non-combatant Russian Labour Corps, did not receive naturalization until 1926, his third attempt, and his brothers only in the 1930s, after Scott's death.[120] Scott's vindictiveness towards Alder and the Saville brothers, like his obstruction of Erickson's case, partook of retaliation for minor transgressions of a sort overlooked before the war. By 1916, however, press propaganda labelled Jewish Londoners who resisted conscription unpatriotic shirkers. This apparently influenced Scott's efforts to force local Jews into the military and later to have them deported.[121] These episodes corroborate scholarly conclusions that xenophobia against enemy aliens spread to implicate all aliens by the war's end, and that prewar anti-Semitism simply compounded wartime anti-Germanism, isolating British Jews and other aliens in the postwar years.[122]

## Citizens of the town: the *Lusitania* riots

Mistreatment of friendly aliens pales, however, compared with the wartime experiences of South Shields' German community. War produced increasingly harsh measures against Germans, Austrians, Bulgarians and Turkish subjects, who made up fully a quarter of aliens in the country. Scholars blame right-wing press demagoguery and national state policies for fomenting particular hostility toward Germans. In South Shields, as geopolitical conflict overshadowed local ties and relationships, Germans became subject to harassment and violence. Internment proceeded sporadically from 1914, when the government also mandated closure of clubs, restaurants and newspapers, and forbade enemy aliens to change their surnames. Organized boycotts and campaigns targeted the German press and churches, accompanied by wholesale firings and evictions. Legislation in 1916 forbade enemy aliens from doing business in Britain, expropriating their property. After May 1917, when Tyneside became a 'prohibited area', enemy aliens could remain only as hardship cases such as invalids, women and children. In addition, six significant episodes of crowd violence occurred nationally, in August 1914, October 1914, May 1915 in response to the sinking of the *Lusitania*, June 1916 upon Kitchener's death, allegedly at the hands of saboteurs, July 1917 in response to a lethal air raid, and September 1918.[123]

'War fever' met a mixed reception on Tyneside, reflecting the multiple social fissures dividing the town. Early in the war, the German congregation arrived one Sunday for services to find the church nailed shut with no explanation.[124] After Pastor Singer's arrest as an enemy alien, local shipbuilding scion Charles Rennoldson, describing Pastor Singer as 'a friend', and Mr T.T. Anderson 'gave bail for him', provoking 'a good deal of anger' in some townspeople.[125]

By far the worst episodes of Germanophobia in South Shields and nationally remained the riots of May 1915, among the most severe of the twentieth century.[126] Local conflicts prompted by world events, the '*Lusitania* riots', as they were called, involved attacks on Germans in Britain prompted by the German sinking of the British *SS Lusitania* on 7 May 1915. Violence against Germans or alleged Germans and other aliens spread from town to town, and eventually to South Shields. In Liverpool, home port of the *Lusitania*, thus of many dead and bereaved, pillaging of German homes and businesses began the day after the tragedy, on Saturday 8 May, incited by the Unionist press. It continued sporadically until the worst rioting the following Saturday, 15 May. This coincided with Horatio Bottomley's bloodcurdling editorial in *John Bull* calling for a 'National Vendetta' against Germans in Britain. By Monday 10 May, pork butchers and other aliens such as Chinese and Scandinavians came under attack. Violence in Merseyside, reported in Tuesday's and Wednesday's newspapers, spread by 12 May to London, where crowds numbering up to 5000 looted and destroyed fully 2000 premises including those owned by non-Germans such as Italians, Russians, Jews and native Britons. As days passed, rioting spread to Manchester and other Northern and Midlands towns, South Wales and the Northeast, taking a particular character in each. Crowds in Manchester and Salford, for example, attacked naturalized British subjects, while a London crowd dispersed when one prospective victim produced his naturalization certificate.[127]

In South Shields as elsewhere, the *Lusitania* tragedy provided the catalyst for attacks on migrants already vulnerable due to state sanction and jingoistic demagoguery. Violence against Germans developed locally after press reports of rioting elsewhere and of punitive government measures. Wednesday 12 May, after Prime Minister Asquith publicly entertained the 'possibility of segregation of alien enemies', saw the first local incident, a paving stone thrown through the window of J.R. Cook's pork butcher shop in Ocean Road.[128] Rioting reached South Shields on Saturday 15 May, a week after Liverpool.[129] The local newspaper called the actions 'premeditated' reporting 'mischief in the air all through the day'. By Saturday evening, a crowd numbering 6000 or 7000 people, a significant proportion of the town's population of approximately 100,000, formed in the Market Square. Amid 'shrill cries of the women ... "Remember the *Lusitania*!" ... a volley of stones' shattered the windows of Frederick Seitz's pork butcher shop and his family's residence above.[130] 'Ringleaders' of this crowd then moved eastwards into the Mile End Road, breaking the windows of butchers John Sieber and John Hertrich.[131] In other parts of the town, women and children, disgorged from the Chichester cinema, threw stones through plate glass windows in Frederick Keith's butcher shop in John Clay Street, and vandals broke the windows of Frederick Fischer's shop in Westoe Road. A crowd gathered at 10 p.m. in Frederick Street, about a mile south of the Market Place, shattering the plate glass window of John George Fischer's pork butcher shop. Of 12 shops attacked, four belonged to members of the German Evangelical congregation: Frederick Seitz, Frederick Keith, John F. Sieber and John Hertrich. All but Seitz were naturalized British subjects.[132]

The riots became the occasion for public debate about the rights of local Germans. Like national authorities, who deplored rather than encouraged the rioters, local worthies allied with the riots' targets, bespeaking solidarity among the town's possessing classes.[133] For even at its height, Germanophobic violence did not reflect local consensus: writing to the *Shields Gazette*, 'Golden Rule' deplored 'curiously named "patriotism" ... to visit upon one class of people punishment due to the crimes of another'.[134] The trials themselves involved elite efforts to reassert local identity and collective sanction.

Scholars suggest that xenophobic violence in Britain differed from contemporaneous pogroms or lynchings because local elites exercised a restraining influence in the former case and covert encouragement in the latter.[135] Trial testimony after the riots of 1915 affirms this, revealing local authorities' ambivalence rather than monolithic hostility towards the Germans in their midst. Chief Constable Scott scolded the nine defendants charged with unlawful assembly, riotous behaviour, obstructing the police, riotous assembly and disturbing the peace: 'there was only one alien enemy amongst the owners of the shops attacked'. The rest, naturalized 'descendants of Germans', as he put it, 'may only move about with my permission... restrictions by which they are sufficiently punished'. This implied that German descent remained a punishable offense, but not as damning as German nationality. Echoing magistrates in other towns, clergy and the respectable press, Alderman Readhead, presiding at Police Court, demanded rhetorically why the defendants had not enlisted, continuing, 'You were not fighting the Germans, although these men have German names. They are citizens of the town.' Readhead sought to distance the rioters from other townspeople, arguing that South Shields was 'last to break out in this fashion, the example having been set by Newcastle and various other places'. Only Thompson's counsel defended the rioters 'for I have seen what the Germans have done to the people of Belgium'. This comment hardly reflected on local social relations, but showed instead how wartime propaganda contaminated them.[136]

Nationally, the *Lusitania* riots prompted wholesale internment of male enemy aliens of military age, 32,440 by autumn 1915. This amounted to over one-tenth of aliens in Britain and nearly all Germans and Austrians of military age. Ten thousand German-born women, children and infirm men were deported.[137] British-born wives and children remained in Britain, subject to restrictive surveillance, along with a small number of long-resident men, including those too frail to travel.[138] In September, two local women chose to leave the country to join their husbands, who, like the more prominent Sir Edgar Speyer, took refuge from internment in the United States. British-born Hannah Zaganowsky, wife of Frank Zaganowsky and landlady of the elusive Teodolf Mattison, and Ellen Gustinger née Benson, Swedish-born wife of Harry Gustinger, requested permission in autumn 1915 to travel to Philadelphia to join their husbands there. These women were not aliens, but rather

British subjects, wives of naturalized men. Yet the Home Office, in issuing embarkation permits, simultaneously withheld their British passports, implicitly depriving them of the right to return. Ellen Gustinger sailed from Liverpool to Philadelphia on Saturday 11 September 1915.[139]

Even as the war turned in the Allies' favour, measures against aliens became more punitive. Unprecedented infringements on civil liberties and due process became normalized, retained and reaffirmed in postwar aliens legislation. The British Nationality and Status of Aliens Act, 1918, empowered the Home Secretary to revoke naturalization certificates. In summer 1918, government jobs closed to all but sons of natural-born British subjects. Sanctions against Germans continued and even intensified after the peace, applying the value of confiscated German property to Germany's reparations assessment.[140] At the war's end deportation, including English-born dependents, sundered families, reducing Germans in Britain by more than one-half: of 57,000 Germans in 1914 a mere 22,254, less than 40 per cent, remained in 1919, 12,358 by the 1921 census.[141] In South Shields numbers fell comparably, from 255, 25 of them naturalized, in 1911, to 74, of whom 34 were naturalized, in 1921.[142] Locally, Joseph Havelock Wilson, president of the seamen's union and local parliamentary candidate, built his political career by exploiting local men lost at sea through enemy action to inflame Germanophobia and jingoism.[143]

In light of these events, scholars recognize the First World War as a moment when British society became especially inhospitable, assimilating all aliens to the suspect position of enemies. One-quarter of 283,000 aliens in Britain had been defined as enemies, most of them Germans, and a further 95,541, or one-third (34 per cent) were Russians, most Jewish. Between them they accounted for more than half of Britain's alien population. Wartime anti-Germanism built on and reinforced prewar anti-Semitism.[144] The chilling impact showed in low numbers naturalized in the 1920s and early 1930s. By 1930 the percentage of migrants in Britain, including the Irish, proved the lowest in Europe.[145] As late as 1929 'foreign' personnel remained barred from Admiralty shipyards including Tyneside firms Swan Hunter Wigham and Richardson's Wallsend shipyard and dry docks.[146] South Shields' most vibrant, affluent and well-integrated Victorian migrant communities, 'citizens of the town', had been defamiliarized, stigmatized and dis-integrated, not through local cultural processes but the influence of national agendas and global events.

## Closing British society

Scholarly focus on top-down processes of state-dominated national identity have neglected everyday practices of inclusion, integration and self-naturalization. To mariners and other migrants, the sea constituted less a natural boundary than a contact zone or borderland reconciling economic opportunity with the maintenance of personal and compatriot networks and family ties. National commitments and even fixed identities remained irrelevant or encumbering. If 'freedom to move about...is a condition of freedom more generally',[147] then anonymity, invisibility, shape-shifting and fabulation permitted individuals to enjoy mobility, freedom and autonomy, as well as transnational personal relationships, in spite of increasingly obstructive national borders. By century's end, however, state formation, driven by global competition for imperial and industrial advantage, curtailed migrants' options to move freely. This impeded their ability to join British society either formally through legal naturalization or informally through unofficial practices of 'self-naturalization'.

With the new century, local integration became increasingly irrelevant to relations between migrants and the British state. Service to state and industry rather than relations with one's neighbours became the test of fitness. From 1903 the state increasingly restricted naturalization to categories of applicants such as mariners and soldiers accountable to them alone. This detached incorporation into British society from localities and civilians in favour of state and industrial agendas. State exactions and exclusions conflicted with the survival strategies as well as the loyalties and sensibilities of an unprecedentedly mobile and global working class, migrants and natives alike.

Effects of British and European state formation and empire building, exclusion, surveillance and policing cut across the liberties and freedoms mariners and other migrants had enjoyed ashore in Britain as well as at sea. Peripatetic men of the world who passed through South Shields in the course of maritime labour found themselves forced to choose between their globally mobile livelihoods and exclusive national allegiances. Shifting state and industrial agendas increasingly impinged on local social relations as well: migrants became subjected to evermore intensive scrutiny with each decade of the twentieth century. From the late nineteenth century onwards, the British state marginalized and excluded in turn a diverse array of people, including non-resident mariners, non-British mariners, mainly Scandinavians, then Jews and Germans. When war came home to South Shields, geopolitical rivalries eclipsed and even reversed longstanding customary practices and local affiliations. Migrants like British natives became subject to unprecedented coercion, surveillance and control, and, for those styled enemies, internment and exclusion.

The foregoing illustrates how British society gradually closed to long-distance migrants in the decades between 1870 and 1920, corroborating scholars' findings that social mobility and openness diminished in this period.[148] Common to other European societies, closure reflected structural contexts of industrial and imperial competition and war.[149] For longstanding residents such as Germans, it proved catastrophic. This problematizes understandings of British culture as parochial, closed and defensive. Hundreds of Scandinavians without a friend in South Shields received naturalization in the early years of the century, meeting no apparent local opposition. In contrast, Germans with deep and longstanding personal ties within the local community were uprooted, not through the operation of local custom and culture, but in spite of it. Local people did not entirely control whether their society remained open to migrants or not, and their control diminished from the nineteenth to the twentieth centuries.

# 8
# I Give My Missus the 28 Shillings: Everyday Forms of Accommodation

'I said to the wife', Nagi Mohamed reported, ' "Howay and see that man about a job ..." [but] His missus came down and say he's not in.' Collecting his unemployment money in the afternoon, Nagi Mohamed took it directly to his wife Lauretta, emulating working-class men's cultural practice of handing over their pay packets: 'I go straight home and give my missus the 28 shillings.' Later, Nagi Mohamed stopped for a drink at the Hop Pole pub, placed a bet with bookmaker Robert Owen Stokes, and encountered his elder son Hamed, a schoolboy, running an errand for Lauretta: 'my son came along and say, "Da, I want to buy some cakes".' In the evening, Nagi Mohamed suspended a game of bagatelle in an Arab-run establishment, Athraby's in Holborn, to take Lauretta to the cinema.[1] Rich in local vernacular and cultural practice, Nagi Mohamed's account of an ordinary day affords an intimate glimpse into everyday forms of cultural accommodation and acculturation in Britain's interracial and multicultural communities.[2] Nagi Mohamed conveyed details lost to the record of previous migrants: specifically how they adopted and adapted local cultural practices as they settled and married in South Shields.

Although hundreds of settlers and sojourners from the colonies lived in South Shields in the nineteenth century, they became perceived as a social problem after the turn of the century. In the same decades when naturalized Germans and British Jews became assimilated to aliens, Britain became unwelcoming to colonized migrants. While migrant communities developed relatively unmolested in the nineteenth century, later newcomers, even nominal British subjects, became subject to disruptive institutional intervention. Spectacular episodes of conflict have captured scholarly attention, but Nagi Mohamed's narrative illustrated ongoing processes of integration and incorporation remained available to colonized migrants in the 1920s and 1930s as they were previously. These included intermarriage, co-residence and eventually naturalization.

This work departs from but also builds on that of other scholars, who generally examined twentieth-century communities of colour without commensurate scrutiny of previous migrants.[3] No effort to discredit their meticulous work, much of which relied on oral interviews and newspapers, what follows contextualizes previous findings in light of further research, and within the longer history of migration to the locality. Municipal and other records reveal a much larger and more stable migrant population than hitherto understood. Narrating colonized people's story into the ongoing history of migration to South Shields and Britain reveals twentieth-century tensions stemmed from changing geopolitical and institutional contexts rather than migrants' presence or characteristics. For as Nagi Mohamed's testimony reveals, cultural practices remained protean, flexible and syncretic.

Colonized subjects present during the Victorian heyday of 'free trade imperialism' excited little apparent hostility, thus received minimal attention: scholars once thought they had disappeared altogether.[4] Revived empire building at the *fin de siècle*, however, intensified discursive and ideological distinctions between colonizers and colonized, often expressed as 'race'.[5] Paradoxically, it simultaneously encouraged and enabled increasing numbers of newly colonized people to settle in Britain.[6] Traversing the spatial distance between colony and metropole, such migrants threatened the imperial appropriation geographical separation reinforced and obscured. Their presence became problematical, thus remarked, in a previously silent record. Nagi Mohamed's daily interactions and cultural adaptations, while continuous with those of European migrants preceding him, could only partly mitigate the adversarial structural relations imperial political economy created.

A major destination for colonized mariners, South Shields has benefited from several scholarly treatments. Early accounts argued that migrants from the colonies coexisted peacefully with local working people. They documented how local government, through slum clearance in the mid-1930s, perpetrated institutional discrimination and segregation.[7] Northeastern isolation and deprivation, another asserted, led ordinary Tynesiders to identify with the underdog, rendering them receptive to colonized migrants: 'intensely proud' of a 'reputation for racial tolerance'.[8] Another depicted the Yemeni community as geographically segregated, first in Holborn and later Laygate, subject to persistent racial attacks culminating in the 1930 trial and deportation of community leader Ali Said.[9] Only one scholar linked the campaign against Ali Said to broader processes of class politics, stressing how employers, state and union manipulated racial tension to obscure economic and political stakes.[10] The most recent emphasized popular racism instead, depicting a Yemeni community largely on the defensive, isolated from local society.[11] Studies of Muslims in present-day Britain, particularly of the Yemenis and Somalis making up the bulk of South Shields' colonized migrants, rarely acknowledge they lived in Britain before 1945. Contemporary Somalis, influenced by Islamism, deprecate or deny prewar migrants such as Nagi Mohamed who married local women or assimilated forbidden practices such as alcohol use.[12] History and fiction alike have depicted interwar South Shields as racially polarized.[13]

Analysis will show that local social relations actually proved similar to those of previous migrants, involving processes of integration into civil society, business relations, intermarriage and spatial dispersal. Acculturation included local institutions' accommodation of Muslim religious observance and cultural practices. Like Jews and Germans, however, colonized migrants suffered a series of attacks, originating with national and municipal authorities and the seamen's union, but structured by employers' divisive practice of pitting super-exploited colonized mariners against British ones.[14] Beginning during the First World War, punctuated by riots in 1919 and 1930, repeated assaults stigmatized and isolated colonized migrants, destabilizing their lives and livelihoods and partially derailing processes of integration.

Conflicts between colonized migrants and native Britons have often been treated as *sui generis*, attributed to racial or cultural difference, as if race and culture themselves had no histories.[15] If apparent 'racial' similarity failed to protect Scandinavians, Jews or Germans from xenophobia and violence, imputed racial difference hardly offers sufficient explanation for antipathy towards colonized migrants. The creation of difference itself reflects anterior processes of power and inequality, in the British case the super-exploitation of colonized workers kept geographically separated from native British ones.[16] Hostility to minorities has simply displaced tensions within larger social formations: truly marginal people pose no threat. Attributing conflict to difference alone risks essentializing violence as inherent in intercultural contact. It spuriously reifies fluid identities and differences, denying individual agency.[17]

Explaining the corrosive antagonism and violence recurring in twentieth-century South Shields and Britain requires refocusing scholarly attention from its objects, whether German, Jewish or colonized, to the global and local processes creating conditions for friction between 1915 and the 1930s. Far from disrupting a previously homogeneous and harmonious society, colonized mariners who arrived in South Shields and Britain during and after the Great War confronted a social formation riven with inequality and conflict. While scholars and nationalists debate the boundaries of Britishness, memoirs of Shields natives show local birth proved no protection from social exclusion or petty cruelty.[18] Divisive attacks on colonized migrants occurred in the course of a broader ruling-class assault on workers' militancy that included destruction of syndicalist organizations such as the Minority Movements and co-optation of others such as the seamen's union.[19] For officials, colonized workers' appearance in Britain represented an alarming escape from colonial subordination, while for the white working class they portended deterioration to colonial standards of pay and working conditions. This context restores contingency to relations between colonized migrants and other local people, reconciling individual responsibility with impersonal structural changes such as imperial instability and global depression.

## Fruits of surveillance

Reconstructing migrants' arrival and settlement after 1901 demands resort to less comprehensive sources than the manuscript censuses (CEBs), which remain unavailable.[20] Registers of those eligible to vote, although omitting birthplaces, ages and other data found in the censuses, contain the name and address of each elector ward by ward and street by street. Like the CEBS, they reveal the presence and distribution of male householders established as overseas-born through other records or through surname analysis. After 1918, they include other adults including women.[21] Using nominal evidence entails a leap of faith, but no larger than that taken by other scholars in the absence of better evidence.[22] Surviving naturalization documents supplement the electoral rolls. Together these sources show that ongoing processes of migration, intermarriage and spatial dispersal continued after 1901, albeit checked and distorted repeatedly by overt state intervention.

Unlike nineteenth-century migrants, their affairs gleaned from relatively opaque sources, South Shields' colonized residents became subject to surveillance and active interference by local and national states. This renders them better documented in some respects than prior migrants, even though comparable records remain unavailable. In the twentieth century, colonized people, with Germans and others, became subject to intensified bureaucratic scrutiny; like Germans and Jews, they also faced ongoing efforts to deport them or otherwise control their movements. These processes generated abundant documentation, enabling a rich reconstruction of community formation, internal dynamics and external relations.

In the same decades as people in South Shields found their choices shaped and sometimes thwarted by an increasingly invasive national state, municipal state building also impinged on migrants and natives. Migrants' depiction in the resultant records proved all too predictable. From 1875 successive Medical Officers of Health and from 1881 chief constables produced annual reports in which mariners from overseas as well as the native poor figured as vectors of disease and disorder. Records of slum clearance reveal how municipal policy in the 1930s reproduced imperial spatial dynamics, attempting although failing to segregate and contain colonized residents. Materials generated by isolated episodes of conflict and violence illuminate otherwise invisible dynamics between migrants and natives both humble and powerful. Together this evidence documents everyday forms of integration, accommodation and acculturation as well as of subordination and exclusion.

## Exotic disorder

Substantial local state formation began only late in the nineteenth century, in the context of ongoing migration and in dialogue with national-level panic over its acceleration. Local intervention anticipated and reinforced early twentieth-century controls on merchant seamen and aliens generally. Seamen's boarding houses and common lodginghouses became increasingly confined to dockside areas, shown in Table 8.1 and Map 8.1. Eleven of the town's 76 seamen's boarding houses remained in the hands of apparent overseas migrants in 1900, indicating the survival of compatriot networks. These included Frederick Sveden, a Swede operating 50 Heron Street in Shields Ward, and Samuel Camilleri, Maltese proprietor of 1 Nile Street, in Holborn Ward. In contrast to the relative dispersal of seamen's boarding houses, common lodging houses, with no apparent migrant proprietors, clustered exclusively in the riverside wards of Shields, St Hilda and Holborn, rendering their inhabitants even more segregated than seafarers.[23]

Annual reports by Medical Officers of Health and chief constables depicted criminality and disease as external to local society, entering the town via mariners and other sojourners. From 1874 a series of Borough Medical Officers not only pursued slum clearance but also focused

*Table 8.1* Common lodging houses and seamen's boarding houses, 1900

| | Common lodging houses | Inmates | Average beds | Seamen's boarding houses | Inmates | Average beds |
|---|---|---|---|---|---|---|
| Shields | 16 | 408 | 25 | 5 | 48 | 9.6 |
| St Hilda | 2 | 56 | 28 | 7 | 82 | 11.7 |
| Holborn | 6 | 237 | 39.5 | 41 | 445 | 10.85 |
| Beacon | – | – | – | 2 | 11 | 5.5 |
| Bents | – | – | – | 3 | 16 | 5.3 |
| Laygate | – | – | – | 3 | 15 | 5 |
| Rekendyke | – | – | – | 7 | 56 | 8 |
| Deans | – | – | – | 6 | 68 | 1.1 |
| Tyne Dock | – | – | – | 2 | 14 | 7 |
| Totals | 24 | 701 | 28.2 | 76 | 755 | 9.9 |

*Source*: *Corporation Minutes*, August 1900, 764–7.

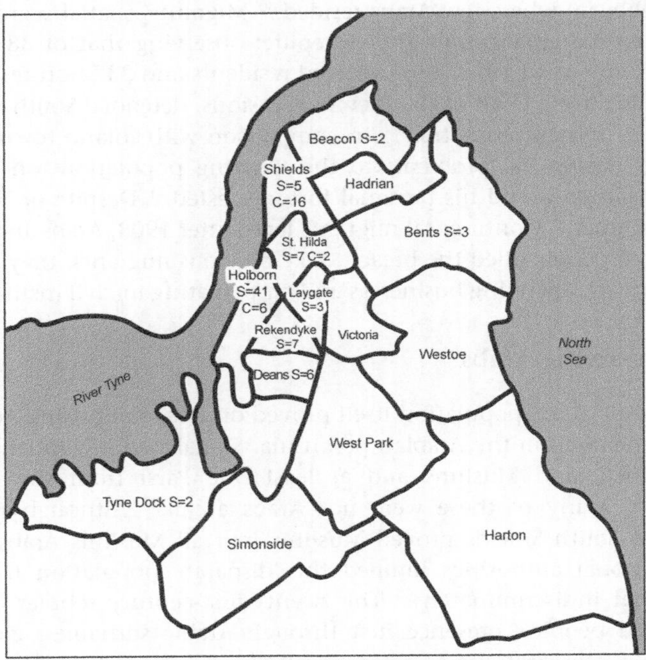


*Map 8.1* Seamen's boarding houses (S) and common lodging houses (C), 1900

on medical inspection of ships in port, by 1902 giving 'special attention' to emigrant passengers.[24] A. Campbell Munro, Medical Officer of Health in the 1890s, attributed 'much' illness in the 'sea-port town' to 'importations from the Continent', while his successor John J. Boyd in 1903 blamed smallpox, whose resurgence actually dated to 1880, on 'tramps and casual labourers... these parasites on society'.[25] From 1896, police tabulated resident and non-resident drunks separately, and until 1911 distinguished Scottish, Welsh and Irish from English workhouse inmates.[26] This divisive discourse, no doubt influenced by anti-Semitic xenophobia emanating from London, also reflected an effort to neutralize and contain *fin de siècle* political democratization.[27] Migrants threatened to generalize values and expectations interregionally and globally, endangering existing power relations.[28] Giving this discourse an Orientalist twist, Medical Officer of Health W. Campbell Lyons in the 1920s attempted to minimize local tuberculosis cases by attributing the town's high numbers to 'low powers of resistance' among the town's so-called Arab population.[29] Yet rates proved higher in Jarrow and Hebburn, where few Arabs resided.[30] Migrants' spatial segregation deepened marginalization and disrepute: observing that of 383 cases of drunkenness in 1918, 146 involved residents and 237 non-residents, James Readhead, chair of the Brewster Sessions, defended South Shields against 'a certain reputation... in comparison with inland towns', displacing local social problems to the 'floating population' on whom local livelihoods and his personal fortune rested.[31] Despite or because of impediments Continental migrants faced after 1903, Arabs and other colonized people filled the breach. Like previous migrants, they settled and married, operating businesses and participating in civil institutions.

## Who were the Arabs?

The town's 'Arab' population itself proved diverse, comprising Adenese and Yemenis from the Arabian peninsula, Somalis and Egyptians from East Africa, and Muslims and at least one Parsi from the Indian diaspora. Many of these were not Arabs at all.[32] Although not all Arabs in South Shields proved Muslims, nor all Muslims Arabs, local and national authorities lumped this disparate population together somewhat indiscriminately.[33] The twenty-first-century scholar detects colonized people's presence first through Arabic surnames, gleaning but dimly the contours of internal relations. Records from the 1930s show most originated in Aden, Sheikh Othman and elsewhere in the Yemen, and in British Somaliland, with a scattering from other British

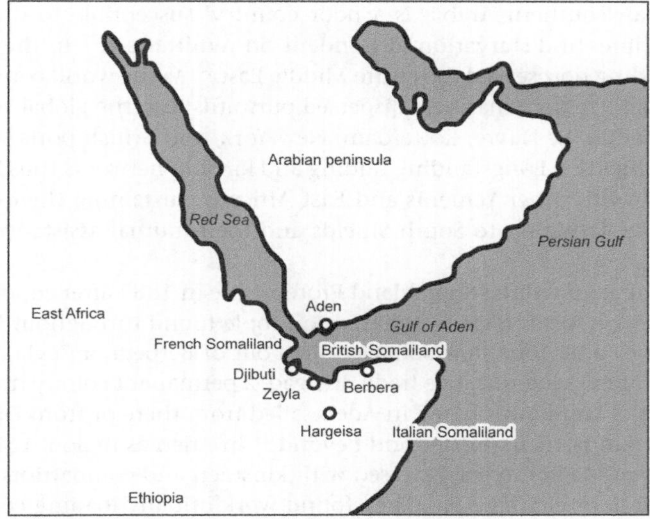


*Map 8.2* Aden and environs

possessions (Map 8.2).[34] The latter included Egyptians such as boarding housekeepers Faid Abdula and his brother Nassar, Kashmiris and other Indians such as Ghulam Rasul, Mande and Timne from Sierra Leone such as Joe Fanday aka Samuel Grant, and men from the Caribbean such as Barbadian James Perla.[35]

Gateway to the once opulent Ottoman province of Arabia Felix or Yemen, and critical crossroads of Indian and African trade, Aden came under British control in 1839 after a series of imperial intrigues. Withstanding indigenous rebellions in 1841 and 1858, the cosmopolitan British Settlement numbered 20,000 by the 1850s, including 100 transported convicts. Its water came from Sheikh Othman 4 miles distant, while Somali traders brought meat across the Red Sea from an annual fair at Berbera.[36] Aden became a port of call for the Peninsula and Oriental steamship company, the P&O, linking Britain to India through the Suez Canal. The port's historically diverse population included Jews, Indians, Persians and Africans, some descended from Somalis who had taken Adenese wives.[37] From 1900, the British merchant navy began recruiting Yemenis via middlemen for menial shipboard jobs as firemen, greasers and donkeymen.[38] 'It has been the custom of Arabs from Aden and the Aden Protectorate, for many generations, to seek their livelihood on the sea', wrote Sir Bernard Reilly, Governor of Aden in the

1930s, as 'southern Arabia is a poor country' susceptible to drought, crop failures and starvation, dependent on remittances.[39] In the 1920s the bustling port served the entire Middle East.[40] As the world converged on Yemen, Yemeni mariners dispersed outwards into the global system, to Marseilles, Le Havre, Rotterdam, New York, and British ports such as South Shields.[41] Longstanding trading and kinship networks thus bound Adenese with other Yemenis and East Africans, sustaining their collective transplantation to South Shields and their mutual assistance once there.

Britain acquired the Somaliland Protectorate in 1887 after concluding treaties with local rulers.[42] A diasporic people found throughout Northeast Africa and Aden, few Somalis sailed out of Berbera or Zeyla, which supported no long-distance trade. Instead, a permanent colony numbering tens of thousands based in Aden sailed from there or from Djibouti or Egyptian ports to Europe and beyond.[43] In Aden as in South Shields, Somalis resided or at least messed with kinsmen and compatriots at the *mokhbâzah* or eatinghouse. They found work initially loading coal and cargo, progressing to servants, bootboys, punkah coolies, policemen, detectives and traders back to Somaliland. Some eventually became firemen on steamships plying between Europe and India, forming networks extending from Aden to Liverpool, Manchester, Cardiff and South Shields.[44]

How and when particular men first arrived in South Shields remains obscure. Despite intriguing nineteenth-century figures such as James Brown, a 25-year-old Egyptian-born second mate with a possibly Anglicized name, no persons with Arabic names appeared in the census of 1901.[45] Two men, Syed Mahdi and Ahmed Alwin, claimed in the 1920s to have arrived in 1909.[46] That year, Arabs began appearing before the Town Council pursuing business licenses, including Ali Said, who obtained a boarding house license for 1 Nile Street.[47] Only in 1910 had an Arabic surnamed individual amassed sufficient property to exercise the parochial franchise: Alexander Said, possibly the same person, who operated a shop in 59 Commercial Road near the docks, residing in Napier Street, Tyne Dock. In 1912, Ali Hassan opened a boarding house for eight men at 93 East Holborn, and Ali Said's wife Mary Ellen premises for 19 men at 79a East Holborn.[48] A.W. Ruddock, an official of the Shipping Federation, represented a series of Arabs operating a boarding house at Point Ferry Approach in West Holborn, suggesting Federation sponsorship of these premises. This betrayed employers' interest in maintaining a pool of vulnerable labour near at hand.[49] Transfers of existing premises such as 1 Nile Street, a substantial boarding house in the waterside district of Holborn, from Maltese Samuel Camillieri, who held it in 1901, to Ali Said, or 20 Nelson's Bank from Frank Zaganowsky to Mohamed Muckble, suggests colonized mariners filled a vacuum in the labour market created by Continental mariners' exclusion after 1903.[50] Like German pork butchers, merchants such as Ali Said enjoyed access to capital, insulating them from labour market discrimination, as from vulnerability to deportation when unemployed.[51] Effectively, Arab boarding housekeepers joined the maritime service sector that offered mobile mariners a foothold in South Shields while simultaneously living from them.

## Civil society

Indicating Arabs' like other migrants' integration into civil society, from 1914 individuals with Arabic names routinely appeared as plaintiffs and defendants in civil proceedings. Of approximately 1800 civil prosecutions between 1914 and 1928, Arabs appeared as plaintiffs in 17 cases and defendants in 33. Only seven of these involved an Arab prosecuting another Arab. Much routine business, including business gone awry, thus appears transacted across ethnic lines, not exclusively among Arabs, who took irresolvable internal disputes as well as those with non-Arabs to British courts.[52] Prosecutions of absconding seamen indicate that by 1914 Arabs like other Shields residents acted as employment agents for European seamen. Abdulla Said of 63 Thrift Street, for example, prosecuted William Ash and N. Wayang, both inmates of his boarding house, who '[F]ailed to join the ss Dauntless after negotiating' wage advances on 22 January 1917. Faid Abdula prosecuted Toby Anderson on 23 December 1918, and Mohamed Muckble George Brown on 24 August 1918. David Evans prosecuted Mossem Mohamed and Elizabeth White pursued Hafin Hassan for similar offenses in September 1918.[53] This challenges the view that Arab boarding housekeepers accommodated only other Arabs, creating a closed and isolated community. Conversely, it shows Arab mariners did not depend exclusively on fellow Arabs for accommodation or other services.[54] Instead, it shows Arabs took part in local society: like migrants before them they transacted business, acquired property, exercised the franchise and resorted to the courts.

Scholars agree with contemporaries, although precise documentation remains elusive, that the number of Arabs in British merchant ships skyrocketed as British seamen abandoned them for the trenches of Flanders.[55]. Seven hundred Arabs allegedly 'lost their lives through enemy action' sailing from the Tyne.[56] To serve them, migrant businessmen and boarding housekeepers expanded their operations during the war. The municipality in 1915 and 1916 granted a series of petitions to Arab boarding housekeepers for licensing or expansion of their premises.[57] By the end of the Great War, South Shields had eight Arab boarding houses accommodating hundreds of men, and some Arabs claimed 10 or 15 years' local residence.[58] Local officials referred to them as a 'colony', implying stability and coherence.[59]

Fluctuating through the 1920s and 1930s, the community remained substantial. As in the nineteenth century, sojourners whose mobility connected Shields with the wider world continued to confound efforts to quantify or otherwise measure migrant communities in this seaport town, especially as intermittent unemployment put large numbers 'on the beach'. Table 8.2 shows periodic snapshots of this population in tallies taken under the spuriously named Coloured Alien Seamen Order, which redefined colonial subjects as aliens.[60] Numbers peaked with unemployment, diminishing gradually as men regularized their status, but consistently amounted to hundreds.[61]

These figures show the magnitude and diversity of this population, comparable to overseas-origin mariners in 1891 (347) and 1901 (503) in Table 4.8, or to Scandinavians (570) and Germans (252) in 1901 in Table 3.1. In addition to Yemenis, who made up the bulk, smaller numbers of Somalis and other Africans, Indians, Malays and men from the Caribbean lived in and sailed out of South Shields. By 1939 the number of Yemenis or 'Arabs' registered in South Shields dropped absolutely and proportionally, shown in Table 8.2, while other groups grew, from 20 to 52 in the case of Somalis. Although Yemenis still predominated, the increase in other groups suggests zealous enforcement against them may have produced a shortage of abusable racialized mariners, a shortage Somalis and other colonized mariners filled. In 1935, when Adan Eroboy and Omar Mohamed wrote to protest colonized mariners' exclusion from vessels subsidized under the British Shipping Assistance Act, they represented 46 Somalis residing in South Shields.[62] A small but unspecified number of Mende and Timne men from Sierra Leone also lived there.[63] In July 1930, 620 'coloured' men remained workless, including 15 Sierra Leoneans, 12 from Jamaica and St Lucia, three from Cape Verde, 30 Somalis and 560 Adenese.[64] Proportions remained similar in subsequent years, shown in Table 8.2. Like previous migrants, Arabs and other colonized settlers thus formed a relatively stable core around which a larger population of sojourners ebbed and flowed. Similarly, the heart of the community located in Holborn anchored a larger population scattered through the town.

*Table 8.2* Composition of population registered as Coloured Alien Seamen in South Shields, 1925–39

| | Arabs | Somalis | Other Africans | Indians | Malays | West Indians | Miscellaneous | Total |
|---|---|---|---|---|---|---|---|---|
| 1925 | – | – | – | – | – | – | – | 1157 |
| 1926 | – | – | – | – | – | – | – | 56 |
| 1927 | – | – | – | – | – | – | – | 42 |
| 1928 | – | – | – | – | – | – | – | 45 |
| 1930 | 470 | 20 | – | – | – | – | – | 490 |
| 1931 | 316 | 20 | 10 | 18 | 12 | 10 | 6 | 392 |
| 1932 | 382 | 27 | 6 | 24 | 5 | 14 | 15 | 473 |
| 1933 | – | – | – | – | – | – | – | 763 |
| 1934 | – | – | – | – | – | – | – | 691 |
| 1935 | 632 | 88 | 22 | 49 | 15 | 21 | 24 | 851 |
| 1936 | 501 | 56 | 24 | 39 | 16 | 12 | 27 | 675 |
| 1937 | 296 | 40 | 23 | 30 | 8 | 5 | 19 | 421 |
| 1938 | 171 | 47 | 26 | 35 | 11 | 4 | 13 | 307 |
| 1939 | 136 | 52 | 25 | 31 | 8 | 3 | 13 | 268 |

*Source*: For 1925–28: 'Statistical Summaries', 15 May 1928, HO45/13392/493912/55; for 1930, HO45/14299/562898/72; for 1931 and 1932, 'Return of the Coloured Alien Seamen in the United Kingdom on 1st January 1931 and 1st January 1932', and for July 1931–January 1939, IOR L/E/9/972. Totals of men registered and deferred have been combined. These figures differ slightly from those in D. Byrne (1976–77) 'The 1930 "Arab riot": A Race Riot That Never Was', *Race and Class* 18: 265, derived from chief constables' reports apparently tallied in December, but the trend is the same.

## An Arab quarter?

By 1928, despite Scandinavians' continuing visibility, the 'Arab quarter' in South Shields formed the only discernable 'foreign quarters' in Tyneside: 'a couple of streets or so, frequented by stokers off the Oriental boats and by those who cater for them'.[65] This migrant service sector of cafes and boarding houses remained on the riverside, but Arabs like previous overseas migrants before them resided throughout the town, and in much larger numbers than scholars or contemporaries thought. Although union, state and even some scholars portrayed colonized migrants as sojourners isolated from local society, electoral rolls enable partial reconstruction of the most stable. These enjoyed substantial spatial and marital integration with other local residents, including previous migrants and their descendants.[66]

Since many colonized people had European names, those most visible in the record proved those with Arabic surnames. Colonized men with European or Anglicized names, including most from the Caribbean and many Africans, such as Joe Fanday, aka Samuel Grant, and Joseph Perla, remain hidden in nominal sources such as electoral rolls, unless somehow identified. Ship's runner Benjamin George Franklin, for instance, known to Nagi Mohamed and Lauretta as 'The Malayo', was identified by deponent Jane Macey as 'an Arab' and by Frederick Elgar as 'a coloured man'.[67] In 1918, when the franchise was broadened to most adult men, to married women and to single women over 30, many more European migrants and their descendants such as Harry Kwist, Enrique and Mary Zarraga, and Andrew Erickson appeared in the electoral roll. So did a substantial Arabic-surnamed population not only living in the town but sufficiently established to vote.

Like Germans and Jews in 1871, Arabs initially clustered in the dockside Holborn district, but unlike previous migrants, their spatial dispersal was inhibited, first by licensing confining seamen's boarding houses to the riverside, and in the 1930s by a deliberate municipal policy of racial segregation, discussed below. Still, as Table 8.3 shows, Arab electors as early as 1918 lived in eight of South Shields' 14 wards, albeit most in Holborn Ward, and by the mid-1930s in all but the outermost suburban wards. In 1918, 40 men and two apparently British wives appeared: Ali Said and his wife Mary Ellen resided at 1 Henry Nelson Street in Ocean Road, while Mary Ellen operated a boarding house at 79a East Holborn. Silem Barras, licensed in 1915 for the boarding house at Point Ferry Approach, lived in 1918 with his wife Winifred in nearby Harrisons Court. Brothers Faid and Nassar Abdula operated a boarding

*Table 8.3* Spatial distribution of Arabic-surnamed electors

| Ward | 1910–15 | 1918 | | 1925 | | 1930 | | 1934 | | 1936 | | 1939 | |
|---|---|---|---|---|---|---|---|---|---|---|---|---|---|
| | | men | women | men | women | men | women | men | women | men | women | men | women |
| Shields | – | 7 | – | 6 | | 11 | 11 | 6 | 4 | 2 | 2 | 5 | 2 |
| Beacon | – | 1 | – | 1 | – | – | – | 3 | 2 | 1 | 1 | 1 | 1 |
| St. Hilda | – | 1 | – | 1 | – | 7 | 6 | 10 | 7 | 1 | 2 | 2 | 1 |
| Hadrian | – | 1 | 1 | 2 | – | 5 | 4 | 4 | 4 | 6 | 7 | 8 | 9 |
| Holborn | 1 | 26 | 2 | 34 | 6 | 48 | 33 | 78 | 46 | 6 | 4 | 49 | 25 |
| Laygate | – | 2 | – | – | – | 2 | 1 | 11 | 8 | 1 | 2 | 25 | 15 |
| Victoria | – | – | – | – | – | – | – | 1 | 2 | 1 | 1 | 4 | 5 |
| Bents | 1 | – | – | – | – | 1 | 1 | 5 | 4 | 3 | 3 | 7 | 6 |
| Rekendyke | – | 1 | – | – | – | 2 | 3 | 4 | 4 | 2 | 3 | 10 | 8 |
| Westoe | – | – | – | – | – | – | – | – | – | – | – | – | – |
| Deans | – | – | – | – | – | – | – | 6 | 3 | – | 2 | 2 | 2 |
| Tyne Dock | 2 | – | – | 2 | – | 3 | 3 | 2 | 1 | 1 | – | 2 | 1 |
| Simonside | – | – | – | – | – | – | – | 3 | 3 | – | – | 2 | 2 |
| West Park | – | 1 | – | – | – | – | – | – | 1 | – | – | – | – |
| E. Boldon | – | – | – | – | – | – | – | – | 1 | 1 | 2 | – | – |
| Cleadon | – | – | – | – | – | – | – | – | – | – | 1 | – | – |
| Total | 4 | 40 | 2[a] | 46 | 6 | 79 | 62 | 133 | 90 | 25 | 30 | 117 | 77 |

*Note*: [a] Mary Ellen Said was found in Hadrian, where she resided, and Holborn, where she operated a boarding house, but counted only once here.

house at 62–63 Thrift Street north of the Market Place, premises formerly occupied by Magdalena Birkett. By 1925, Arab electors in Holborn had increased, and the number of married men had tripled, from two to six. The number of men nearly doubled by 1930 and again by 1934, while the proportion married skyrocketed. By 1930 the vast bulk of male electors, 62 of 79, had married apparently local women. They resided in seven of the town's 16 electoral wards, possibly an effect of working-class matrilocal marriage customs.[68] By 1934 their numbers had risen again, to 90 of 133. By 1939, as Table 8.3 shows, less than half of Arab men, 49 of 117, remained in Holborn, in spite of municipal efforts to impede their dispersal. Arabs' numbers and rates of dispersal between 1910 and 1939 compare roughly to those of Germans or Scandinavians in the 30-year period 1851 to 1881, when Germans grew from 9 to 115, and Scandinavians from 6 to 154, per Table 3.1. If the number of married women indicates the number of households, 62 Arab households in 1930 compare to 59 German ones in 1871 shown in Table 3.2, while 90 Arab households in 1934 and 77 in 1939 compare to 83 German ones in 1881, 131 in 1891 and 165 in 1901. Arabs did not therefore arrive and settle in unprecedentedly large numbers: other factors must explain their persecution.

In addition to spatial dispersal, informal forms of naturalization and self-naturalization remained available to Arabs as to Victorian migrants. Like Mohamed Muckble and Yussif Hersi Sulliman, who had transliterated their surnames to resemble local names Muckle and Sullivan, Monsoor Fareh had Anglicized his name, appearing in the 1925 electoral roll as Morris, as did Mahomed Mosley in 1934 and Ahmed Sherrif in 1925.[69] Several appeared in the electoral rolls before their formal naturalization: Mahomed Mosley, naturalized in 1937, appeared with his wife Isabella in 1934, as did Ahmed Awad and his wife Christina in 1930, although Ahmed received naturalization only in 1936.[70] Local officials apparently treated such men as local and British, as they had Reynold Erickson and Thomas Rogers in the previous century.

Electoral rolls not only reveal where people lived, but that they exercised political power. The sharp drop between 1934 and 1936, shown in Table 8.3, flanked the notorious slum clearance displacing and segregating Holborn's multiracial population. It tells the story of the community's dramatic disenfranchisement. Rolls for 1935 remain incomplete, but those for 1936 show a radical diminution not only in Holborn Ward, where numbers dropped from 133 men and 90 women to 25 men and 30 women, but throughout the town. This represented a decrease of 81.4 per cent for men and two-thirds for women, 75 per cent overall. In comparison, Germans diminished 71 per cent, from 255 to 74, between 1911 and 1921. Although Arab electors' numbers began to recover, by the end of the decade the total still stood below those in 1934: 117 men and 77 women. Still, in spite of massive disruption slum clearance wrought, Table 8.3 shows Arabs continued to disperse spatially and vote in gradually recovering numbers.

The community extended beyond those enfranchised however. In 1932 it included confectioner C. Ahmed in Green Street, Mrs Grace Abdulla, a shopkeeper in 44 Wilson Street, both in Laygate Ward, and A. Cassem, a hairdresser plying his trade at 59 East Holborn.[71] Others such as Ejmal Mackmute, a hairdresser located in Mile End Road, and Ahmed Alwin, a tobacconist, likely served a clientele beyond the Arab community.[72] Even single men did not necessarily live in a homosocial compatriot enclave: until 1934 and again by 1939, as Table 8.3 shows, single men dispersed nearly as widely as married ones.[73] Electoral rolls also reveal co-residence between Arab and apparently British people: Mahomet Dollah, residing in Slake Terrace, Tyne Dock, in 1925, shared an address with Thomas Frederick Thompson and William Watkinson, the former a mariner but the latter not, while Ahmed Ali lived in the 38 Dock Street lodging house of Henry Vallack, along with apparently British lodgers including two couples.[74] The impact of relative integration showed when police reported in 1930 that of 19 Arabs in their custody, all 'understand English when you speak to them and a number of them talk English fairly well'.[75]

These data demand revising several assumptions about colonized settlers in Britain and South Shields. First, they undermine the widespread view that Arabs were informally segregated exclusively in the disreputable and unhealthy dockside Holborn Ward, to be displaced and re-isolated en bloc by slum clearance later in the 1930s.[76] Unlike Cardiff and Liverpool, where rioters in 1919 pillaged the houses of interracial couples, deterring landlords outside the maritime districts from renting to them, there appear not to have been 'no-go' areas for Arabs in South Shields.[77] Table 8.3 and Map 8.3 show Arab-surnamed householders appeared by the 1930s in nearly every ward. Second, the number of married women, 62 in 1930, 90 in 1934 and 77 in 1939, with the census of slumdwellers discussed below, show contemporary estimates that the town's resident Arab families numbered between 40 and 50 in 1930 and 71 in 1934 undercounted substantially, probably because they ignored areas outside Holborn.[78] Undeterred by decades of vocal public disapproval, local women continued to marry migrant husbands in increasing numbers, and these couples gradually dispersed throughout

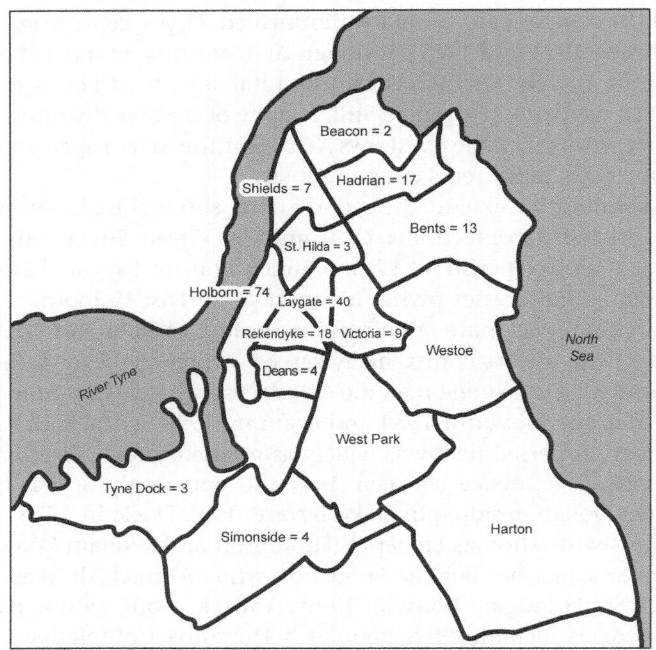


*Map 8.3* Spatial distribution of Arabic-surnamed electors, 1939

South Shields. Analysis reveals a town less residentially segregated than hitherto understood, colonized residents far from uniformly shunned and disreputable in their neighbours' eyes. Instead they appear approximately as broadly distributed as nineteenth-century migrants mapped in Chapter 3, although most remained near the docks because men worked in the maritime industry.

Electoral rolls reveal a privileged and stable portion of the working and commercial classes. Those of slum clearance reflect a population in which Arab-surnamed householders inhabited the same streets, buildings and houses as other townspeople. Analysing people displaced through demolition in the 1930s, reflected in Table 8.4 and Map 8.4, show that even in Holborn, the 'Arab quarter', Arab-headed households made up a small minority. Of 2829 families about to be displaced, 198, only 7 per cent, had an Arabic-surnamed householder, sometimes a woman. Nor did Arabs reside exclusively in this imputed ghetto. Although scholars have focused on the controversial clearance of Holborn, which accounted for 144 Arab households, a further 54, or

*Table 8.4* Distribution of Arab households in slum clearance areas, 1931–35

| Ward | Total persons | Total households | Arab-headed households | % Arab households |
|---|---|---|---|---|
| Shields | 3636 | 958 | 11 | 1.1 |
| Hilda | 1673 | 548 | 14 | 2.5 |
| Laygate | 1171 | 376 | 29 | 7.7 |
| Holborn | 2536 | 1071 | 144 | 13.4 |
| Simonside | 421 | 119 | 0 | 0 |
| Harton Colliery | 537 | 129 | 0 | 0 |
| Totals | 9974 | 3201 | 198 | 6 |

*Source*: 'Register of Houses in Clearance Areas, 1931–1935', TWAS T28/20–24. Occupiers were listed only if their tenancies exceeded one month, so these records remain an undercount of the most mobile. Laygate Square, 1933, Drake Street, 1933, TWAS T95/278.

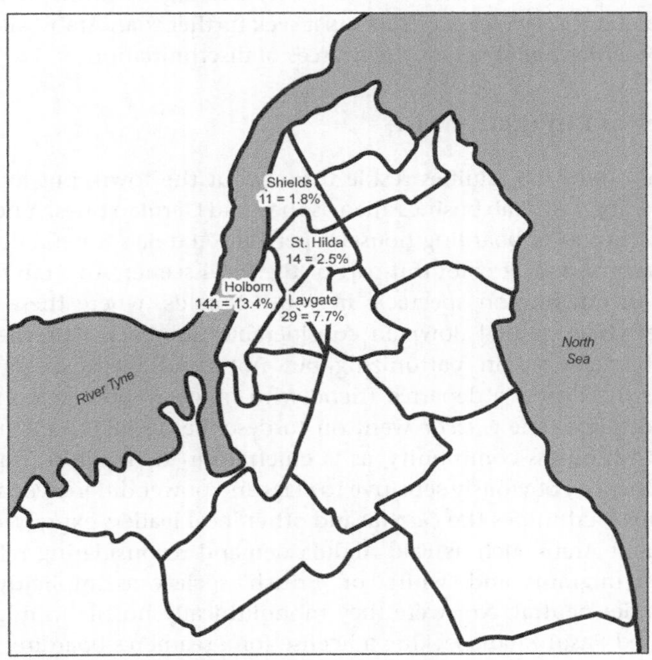


*Map 8.4* Location of Arab households in slum clearance areas

27 per cent, lived in Laygate, Hilda or Shields Wards. The overwhelming majority of these households consisted of two or more persons, that is, they were families. The vast bulk, 141, or 71 per cent, shared tenemented houses with apparent Britons.[79] Far from a perfectly random distribution, this indicates substantial integration. Despite vocal complaints in 1937 and 1940 about sharing new council housing with Arabs, no evidence appears of prior 'white flight' leaving whole streets occupied by Arabs.[80] Empirical data, however partial, thus suggest Arab families in these four wards alone amounted to at least three to four times contemporary estimates of the town's entire Arab population.[81] This calls into question the view of South Shields Arabs as transients largely isolated from local society through spatial segregation and unbridgeable linguistic, cultural and confessional differences. Comparing these figures with nineteenth-century migrants in Table 3.2 shows 198 Arab households exceeded the maximum nineteenth-century German total of 165, but came nowhere near the total of all overseas-origin households, 205 in 1881, 358 in 1891 and 581 in 1901. Bearing in mind that most Arabs had British wives, scholars must seek further than Arabs' allegedly unprecedented numbers for the sources of discrimination.

## A chieftain in their midst

Not only did Arab families reside throughout the town, but local oligarchs embraced Arab businessmen as they had German ones. A newspaper description of boarding housekeeper Faid Abdula's funeral depicted Arabs as a normal if colourful part of the local scene: 'An Arab funeral is not an uncommon spectacle in South Shields, where these dusky Orientals have settled down in considerable numbers.' The rite itself they characterized in patronizing but not hostile terms: 'the Arab mourns the loss of a departed friend with much weird ceremony and lavish display'. The *Gazette* went on to describe Abdula, a member of the local business community, as 'a chieftain in their midst ... a superior influence', obviously sensitive to class and power differences among the Arabs.[82] Affinities the *Gazette* and other local leaders expressed with prominent Arabs such as Faid Abdula demand reconsidering relations between migrants and 'white' or 'British' society as implicitly class and gender neutral. Nor were they monolithically hostile to migrants. Mohamed Rasul Khan, seeking a license for a seamen's boarding house in 11 Market Place, Frederick Seitz's former premises, offered three local men as references: the manager of a boot company, another Market Place merchant, Mr Richardson, and port chaplain Frederic Matthews.[83]

The 1920s and 1930s saw intense class warfare in South Shields and Britain, in which migrants from the colonies became implicated. Paeans to Faid Abdula reveal relations between colonized settlers and South Shields natives not simply as racially dichotomous or polarized, but cross-cut by gendered, sexual and class solidarities, antipathies and other dynamics. Class and commerce proved apparent solvents of cultural and racial barriers for affluent Arabs as for nineteenth-century merchants.[84]

Local authorities and institutions accommodated the migrants in turn. Until 1928, Muslims obtained a 'concession... whereby animals could be slaughtered in their houses for religious observances'.[85] After this the council licensed Abdu Osman, a butcher, to use the Council abattoirs to produce meat for observant Muslims.[86] In the late 1930s, slaughtermen licensed by the municipality included Sallah Nagi at 10 Chapter Row, Gullan Hasan Shah at 1 Thrift Street and Abdul Mussen at 9 Spring Lane. Mahomed Ali continued to hold a license in the late 1940s.[87] The courts provided a copy of the Qur'an for swearing oaths. A section of the Harton Cemetery was set aside for Muslim burials, bodies prepared by a local undertaker, A.W. Wilson of Derby Street. The local hospital performed circumcisions.[88] When Arabs entered Harton Workhouse en masse in October 1930, their dietary strictures were 'taken into consideration', while the local imam garnered public sympathy for refusing to duplicate his Muslim wedding rite with a British civil marriage.[89] The Muslim community used public spaces such as the National Union of Seamen's Unity Hall and the Mill Dam for religious celebrations, and the streets of South Shields for colourful processions complete with flags, banners and turbaned participants chanting Qur'anic verses. When not fomenting ill feeling, the *Shields Gazette* celebrated the 'cosmopolitan flavour' of such events, 'snapped' by holidaymakers.[90] Although one scholar has emphasized hostile letters to the *Gazette*, another reported the preponderance defended the Arabs.[91] Local attorneys such as James Muir Smith and Victor Grunhut, the latter of German origin, frequently represented Arabs in court.[92] Mutual accommodation and even sympathy, official and informal, show cultural differences proved no more insuperable in the twentieth century than in the nineteenth century. If local officials had wished to make life difficult for colonized settlers, concessions such as circumcision, parade permits and butchers' licenses could have been withheld easily.

In disputes over access to work in the depressed maritime labour market of the 1920s and 1930s, tellingly, Arab mariners living in South Shields received preference over those residing a mere 10 miles down the coast in Sunderland. That is, one became a 'local man' simply by residing in the port and need not be British nor 'white'. This customary practice dated from at least the strikes of the early nineteenth century, when locals rebuffed mariners from Yorkshire as 'foreigners'.[93] During a crisis precipitated by the British Shipping Assistance Act, 1935, Ahmed Mohamed, who had been sailing out of South Shields for some time but living in Sunderland, reported an encounter with another Arab 'who asked him what had he come to Shields to sign on for, because he lived in Sunderland'.[94] Like those of nineteenth-century migrants, Ahmed Mohamed's unfortunate experience stemmed less from formal status or origins than local relationships.[95]

As Mohamed Nagi's case illustrated, the most stable and integrated colonized settlers married. Like Europeans and other migrants before them, they established families and homes in South Shields. Unlike highly endogamous Germans and Jews, however, Arab householders, like most other men from abroad, married in Britain. Relationships with local women eased their integration and incorporation into local society.

## He treated me as a husband would

Women in South Shields as elsewhere in Britain married Arab and other colonized migrants as their mothers and grandmothers had married Germans, Swedes and Spaniards. The First World War, however, appears a pivot during and after which the disadvantages to a Shieldswoman of a migrant husband began to overshadow the benefit to a migrant man of a locally born wife. In a country at war, exogamous marriages, no longer apparently benign, began to attract public disapproval, state penalties and even popular violence against British women married to Germans. By war's end, while continuing to perform the same integrating and stabilizing functions, exogamous women had been reconstructed by the state and in national discourse as betrayers of the nation.[96] Suspicion of exogamous women coloured responses to those marrying the colonized men who formed an increasing proportion of maritime labour and port populations during and after the war. Scholars viewing such relationships from the outside have focused on public disapproval and racist rhetoric, including the riots of 1919, directed in some towns against interracial couples.[97] The most sensitive contemporaries, however, observed husbands and wives negotiated cultural differences through everyday practices in the intimacy of the domestic sphere.[98]

Moral outrage aplenty greeted mixed couples in South Shields as elsewhere, expressed through abusive letters to the *Shields Gazette* and offensive comments by local officials.[99] Like wives of Kru men in Liverpool, such women often found themselves shunned by family and friends, although reconciliation commonly followed.[100] That women contracted such marriages at all suggests a degree of support in obtaining witnesses for the ceremony and clergymen or other officials to perform it. Mixed couples in other towns met through the same social networks that brought previous migrants together with local women: friends, neighbours, relatives and co-workers.[101] Anthropologist Sydney Collins found multiple instances in South Shields of two, three or four sisters all married to men of colour, sometimes brothers or kinsmen. This suggested parents' response to the first marriage signalled to their other daughters such unions' acceptability. This marriage pattern, conversely, proved compatible with many colonized men's understandings that marriage united clans and families as much as individuals.[102]

Migrant men derived numerous advantages from associating with and marrying local women. These included access to kin, social and church networks, bona fides with the British state, and claims on that state through British-born wives and children such as Nagi Mohamed's son Hamed. Marriage offered them the attentive solicitude of a spouse in mastering language, cultural practices and bureaucracy.[103] Like Home Office officials evaluating candidates for naturalization, local magistrates tended to give married men the benefit of the doubt in claiming British nationality for purposes of working and living in Britain. This repeatedly frustrated central state enforcers such as immigration officers as well as Chief Constable Scott. 'Married Arabs' garnered sympathy in debates about measures such as the union's 1930 introduction of a discriminatory 'rota' or quota for Arab and Somali mariners, or discrimination resulting from the British Shipping Assistance Act of 1935. In contrast to single men, colonized householders were represented by the union and recognized by the state as legitimate members of local society and the maritime workforce.[104] Rigidly excluded from responsible jobs aboard ship and from most shore employment, colonized mariners, like upwardly mobile working-class men, found greater success marrying into the white working class than working their way into it.[105]

Evidence from South Shields affirms that outsiders found such marriages threatening, but those exploring the content of such marriages from the inside out, often through interviews with the couples involved, almost universally portrayed them as loving and stable relationships in which wives felt valued and children nurtured. Relations between such couples appeared little different from other marriages, although scrutiny and surveillance yielded more information about them. Women in

South Shields as elsewhere appear to have contracted marriages with colonized men for much the same reasons as others married local or migrant men.[106] Deposed Lauretta Lee of her common law husband Nagi Mohamed, 'He has always been kind to me. He treated me as a husband would.'[107] 'Coloured' men were almost universally acknowledged and represented as faithful and generous husbands, good providers active in childrearing. Through such 'kindness', men of colour might bid up the marriage market for local women, undermining white men's dominant position resting on wages and cultural capital.[108] A woman might balance enhanced power in her marriage against the loss of status exogamy might bring.[109] This apparent shift in the terms of local gender relations may have underlain local women's receptivity and white men's hostility to colonized men.

While Nagi Mohamed's mastery of local argot and adherence to the British custom of handing his wages to 'the missus' indicate his conformity to local cultural norms, other evidence corroborates scholars' findings that British wives in turn assimilated to Arab, African and other colonized husbands' cultural practices and expectations. Surveying South Shields' interracial couples between 1949 and 1952, Collins found native wives had accommodated to their migrant husbands' preferences, particularly in the matter of home furnishings and cuisine: wall decorations included 'decorated Koranic verses written in Arabic letters' and pictures of Muslim holy sites such as Mecca and Medina.[110] Wives sometimes learned to prepare 'Moslem' dishes, but more often adapted their own recipes to exclude proscribed foods such as pork in favour of mutton or chicken, while adding spices or rice to English recipes. Some women also participated in religious ritual and abstained from forbidden activities such as dancing and consuming alcohol. Beyond the private sphere, Collins found women acted as cultural mediators and interlocutors between their husbands and communities and local society. As in the working class generally, wives took responsibility for finding lodging, a delicate matter when some proprietors refused to rent to men of colour.[111] Like Louise Anderson, Arabs' wives wrote letters on men's behalf and translated for husbands in transactions with employers and in other public matters: Lauretta Lee read the *Journal of Commerce* to Nagi Mohamed.[112]

These processes dated from the Great War at least. When Hassan Mohamand threw a rock though the window of her house at 91 E. Holborn, Elizabeth Zaid, wife of boarding housekeeper Abdul Zaid, reproved him in Arabic.[113] Margaret or Maggie Abdula, married to Faid Abdula, had picked up enough Arabic in her years of serving meals to her boarders to recognize the word 'Kolo', which she translated as 'all'.[114] After Faid Abdula's death, 'Following the custom of the Arabs they sat up all night in the same room as the dead man she [his wife] being present on the first night.'[115] Relations with other local people appear to have been cordial: when the body was discovered, Maggie took the baby to a neighbour's house.[116] Colonized migrants' pattern and trajectory of settlement thus appear continuous with those of other overseas migrants: marrying into the local population, establishing stable households, and accepted as part of local society by their neighbours, even by some of the elite. Exogamy remained a cultural practice local women had engaged in for generations.

Mutual cultural assimilation, no doubt common to other exogamous marriages, became publicly visible in the Muslim community. While European migrants other than Jews and Germans tended to join an existing congregation such as St Bede's Roman Catholic Church, many Muslims' wives converted to Islam.[117] Community leader Yussif Hersi Sulliman estimated in 1938 that women accounted for 20 of the town's 645 'Moslems'.[118] Wives also defended their families and communities vocally, writing to the *Gazette* to repudiate racist letters to the editor, and sending a delegation to the mayor in 1937 to demand their share of new council housing.[119] This open embrace of their husbands' culture may have threatened some observers.

This rich qualitative evidence prompts analogous questions about earlier migrants. One wonders how many wives of Norwegians or Spaniards learned their husbands' languages, adapted their recipes, changed their religions or identified with their husbands' communities. Did British wives' accommodation to Swedish or Estonian lifeways create local consternation? Lacking the infrastructure of a mosque or the German mission, such adaptations might remain relatively unobserved, thus lost to the record. Available evidence cannot answer these questions for South Shields, but perhaps research on other communities may one day do so.[120] Couples' mutual cultural adaptation problematizes cultural incompatibility as the root of antipathy to colonized migrants. It demands seeking elsewhere for the sources of conflicts between migrants and natives.

In the twentieth century as in the nineteenth century, women other than wives facilitated integration and defended migrants: the *Shields Gazette* reported an altercation between Dana Sharp, a servant in an Arab boarding house, and two other women, Elizabeth Jenkins and her mother Mrs Donkin. In court the women 'denied having provoked her by making some remark about the Arabs'. Fined for behaving in a disorderly manner and using threatening language, Sharp had the last word, declaring 'I wouldn't leave the Arab house for 20 of you. I'm probably going to marry one tomorrow. Happy days.'[121] Eva Shiel testified in court on behalf of her employer, Abdul Nagi, after a hostile crowd vandalized his shop in 36 Waterloo Vale.[122] Landladies continued to serve as advisers and confidantes, reflected in the honorific 'missus'.[123] Exogamous marriages and other relationships between local women and migrant men thus exhibited continuities between those antedating and following the First World War. While the state and migrants themselves continued to rely on women, both native and otherwise, for practical as well as cultural assistance, women's function as gatekeepers to local society left them exposed as state policy towards migrants grew hostile in the twentieth century.

## Wives out of place

Because these marriages transgressed imperial hierarchies, the state penalized them, straining relationships. Nassar Abdula, 23, brother of Faid Abdula, 25, became a suspect in his brother's March 1919 murder because Nassar openly resented Faid's marriage to Maggie, a local woman: 'there was always this bickering and quarrelling about the white wife and also about the money'. The brothers were in business together, and the marriage in January 1918, followed in due course by the birth in South Shields of a son, signalled Faid Abdula's resolve to remain in Britain rather than return to Egypt as he and his brother planned, for 'if they returned to their own country a white wife would be out of place'.[124]

As this comment suggests, strains in the Abdula brothers' relationship stemmed in part from the British imperial state's hostility to marriages between British women and colonial subjects, and its efforts to discourage or penalize them.[125] While the contemporaneous German state annulled such marriages in Southwest Africa, the British state took indirect measures, destabilizing them by barring British or white wives from returning with their husbands to the colonies.[126] Asked, 'Did you know that if your husband returned to his own country he would be unable to take you?' Margaret Abdula responded, 'I did not know that.'[127] Such measures undermined the rights of such couples, creating a new social problem: that of men forced from Britain abandoning wives and children, 'an insult to the women of our land' that burdened local poor relief.[128] This possibly discouraged local marriages, for Table 8.5 shows a smaller proportion of Arabs married than any other group naturalized, including mariners admitted under special terms between 1903 and 1914.[129] The common observation that Somalis did not marry in Britain

*Table 8.5* Naturalization applicants, single versus married, 1879–1939

| | Yemeni/Arab/ Indian/Turk | | | Others | | |
|---|---|---|---|---|---|---|
| | married[a] | single | % married | married | single | % married |
| 1879–1902 | – | – | – | 49 | 51 | 96 |
| 1903–15 | – | – | – | 162 | 234 | 69 |
| 1915–30 | – | – | – | 38 | 48 | 79 |
| 1931–35 | 4 | 8 | 50 | 60 | 93 | 64.5 |
| 1936 | 16 | 99 | 16 | 26 | 39 | 67 |
| 1937 | 11 | 66 | 17 | 4 | 12 | 33 |
| 1938 | 9 | 35 | 26 | 12 | 16 | 75 |
| 1939 | 6 | 20 | 30 | 7 | 8 | 87.5 |

*Note*: [a] Six widowers and one legally separated man were counted as married on the assumption that they might have similarities to married men such as children or other kin in South Shields.

may have resulted from their even more tenuous status, rendering them less than desirable husbands.[130] While treating them as aliens for purposes of employment, the Home Office nonetheless forbade Somalis as well as West African Mende and Timne from pursuing naturalization at all.[131]

While the bulk of men stable enough to vote also married by the 1930s, naturalizations under duress of increasing restrictions rendered visible a hitherto hidden and likely more fluid population of single Arab mariners resembling the 'invisible men' of the *fin de siècle*.[132] In spite of deepening hostility from state, municipality and union, such men apparently possessed sufficient claim to residence in South Shields to attain naturalization. Yet few had married in Britain. Table 8.5 shows that well over half of men of all other origins married before pursuing naturalization, while a minority of Arabs had done so.[133] The disproportion of single to married Arabs suggests threats to exclude them from employment after 1935, like the legislation of 1903, prompted single men with few local ties to seek naturalization who would not otherwise have done so. It also suggests state penalties possibly discouraged Arabs and other colonized men from marrying. Since intermarriage facilitated migrants' integration, as wives' kin and networks replaced or supplemented those of men's places of origin, depressed rates of marriage may have rendered colonized migrants less familiar to local people than Germans, Scandinavians and other previous migrants, who almost universally married.[134] Perhaps, then, it was not intermarriage with local women but rather insufficient intermarriage that rendered colonized men unfamiliar and subject to suspicion. It also left them more dependent on boarding houses and services segregated at the riverside.

## Respectable men of means

Arabs not only integrated into local society through marriage, business relations and other practices, but also reconstructed communal cultural practices and institutions. Through these, like Germans, Jews and Norwegians before them, they articulated local with national and global compatriot networks. Arabs' boarding houses, cafes and houses of worship presented an iteration of the institutions and practices sustaining nineteenth-century migrants.[135] Their networks differed from Continental ones in three critical respects however. First, whether merchants or mariners, they brought almost no women with them. Second, Arab businesses did not disperse throughout the town, but remained concentrated largely in Holborn. Third, Arab establishments apparently ministered to an almost entirely male and Arab clientele rather than to townspeople at large. While Arabs married and single gradually dispersed throughout the town, the Arab service sector remained in Holborn near the docks, the shipping offices and the union quarters on the Mill Dam, where seafarers assembled daily seeking work. Even married men such as Nagi Mohamed maintained homosocial cultural practices and personal ties through frequenting compatriot enterprises such as the White House at 1 West Holborn where he took his midday meal on 17 May 1929, Sophie's at 4 Thrift Street or Athraby's at 27 East Holborn, where Lauretta found him playing bagatelle that evening.[136]

Like nineteenth-century migrant institutions, Arab boarding houses drew on networks of capital, information and mutual support spanning Britain, Arabia and beyond.[137] After Faid Abdula's death, Abdulla Sartar of Cardiff rented the Abdula brothers' erstwhile boarding house in 63 Thrift Street, but delegated Monsair Seyd, to whom Faid owed £200, to manage it.[138] In spring 1935, Abdul Mohamed, an Adenese trader described as 'a respectable man with sufficient means', travelled to Britain to stay with Salem Abuzed, his former business partner at 1 West Holborn, now a boarding housekeeper at 25 East Holborn. While there he hoped to visit friends and collect debts amounting to approximately £300.[139]

Boarding housekeepers provided an array of services for sojourning Arab mariners, offering familiar company, accustomed food and facilities for religious observance. They also assisted men in obtaining jobs as well as identity documents and other paperwork the state increasingly demanded.[140] In 1928, Ali Hamed, of 95 West Holborn, travelled to London to visit the High Commissioner for India, designated protector of Asian subjects in Britain, to obtain documents for brothers Saleh and Mohamed Nassir, also from Dheli, Aden. The authorities knew Ali Hamed as he frequently secured documents for Arabs in South Shields. Ali Hamed also attempted to negotiate exemption for his clients from the 1930 rota.[141] Boarding housekeepers also provided financial and other services: 'it was the custom for Arab seamen to leave their savings with the boardinghousekeeper when they went to sea....' Faid and Nassar Abdula allegedly held between £400 and £500 on behalf of 60 or 70 boarders.[142]

Boarding houses provided a social safety net for colonized mariners far from home. Proprietors maintained clients at their own expense during periods of unemployment, in anticipation of repayment when men found work. 'The charity of his compatriots' shielded an unemployed man from efforts to deport him if he sought relief.[143] In a dramatic illustration of the responsibility boarding housekeepers took for sustaining the maritime workforce, 97 unemployed Arab mariners denied outdoor relief payments entered the South Shields workhouse briefly in autumn 1930.[144] Simultaneous appeals from local boarding housekeepers showed many were owed substantial sums by men they had continued to support during months and sometimes years of unemployment.[145]

Consistent with their affinity for Faid Abdula, local officials initially recognized the service boarding housekeepers performed for local industry. In the early 1920s, the British and Foreign Sailors' Society, a maritime charity, paid maintenance for unemployed mariners directly to the boarding housekeepers.[146] In May 1928, Mohamed Methana sought reimbursement from the local Public Assistance Committee (PAC) in respect of Ali Osram, whom he had supported in lieu of public assistance. The PAC duly collected the money for him from the Shipping Federation, an employers' cartel.[147] Local officials' accommodation to Arabs' cultural practices may have stemmed from mutual interest in colonized mariners' labour. Overt racial polarization and exclusion thus remained somewhat qualified in South Shields by the stake town authorities shared with employers and boarding housekeepers in these vulnerable workers.

As Table 8.6 shows, by mid-century, Arabs operated more boarding houses than any other migrant group, while the nationality of

*Table 8.6* Seamen's boarding houses and beds in South Shields by purported nationality, 1929–39

| | British | | Russian | | Scandinavian | | Arab | | Coloured | | Maltese | | Totals | |
|---|---|---|---|---|---|---|---|---|---|---|---|---|---|---|
| | houses | beds | houses | beds | houses | beds | houses | beds | houses | beds | houses | beds | houses | beds |
| 1929 | 15 | 117 | 2 | 28 | 6 | 81 | 14 | 268 | 1 | 18 | 2 | 29 | 40 | 541 |
| 1930 | 13 | 88 | 2 | 20 | 6 | 80 | 11 | 233 | 1 | 18 | 21 | 20 | 34 | 467 |
| 1931 | 13 | 83 | 2 | 28 | 6 | 78 | 10 | 210 | 1 | 18 | 1 | 20 | 31 | 421 |
| 1932 | 11 | 78 | 2 | 28 | 6 | 79 | 10 | 199 | 1 | 18 | 1 | 20 | 31 | 421 |
| 1933 | 10 | 75 | 2 | 28 | 5 | 56 | 10 | 218 | 1 | 18 | 1 | 20 | 29 | 415 |
| 1934 | 9 | 76 | 2 | 16 | 2 | 20 | 9 | 187 | 1 | 18 | 1 | 20 | 24 | 337 |
| 1935 | 5 | 41 | 2 | 16 | 2 | 20 | 9 | 248 | 1 | 18 | – | – | – | – |
| 1936 | 3 | 25 | 2 | 16 | 2 | 20 | 9 | 217 | 9 | 116 | – | – | – | – |
| 1937 | 3 | 24 | 2 | 16 | 2 | 20 | 6 | 168 | 9 | 123 | – | – | – | – |
| 1938 | 3 | 30 | 2 | 16 | 1 | 10 | 7 | 183 | 8 | 120 | – | – | – | – |
| 1939 | 4 | 33 | 2 | 16 | 1 | 10 | 5 | 138 | 8 | 120 | – | – | – | – |

*Source*: *Report of the Police Establishment*, 1929–39, STCL.

prospective residents had become prescribed, at least nominally. These figures also show that as official efforts to exclude Arab mariners in the 1930s reduced the number of their boarding houses and beds, those accommodating 'coloured' mariners rose.[148] Like figures on 'Coloured Alien Seamen' above, this suggests repression against Arabs simply increased demand for other exploitable colonized mariners to fill the least desirable shipboard jobs. How closely these classifications reflected actual residence patterns remains opaque: some colonized mariners apparently preferred to reside among clansmen.[149] Just as segregated council housing never proved adequate to rehouse displaced families of colour, the number of beds in licensed facilities fell short of the supply necessary to keep colonized mariners separated from local people. Chief Constable Wilkie complained in 1929 that many ended up seeking accommodation in Temperance Hotels and common lodging houses, where some such as Nagi Mohamed apparently acquired their taste for alcohol, tobacco, gambling and other local cultural practices that repelled the devout.[150] Although numerous licenses were cancelled in 1936 due to apparent demolition of the properties, several survived the war, including premises at 2 Regent Street, licensed to Mongo Allia on 18 March 1936, transferred to Said Mabrouk on 19 April 1939, and to Mohamed Said on 14 April 1955, who held it until the property's demolition in 1969.[151]

Local officials recognized these institutions' importance to the town's major industry. On the eve of slum clearance in 1933, John Reid, Borough Engineer, proposed building 'special houses' for 126 single men among 400 displaced men, women and children. These would be 'let to the boarding masters' losing premises to demolition. Passing this request to the Ministry of Health, the Town Clerk asserted the 'desirability... that these men should continue to be housed in the riverside district', not 'scattered throughout the borough' although, of course, they already were. Although the Ministry of Health insisted they could not subsidize them, they agreed that 'lodginghouses can normally be provided on a self-supporting basis'.[152] Local and national support for boarding houses and boarding housekeepers occurred at the same historical moment when Home Office policy, instigated by the Board of Trade and the seamen's union but carried out by local police, grew increasingly hostile.[153] To the degree they clashed with the agendas of an invasive and aspirationally manipulative state apparatus, the inner workings of Arabs' compatriot networks and institutions became objects of suspicion and eventually attack.

## Drifting to South Shields

In spite of their many similarities to Victorian migrants, Arab settlers became subject to unprecedented levels of central government scrutiny and harassment in which local government, first police and later the municipality, became increasingly involved. Although scholars have identified interracial marriage as the catalyst for twentieth-century conflicts, authorities, local and national, appeared less bothered by men so integrated into the community than by the boarding houses at the riverside. Despite affinities for men such as Faid Abdula, official suspicion and surveillance focused on boarding housekeepers, mainly because the compatriot service sector remained independent of and illegible to the state.[154] Hostile parties alleged boarding housekeepers evaded union-mandated hiring procedures, whereby men assembled publicly on the Mill Dam for selection by local officials of the Board of Trade, the National Union of Seamen and the Shipping Federation, all of whom discriminated against mariners of colour. Instead, boarding housekeepers contracted directly with companies or officers of individual ships to supply crews, receiving a 'commission' from each man hired.[155] Despite possibly well-founded concerns about trafficking, official attacks on colonized mariners rendered them more rather than less vulnerable to boarding housekeepers and other middlemen.[156]

While birthplaces of successive children yield clues to nineteenth-century migration patterns, state efforts to control twentieth-century migration enable reconstruction of the indirect routes colonized mariners took to South Shields. Authorities suspected British Somalis of 'slipping over the frontier' to the French port of Djibouti where they allegedly got work on ships heading for Marseilles. From there they travelled as passengers, and 'sooner or later they are thrown up at some European seaport' such as Havre, Antwerp, Cardiff or South Shields.[157] The South Shields Mercantile Marine Superintendent in 1920 reported that Arab seamen were 'discharged at Marseilles, pay their fares to England, and drift to South Shields'.[158] Rather than drift, colonized mariners quite sensibly left London, where ocean liners offered them poorly paid contract labour, for Cardiff and South Shields with relatively well-paid work on tramp steamers and Home and Coasting vessels.[159] Like the invisible men of the *fin de siècle*, such mariners remained elusive to the authorities and the historical record, perhaps deliberately so: focused on getting a living, their sojourns in South Shields often remained brief and their purposes instrumental. A series of state and union interventions destabilized, stigmatized, criminalized and finally segregated this population, sojourner and settler alike.

Like attacks on Jews and Germans, pressure on colonized migrants came initially from the imperial state via local police. Although exclusionary measures such as wartime and postwar aliens registration, the Coloured Alien Seamen Order, 1925, the rota of 1930, and the protectionist British Shipping Assistance Act, 1935 originated with the central state and other national bodies such as the union and employers, enforcement fell to local officials.[160] In wartime South Shields, police made Arabs, like Germans, objects of punitive measures. In 1917, Scott prosecuted three boarding housekeepers who had lived in South Shields for years, among them Ali Said. He sought to make an example of them, for as 'Boarding House Keepers, they would have considerable influence among the Arabs'.[161] As in the cases of J.F. Erickson, John Alder and the Saville brothers, Scott abused an ambiguous central state directive to pursue personal agendas.

This episode illuminates several points: first, the xenophobic climate of the twentieth century, intensified in wartime, legitimated harassing an ever-widening array of migrants; second, migration patterns proved sufficiently well established to be known to local authorities and third, the Arab community in South Shields already possessed discernable internal structures that outsiders such as Scott sought to manipulate.[162] The press and local officials such as police did not treat migrants as a monolith: they recognized internal divisions and distinctions, approving some, deprecating others and accurately identifying community leaders. Although space precludes thorough discussion of their causes, course and outcomes, riots in January and February 1919 and again in August 1930 stemmed specifically from competition for employment, not generalized antipathy based on racial or cultural difference. Unlike the larger and more destructive *Lusitania* riots, they remained geographically contained on the Mill Dam.[163] This problematizes views of South Shields as a racially polarized community, suggesting relations between Arabs and others, migrants and natives, remained complex.

As national authorities pressed local ones to exclude and criminalize colonized mariners, local police in particular assumed an increasingly adversarial stance that put them at odds with local values. In March 1924, defence counsel J. Muir Smith persuaded South Shields magistrates that 'it was up to the prosecution to prove' seamen Abdullah Ahmed aka Hassan Karika aka Hassan Yaya was not an Adenese British subject entitled to land in South Shields. The Home Office reacted by scolding the magistrates while advising Chief Constable Scott and

J.W. Oldfield, H.M. Immigration Officer, to prosecute future cases using the legislation of 1920, which apparently dispensed with the presumption of innocence.[164] Prosecutions of boarding housekeepers skyrocketed from none in 1925 to 1522 in 1926 and 1624 in 1927, remarkable when only 38 to 42 such establishments existed in the town.[165] Resultant alienation between police and the community emerged in the 'extreme difficulty Police found in obtaining reliable evidence from co-patriots of the accused' while investigating the 1929 murder of Benjamin George Franklin.[166] Global economic instability, unemployment, and union, employers' and state policies thus opened fissures in local society. South Shields' Arab community, like other migrant communities, thus took shape within a web of global, national and local relationships and processes, including empire building, depression and war. This context shaped the mixed and often hostile reception twentieth-century migrants encountered, including defamation by the press and local officialdom as well as sporadic outbreaks of harassment and violence. Although far less destructive than the *Lusitania* riots that drove Germans from South Shields and Britain, these events have haunted migrants in South Shields, overshadowing persistent cultural processes continuous with those integrating nineteenth-century migrants.[167]

## Suitable premises near the river

By the 1930s, many municipal authorities joined the police in overt hostility towards colonized migrants. Slum clearance of Holborn's multicultural and multiracial population became a means to impose racial segregation, removing white residents to suburban housing estates while rehousing and thereby containing 'coloured' residents in Holborn. On 15 May 1933 the Housing and Town Planning Committee 'considered…provision of houses for coloured persons and aliens displaced from clearance areas', and in March 1934 asked the borough engineer to provide plans for 'suitable premises near the River' to rehouse mariners.[168] These measures, importing and reproducing spatial segregation from Britain's overseas colonies, proved controversial at the time, and have remained so.[169] This episode has become notorious because town authorities actively intervened to segregate the Arab and 'coloured' population. Yet the records it generated reveal the community disrupted proved highly mixed, not homogeneously Arab, shown in Table 8.4. Segregation ultimately failed because the municipality never produced enough new housing to accommodate those displaced, who simply moved into adjacent, mixed neighbourhoods, principally

Laygate. Although the council refused to let public housing outside Holborn to families of colour, Table 8.3 shows the bulk of Arabic-surnamed electors, 120 or 62 per cent, resided outside Holborn by 1939, and only 74, or 38 per cent of the total, in Holborn.[170] Further, some white residents actively chose to remain in Holborn because they enjoyed relations of interdependence with the Arab population.

Social integration cannot, of course, be read off of geographical integration unproblematically, but since those advocating spatial segregation overtly intended it to produce social segregation, protests against it provide further evidence of a community mixed in class and culture.[171] Two elderly English sisters, Miss Telford, a tobacconist at 117 East Holborn, and her sister, the widowed Mrs Soderlund, a grocer at 115 East Holborn, requested relocation, not in a distant housing estate, but in the 'Arab' estate nearby. Proprietors of an 'old and established business', they expressed the hope that 'they will be given the option of taking a shop in the same district as it is intended to place the Arabs' on whom their livelihoods depended.[172] Records thus reveal Holborn not simply as an Arab ghetto, but a mixed community before and after slum clearance, whose collective *esprit* transcended cultural or racial difference.

Scholars conclude nonetheless that overt efforts at segregation retarded the 'centripetal' tendency for migrants to integrate into the town both spatially and culturally, as Nagi Mohamed and previous migrants had. It also legitimated segregation promoted by bigots on the Town Council and in letters to the *Gazette*. White neighbours who had long resided in Holborn with the Arabs now demanded segregated housing.[173] Demolishing the fabric of Holborn's multicultural community climaxed almost two decades of calumny, riots, deportations, police harassment and coercive central government measures. The Arab community turned inwards, responding with a Muslim religious revival stressing differences from their neighbours while retreating from political engagement. In the process, Muslim men began to be shamed for accommodating to British customs as innocuous as Western dress, much less tobacco or gambling. The community began celebrating festivals publicly, involving processions of chanting, robed and turbaned men, women and children.[174] These developments resembled those in Liverpool. There, Kru mariners' occupational mobility, enforced by state and employers' efforts to marginalize them, produced 'reactive ethnicity' for mutual defence and aid.[175] Racial segregation and conflict as well as cultural accommodation and integration thus proved subject to local, national, imperial and global historical processes.

## Culture and struggle

Union and state discourses treating colonized migrants as an illegitimate and excludable 'floating population' have deceived scholars into minimizing their numbers and spatial and cultural integration, while overestimating their isolation from local society. Colonized subjects' relegation to the lowest strata of the maritime workforce, reinforced by imperial distortions in the global labour market, did render them, like the Irish, less welcome than nineteenth-century merchants and artisans. Occupational segregation impeded Arab and other colonized mariners from forming shipboard friendships that integrated nineteenth-century migrants. Municipal ambivalence, offering concessions such as halal butchering while hounding and segregating colonized mariners, bespeaks their ambiguous position: essential to the health of the local and imperial economy but subordinate and super-exploited within it. Still, little evidence appears of monolithic hostility.

Gross underestimates of their numbers and erroneous assumptions about their composition and spatial distribution have obscured Arabs' integration with local people. Despite periodic violence provoked by competition for seafaring jobs, often by specific agents, informal processes of everyday integration continued in interwar South Shields. Businessmen providing services to local industry continued to be welcome, while public spectacles such as funerals garnered sympathetic if Orientalist press coverage. This evidence demands revisiting assumptions that populations in other towns remained marginal and ghettoized. It also demands looking elsewhere than cultural difference for the sources of conflict between migrants and other residents. Arabs such as Nagi Mohamed and the Muckbles participated in local cultural practices such as drinking, betting and baptizing their children, until polarized by repeated attacks in the 1930s.

In this respect, women's centrality as gatekeepers to British society cannot be overemphasized and merits further research. Exogamous couples in interwar South Shields acquired their precarious social position due to the cumulative effects of *fin de siècle* anti-Semitism and wartime Germanophobia, as well as their challenge to the discourses, practices and power relations sustaining imperial wealth and might. This historical and structural context renders animus towards wives of Arabs and other colonized men continuous with and shaped by nineteenth- and twentieth-century cultural and structural shifts rather than racial difference alone. It reveals a gender struggle inextricable from what has commonly been understood as racial polarization. By 1930 the vast majority of Arabs stable enough to vote had married, and little evidence appears that exogamous couples confronted wholesale ostracism. Everyday relations exhibited significant mutual cultural accommodation: British wives and colonized husbands alike adapted, wives to their husbands' dietary and other preferences and husbands to local custom including the disposition of the pay packet and leisure activities. Despite state-imposed impediments, Arabs gradually dispersed through the town, like European and colonized migrants before them. Local people continued to incorporate migrants through everyday practices such as business transactions, marriage and daily interactions in street and neighbourhood. This calls into question views of South Shields Arabs as transients isolated from local society through spatial segregation and unbridgeable linguistic, cultural and confessional differences.

This neither excuses nor minimizes the hardships Arabs faced. It undertakes to explain conflicts without recourse to simplistic universalisms such as 'difference'—blaming the victim—or 'intolerance'—blaming the British. Blows the migrant community suffered at official hands simultaneously damaged and reconfigured everyday forms of customary inclusion and integration. Influenced by union campaigns and central government policies, local decision makers increasingly embraced exclusionary agendas. Like the *Lusitania* riots of 1915 and wartime xenophobia, the riots on the Mill Dam in 1919 and 1930 and the controversial segregation of public housing chilled and checked ongoing processes of integration. With their defensive revival of Islam, in which British-born women participated publicly, the community became more visible and apparently more culturally alien in the late 1930s. Still, scores of Arabs in the same years obtained naturalization, thwarting state and union efforts to exclude them. Despite repeated assaults, South Shields' multicultural community remained resilient, embedded in global webs of relationships. National, global and local structural dynamics continued to shape relations between migrants and natives until another global war transformed these relations, altering South Shields, Britain and the world anew.

# Conclusion: Global Migrants in Provincial England

Violence and other expressions of hostility have punctuated the history of migrants to Britain. These traumatic events have haunted historical memory: their acknowledgement constituted an important step towards making Britain's history and its multicultural society whole. This work has sought to recover for the past, present and future an alternative, usable historical legacy of inclusion, integration and cultural exchange. Reconstructing migration to, from and through South Shields between 1841 and 1939 debunks views of more recent migrants as disruptive to a mythically harmonious, static and homogeneous society. Instead, investigating migrants' relations with other migrants and native Britons reveals South Shields' population remained fluid and its culture protean in the century before 1939.

Analysing the whole migrant population rather than visible 'ethno-cultural groups' shows multifarious relationships formed between migrants and natives, integrating globally mobile newcomers into local society through work, marriage, civic participation and other social relations. Sons and daughters of these migrants such as Victor Grunhut became pillars of the local community. Overseas migrants to South Shields encountered not simply tolerance or coexistence but mutual cultural accommodation, integration and incorporation into local kin, occupational and other social networks. Examining local relations through global processes and vice versa shows migrant-native relations in South Shields hardly reflected rigid binarisms created by cultural, confessional or racial differences. Instead, local relations remained relatively open and fluid, responding to class, gender, social and sexual dynamics and local, national, imperial and global ones. Migrants generated conflict and contention only in certain relations.

## Provincial England

Recognizing how global processes shaped local history poses a challenge to the insular interpretation of British history and culture. Portraying Britain and especially provincial England as closed societies, unworldly and hostile to newcomers, has been used to explain conflicts over immigration, especially since 1948. Yet the history of South Shields reveals local populations remained fluid and diverse, replenished and reconfigured by migration from overseas as well as elsewhere in Britain. The hundreds of households containing return migrants show global mobility and cosmopolitanism characterized many Britons living in provincial England, belying their habitual portrayal as parochial and culturally homogeneous.

## Culture as process

Cultural difference thus requires reconsideration as an obstacle to social harmony. Explanations for conflict have often rested on the premise of insuperable cultural barriers between migrants and natives. Apparent differences of language or lifeways, however, proved no impediment to Jewish, German or Basque shopkeepers and artisans establishing businesses and other institutions in the town, or forging friendships sustaining naturalization. Analysing migrant-native relations in South Shields shows local cultures proved flexible, mutable, syncretic and protean, hardly the stuff of which insurmountable barriers are made. Local cultural practices of inclusion, permeability and fluidity belie fictions of cultural stasis, purity, fragility and defensiveness.

Cultural traditions of openness and inclusion did not operate in a vacuum, however. Ongoing discursive construction and reproduction of familiar and foreign cultural identities occurred through national-level census procedures, global and local labour market shifts, national and local state formation and housing policies. What made the difference between inclusion in the nineteenth century and exclusion in the twentieth? Not factors endogenous to local relations, but the impact of geopolitics. Economic expansion and instability, nation building in Britain and elsewhere, imperial competition and decline, world war and global depression impinged on and transformed local cultures. Jews and other minorities from Schleswigers to Finns fled Continental empire building, painful reminders of burgeoning European powers' encroachment on British imperial dominance. Migrants from Britain's own colonies challenged the geographical segregation reinforcing imperial extraction. As ongoing struggles imbued 'difference' with shifting political meanings, migrants could move from inclusion to exclusion and sometimes back again. Attacks on Germans who had lived for decades in South Shields show global events such as the First World War dramatically altered local relations. Other long-time residents met harassment and threats of exclusion, not due to personal or cultural characteristics, but due to a transformed geopolitical context and its local effects. Institutional discrimination, especially against Jews, Germans and Arabs, escalated into violence in 1915, 1919 and 1930. Such events, although national or even global in scope, reflected local power relations as well. Still, processes of everyday integration continued, through business transactions, friendships, naturalizations, and especially marriage and family formation. This history has several lessons for the study of migration in Britain and more generally.

## A plea for empirical investigation

First, scholars can no longer rely on episodes of conflict to identify significant migrant populations. Neglecting the volume and spatial distribution, much less the reception and experiences of more stable and affluent migrants who comprised the bulk of those arriving in the Victorian period has produced unfounded generalizations about popular responses to migrants. Focusing on flashpoints of conflict such as those provoked by the Irish in the 1840s and the Jews in the 1890s has skewed scholarship towards seeing migrants universally as objects of popular hostility. Aggregate figures, although flawed, coupled with analysis of evidence contained in censuses, electoral rolls and other sources, yields results at surprising variance from assumptions based on conflict alone. Naturalization case records offer a particularly rich source not only for reconstructing everyday relations, but the networks and composition of migrant populations in particular towns. We need more systematic studies of migrants from overseas, both colonized and otherwise. Apart from the Jews and the Irish, mid-century overseas migrant populations remain almost entirely uninvestigated: the few exceptions focus almost exclusively on London. Greater attention to other major groups remains in order; for a start, the well-known but neglected cases of Germans in Bradford and Orthodox Jews in Gateshead. The point is not that scholars ought to produce 'recuperative' histories in which unsung groups get their 15 minutes of fame, but rather, that in the absence of accurate data, interpretations may err. Attention is thus long overdue to the increasing numbers of overseas migrants who contributed to British society and culture in the century before 1939, a rich and fertile field for future research.

## No closed communities

Second, scholars must reconsider models of 'ethnic' or 'race' relations that approach migrants and natives as distinct and bounded communities. Neither South Shields nor its constituent migrant networks proved closed communities. Even the German Seamen's Mission, to all appearances a classic migrant institution, partook in global, regional and local networks including natives as well as migrants of many lands. This evidence of ongoing circulation to and through South Shields and commensurate movement of local men and women into the wider world and often back again complicates views of migrants and natives as mutually exclusive populations. Rather than assuming friction between homogeneous closed communities, scholars must ask instead what social ties or fissures, from kinship, class and gender to region, sexuality and occupation bound migrants with natives or divided migrant from migrant and native from native. In this endeavour it appears time to reconsider the recently unfashionable dynamic of class, or, more properly, social formation, including gender and sexual relations among others.

## Bringing social formation back in

In contrast to the pauperized Irish and destitute *fin de siècle* Jews, or even to strike-breaking Yorkshiremen and Shetlanders, mid-Victorian migrants, despite their significant numbers, provoked so little outcry that historians have almost entirely overlooked them. The key to this puzzle lies obviously with the skills and capital that Germans, mid-century Jews and other overseas migrants contributed to the making of Victorian South Shields. This in turn may explain their failure to attract attention from scholars who look for conflict to find migrants. Such migrants' relatively seamless integration into local society not only challenges explanations for conflict proposing xenophobia or intolerance as ahistorical constants. It also demands greater attention to wealth, skills and other resources as variables affecting migrants' reception.

Reconstructing the town's whole migrant population, to the extent evidence permits, shows the more affluent also proved the most stable, while proletarians such as labourers and mariners more often moved on. In this respect, long-distance migration patterns appear continuous with rather than different from those of internal migrants, rendering national borders somewhat irrelevant to migration processes and indeed the study of migration. Given Britain's notoriously class-stratified society this should hardly surprise, yet despite some lip service, class analysis has proven almost entirely absent from the study of 'immigrants and minorities'. Greater attention to the varied responses affluent migrants received would enrich scholars' understanding not only of migration but of British society.

In addition to class and imperial competition, gender relations, a constant sub-theme of scholarship on colonized migrants, merits further scholarly attention. The hysterical bigotry some exogamous couples evoked conveyed the unspoken realization that British society and possibly others remained more permeable through gender and sexual relations than the vaunted secular values of hard work or civic participation. As in other areas of historical inquiry, gender struggle and negotiation thus emerge as central dynamics of human mobility. Reconstructing where different migrants and migrant groups fit into local and global social formation could begin to fill the numerous gaps that currently render the history of overseas migration a random patchwork with yawning empty spaces such as Britain's Victorian period.

## South Shields globalized

Finally, South Shields holds lessons for industrial societies in the toils of what is currently styled globalization. Not only did the town attract migrants from all over the world, its industrial structure proved, arguably, paradigmatic for long-distance migrants in industrial societies. While West coast ports such as Bristol, Liverpool and Manchester depended on the slave economy and the 'first' Industrial Revolution based on textile production and consumer goods, Tyneside exemplified export-based and extractive economies prevalent in the 'second' Industrial Revolution, and common to the Continent, the United States and elsewhere. The region's disproportionate stake in a handful of industries rendered local working people, migrant and native, vulnerable to geopolitics, technological change and foreign competition. This lack of local control or accountability has characterized industrial societies increasingly oriented to global markets in the late nineteenth, twentieth and twenty-first centuries. This renders South Shields illuminating for understanding ongoing processes of globalization accompanied by unprecedented levels of transnational migration.

The history of migration to South Shields shows Britain never was a homogeneous, closed society, detached from global flows of population or cultural influence. Instead, it reveals local society and culture remain plural and dynamic, embedded in circuits of people, goods, ideas, power and interest, local and global as well as national and imperial. Local relations and how they changed prove inexplicable without recourse to global contexts as well as national and imperial ones. The impacts of these world-scale changes and how people responded to and coped with them cannot be understood, conversely, without examining their local histories. Geopolitics impinged on migrants and natives alike in the most intimate areas of their daily lives: where they lived, who they married, what work they could find and how their children fared. Yet by 1948, as the Empire Windrush brought some of the first postwar migrants to British shores, these relationships and events had been erased from popular memory and scholarship alike.

# Appendix: Was the Referee Process Corrupt?

Audiences have wondered whether referees were bribed to support naturalization claims. There was no evidence for this. First, the police investigated thoroughly each referee and his relationship to the memorialist. They even rejected some, as discussed above. Further, of a total of 676 referees, only 64, or barely 9 per cent, vouched for more than one applicant. Of these the vast bulk, or 50, vouched for no more than two. Six supported three, and eight supported as many as four, half of these four brothers.

This evidence hardly indicates a traffic in references, but was explained in many cases by a referee's professional position: Charles Bellem, NSFU District Secretary, supported three mariners. Family connections explain why Richard Goodwin, a builder, supported both Isaac and Jacob Pearlman. Ten of the 64 can be accounted for among those vouching for two or more of the four brothers mentioned above. In some instances the occasions occurred decades apart: auctioneer John Thomas Reed supported Ernest Dabbert in 1989 and another man in the 1930s, and cycle agent James John Runcieman first vouched for Paul Arthur Eggert in 1893 and another mariner in 1929. One could hardly live off the proceeds of such an intermittent traffic!

Conversely, of the 158 memorialists who shared a referee with one or more other migrants, little evidence appeared of systematic much less corrupt practice. Butchers, landladies, mariners and kin form the only discernable patterns, reflecting the larger pool. There was, however, a somewhat higher probability that one or more referees had or would some day vouch for another migrant. Eighty, or 51 per cent, presented at least one repeat referee. Yet as each memorialist presented four or more referees, this remains a small proportion overall.

# Notes

## Introduction: Migration and Cultural Change

1. P. Bidwell and S. Speak (1994) *Excavations at South Shields Roman Fort*, vol. I (Newcastle upon Tyne: Society of Antiquaries of Newcastle Upon Tyne with Tyne and Wear Museums), esp. 13; P. Salway and J. Blair (1988 [1984]) *Roman and Anglo-Saxon Britain* (Oxford: Oxford University Press), 1, 8.
2. B. Dobson and D.J. Breeze (2000) *Hadrian's Wall* 4th edn (Harmondsworth: Penguin), xv, 149; M. Baud and W. van Schendel (1997) 'Toward a Comparative History of Borderlands', *Journal of World History* 8, 2: 211–42. Thanks to Linda Darling for the latter.
3. In 1911 nearly half County Durham's working people were employed in one of the first four. D.J. Rowe (1990) 'The North-East', in F.M.L. Thompson (ed.) *The Cambridge Social History of Britain 1750–1950* (Cambridge: Cambridge University Press), 430.
4. See P. Gilroy (1991 [1987]) *'There Ain't No Black in the Union Jack': The Cultural Politics of Race and Nation* (Chicago: University of Chicago Press); K. Paul (1997) *Whitewashing Britain: Race and Citizenship in the Postwar Era* (Ithaca: Cornell University Press); I.R.G. Spencer (1997) *British Immigration Policy Since 1939: The Making of Multi-Racial Britain* (London: Routledge); C. Waters (1997) '"Dark Strangers" in our Midst: Discourses of Race and Nation in Britain, 1947–1963', *Journal of British Studies* 36: 207–38. Negative views of migration originated with Ferdinand Tönnies, reinforced by modernization theory, per J.H. Jackson (1997) *Migration and Urbanization in the Ruhr Valley, 1821–1914* (Atlantic Highlands: Humanities), 19–20.
5. A. Sivanandan (1982) *A Different Hunger: Writings on Black Resistance* (London: Pluto), 99–140; P. Gordon (1985) *Policing Immigration: Britain's Internal Controls* (London: Pluto), 40; R. Hansen (2000) *Citizenship and Immigration in Post-War Britain: The Institutional Origins of a Multicultural Nation* (Oxford: Oxford University Press), esp. 182–5. On analogous cases, see S. Castles and G. Kosack (1973) *Immigrant Workers and Class Structure in Western Europe* (Oxford: Oxford University Press), 441–3.
6. S. Hall, C. Crichter, T. Jefferson, J. Clarke and B. Roberts (1978) *Policing the Crisis: Mugging, the State, and Law and Order* (London: Macmillan); T. Asad (1990) 'Multiculturalism and British Identity in the Wake of the Rushdie Affair', *Politics and Society* 18, 4: 455–80, esp. 461–2; C. Husband (1994) 'The Political Context of Muslim Communities' Participation in British Society', B. Lewis and D. Schnapper (eds) *Muslims in Europe* (London: Pinter/St Martin's Press), 79–97; G. Lewis and S. Neal (2005) 'Introduction: Contemporary Political Contexts, Changing Terrains, and Revisited Discourses', *Ethnic and Racial Studies* 28, 3: 423–44. On asylum seekers, see T. Kushner

(2006) 'Great Britons: Immigration, History and Memory', in K. Burrell and P. Panayi (eds) *Histories and Memories: Migrants and their History in Britain* (London: Tauris), 18–34.

7. See 'Thousands Apply for Passports to Beat Start of UK Citizenship Test', *Guardian* (Wednesday 24 May 2006); 'British Court Says Banning Muslim Gown Violates Student's Rights', *New York Times* (3 March 2005), A13; R. Doty (1996) 'Sovereignty and the Nation: Constructing the Boundaries of National Identity', in T.J. Biersteker and C. Weber (eds) *State Sovereignty as Social Construct* (Cambridge: Cambridge University Press), 121–47; Waters, '"Dark Strangers" in Our Midst'. For a more critical literature, see R. Colls and P. Dodd (eds) (1986) *Englishness: Politics and Culture 1880–1920* (London: Croom Helm); L. Colley (1992) *Britons: Forging the Nation 1707–1837* (New Haven: Yale University Press).
8. P. Harris (1981) 'Oldham, Capital of Racial Tension', *Observer* (10 June 2001), 6; Campaign Against Racism and Fascism, *Southall: The Birth of a Black Community* (London: Institute of Race Relations and Southall Rights); Gilroy, *'There Ain't No Black in the Union Jack'*, esp. 72–108; Castles and Kosack, *Immigrant Workers and Class Structure*, 12.
9. J. Gillis (2004) *Islands of the Mind: How the Human Imagination Created the Atlantic World* (New York: Palgrave Macmillan), 114–15; V. Ware (1992) *Beyond the Pale: White Women, Racism, and History* (London: Verso), 12. On longstanding cultural pluralism, see J. Nelson (2003) 'England and the Continent in the 9th Century II, The Vikings and Others', Presidential Address, *Transactions of the Royal Historical Society* 6th ser., xiii (Cambridge: Cambridge University Press), esp. 14, 26–8; G.W.S. Barrow (1969) 'Northern English Society in the Twelfth and Thirteenth Centuries', *Northern History* 4: 1–28.
10. R. Samuel (1998) *Island Stories: Unravelling Britain* Theatres of Memory vol. 2 (London: Verso).
11. Hansen, *Citizenship and Immigration in Post-War Britain*, 181. For critiques, see essays in R. Samuel (ed.) (1989) *Patriotism: The Making and Unmaking of British National Identity* vol. I (London: Routledge).
12. Asad, 'Multiculturalism and British Identity', 458–63; L. Colley, 'British Values, Whatever They Are, Won't Hold Us Together', *Guardian* (18 May 2006), 35.
13. See A.L. Stoler (1995) *Race and the Education of Desire: Foucault's History of Sexuality and the Colonial Order of Things* (Durham: Duke University Press).
14. On fabricated 'cultural identities', see E. Hobsbawm and T. Ranger (eds) (1983) *The Invention of Tradition* (Cambridge: Cambridge University Press); S. Meacham (1999) *Regaining Paradise: Englishness and the Early Garden City Movement* (New Haven: Yale University Press).
15. M.G.H. Pittock (1997) *Inventing and Resisting Britain: Cultural Identities in Britain and Ireland, 1685–1789* (London: Macmillan); H. Kearney (1989) *The British Isles: A History of Four Nations* (Cambridge: Cambridge University Press); P. Hudson (1989) 'The Regional Perspective', in P. Hudson (ed.) *Regions and Industries: Perspectives on the Industrial Revolution Britain* (Cambridge: Cambridge University Press), esp. 15, 18; Samuel, *Island Stories*, 21–40, 153–71; Y. Ali (1992) 'Muslim Women and the Politics of Ethnicity and Culture in Northern England', in G. Sanghaza and N. Yuval-Davis

(eds) *Refusing Holy Orders: Women and Fundamentalism in Britain* (London: Virago), esp. 107–8.

16. E.P. Thompson (1991) *Customs in Common: Studies in Traditional Popular Culture* (New York: New Press), esp. 1–15, 179.
17. E.R. Wolf (1982) *Europe and the People Without History* (Berkeley: University of California Press).
18. M.J. Hickman (1999) 'Alternative Historiographies of the Irish in Britain: A Critique of the Segregation/Assimilation Model', in R. Swift and S. Gilley (eds) *The Irish in Victorian Britain: The Local Dimension* (Dublin: Four Courts), 243–4.
19. S. Hall (1991) 'The Local and the Global: Globalization and Ethnicity', and 'Old and New Identities, Old and New Ethnicities', in A. King (ed.) *Culture, Globalization and The World-System: Contemporary Conditions for the Representation of Identity* (London: Macmillan), 19–68; B. Crick (ed.) (1991) *National Identities: The Constitution of the United Kingdom* (London: Blackwell). This is also the conclusion to be drawn from N. Dirks (ed.) (1992) *Colonialism and Culture* (Ann Arbor: University of Michigan Press).
20. Gillis, *Islands of the Mind, passim*; I. Land (2007) 'Tidal Waves: The New Coastal History', *Journal of Social History* 40, 3: 731–43; N. Steensgaard (1987) 'The Indian Ocean Network and the Emerging World-Economy c1500–1750', in S. Chandra (ed.) *The Indian Ocean: Explorations in History, Commerce and Politics* (London: Sage), esp. 126–7; indebted to F. Braudel (1972) *The Mediterranean and the Mediterranean World in the Age of Philip II* (New York: Harper & Row). On 'contact zones', see M.L. Pratt (1992) *Imperial Eyes: Studies in Travel Writing and Transculturation* (London: Routledge), 4, 6; Baud and van Schendel, 'Toward a Comparative History of Borderlands', esp. 216, 225–6.
21. N. Chaudhuri (1992) 'Shawls, Jewelry, Curry, and Rice in Victorian Britain', in M. Strobel and N. Chaudhuri (eds) *Western Women and Imperialism: Complicity and Resistance* (Bloomington: Indiana University Press), 231–46; A. Burton (1998) *The Heart of the Empire: Indians and the Colonial Encounter in Late-Victorian Britain* (Berkeley: University of California Press); P. Gilroy (1993) *The Black Atlantic: Modernity and Double Consciousness* (Cambridge: Harvard University Press); C. Hall and S.O. Rose (eds) (2006) *At Home With The Empire: Metropolitan Culture and the Imperial World* (Cambridge: Cambridge University Press); F. Cooper and A.L. Stoler (1989) 'Introduction: Tensions of Empire: Colonial Control and Visions of Rule', *American Ethnologist* 16, 4: 600–21.
22. J. van Lottum (2007) *Across the North Sea: The Impact of the Dutch Republic on International Labour Migration, c. 1550–1850* (Amsterdam: Aksant); D. Kirby and M. Hinkkanen (2000) *The Baltic and the North Seas* (London: Routledge).
23. S. Maza (1996) 'Stories in History: Cultural Narratives in Recent Works in European History', *American Historical Review* 101, 5: 1493–1515, esp. 1500–3. The reference is, of course, to Hall, 'The Local and the Global'.
24. On the state of play in historical demography, see S. Hochstadt (1999) *Mobility and Modernity: Migration in Germany, 1820–1989* (Ann Arbor: University of Michigan Press), 1–54; also L.P. Moch (1992) *Moving Europeans: Migration in Western Europe Since 1650* (Bloomington: Indiana University Press); Jackson, *Migration and Urbanization in the Ruhr Valley*.

25. P.S. Wells (1999) *The Barbarians Speak: How the Conquered Peoples Shaped Roman Europe* (Princeton: Princeton University Press), 193, 264; R. Bartlett (1993) *The Making of Europe: Conquest, Colonization and Cultural Change, 950–1350* (Princeton: Princeton University Press).
26. A. Redford (1964 [1926]) *Labour Migration in England, 1800–1850* 2nd edn, W.H. Chaloner (ed. and rev.) (Manchester: Manchester University Press), xiii, 4–5, 64–5, 165, 183; E.G. Ravenstein (1885 and 1889) 'The Laws of Migration', *Journal of the Royal Statistical Society* 48: 167–227, and 52: 241–301; L.P. Moch (1989) 'The Importance of Mundane Movements: Small Towns, Nearby Places and Individual Itineraries in the History of Migration', in P.E. Ogden and P.E. White (eds) *Migrants in Modern France: Population Mobility in the Later Nineteenth and Twentieth Centuries* (London: Unwin Hyman), 97–117; I. Whyte (2000) *Migration and Society in Britain: 1550–1830* (London: Macmillan/St Martin's), 12, 33, 143, 173.
27. Redford, *Labour Migration in England*, 165; D.I. Kertzer and D.P. Hogan (1989) *Family, Political Economy, and Demographic Change: The Tranformation of Life in Casalecchio, Italy, 1861–1921* (Madison: University of Wisconsin Press), 66; Jackson, *Migration and Urbanization in the Ruhr Valley*, 23–4.
28. Wolf, *Europe and the People Without History*; G. Wang (ed.) (1997) *Global History and Migrations* (Boulder: Westview).
29. L.P. Moch and D. Hoerder (1996) *European Migrants: Global and Local Perspectives* (Boston: Northeastern University Press); G. Noiriel (1996 [1988]) *The French Melting Pot: Immigration, Citizenship, and National Identity* (Minneapolis: University of Minnesota Press).
30. U. Herbert (1990) *A History of Foreign Labor in Germany 1880–1980: Seasonal Workers/Forced Laborers/Guest Workers* (Ann Arbor: University of Michigan Press), esp. 46, 54–7; Noiriel, *The French Melting Pot*, 227–57 and *passim*; C. Klessman (1986) 'Comparative Immigrant History: Polish Workers in the Ruhr Area and the North of France', *Journal of Social History* 20: 336–7.
31. Moch, *Moving Europeans*, 18, 127; L.P. Moch and L. Tilly (1985) 'Joining the Urban World: Occupation, Family and Migration in Three French Cities', *Comparative Studies in Society and History* 27, 1: 33–56; Hochstadt, *Mobility and Modernity*, 12; C. Guerin-Gonzalez and C. Strikwerda (eds) (1993) *The Politics of Immigrant Workers: Labor Activism and Migration in the World Economy Since 1830* (London: Holmes & Meier), 12–13. On Scots, see Ravenstein, 'The Laws of Migration', Pt. 1, esp. 179.
32. Moch, *Moving Europeans*, 104–5; Redford, *Labour Migration in England*, 132–3.
33. A.R. Zolberg, 'Global Movements, Global Walls: Responses to Migration, 1855–1925', in Wang, *Global History and Migrations*, 279–307.
34. F. Thistlethwaite (1960) 'Migration from Europe Overseas in the Nineteenth and Twentieth Centuries', reprinted in R. Vecoli and S.M. Sinke (eds) (1991) *A Century of European Migrations, 1830–1930* (Urbana: University of Illinois Press), 17–57; H. Southall (1991) 'The Tramping Artisan Revisits', *Economic History Review* 44, 2: 272–96; C. Stephenson (1979) 'A Gathering of Strangers? Mobility, Social Structure, and Political Participation in the Formation of Nineteenth-Century American Workingclass Culture', in M. Cantor (ed.) *American Workingclass Culture: Explorations in American*

*Labor and Social History* (Westport: Greenwood), 31–60; M. Mamdani (1996) *Citizen and Subject: Contemporary Africa & the Legacy of Late Colonialism* (Princeton: Princeton University Press), 193.

35. Scholars contesting dichotomies between migrants and immigrants include A. Zolberg (1978) 'International Migration Policies in a Changing World System', in W.H. McNeill and R.S. Adams (eds) *Human Migration: Patterns and Policies* (Bloomington: Indiana University Press), 241–86; Thistlethwaite, 'Migration from Europe Overseas in the Nineteenth and Twentieth Centuries', 35–9; A. Shaw (1994) 'The Pakistani Community in Oxford', in R. Ballard (ed.) *Desh Pardesh: The South Asian Presence in Britain* (London: Hurst), 35–57.
36. M. Anderson (1971) *Family Structure in Nineteenth Century Lancashire* (Cambridge: Cambridge University Press); J. Foster (1974) *Class Struggle and the Industrial Revolution: Early Industrial Capitalism in Three English Towns* (London: Methuen). For US parallels, see J. Bodnar (1985) *The Transplanted: A History of Immigrants in Urban America* (Bloomington: Indiana University Press); D.R. Gabaccia (1988) *Militants and Migrants: Rural Sicilians Become American Workers* (New Brunswick: Rutgers).
37. For critiques, see C. Holmes, Foreword to N. Merriman (ed.) (1993) *The Peopling of London: Fifteen Thousand Years of Settlement From Overseas* (London: Museum of London), ix; Kushner, 'Great Briton', 25, 29.
38. C.G. Pooley (1977) 'The Residential Segregation of Migrant Communities in Mid-Victorian Liverpool', *Transactions of the Institute of British Geographers* 2nd ser. 2: 366.
39. *1931 General Census Report* (London: HMSO, 1950), Table LXX: 'Birthplaces of the Population... 1851–1931', 169. On the fallacy of 'numbers', see L. Tabili, 'A Homogeneous Society? Britain's Internal "Others", 1800-Present', in Hall and Rose *At Home With The Empire*, 53–76.
40. W. Cunningham (1969 [1897]) *Alien Immigrants to England* (London: Frank Cass). Notably, this work was reprinted in the 1960s, amid alarm over post-colonial migration.
41. C. Holmes (1991) 'Building the Nation: The Contributions of Immigrants and Refugees to British Society', *BSA Journal*: 725–34; C. Holmes (1988) *John Bull's Island: Immigration and British Society, 1871–1971* (Basingstoke: Macmillan Educational); K. Lunn (ed.) (1980) *Hosts, Immigrants and Minorities: Historical Responses to Newcomers in British Society, 1870–1914* (Folkstone: Dawson).
42. P. Fryer (1984) *Staying Power: The History of Black People in Britain* (London: Pluto); R. Visram (1986) *Ayahs, Lascars and Princes: Indians in Britain, 1700–1947* (London: Pluto); J. Green (1998) *Black Edwardians: Black People in Britain 1901–1914* (London: Frank Cass); M.H. Fisher, S. Lahiri and S. Thandi (2007) *A South-Asian History of Britain: Four Centuries of Peoples from the Indian Sub-Continent* (Westport: Greenwood).
43. On Jewish impact, see B. Williams (1976) *The Making of Manchester Jewry 1740–1875* (Manchester: Manchester University Press), vi–viii; M. Kaplan (1991) *The Making of the Jewish Middle Class: Women, Family, and Identity in Imperial Germany* (Oxford: Oxford University Press).
44. Burrell and Panayi, 'Immigration, History and Memory in Britain', in *Histories and Memories*, 3–8; D. Feldman (2000) 'Migration', in M. Daunton

(ed.) *The Cambridge Urban History of Britain vol. III 1840–1950* (Cambridge: Cambridge University Press), 185–206.

45. Efforts to stimulate such include T. Kushner (1993) 'Jew and Non-Jew in the East End of London: Towards an Anthropology of "Everyday" Relations', in G. Alderman and C. Holmes (eds) *Outsiders and Outcasts: Essays in Honour of William J. Fishman* (London: Duckworth), 32–52; and N. Deakin (1978) 'The Vitality of a Tradition', in C. Holmes (ed.) *Immigrants and Minorities in British Society* (London: George Allen & Unwin), 158–85.
46. C. Holmes (1994) 'Historians and Immigration', in M. Drake (ed.) *Time, Family and Community: Perspectives on Family and Community in History* (Oxford: Blackwell), 165–80, remaining valid.
47. P. Panayi labelled conflict-focused approaches 'Anglocentric', in (1996) 'The Historiography of Immigrants and Ethnic Minorities: Britain Compared with the USA', *Ethnic and Racial Studies* 19, 4: 829. Also see D. Lorimer (2003) 'Reconstructing Victorian Racial Discourse: Images of Race, the Language of Race Relations, and the Context of Black Resistance', in G.H. Gerzina (ed.) *Black Victorians/Black Victoriana* (New Brunswick: Rutgers), 187–203; Hickman, 'Alternative Historiographies', 273; Ballard, *Desh Pardesh*, viii.
48. R. Lomas (1992) *North-East England in the Middle Ages* (Edinburgh: John Donald), 197–8, 206.
49. On the 'second' Industrial Revolution, see D.S. Landes (1969) *The Unbound Prometheus; Technological Change and Industrial Development in Western Europe From 1750 to the Present* (Cambridge: Cambridge University Press); G. Barraclough (1964) *An Introduction to Contemporary History* (Harmondsworth: Penguin).
50. On Cardiff, see K.L. Little (1972 [1948]) *Negroes in Britain: A Study of Racial Relations in English Society* (London: Routledge & Kegan Paul); on London, M. Banton (1955) *The Coloured Quarter: Negro Immigrants in an English City* (London: Jonathan Cape); on Liverpool, C. Wilson (1992) 'A Hidden History: The Black Experience in Liverpool, England, 1919–1945' (Dissertation, University of North Carolina); D. Frost (1999) *Work and Community Among West African Migrant Workers Since the Nineteenth Century* (Liverpool: Liverpool University Press).
51. D.J. Rowe (1971) called for a scholarship on migration to the North-east, to little avail, in 'The Economy of the North-East in the Nineteenth Century: A Survey with a Bibliography of Works Published Since 1945', *Northern History* 6: 120–1. This book has nonetheless benefited from three significant works: S. Collins (1957) *Coloured Minorities in Britain: Studies in British Race Relations Based on African, West Indian, and Asian Immigrants* (London: Lutterworth); Foster, *Class Struggle and the Industrial Revolution;* and R. Lawless (1995) *From Ta'izz to Tyneside: An Arab Community in the North-East of England During the Early Twentieth Century* (Exeter: University of Exeter Press).
52. Redford, *Labour Migration in England*, 19; Feldman, 'Migration', 185.
53. On 'ethnocultural groups', see Stephenson, 'A Gathering of Strangers?', 34.

54. On microhistory methodology, see E. Muir and G. Ruggiero (eds) (1991) *Microhistory and the Lost Peoples of Europe* (Baltimore: Johns Hopkins University Press).
55. Foster, *Class Struggle and the Industrial Revolution*, 125–7.

## 1 Aal Tegither, Like the Folks O'Sheels: Colonizers, Invaders, Settlers and Sojourners in the Making of an Industrial Town

1. W. Clark Russell (1883) *The North-East Ports and Bristol Channel: Sketches of the Towns, Docks, Ports, and Industries of Newcastle-upon-Tyne, Sunderland, the Hartlepools, Middlesbro', Bristol, Cardiff, Newport, and Swansea* 2nd edn (Newcastle-upon-Tyne: Andrew Reid), 7, 18, 24–5.
2. Quote, G.B. Hodgson (1996 [1903]) from *The Borough of South Shields: From the Earliest Period to the Close of the Nineteenth Century* (South Shields: South Tyneside Libraries), 8, also 32.
3. Quotes from D.J. Rowe (1990) 'The North-East', repudiating them in F.M.L. Thompson (ed.) *The Cambridge Social History of Britain 1750–1950 Vol. I: Regions and Communities* (Cambridge: Cambridge University Press), 433–6; except for 'a race apart', Hodgson, *The Borough of South Shields*, 4–5; and the proverb, on the title page of W. Brockie (1857) *Family Names of the Folks of Shields Traced to their Origins, with Brief Notice of Distinguished Persons, to Which is Appended a Dissertation on the Origin of the Britannic Race* (South Shields: T.F. Brockie & Co.), 1. The definition of the Northeast remains subject to interpretation, but its core consists of the northernmost counties of Durham and Northumberland, separated by the River Tyne. See Rowe, 'The North-East', 416–17.
4. Quote is from H.A. Mess (1928) *Industrial Tyneside: A Social Survey* (London: Ernest Benn), 25; also see Rowe, 'The North-East', 415–70, esp. 425, 435–9; D.J. Rowe (1971) 'The Economy of the North-East in the Nineteenth Century: A Survey', *Northern History* 6: 118; H. Jewell (1994) *The North-South Divide: The Origins of Northern Consciousness in England* (Manchester: Manchester University Press), 20–1, 212; R. Samuel (1998) 'North and South', in *Island Stories: Unravelling Britain,* Theatres of Memory, Vol. 2 (London: Verso), 153–71, esp. 158; R. Colls and B. Lancaster (eds) (2005 [1992]) *Geordies: Roots of Regionalism* (Newcastle upon Tyne: Northumbria University Press), xii–xiii, 10, 12–17. On the derivation of 'Geordie', see F. Graham (ed.) (1987) *The New Geordie Dictionary* (Northumberland: Butler Publishing), 4.
5. Rowe argued much the same in 'The North-East', esp. 436–9, 469.
6. R. Feacham (1965) *The North Britons: The Prehistory of a Border People* (London: Hutchinson), 41. For prehistory, see R. Miket and C. Burgess (eds) (1984) *Between and Beyond the Walls: Essays on the Prehistory of North Britain in Honour of George Jobey* (Edinburgh: John Donald).
7. P. Bidwell and S. Speak (1994) *Excavations at South Shields Roman Fort* Vol. 1 (Newcastle: Society of Antiquaries), 13–16, 20, 27, 29–31, 42; D.J. Breeze and B. Dobson (2000) *Hadrian's Wall* 4th edn (London: Penguin), 7–9, 147, 226, 230, 262, 274, 293; M.E. Jones (1996) *The End of Roman*

*Britain* (Ithaca: Cornell University Press), 16–17. On whether the fort's putative name, Arbeia, referred to Mesopotamian barcarii, lightermen from the province Arbaye, see N. Hodgson (2005) 'The Roman Place-Names Arbeia and Corstopitum: A Response to the Response', *Archaeologia Aeliana* 5th ser. xxxiv: 151–2.

8. M.E. Snape, P. Bidwell, A. Croom and J. Langston (1994) 'An Excavation in the Roman Cemetery at South Shields', *Archaeologia Aeliana* ser. 5, 22: 43–66, esp. 63; B.R. Hartley and R.L. Fitts (1980) *The Brigantes* (Gloucester: Alan Sutton), 87–8, 95, 106–8; P. Salway (1965) *Frontier People of Roman Britain* (Cambridge: Cambridge University Press), 24, 25, 60, 62–6, 202, 243, 256–8.
9. The quote is from K. Fairless, 'Three Religious Cults from the Northern Frontier Region', in Miket and Burgess, *Between and Beyond the Walls*, 239–40. Salway, *Frontier People*, 62; also see Breeze and Dobson, *Hadrian's Wall*, 281–2, 285–6.
10. Hodgson, *Borough of South Shields*, 10, 19–20, 28, 126; Bidwell and Speak, *Excavations at South Shields Roman Fort*, 11. Thanks to Peter Hepplewhite for assistance in locating the Wrekendyke.
11. M.E. Cornford (1907), 'Religious Houses', in W. Page (ed.) *A History of Durham, Vol. II, The Victoria History of the Counties of England* (London: Archibald Constable & Company), 80–1, hereinafter *Victoria County History*; Hodgson *Borough of South Shields*, 32–3. Deira corresponded roughly to modern Yorkshire. R. Lomas (1992) *North-East England in the Middle Ages* (Edinburgh: John Donald), 1–3. Also Higham, *Northern Counties*, 258–69. On Lawes, see R.E. Hooppell (1878) 'On the Discovery and Exploration of Roman Remains at South Shields in the Years 1875–6', *Natural History Transactions of Northumberland, Durham, and Newcastle-upon-Tyne* 8: 138.
12. Higham *Northern Counties*, 299.
13. Hodgson, *The Borough of South Shields*, 34–6.
14. Jewell, *The North-South Divide*, 20–1; more generally, Higham, *Northern Counties*, 286–315.
15. G.W.S. Barrow (1969) 'Northern English Society in the Twelfth and Thirteenth Centuries', *Northern History* 4: 25–6; Jewell, *North-South Divide*, 4–5, 23.
16. N. Evans (1989) 'Two Paths to Economic Development: Wales and the North-East of England', in P. Hudson (ed.) *Regions and Industries: A Perspective on the Industrial Revolution in Britain* (Cambridge: Cambridge University Press), 211; also see 201–27, esp. 204–5. Also see I. Leister (1975) *The Sea Coal Mine and the Durham Miner* (Department of Geography, University of Durham Occasional Publications, new ser., No. 5), 6.
17. J.W. House (1969) *The North East* (Newton Abbott: David & Charles), 45.
18. *Pigott's Directory 1828–1829*, 176.
19. Hodgson, *The Borough of South Shields*, 38–40.
20. Quotes from Hodgson, *Borough of South Shields*, 40–1. Also see 36–44. For seventeenth-century documents, see Surtees Society (1901) *Extracts from the Record of the Company of Hostmen of Newcastle-upon-Tyne* (Durham: Andrews), esp. 29, 35, 71, 89–93, 106, 111, 123, 155–6, 181, 189.
21. J. Ellis (1980) 'The Decline and Fall of the Tyneside Salt Industry, 1660–1790: A Re-examination', *Economic History Review* 2nd ser., 33, 1: 45–58;

M. Sellers, 'Industries', in *Victoria County History*, 294–7; E.W. Hughes (1934) *Studies in Administration and Finance, 1558–1825* (Manchester: University of Manchester Press), 8–9, 408; Hodgson, *The Borough of South Shields*, 8, 79. Fishing, also an extractive export industry, for reasons of space will not be discussed.

22. Ellis, 'Decline and Fall of the Tyneside Salt Industry', 50–6.
23. Hodgson, *The Borough of South Shields*, 116, 122.
24. Elliott, 'Tyneside: A Study', 229, 231, 233; Sellers, 'Industries', 275, 304–11; *White's Directory 1827*, 282; Hughes, *Studies in Administration and Finance*, 408, 430. On Cookson, see N. McCord and D.J. Rowe (1977) 'Industrialisation and Urban Growth in North-East England', *International Review of Social History* 22: 38–9.
25. Hodgson, *Borough of South Shields*, 139, also 357–8, 361, 364; Mess, *Industrial Tyneside*, 40.
26. F. Atkinson (1977) *Life and Tradition in Northumberland and Durham* (London: Dent), 116, also 117–21; J.E. Waltham and W.D. Holmes (1974) *North East England* (Cambridge: Cambridge University Press), 59; Sellers, 'Industries', 301–2; Hughes, *Studies in Administration and Finance*, 430. The Solvay process was pioneered by German migrant Ludwig Mond. Mess, *Industrial Tyneside*, 39.
27. F. Bradshaw, 'Social and Economic History', in *Victoria County History*, 257; *White's Directory 1827*, 292; Brockie, *Family Names of the Folks of Shields*, 33; Hodgson, *Borough of South Shields*, 320; Elliott, 'Tyneside: A Study', 234.
28. Hodgson, *Borough of South Shields*, 407–8; Evans, 'Two Paths to Economic Development', 211, 214.
29. On Simon Temple, the coal entrepreneur, son of Simon Temple the shipbuilder, see Hodgson, *Borough of South Shields*, 320, 366, 372.
30. Leister, *The Sea Coal Mine and the Durham Miner*, 1, 5; Elliott, 'Tyneside: A Study', 228, 235.
31. J.W. House (1954) *North-Eastern England: Population Movements and the Landscape Since the Early Nineteenth Century* (Newcastle: Department of Geography, King's College in the University of Durham), 35–6; Rodwell Jones, *North England*, 1, 6; Leister, *Sea Coal Mine and the Durham Miner*, 5.
32. D. Levine and K. Wrightson (1991) *The Making of an Industrial Society: Whickham 1560–1765* (Oxford: Clarendon Press), 8; P. Dollinger (1970) *The German Hansa*, eds and trans D.S. Ault and J.H. Steinberg (London: Macmillan), 86, 243; C.M. Fraser (1969) 'The Pattern of Trade in the North-East of England, 1265–1350', *Northern History* 4: 58–9, 64; J.B. Blake (1967) 'The Medieval Coal Trade of North East England: Some Fourteenth Century Evidence', *Northern History* 2: 8–9, 12–14, 17; Leister, *Sea Coal Mine and the Durham Miner*, 5.
33. B. Dietz (1986) 'The North-East Coal Trade, 1550–1750: Measures, Markets, and the Metropolis', *Northern History* 22: 282–9; Evans, 'Two Paths to Economic Development', 204.
34. Leister, *Sea Coal Mine and the Durham Miner*, 4; House, *North-Eastern England*, 35; Rodwell Jones, *Northern England*, 21–3, 26; Levine and Wrightson, *Making of an Industrial Society*, 9.
35. Quote from Hodgson, *Borough of South Shields*, 291; Leister, *Sea Coal Mine and the Durham Miner*, 17; R.I. Hodgson (1978) 'Demographic Trends in

County Durham, 1560–1801: Data Sources and Preliminary Findings with Particular Reference to North Durham', *University of Manchester School of Geography Research Papers* 5: 18, 31–2; Bradshaw, 'Social and Economic History', 242; Sellers, 'Industries', 276, 281, 288, 293.

36. Quotes from Daniel Defoe, *A Tour thro' Great Britain, 1742,* S. Richardson (ed.) (1975) 4 vols (New York: Garland), 200. The painting is held by the National Gallery of Art, Washington, DC, Widener Collection 1942.9.86; Rodwell Jones, *Northern England,* 23, 32, 27; Elliott, 'Tyneside: A Study', 230, 233.
37. G. Head (1968 [1836]) *A Home Tour Through the Manufacturing Districts of England in the Summer of 1935*, 2nd edn with a new introduction by W.H. Chaloner (New York: Augustus Kelley), 346–8.
38. By 1903 the Harton Coal Company owned the last four. Hodgson, *Borough of South Shields,* 372–3, 381; R.W. Johnson and R. Aughton (1934) *The Tyne: Its Trade and Facilities* (Newcastle upon Tyne: Andrew Reid), 121.
39. McCord and Rowe, 'Industrialisation and Urban Growth', 34; Johnson and Aughton (1934) *The Tyne,* 131; Elliott, 'Tyneside: A Study', 233, 235.
40. House, *The North East,* 47; Russell, *The North East Ports,* 136, reproducing statistics from the Annual Parliamentary Statement of the Navigation and Shipping of the United Kingdom for the year 1882. Figures for inward voyages were similar.
41. Mess, *Industrial Tyneside,* 41; Rodwell Jones, *Northern England,* 20, 33.
42. *White's Directory 1827,* 277–8, 281–2; the collieries were Templetown and Hilda. Other quotes from Hodgson, *Borough of South Shields,* 136. Also see 2, 73, 116–17, 161, 179; House, *North East England,* 12–14; *Pigott's Directory 1834,* 22, 170; *Robson's Directory 1839,* 123; D.B. Reid (1845) *Report on the State of Newcastle-upon-Tyne and other Towns* (London: W. Clowes and Sons for HMSO), 111; R.W. Rennison (1999) 'The Market Place, South Shields', *Archaeologia Aeliana* 5th ser. 27: 171–2.
43. Hodgson, *Borough of South Shields,* 181.
44. Head, *A Home Tour,* 348.
45. Reid, *Report on the State of Newcastle-upon-Tyne,* 111; Hodgson, *Borough of South Shields,* 179.
46. Elliott, 'Tyneside: A Study', 227, 230, 235; Russell, *The North-East Ports and Bristol Channel,* 7.
47. Hodgson, *Borough of South Shields,* 72, 76–7, 88.
48. Quote is from Johnson, *Making of the Tyne,* 191, also see 6, 53–4, 191; White's *Directory, 1927,* cvi, cxxi; Hodgson, *Borough of South Shields,* 88–9, 290, 292–3, 332; N. McCord (1972) 'Some Aspects of North-East England in the Nineteenth Century', *Northern History* 12: 77; A.G. Kenwood (1971) 'Capital Investment in Docks, Harbours, and River Improvements in North-Eastern England, 1825–1850', *Journal of Transport History* new ser. 1, 2: 75, 77, 79.
49. Hodgson, *Borough of South Shields,* 103, 288; Mess, *Industrial Tyneside,* 47.
50. McCord, 'Some Aspects of North-East England', 77, 80; Bradshaw, 'Social and Economic History', 234, 257. Hodgson, *Borough of South Shields,* 181; Kenwood, 'Capital Investment', 79; Johnson and Aughton (1934) *The Tyne,* 1–2, 131–3.

51. Improvements begin only in 1859–60, per Elliott, 'Tyneside: A Study', 227, 235. Also see E. Allen, J.F. Clarke, N. McCord and D.J. Rowe (1971) *The North-East Engineers' Strikes of 1871: The Nine Hours' League* (Newcastle upon Tyne: Frank Graham), 25; S. Pollard and P. Robertson (1979) *The British Shipbuilding Industry, 1870–1914* (Cambridge: Harvard University Press), 63.
52. Johnson, *The Making of the Tyne*, 73–9, 190; Russell, *North-East Ports and Bristol Channel*, 15–18.
53. Johnson and Aughton (1925) *The Tyne*, 36; Russell, *North-East Ports and Bristol Channel*, 17.
54. House, *North-Eastern England*, 41–5; Johnson, *Making of the Tyne*, 37, also 5, 6, 48; N. McCord (1995) 'Some Aspects of Change in the Nineteenth-Century North East', *Northern History* 31: 241–6, 266.
55. Hodgson, *Borough of South Shields*, 291, 293, 317; *Pigot's Directory 1834*, 169; W.G. Armstrong et al., *The Industrial Resources of the District of the Three Northern Rivers: Tyne, Wear, and Tees*, 3–5. D.J. Starkey (ed.) with R. Gorski, S. Milward and T. Pawlyn (1999) *Shipping Movements in the Ports of the United Kingdom, 1871–1913: A Statistical Profile* (Exeter: University of Exeter Press), 28–9.
56. Russell, *North East Ports*, 136, reproducing statistics from the Annual Parliamentary Statement of the Navigation and Shipping of the United Kingdom for the year 1882. Figures for inward voyages were similar.
57. Foster, *Class Struggle and the Industrial Revolution*, 90; J. Foster (1968) 'Nineteenth Century Towns—A Class Dimension', in John Dyos (ed.) *The Study of Urban History* (New York: St Martin's Press), 292–3; McCord, 'Some Aspects of Change', 251; S.P. Ville (1989) 'Patterns of Shipping Investment in the Port of Newcastle upon Tyne, 1750–1850', *Northern History* 25: 207–16, 219–20.
58. W.G. East, 'England in the Eighteenth Century', in H.C. Darby, *Historical Geography of England Before 1800: Fourteen Studies* (Cambridge: Cambridge University Press, 1951), 510; Pollard and Robertson, *British Shipbuilding Industry*, 63.
59. Sellers, 'Industries', 302–6; Hodgson, *Borough of South Shields*, 135, 320–1, 324; D. Dougan (1968) *The History of North East Shipbuilding* (London: George Allen & Unwin), 23–4.
60. Dougan, *History of North East Shipbuilding*, 62, 77, 84, 95, 214; House, *The North East*, 47; McCord, 'Some Aspects of Change', 246; Sellers, 'Industries', 306. From 1886 Armstrong's Elswick yard produced ships for Austria, Italy, China, Spain, Romania, Argentina and Norway. Between 1890 and 1916, Armstrong's built battleships for Britain and the colonies, China, the Netherlands, Chile and Japan. Hawthorn Leslie of Hebburn built ships for Russia and Swan Hunter for Britain, Chile, Portugal, Turkey, Brazil and the United States. In 1897 Armstrong Mitchell merged with Sir Joseph Whitworth & Co. to form Sir W.G. Armstrong, Whitworth, which equipped the Japanese fleet of 1905. Pollard and Robinson, *British Shipbuilding*, 89–91; also see 51, 63.
61. Mess, *Industrial Tyneside*, 51, 55.
62. Dougan, *History of North East Shipbuilding*, 77, 84.
63. Pollard and Robertson, *British Shipbuilding Industry*, 51; House, *North East*, 173.

64. Johnson (1895) *Making of the Tyne*, 63.
65. Quotes from Hodgson, *Borough of South Shields*, 326, 324, also see 327; Sellers, 'Industries', 306–7; Dougan, *History of North East Shipbuilding*, 23–4, 29–30, 38, 72–3, 240–1.
66. Elliott, 'Tyneside: A Study', 234; Sellers, 'Industries', 306; Johnson, *Making of the Tyne*, 249.
67. Hodgson, 'Demographic Trends', 11, 15, 18, also 6–7, 28.
68. Quote from House, *North East*, 45; A.R. Zolberg, 'Global Movements, Global Walls: Responses to Migration, 1855–1925', in Wang, *Global History and Migrations*, 279–307.
69. House, *North East*, 44, also 38, 46.
70. Redford, *Labour Migration in England*, 16. Only 10.5 per cent of the French population lived in such towns, while 71.5 per cent of Prussia's population remained rural. Ibid., 6.
71. Figures are from Hodgson, *The Borough of South Shields*, 179.
72. Quote from Mess, *Industrial Tyneside*, 28; House, *North-Eastern England*, 38; D.J. Rowe (1973) 'Occupations in Northumberland and Durham, 1851–1911', *Northern History* 8: 128. Also see H. Southall (1988) 'The Origins of the Depressed Areas: Unemployment, Growth, and Regional Economic Structure in Britain Before 1914', *Economic History Review* 2nd ser. 41, 2: 252–4; Atkinson, *Life and Tradition*, 119.
73. T.P. MacDermott (1982) 'The Irish in Nineteenth Century Tyneside', *North-east Labour History Bulletin* 16: 43–6; D. Steele (1976) 'The Irish Presence in the North of England, 1850–1914', *Northern History* 12: 220–41.
74. Mess, *Industrial Tyneside*, 34.
75. Board of Trade Memorandum, 23 June 1903, The National Archives (hereafter TNA) MT9/756.M9996.
76. Rowe, 'The North-East', 430; Foster, *Class Struggle and the Industrial Revolution*, 88, 90, 94, 120–3; House, *North-Eastern England*, 60.
77. L. Tabili (1994) *'We Ask for British Justice': Workers and Racial Difference in Late Imperial Britain* (Ithaca: Cornell University Press), 41–57.
78. Foster, *Class Struggle and the Industrial Revolution*, 90–1, 94–5; R. Foulke (1986) 'Life in the Dying World of Sail, 1870–1910', in P.A. Carlson (ed.) *Costerus* 53, new ser. (Amsterdam: Rodopi), 72–115, esp. 94.
79. Thomas Wilson, Assistant Overseer for the Township of Westoe to the Ministry of Health, 3 November 1932, TNA Papers of the Ministry of Health MH12/3201.
80. D.M. Williams (1992) 'The Quality, Skill and Supply of Maritime Labour: Causes of Concern in Britain, 1850–1914', in L.R. Fischer, H. Hamre, P. Holm and J.R. Bruijn (eds) *The North Sea: Twelve Essays on Social History of Maritime Labour* (Stavanger: Stavanger Maritime Museum), 46, 52.
81. Hodgson, *Borough of South Shields*, 161.
82. On shipboard racial divisions, see T. Lane (1986) *Grey Dawn Breaking: British Merchant Seafarers in the Late Twentieth Century* (Manchester: Manchester University Press); Tabili, *'We Ask for British Justice'*, 36–57; L. Tabili (1996) '"A Maritime Race": Masculinity and the Racial Division of Labor in British Merchant Ships, 1900–1939', in M.S. Creighton and L. Norling (eds) *Iron Men, Wooden Women: Gender and Seafaring in the Atlantic World, 1700–1920* (Baltimore: Johns Hopkins University Press), 169–88.

83. Crew list of the *SS Newburn*, owned by the Newcastle Steamship Company, registry no. 118634, Tyne & Wear Archives Service (hereafter TWAS) 1496/2. Two apprentices who began the voyage deserted in Newport. Able Seaman was a job description.
84. Mess, *Industrial Tyneside*, 52, 55; Foster, *Class Struggle and the Industrial Revolution*, 90–1; K. McClelland (1987) 'Time to Work, Time to Live: Some Aspects of Work and the Re-formation of Class in Britain, 1850–1880', in P. Joyce (ed.) *The Historical Meanings of Work* (Cambridge: Cambridge University Press), 185–6.
85. H. Beynon and T. Austrin (1994) *Masters and Servants: Class and Patronage in the Making of a Labour Organisation: The Durham Miners and the English Political Tradition* (London: Rivers Oram), on the bond, xv, 29–50; on accidents and labour strife, 120–40, 272–3, 279 and *passim*; on wages, 12–27, 36, 73, 75 and *passim*.
86. McCord, 'Some Aspects of North-East England', 75; McCord, 'Some Aspects of Change', 250.
87. Foster, *Class Struggle and the Industrial Revolution*, 90–1.
88. House, *North-Eastern England*, 38, 40; Hodgson, *Borough of South Shields*, 302; J. Carney, R. Hudson, G. Ive and J. Lewis (1976) 'Regional Underdevelopment in Late Capitalism: A Study of the Northeast of England', in I. Masser (ed.) *Theory and Practice in Regional Science* (London: Pion/Academic Press), 11–29.
89. The first quote is from Redford, *Labour Migration in England*, 156–9; the second from McCord, 'Some Aspects of North-East England', 84–6; the third from Foster, 'Nineteenth Century Towns—A Class Dimension', 290, 299.
90. Mess, *Industrial Tyneside*, 41, 43; P. Hudson, 'The Regional Perspective', in *Regions and Industries*, 36; House, *North-Eastern England*, 13–14, 36, 43; Southall, 'Origins of the Depressed Areas', 245–8, 250–1, 253–4, 256–7; Carney et al., 'Regional Underdevelopment in Late Capitalism', 19–20. Also see Leister, *Sea Coal Mine and the Durham Miner*, 9.
91. Foster, *Class Struggle in the Industrial Revolution*, 5, 95–6; D.M. Goodfellow (1940) *Tyneside: The Social Facts* (Newcastle-on-Tyne: Cooperative Printing Society), 18–19, 26–7, 73–4; Southall, 'Origins of the Depressed Areas', 257. Witness the running battle between successive Medical Officers of Health and the South Shields Water Company regarding waterborne sanitation. J. Spear, Medical Officer of Health for the Borough (1876) *Report on the Health of South Shields for the Year 1875* (South Shields: Joseph R. Lackland), 5, 6–8 (hereafter *Medical Officer of Health Report)*; J. Spear, *Medical Officer of Health Report* for 1876, Appendix B, 'Mortality Amongst Men Engaged in Various Occupations', 51; A. Campbell Munro, *Medical Officer of Health Report* for 1884, 5, 16, all held by South Tyneside Central Library (hereafter STCL).
92. Carney et al., 'Regional Underdevelopment in Late Capitalism', 21; Rowe, 'The North-East', 462; R.L. Martin (2004) 'Contemporary Debate over the North-South Divide', in A.R.H. Baker (ed.) *Geographies of England: The North-South Divide, Material and Imagined* (Cambridge: Cambridge University Press), 18–19, 392–4.
93. Mess, *Industrial Tyneside*, 77–93, 96, 101, 104–11, quote 166; Rowe, 'The North-East', 439–60. On overcrowding, see M. Daunton (1985) *House and*

*Home in the Victorian City: Working-Class Housing 1850—1914* (London: Edward Arnold), 79–82; Goodfellow, *Tyneside: The Social Facts.*

94. Sellers, 'Industries', 306–7; Dougan, *History of North East Shipbuilding*, 240–1; Jarrow was a virtual company town for Palmer's Shipbuilding Company, Ltd, while Hebburn's fortunes were tied to Hawthorn Leslie.
95. Hunter, 'Labour in Local Government in Tyneside, 1883–1921', in M. Calcott and R. Challinor (eds) *Working Class Politics in North East England* (n.p.: North East Group for the Study of Labour History, 1983), 23–62.
96. Foster, *Class Struggle and the Industrial Revolution*, 121–3; Hodgson, *Borough of South Shields*, 147, 168–71, 321, 479. Charles Mark Palmer of Palmers Shipbuilding Company was MP for Jarrow, where his firm was the major employer. Dougan, *History of North East Shipbuilding*, 85.
97. Hodgson, *Borough of South Shields*, ix, xi, 128–9, 167, 168, 178, 218, 230, 232, 272, 325, 443; *Robson's Directory 1838*, 123. Viscount Walter Runciman, MP 1899–1900, 1902–18, 1924–37, son of a Shields shipowner, served as President of the Board of Trade in 1914–16 and 1931–37. In the 1930s the family firm continued to operate out of the Moor Buildings in Pilgrim Street, Newcastle. See Johnson and Aughton (1934) *The Tyne*, 83–103.
98. L. Olsover (1981) *The Jewish Communities of North-East England* (Gateshead: Ashley Mark), 258.
99. J. Foster (1970) 'South Shields Labour Movement in the 1830's and 1840's', *North East Labour History Bulletin* 4: 5; Beynon and Austrin, *Masters and Servants*, 66, 92–101.
100. Quote from J. Foster, 'Nineteenth Century Towns—A Class Dimension', 282; see also Foster, 'South Shields Labour Movement', 5, 8; Carney et al., 'Regional Underdevelopment in Late Capitalism', 19–20; F. Broeze (1984) 'Underdevelopment and Dependency: Maritime India During the Raj', *Modern Asian Studies* 18, 3: 429–57; Mess, *Industrial Tyneside*, 26.
101. McCord, 'Some Aspects of North-East England', 78–80; Carney et al., 'Regional Underdevelopment in Late Capitalism', 17, 22.
102. This characterization of globalization is derived from S. Sassen (2001) *The Global City* (Princeton: Princeton University Press), 340: 1991 edition quoted in J. Eade (1997) *Living the Global City: Globalization as a Local Process* (London: Routledge), 12.
103. Mess, *Industrial Tyneside*, 18; Rodwell Jones, *North England*, 8.
104. Southall, 'Origins of the Depressed Areas', 254, 256–7.
105. Dougan, *History of North East Shipbuilding*, 16, 122, 124, 129, 131, 135, 137, 141, 153; Pollard and Robertson, *British Shipbuilding Industry*, 51; R.W. Johnson and R. Aughton (1930) *The Tyne: Its Trade and Facilities* (Newcastle upon Tyne: Andrew Reid & Company), 53.
106. C.A. Brown (2003) *'We Were All Slaves': African Miners, Culture, and Resistance at the Enugu Government Colliery* (Portsmouth, New Hampshire: Heinemann), 107.
107. Ministry of Labour (1934) *Reports of Investigations into the Industrial Conditions in Certain Depressed Areas* (London: HMSO), part II: Durham and Tyneside, by D.E. Wallace, 73, 81; Rowe, 'The North-East', 430.
108. Allen, 'The Regional Problem in Retrospect', 4; Rowe, 'The North-East', 430; Johnson and Aughton (1934) *The Tyne*, 42. On resultant labour conflicts, see Robinson, *Tommy Turnbull*.

109. Dougan, *History of North East Shipbuilding*, 62, 95, 214; House, *The North East*, 47; McCord, 'Some Aspects of Change', 246; Wallace, 'Durham and Tyneside', 72, 77, 78, 79; Rowe, 'The North-East', 432.
110. Dougan, *History of North East Shipbuilding*, 16, 122, 124, 129, 131, 135, 137, 141, 153; Pollard and Robertson, *The British Shipbuilding Industry*, 51; Mess, *Industrial Tyneside*, 51; Johnson and Aughton (1930) *The Tyne*, 53.
111. King, *Urbanism, Colonialism and the World-Economy*, 124; Allen, 'The Regional Problem in Retrospect', 4; Tabili, *'We Ask for British Justice'*, 36–9.
112. Dougan, *History of North East Shipbuilding*, 147, 153, 184.
113. Wallace, 'Durham and Tyneside', 81, 83–4; also see (1936) *Special Report of the Commissioner for the Special Areas* (England and Wales) [Cmd 5090] Pt. I (London: HMSO), 9–11.
114. House, *North East*, 44, 52; Mess, *Industrial Tyneside*, 30; House, *North-Eastern England*, 42, 47; Carney et al., 'Regional Underdevelopment in Late Capitalism', 19; D. Friedlander and R.J. Roshier (1966) disputed this, in 'A Study of Internal Migration in England and Wales, Part I: Geographical Patterns of Internal Migration, 1851–1951', *Population Studies* 19, 3: 258–61, 266.
115. Southall, 'Origins of the Depressed Areas', 254.
116. C. Harris and G. Lewis (1993) found post-1945 migrants likewise filled jobs native workers had evacuated, in the least stable and profitable sectors of British industry, in 'Post-War Migration and the Industrial Reserve Army', and 'Black Women's Employment and the British Economy', in W. James and C. Harris (eds) *Inside Babylon: The Caribbean Diaspora in Britain* (London: Verso), 9–54, 73–96.
117. Quote from Wallace, 'Durham and Tyneside', 74–5; W. Campbell Lyons, *Medical Officer of Health Report* for 1922 (n.p., n.d., *c.* 1923), 5.

## 2 A Stable and Homogeneous Population? Overseas Migrants in South Shields, 1841–1901

1. Even sympathetic scholars treat Britain's 'multiracial' or 'multicultural' character as recent and unprecedented. See I.R.G. Spencer (1997) *British Immigration Policy Since 1939: The Making of Multi-Racial Britain* (London: Routledge), xiii; R. Hansen (1992) *Citizenship and Immigration in Post-War Britain* (Oxford: Oxford University Press), 4; W. James (2004) 'The Black Experience in Twentieth Century Britain', in P.D. Morgan and S. Hawkins (eds) *Black Experience and the Empire* (Oxford: Oxford University Press), 347–9. On the reactionary implications, see S. Hochstadt (1999) *Mobility and Modernity: Migration in Germany, 1820–1989* (Ann Arbor: University of Michigan Press), 1–33.
2. See R. Samuel (1998) *Island Stories: Unravelling Britain,* Theatres of Memory, Vol. II (London: Verso); P. Wright (1985) *On Living in an Old Country: The National Past in Contemporary Britain* (London: Verso).
3. L.P. Moch (1989) 'The Importance of Mundane Movements: Small Towns, Nearby Places and Individual Itineraries in the History of Migration', in P.E. Ogden and P.E. White (eds) *Migrants in Modern France: Population Mobility in the Later Nineteenth and Twentieth Centuries* (London: Unwin Hyman), 97–117; J.H. Jackson, Jr (1977) *Migration and Urbanization in the Ruhr Valley*

*1821–1914* (New Jersey: Humanities); F. Neal (1999) 'Irish Settlement in the North-East and North-West of England in the Mid-Nineteenth century', in R. Swift and S. Gilley (eds) *The Irish in Victorian Britain: The Local Dimension* (Dublin: Four Courts), 75–100; E.D. Steele (1976) 'The Irish Presence in the North of England, 1850–1914', *Northern History* 12: 220–41; T.P. MacDermott (1982) 'The Irish in Nineteenth Century Tyneside', *North East Labour History Bulletin* 16: 43–6.

4. On 'values', see G. Lewis and S. Neal (2005) 'Introduction: Contemporary Political Contexts, Changing Terrains, and Revisited Discourses', *Ethnic and Racial Studies* 28, 3:423–44; L. Colley (2006) 'British Values, Whatever They Are, Won't Hold Us Together', *Guardian* (18 May), 35.
5. M. Anderson (1971) *Family Structure in Nineteenth Century Lancashire* (Cambridge: Cambridge University Press); J. Foster (1979 [1974]) *Class Struggle and the Industrial Revolution: Early Industrial Capitalism in Three English Towns* (London: Methuen).
6. I.D. Whyte (2000) *Migration and Society in Britain, 1550–1830* (Basingstoke: Macmillan), 1, 33; P. Laslett (1983) *The World We Have Lost: Further Explored* (London: Methuen), 75, 77; Hochstadt, *Mobility and Modernity*, 1–54, esp. 37–9.
7. A.R. Zolberg (1978) 'International Migration Policies in a Changing World System', in W.H. McNeill and R.S. Adams (eds) *Human Migration: Patterns and Policies* (Bloomington: Indiana University Press), 246–50.
8. P. Clark (1979) 'Migration in England During the Late Seventeenth and Early Eighteenth Centuries', *Past and Present* 83: 59, 72, 85–6, 90; D. Feldman (2003) 'Migrants, Immigrants and Welfare from the Old Poor Law to the Welfare State', *Transactions of the Royal Historical Society* 6th ser. 13 (Cambridge: Cambridge University Press), 87–8, 90, 92; F. Bradshaw (1907) 'Social and Economic History', in W. Page (ed.) *A History of Durham, Vol. II, The Victoria History of the Counties of England* (London: Archibald Constable), 235. On similar measures elsewhere, see Whyte, *Migration and Society in Britain*, 98.
9. R.I. Hodgson (1978) 'Demographic Trends in County Durham, 1560–1801: Data Sources and Preliminary Findings with Particular Reference to North Durham', *University of Manchester School of Geography Research Papers* 5: 32–3. On state constraints, see A. Redford (1964 [1926]) *Labour Migration in England, 1800–1850* 2nd edn, W.H. Chaloner (ed. and rev.) (Manchester: Manchester University Press), 88.
10. E.J. Hobsbawm (1951) 'The Tramping Artisan', *Economic History Review* 2nd ser. 3, 3: 299–320; H. Southall (1991) 'The Tramping Artisan Revisits', *Economic History Review* 44, 2: 272–96. On related Continental customs transgressing national frontiers, see R. Darnton (1982) *The Literary Underground of the Old Regime* (Cambridge: Harvard University Press), 148–66; M.A. Clawson (1980) 'Early Modern Fraternalism and the Patriarchal Family' *Feminist Studies* 6, 2: 368–91.
11. R. Samuel (1973) 'Comers and Goers', in H.J. Dyos and M. Wolff (eds) *The Victorian City: Images and Realities* (London: Routledge & Kegan Paul), 152, also 124–6, 132–4, 138, 144 and *passim*; L.P. Moch (1992) *Moving Europeans: Migration in Western Europe Since 1650* (Bloomington: Indiana University Press), 120–1; Redford, *Labour Migration in England*, 66–7, 143–8; Whyte,

*Migration and Society in Britain*, 166–72; D. Hoerder (1982) 'Immigration and the Working Class: The Remigration Factor', *International Labor and Working Class History* 21:30.

12. Redford, *Labour Migration in England*, 2–3, 128, 174–5; Moch, *Moving Europeans*, 10, 16–18, 98, 104, 115–16, 126–30 and *passim*; T. Hamerow (1958) *Restoration, Revolution, Reaction: Economics and Politics in Germany, 1815–1871* (Princeton: Princeton University Press), 14–15, 246–8, 252–3, 255.
13. F. Thistlethwaite (1960) 'Migration from Europe Overseas in the Nineteenth and Twentieth Centuries', reprinted in R.J. Vecoli and S.M. Sinke (eds) (1991) *A Century of Europe Migrations, 1830–1930* (Urbana: University of Illinois Press), esp. 26–8, 35–6; G. Rosoli (1985) 'Italian Migration to European Countries from Political Unification to World War I', in D. Hoerder (ed.) *Labor Migration in the Atlantic Economies* (Westport: Greenwood), 114; also Hoerder, 'The Remigration Factor'.
14. P.D. Curtin, 'Africa and Global Patterns of Migration'; Y. Ghai, 'Migrant Workers, Markets, and the Law'; and A.R. Zolberg, 'Global Movements, Global Walls: Responses to Migration, 1885–1925', in G. Wang (ed.) (1997) *Global History and Migrations* (Boulder: Westview), 82–3, 157–62, 287–96.
15. L. Tabili (1994) *'We Ask for British Justice': Workers and Racial Difference in Late Imperial Britain* (Ithaca: Cornell University Press); L. Amenda (2006) *Fremde-Hafen-Stadt: Chinesische Migration und ihre Wahrnehmung in Hamburg 1897–1972* (Munich: Dölling und Galitz).
16. Moch, *Moving Europeans*, 13, 16; L.P. Moch, 'Importance of Mundane Movements', 97–8, 115; Whyte, *Migration and Society*, 98, 151; D.R. Gabaccia (1994) 'Worker Internationalism and Italian Labor Migration, 1870–1914', *International Labor and Working Class History* 45: 67.
17. Redford, *Labour Migration in Britain*, 186.
18. D. Friedlander and R.J. Roshier (1966) 'A Study of Internal Migration in England and Wales, Part I: Geographical Patterns of Internal Migration, 1851–1951', *Population Studies* 19, 3: 239–79; J.W. House (1954) *North-Eastern England: Population Movements and the Landscape Since the Early Nineteenth Century* (Newcastle on Tyne: School of Geography, King's College in the University of Durham), 12, 38, 50, 62.
19. On the fallacy dichotomising long-distance and short-distance, internal and international migration, see L.P. Moch and L.A. Tilly (1985) 'Joining the Urban World: Occupation, Family, and Migration in Three French Cities', *Comparative Studies in Society and History* 27, 1: 41, 53; D.E. Baines (1972) 'The Use of Published Census Data in Migration Studies', in E.A. Wrigley (ed.) *Nineteenth-Century Society: Essays in the Use of Quantitative Methods for the Study of Social Data* (Cambridge: Cambridge University Press,), 326; C.G. Pooley and I.D. Whyte (1991) *Migrants, Emigrants, and Immigrants: A Social History of Migration* (London: Routledge), 6, 12, 298.
20. J. Robinson (1996) *Tommy Turnbull: A Miner's Life* (Newcastle: TUPS Books), 1, 13, 16.
21. Redford, *Labour Migration in England*, 94, 106. Passage from Sicily to New York cost less than to northern Germany. Rosoli, 'Italian Migration to European Countries', 98.

22. See Spencer, *British Immigration Policy Since 1939*, xii–xiii; E.D. Steele (1976) 'The Irish Presence in the North of England, 1850–1914', *Northern History* 12: 220–41; W. Kenefick (2006) 'Jewish and Catholic Irish Relations: The Glasgow Waterfront c. 1880–1914', in D. Cesarani and G. Romain (eds) *Jews and Port Cities, 1590–1990: Commerce, Community and Cosmopolitanism* (London: Vallentine Mitchell), 215–234.
23. Figures for Liverpool, Bristol and other towns in 1851 and 1871 come from C.G. Pooley (1977) 'The Residential Segregation of Migrant Communities in Mid-Victorian Liverpool', *Transactions of the Institute of British Geographers* 2nd ser. 2: 366.
24. *1891 Census General Report* PP1893–4 [*c.* 7222] CVI, 65.
25. H.A. Mess (1928) *Industrial Tyneside: A Social Survey* (London: Ernest Benn), 34. London's overseas-born population exceeded both Irish and Scots as early as 1851. Pooley, 'Residential Segregation', 366.
26. Germany had 0.6 per cent in 1871 and 1880, 0.9 per cent in 1890, 1.4 per cent in 1900 and 1.9 per cent in 1910, per U. Herbert (1990 [1986]) *A History of Foreign Labor in Germany, 1880–1980: Seasonal Workers/Forced Laborers/Guest Workers* (trans.W. Templer) (Ann Arbor: University of Michigan Press), 21.
27. Zolberg, 'International Migration Policies', 263.
28. K.A. Schleunes (1990) *The Twisted Road to Auschwitz: Nazi Policy Toward German Jews, 1933–1939* (Urbana: University of Illinois Press), 33.
29. For exhaustive assessment of these censuses, see Wrigley, *Nineteenth-Century Society*.
30. D.P. Hogan and D.I. Kertzer (1985) 'Longitudinal Methods for Historical Migration Research', *Historical Methods* 18: 20–30; and others discussed in Moch, *Moving Europeans*, 19.
31. M. Drake, 'The Census 1801–1891', in Wrigley, *Nineteenth-Century Society*, 7–46; Moch, *Moving Europeans*, 12, 13, 120, 128; Hochstadt, *Mobility and Modernity*, 10–11.
32. D.I. Kertzer and D.P. Hogan (1989) *Family, Political Economy, and Demographic Change: The Tranformation of Life in Casalecchio, Italy, 1861–1921* (Madison: University of Wisconsin Press), 70, 74, 84; Moch, *Moving Europeans*, 136–7; Jackson, *Migration and Urbanization*, 309; Baines, 'Use of Published Census Data', 326; House, *North-Eastern England*, 50.
33. See Table 3.1.
34. E. Buettner (2004) reports that for racially ambiguous Anglo-Indians, a sojourn in Britain proved a critical aspect of the 'whitening' process itself, in *Empire Families: Britons in Late Imperial India* (Oxford: Oxford University Press).
35. C. Hakim (1980) 'Census Reports as Documentary Evidence: The Census Commentaries, 1801–1951', *Sociological Review* new ser. 28, 3: 551–80. Thanks to Bert Barickman for passing me this article. Also see E. Higgs (1987) 'Women, Occupations and Work in the Nineteenth Century', *History Workshop Journal* 23: 61–2; P. Thompson (1985 [1975]) *The Edwardians: The Remaking of British Society* (Chicago: Academy Chicago), 16; P. Levine (2003) *Prostitution, Race & Politics; Policing Venereal Disease in the British Empire* (New York: Routledge), 199–229.

36. E. Higgs (1996) *A Clearer Sense of the Census: The Victorian Censuses and Historical Research* (London: HMSO), 7. In Scotland, schoolmasters also served as enumerators, per Drake, 'The Census 1801–1891', 10–11. On consequent vagaries, see A.J. Taylor (1951) 'The Taking of the Census, 1801–1951', *British Medical Journal* (Saturday, 7 April): 715–20.
37. The National Archives (hereinafter TNA), 'Directions for Enumerators', Census Enumerator's Book, 1841 HO107/297/1; and *1901 Census Report* PP1904 [Cd.2174] CVII, Appx. B, Form of Occupier's Schedule, 321–2; P.M. Tillott, 'Sources of Inaccuracy in the 1851 and 1861 Censuses', in Wrigley, *Nineteenth-Century Society*, 83; S. Lumas (1997) *Making Use of the Census* (Kew: PRO Publications), 5–6, 9. On the 1841 and 1851 censuses, see W.A. Armstrong (1966) 'Social Structure from the Early Census Returns: An Analysis of Enumerators' Books for Censuses after 1841', in D.E.C. Eversley, P. Laslett and E.A. Wrigley (eds) *An Introduction to English Historical Demography: From the Sixteenth to the Nineteenth Century*, with contributions by W.A. Armstrong and L. Ovenall (New York: Basic), 209–37.
38. Harburg, a suburb of Hamburg, birthplace of Peter Brown, RG10/5038 1871 f56; East Indies Barbadoes, birthplace of Margaret Hickis, West Pan Bank, RG9/3788 1861 f75; Ipswich, Norwich, RG9/3788 1861 f99. Also see Tillott, 'Sources of inaccuracy', 108.
39. Lumas, *Making Use of the Census*, 5–6. Catharine Hoyler in 1851, HO107/2399 f392, became Catharine Oiler in 1861, RG9/3791 1861 f11v; Noimun likely Neumann, RG9/3790 1861 f6.
40. See printed 'Directions to Enumerators', in 1841, HO107/297/1 f2; Tillott, 'Sources of Inaccuracy', 90–108.
41. As householders' relationships to other household members were not specified, boarders and such likely remained undercounted. Higgs, *A Clearer Sense of the Census*, 10–11. 'Directions', HO107/297/1 f2; W.A. Armstrong, 'The Use of Information About Occupation', in Wrigley (ed.) *Nineteenth-Century Society*, 224, 424 n. 50.
42. Also see Armstrong, 'The Use of Information About Occupation'; 1841 Census 'Directions' to enumerators, HO107/297/1.
43. For negotiation of these categories, see Drake, 'The Census 1801–1891', 7–46.
44. For aggregate tabulations of Irish, Scots, Welsh and Foreigners for several large towns, see Pooley, 'Residential Segregation', 366.
45. James emphasized colonial subjects' status as internal migrants in 'The Black Experience in Twentieth Century Britain', 349. M.J. Hickman argues the same in 'Alternative Historiographies of the Irish in Britain: A Critique of the Segregation/Assimilation Model', in Swift and Gilley, *The Irish in Victorian Britain: The Local Dimension*, 244–5. On the increasing legal assimilation of colonial subjects with 'aliens' since the 1960s, see Hansen, *Citizenship and Immigration in Post-War Britain*, 180, 188, 201–3, 213, 238 and *passim*.
46. As a check on the 1841 census, all persons reporting foreign birth were sought in the *Index to 1851 Census of South Tyneside*, 2 vols (1988, 1996) (Newcastle: Northumberland and Durham Family History Society). Those

found locally resident ten years later were excluded from the 1841 pool if they proved British.

47. Moch, *Moving Europeans*, 129, 136–7, 142.
48. Lone persons were automatically counted as household heads, except for Matthew Wilson who appeared a lodger.
49. Rayland, HO107/297/20 1841 f19v; Coates, HO107/297/19 1841 f37; Watley, HO107/298/2 1841 f36v.
50. Hagens, HO107/297/19 1841 f31; Coppin, HO107/297/19 1841 f37; Birmingham, HO107/298/6 1841 f23v; Thompson, HO107/297/20 1841 f26v.
51. Testor, HO107/298/8 1841 f5; Hang, HO107/298/5 1841 f25; Shure, HO107/298/2 1841 f40v. Conventions treat household members sharing surnames as kin: see Armstrong, 'Social Structure from the Early Census Returns', 229.
52. Stephenson, HO107/298/3 1841 f19.
53. Mackay, HO107/297/17 1841 f26v.
54. Toshach, HO107/297/20 1841 f34. On Reverend Toshach, see Hodgson, *The Borough of South Shields*, 265; *White's Directory, 1847*, 279 and *Slater's Directory, 1848*, 229.
55. For example, East Indies-born Fanny Drury, niece of Peter Clark RG9/3787 1861 f36v; Nancy Elizabeth, Jamaican-born granddaughter of Elizabeth Phillips, HO107/2399 1851 f106; and Eulalia Thompson, Ram-Ganges-born granddaughter of brewer Robert Kidd, HO107/2399 1851 f278. Local novelist E.B. Dyer (1996 [1930]) depicted two Indian-born orphans deposited with a well-heeled aunt in Tynemouth, in *Jean of Storms* (London: Bettany). Also see Buettner, *Empire Families*; H.J. Dyos and A.B.M. Baker (1968) 'The Possibilities of Computerizing Census Data', in Dyos (ed.) *The Study of Urban History* (New York: St Martin's Press), 103.
56. Moray; Coates; Wilson; Watley; Joseph.
57. Foster, *Class Struggle*, 163, 178, 195; Armstrong, 'Use of Information About Occupation', 224.
58. *White's Directory 1827* listed roughly 1000 of the town's population, 15,165 in 1821 and 16,501 in 1831. Also see G. Shaw and A. Tipper (1988) *British Directories: A Bibliography and Guide to Directories Published in England and Wales (1850–1950) and Scotland (1773–1950)* (Leicester: Leicester University Press), esp. 9–33.
59. *White's Directory 1827*, 293; *Pigot's Directory 1828–1829*, 180; *Pigot's Directory 1834*, 176; *White's Directory 1846*, 337; *Slater's Directory 1848*, 234.
60. *White's Directory 1846*, 317; *White's Slater's Directory 1848*, 230.
61. *Pigot's Directory of Durham 1834*, 'Watch and Clock Makers', 176.
62. Brockie, *The Family Names of the Folks of Shields*, 7. None of the mariners in the 1841 sample appeared among master mariners first listed in *White's Directory, 1846*, 330–1.
63. C.G. Pooley and J. Turnbull (1998) *Migration and Mobility in Britain Since the Eighteenth Century* (London: UCL Press), 326, 328; D.B. Grigg (1994) 'E.G. Ravenstein and the "Laws of Migration"', in M. Drake (ed.) *Time, Family, and Community: Perspectives on Family and Community History* (Oxford: Blackwell/Open University Press), 154–5; Southall, 'The Tramping Artisan Revisits', 279, 281.

64. Quote from Hoerder, 'The Remigration Factor', 36–7; also S. Castles and G. Kosack (1973) *Immigrant Workers and Class Structure in Western Europe* (Oxford: Oxford University Press), 8.
65. Moray, HO107/297/15 1841 f10; Joseph, HO107/298/7 1841 f17v.
66. See, for example, Hardy, RG9/3789 1861 f52v. C.G. Pooley and J.C. Doherty, 'The Longitudinal Study of Migration: Welsh Migration to English Towns in the Nineteenth Century', in Pooley and Whyte, *Migrants, Emigrants, and Immigrants*, 145, 149, 166.
67. M. Anderson (1979) 'Some Problems in the Use of Census-Type Materials for the Study of Family and Kinship Systems', in J. Sundin and E. Söderlund (eds) *Time, Space, and Man: Essays from Microdemography* (Stockholm: Almkvist and Wiksell International/Humanities), 78. R.I. Hodgson described static communities as 'freak... not typical', in 'Demographic Trends in County Durham, 1560–1801', 6–7. Also see Cesarani, 'Introduction', in *Jews and Port Cities, 1590–1990*, 12.
68. Coppin, HO107/2399 1851 f324; Hull, HO107/2399 1851 f161; Joseph, HO107/2399 1851 f340.
69. Those ratios remained between 2:1 and 3:1 until 1891, when they rose to 3.3:1.
70. On gender and other biases, see I. Winchester (1973) 'On Referring to Ordinary Historical Persons', in E.A. Wrigley (ed.) *Identifying People in the Past* (London: Edward Arnold), 22–3.
71. Attrition rates through death ranged from 4 per cent per year to 25 per cent per decade. See Dennis and Daniels, '"Community" and the Social Geography of Victorian Cities', 204–8.
72. In Hathersage, Derbyshire, one-third of those found in 1851 remained in 1861, Tillott, 'Sources of Inaccuracy', 107; but only 12 per cent in Paris, Illinois between 1851 and 1861. Turnover in the United States ranged between 30 per cent and 70 per cent. C. Stephenson (1979) 'A Gathering of Strangers? Mobility, Social Structure, and Political Participation in the Formation of Nineteenth-Century American Workingclass Culture', in M. Cantor (ed.) *American Workingclass Culture: Explorations in American Labor and Social History* (Westport: Greenwood), 32, 41.
73. Samuel, 'Comers and Goers'; Southall, 'The Tramping Artisan Revisits'.
74. Compare to D. Hoerder's finding (1996) that some German union locals turned over 100 per cent in one year, 'From Migrants to Ethnics: Acculturation in a Societal Framework', in D. Hoerder and L.P. Moch (eds) *European Migrants: Global and Local Perspectives* (Boston: Northeastern), 211–262.
75. R.J. Dennis (1977) 'Intercensal Mobility in a Victorian City', *Transactions of the Institute of British Geographers* new ser. 2: esp. 334–5, 354–5, 360–1. On high mobility, see Hochstadt, *Mobility and Modernity*, 37–45; G. Noiriel (1996 [1988]) *The French Melting Pot: Immigration, Citizenship, and National Identity* (Minneapolis: University of Minnesota Press), 110.
76. On 'thickening', see A. Miles (1999) *Social Mobility in Nineteenth- and Early Twentieth-Century England* (New York: St Martin's Press), 63.
77. Moray, HO107/297/15 1841 f10; HO107/2400 1851 f280.
78. Coates, HO107/297/19 1841 f37; HO107/2400 1851 f128.

79. Although Christopher Mackay did not appear in the 1851 census, he remained connected to the town, surfacing in the 1850 electoral roll through owning property in the Market Place. *Register of Electors* for 1850, No. 243, STCL.
80. Arrowsmith, HO107/2399 1851 f588. Only four families surnamed Arrowsmith appeared in the 1851 census, HO107/2399 f140, f161 and f588, and HO107/2400 f81, per *Index to 1851 Census of South Tyneside*. In 1841 four appeared also, enhancing, but by no means guaranteeing, the possibility they were the same individuals.
81. Smith, HO107/297/16 1841 f33v, HO107/2399 1851 f219, RG9/3794 1861 f38v.
82. Hodgson, *Borough of South Shields*, 362–3. Given the frequency of the surname Smith among British Roma, the man may well have been a chief, or so fancied himself. Similarly, Matilda Gradley, born in Berwick at the time of the 1851 census, reported birth in Portugal by 1861. Gradley, HO107/2400 1851 f57v, RG9/3786 1861 f113v.
83. Higgs, *A Clearer Sense of the Census*, 7. James Mather led the campaign against naval impressment. Hodgson, *Borough of South Shields*, 480; 'The Press Gang in the Northern Counties', *Monthly Chronicle of North Country Lore and Legend* 5, 47 (January 1891): 1–4; Foster, *Class Struggle and the Industrial Revolution*, 105. 'Backwardness or evasion' of the 1801 census occurred for fear of 'direct taxation, and more obviously the levy of men in every place'. *1811 Census Abstract of Answers and Returns*, PP1822 XV, International Population Census Publications: Region Europe, Country England and Wales, 1821.1 (microform) (New Haven: Research Publications, 1983 [1970]), xxix; Noiriel, *French Melting Pot*, 283.
84. Drake, 'The Census 1801–1891', 21; Redford, *Labour Migration in England*, 19, 126.
85. M. Anderson suggested longevity in a locality conduced to misreporting one's birthplace as local. See Southall, 'Tramping Artisan Revisits', 292. B. Williams (1976) likewise found a handful of Germans who claimed British birth in 1841, in *The Making of Manchester Jewry, 1740–1875* (Manchester: Manchester University Press), 361.
86. Brockie, *Family Names of the Folks of Shields*, 4.
87. Chiefton Smith reported himself locally born in 1851 so is omitted.
88. *1851 Census Summary Tables*, PP1852–3 [1691-I] LXXXVIII Pt.1, Table XXXIX, 'Birth-Places of the Inhabitants of England and Wales', ccxcv; Table XXXVIII, 'Birth-Places of the People', cclxxxvii; and Table XXXIX, 'Birth-Places of the Inhabitants of England and Wales', ccxcv.
89. Hazard, HO107/2399 1851 f660; McDonald, HO107/2400 1851 f85v; Henderson, HO107/2400 1851 f237; Pearson, HO107/2400 1851 f132; Johnson, HO107/2400 1851 f212v.
90. Knowles, HO107/2399 1851 f222–3; Brown, HO107/2400 1851 f119v; Noel, HO107/2399 1851 f514; Williamson, HO107/2399 1851 f217.
91. Reack, HO107/2400 1851 f152v; Amede, HO107/2399 f560; Jacobs, HO107/2400 1851 f88v.
92. On stepwise migration, see Pooley and Turnbull, *Migration and Mobility*, 325.

93. Gaible, HO107/2400 1851 f14; Bouillet, HO107/2399 1851 f555.
94. Hoyler, HO107/2399 1851 f392; Gray, HO107/2399 1851 f573v.
95. Mather, HO107/2399 1851 f236. See Hodgson, *Borough of South Shields*, 479–80; Foster, *Class Struggle in the Industrial Revolution*, 122–3; *Pigot's Directory, 1834, Robson's Directory, 1839*. *White's Directory* and *Slater's Directory* in 1846 listed James Mather as the proprietor and householder, but Grace was reported head of household in the CEB.
96. Sharp, HO107/2400 1851 f60; Lackey, HO107/2400 1851 f139v.
97. Eulalia Thompson, HO107/2399 1851 f278, and Margaret, John and Mary Elizabeth Phillips, HO107/2399 1851 f224 and HO107/2399 1851 f106v. On this practice, see Buettner, *Empire Families*.
98. Delevoy, HO107/2399 1851 f176v–177.
99. Whole families included Amede, Gaible, Bouillet, Jacobs and Reack.
100. George Gibson, Prussia, HO107/2399 1851 f621; Alfred and Loredda Garbutt, France, HO107/2399 1851 f563; Mary Ann Carl, France, HO107/2399 1851 f673; Thomas Storey, Lisbon, HO107/2400 1851 f118v.
101. Knowles, RG9/3785 1861 f8v; Reick, RG9/3785 1861 f14; Hazard, RG9/3791 1861 f62; Smith, RG9/3794 1861 f38v.
102. Loyd, RG9/3785 1861 f75v; W.N., Union Workhouse, German Street, RG9/3785 1861 f35v.
103. Mather, RG9/3787 1861 f75; Hardy, RG9/3789 1861 f52v; Gray, RG9/3790 1861 f31v.
104. Hughes nee Hoyler, RG9/3791 1861 f17v; Catharine Oiler, RG9/3791 1861 f11v.
105. Lillico, RG9/3790 1861 f56.
106. Muncy, RG9/3787 1861 f23v. Groat household, HO107/2400 1851 f120, per *Index to 1851 Census of South Tyneside*, 29.
107. Bowman/Harper, RG9/3787 1861 f42; HO107/2399 1851 f368; Howse, RG9/3787 1861 f34; HO107/2399 1851 f164; Wright, RG9/3787 1861 f41v; HO107/2399 1851 f236v; *Index to 1851 Census of South Tyneside*, Vol. 1, 45, 51, 108, respectively.
108. Figures from Table 2.1.
109. In comparison, Indian and colonial subjects numbered 51,572, Irish and Scots in England 601,634 and 169,202 respectively. *1861 General Census Report* PP1863 [3221] LIII Pt. 1, 39–40.
110. *1861 General Census Report* PP1863 [3221] LIII, Table 46.
111. M. Williams (1996) found similar diversity in Sheffield, in *Researching Local History: The Human Journey* (London: Longman), 177–8.
112. Moch and Tilly, 'Joining the Urban World', 33, 42, 49, 53; Stephenson, 'A Gathering of Strangers?' 43–4, citing P. Buhle.
113. Armstrong, 'Social Structure from the Early Census Returns', 234–5; W.A. Armstrong, 'The Interpretation of the Census Enumerators' Books for Victorian Towns', in Dyos, *The Study of Urban History*, 73–4; Pooley and Turnbull, *Migration and Mobility*, 13, 304–5, 316; Grigg, 'E.G. Ravenstein and the "Laws of Migration" ', 153.
114. Compare to towns in Armstrong, 'Interpretation of the Census Enumerators' Books', 72, 146–7.
115. Gadola, HO107/2399 1851 f115; Henderson, HO107/2400 1851 f237.

116. Such classifications may prove deceptive, as Hyman Isaacs, co-resident son of general dealer Isaac Jacobs, was no doubt carrying out family business, rendering his placement in class V likely temporary.
117. Of 40 non-mariners, colonial subjects now accounted for only three.
118. This figure includes five teenagers aged 16 to 18 living independently of parents and holding a man's job.
119. *1871 Census Population Abstracts* PP1873 [c. 872] III, Tables 16 and 17, 534–40.
120. Quote from *1861 General Census Report* PP1863 [c. 3221] LIII, 36, 39. Also see Table 24, 808. The largest group of occupied women were 35 domestic servants, ibid.
121. See Hoerder, 'From Migrants to Ethnics', 233.
122. See precise figures in Table 4.8.
123. *Census 1861: Ages, Civil Conditions, Occupations and Birthplaces of the People* PP1863 [c. 3221] LIII Division X-Northern Counties, Table 10, 776–88.
124. On compression, see Foster, *Class Struggle and the Industrial Revolution*, 126–7.
125. Also see A. Fahrmeir (2000) *Citizens and Aliens: Foreigners and the Law in Britain and the German States, 1789–1870* (New York: Berghahn), 218.
126. Register of Persons Entitled to Vote at any Election of a Member to Serve in Parliament... 1851; Register of Persons Entitled to Vote in Any Election of a Member to Serve in Parliament... 1857, STCL.
127. See R. Ashton (1986) *Little Germany: Exile and Asylum in Victorian England* (Oxford: Oxford University Press); W.E. Mosse (ed.) (1991) *Second Chance: Two Centuries of German Speaking Jews in the United Kingdom* (Tübingen: J.C.B. Mohr).

## 3 Migrants' Networks and Local People

1. Birkett, RG11/5020 1881 f34; RG12/4164 1891 f29; RG13/ 4734 1901 f147; Katzenberger, RG13/4737 1901 f146. Magdalena's maiden name was Katzenberger per South Shields' German Church Totenbuch, 26 March 1914, Tyne and Wear Archives (hereafter TWAS) C/SS28/11.
2. 'Model subcultures' discussed in C. Stephenson (1979) 'A Gathering of Strangers? Mobility, Social Structure, and Political Participation in the Formation of Nineteenth-Century American Workingclass Culture', in Milton Cantor (ed.) *American Workingclass Culture: Explorations in American Labor and Social History* (Westport: Greenwood), 36.
3. Jensen, RG10/5033 1871 f108.
4. On 'classic' community formation, see D. Hoerder (1996) 'From Migrants to Ethnics: Acculturation in a Societal Framework', in D. Hoerder and L.P. Moch (eds) *European Migrants: Global and Local Perspectives* (Boston: Northeastern), esp. 244–50. For Britain, see B. Williams (1976) *The Making of Manchester Jewry, 1740–1875* (Manchester: Manchester University Press); M.L. Wong (1989) *Black Liverpudlians: A History of the Chinese Community in Liverpool* (Birkenhead: Liver Press); D. Frost (1999) *Work and Community Among West African Migrant Workers Since the Nineteenth Century* (Liverpool: Liverpool University Press).

5. The scholars in question scrupulously repudiated this view. See K.L. Little (1972 [1948]) *Negroes in Britain: A Study of Race Relations in English Society* (London: Routledge & Kegan Paul), 56; M. Banton (1955) *The Coloured Quarter: Negro Immigrants in an English City* (London: Jonathan Cape), 13; K. Pryce (1970) *Endless Pressure: A Study of West Indian Life-Styles in Bristol* (London: Penguin).
6. L. Silberman and B. Spice (1950) *Colour and Class in Six Liverpool Schools* (Liverpool: Liverpool University Press), 57; G. Rosoli (1985) 'Italian Migration to European Countries from Political Unification to World War I', in D. Hoerder (ed.) *Labor Migration in the Atlantic Economies* (Westport: Greenwood), 98.
7. G. Noiriel (1996 [1988]) *The French Melting Pot: Immigration, Citizenship, and National Identity* (Minneapolis: University of Minnesota Press), 132–3; C. Klessman (1986) 'Comparative Immigrant History: Polish Workers in the Ruhr Area and the North of France', *Journal of Social History* 20: 341–2. On the Irish and Jews in Britain, see R. Dennis and S. Daniels (1994) '"Community" and the Social Geography of Victorian Cities', in M. Drake (ed.) *Time, Family, and Community: Perspectives on Family and Community History* (Oxford: Blackwell), 214, 217; R. Samuel (1998) *Island Stories: Unravelling Britain,* Theatres of Memory, Vol. 2 (London: Verso, 1998), 57.
8. D. Feldman (2000) 'Migration', in M. Daunton (ed.) *Cambridge Urban History of Britain Vol. III 1840–1950* (Cambridge: Cambridge University Press), 192–201.
9. C. Holmes, 'Historians and Immigration', in Drake, *Time, Family and Community,* 166.
10. H.S. Nelli (1967) 'Italians in Urban America: A Study of Ethnic Adjustment', *International Migration Review* 1, 2: 38–55; W.L. Yancey (1985) debunked fetishized ethnicity in 'The Structure of Pluralism: "We're All Italian Around Here, Aren't We, Mrs. O'Brien?"' *Ethnic and Racial Studies* 8, 1: esp. 94–5, 105, 113. In general, I resist the term 'ethnicity', for implicitly reifying cultural practices that proved fluid in South Shields and elsewhere. On confected 'Irish' ethnic stereotypes, see J. Belchem (2002) 'Ethnicity and Labour History: with Special Reference to Irish Migration', in L.H. van Voss and M. van der Linden (eds) *Class and Other Identities: Gender, Religion and Ethnicity in the Writing of European Labour History* (London: Berghahn), 89–100.
11. E. Oliel-Grausz (2006) 'Networks and Communication in the Sephardi Diaspora: An Added Dimension to the Concept of Port Jews and Port Jewries', in D. Cesarani and G. Romain (eds) *Jews and Port Cities, 1590–1990: Commerce, Community and Cosmopolitanism* (London: Vallentine Mitchell), 68, drawing on P.A. Rosental (1990) 'Maintien/rupture: un nouveau couple pur l'analyse des migrations', *Annales ESC* 45: 1403–31.
12. E. Morawska (1991) 'Return Migrations: Theoretical Research Agenda', in R.J. Vecoli and S.M. Sinke (eds) *A Century of Europe Migrations, 1830–1930* (Urbana: University of Illinois Press), 284–5; A. Shaw (1994) 'The Pakistani Community in Oxford', in R. Ballard (ed.) *Desh Pardesh: The South Asian Presence in Britain* (London: Hurst & Company), 35.
13. On kinship colonies, see J. Gjerde, 'Chain Migration from the West Coast of Norway', in Vecoli and Sinke, *A Century of European Migrations,* 158–81;

on chain migration, see D.R. Gabaccia (1988) *Militants and Migrants: Rural Sicilians Become American Workers* (New Brunswick: Rutgers), 76–90 and *passim.*
14. R.J. Dennis (1977) 'Intercensal Mobility in a Victorian City', *Transactions of the Institute of British Geographers* new ser. 2: 354–5; also D. Frost (2000) 'Ambiguous Identities: Constructing and De-constructing Black and White "Scouse" Identities in Twentieth Century Liverpool', in N. Kirk (ed.) *Northern Identities: Historical Interpretations of 'The North' and 'Northernness'* (Aldershot: Ashgate), 195–217.
15. D. Cesarani, 'The Jews of Bristol and Liverpool, 1750–1850: Port Jewish Communities in the Shadow of Slavery', and W. Kenefick, 'Jewish and Catholic Irish Relations: The Glasgow Waterfront c. 1880–1914', in Cesarani and Romain, *Jews and Port Cities,* 141–56, 215–34; C.G. Pooley (1977) in 'The Residential Segregation of Migrant Communities in Mid-Victorian Liverpool', *Transactions of the Institute of British Geographers* 2nd ser. 2: 361–79, esp. 373, found voluntary cohesion as well as discrimination; Little argued, implausibly, that spatial segregation enabled coexistence, in *Negroes in Britain,* 65.
16. D.B. Reid, Esq., MD *(1845) Report on the State of Newcastle-upon-Tyne and other Towns* (London: W. Clowes and Sons for HMSO), 111–12, quoted in J. Foster (1977 [1974]) *Class Struggle and the Industrial Revolution: Early Industrial Capitalism in Three English Towns* (London: Methuen), 128.
17. C.G. Pooley and J. Turnbull (1998) *Migration and Mobility in Britain Since the Eighteenth Century* (London: UCL Press), 316; A. August (1999) *Poor Women's Lives: Gender, Work and Poverty in Late-Victorian London* (Madison/Teaneck: Fairleigh Dickinson), 32, 36, 140 and *passim.*
18. Foster, *Class Struggle and the Industrial Revolution,* 126–9; J. Foster (1970) 'South Shields Labour Movement in the 1830's and 1840's', *North East Labour History* 4: 4–9.
19. W. Brockie (1857) *Family Names of the Folks of Shields Traced to their Origins, with Brief Notice of Distinguished Persons, to Which is Appended a Dissertation on the Origin of the Britannic Race* (South Shields: T.F. Brockie & Co.), 6, 28.
20. J. Robinson (ed.) (1996) *Tommy Turnbull: A Miner's Life* (Newcastle: TUPS Books), 13, 17.
21. Foster, *Class Struggle and the Industrial Revolution,* 120–8.
22. T. Gallagher (1985) 'A Tale of Two Cities: Communal Strife in Glasgow and Liverpool Before 1914', in R. Swift and S. Gilley (eds) *The Irish in the Victorian City* (London: Croom Helm), 109–10; on the Northeast, see D.M. McRaild (2004) *Faith, Fraternity and Fighting: The Orange Order and Irish Migrants in Northern England, c. 1850–1920* (Liverpool: Liverpool University Press), esp. 44–5, 60–4, 123, 162–3, 185, 198–9.
23. Quotes from J. Foster (1968) 'Nineteenth Century Towns—A Class Dimension', in H.J. Dyos (ed.) *The Study of Urban History* (New York: St Martin's Press), 297. In contrast, see Pooley, 'Residential Segregation of Migrant Communities', 369.
24. The percentages were 14 per cent in 1841, 13 per cent in 1851, 21 per cent in 1861, 16.5 per cent in 1871, 16 per cent in 1881, 18 per cent in 1891 and 17 per cent in 1901.

25. Henry, RG12/4155 1891 f19; Jacobson, RG12/4158 1891 f122; Thorkeldson, RG12/4155 1891 f22v.
26. Corneliason, RG12/4158 1891 f23.
27. Few migrant households' sole British-born members were children, in any case; less than 5 per cent in 1871 and less than 6 per cent in 1891. On schools and social services disciplining parents, see A. Davin (1996) *Growing Up Poor: Home, School and Street in London 1870–1914* (London: Rivers Oram), esp. 86–7, 93–4, 199–217; E. Ross (1985) '"Not the Sort that Would Sit on the Doorstep": Respectability in Pre-World War I London Neighborhoods', *International Labor and Working Class History* 27: 40–1, 48–9.
28. Sveden, RG12/4154 1891 f72v. Also see Harild, RG12/4153 1891 f62; Hartung, RG12/4160 1891 f39.
29. Bouillet, HO107/2399 1851 f555.
30. L.P. Moch (1992) *Moving Europeans: Migration in Western Europe Since 1650* (Bloomington: Indiana University Press), 136–7, 142.
31. See Table 2.2.
32. L. Frader (1998) 'Doing Capitalism's Work: Women in the Western European Industrial Economy', in R. Bridenthal, S.M. Stuard and M.E. Wiesner (eds) *Becoming Visible: Women in European History* 3rd edn (Boston: Houghton Mifflin), 295–325; Moch, *Moving Europeans,* 104, 148–9; A.R. Zolberg (1997) 'Global Movements, Global Walls: Responses to Migration, 1855–1925', in G. Wang (ed.) *Global History and Migrations* (Boulder: Westview), 283–93. On the *nulla osta,* or permission to leave, see Gabaccia, *Militants and Migrants,* 22. L. Tabili (2006) 'A Homogeneous Society? Britain's Internal "Others", 1800–Present', in S.O. Rose and C. Hall (eds) *At Home With The Empire: Metropolitan Culture and the Imperial World* (Cambridge: Cambridge University Press), esp. 65–7; also Chapter 7 below; D. Feldman (1994) *Englishmen and Jews: Social Relations and Political Culture 1840–1914* (New Haven: Yale University Press), 157.
33. L. Tabili (1994) *'We Ask for British Justice': Workers and Racial Difference in Late Imperial Britain* (Ithaca: Cornell University Press), 47, 127 and *passim.*
34. On close- versus loose-knit networks, see Elizabeth Bott (1957) *Family and Social Network* (London: Tavistock), 58–99.
35. On these patterns, see D. Gabaccia (1994) *From the Other Side: Women, Gender, and Immigrant Life in the United States, 1820–1990* (Bloomington: Indiana University Press), 152 fn.3, also 6, 63; also C. Holmes, *Historians and Immigration,* 169.
36. P. Panayi (1996) *Germans in Britain Since 1500* (London: Hambledon), 1–8, 75; C. Holmes (1991) 'Immigrants and Refugees in Britain', in W.E. Mosse (ed.) *Second Chance: Two Centuries of German Speaking Jews in the United Kingdom* (Tübingen: J.C.B. Mohr), 11; H. Kellenbenz (1978) 'German Immigrants in England', in C. Holmes (ed.) *Immigrants and Minorities in British Society* (London: George Allen & Unwin), 63–80.
37. P. Panayi (1994) *Immigration, Ethnicity and Racism in Britain 1815–1945* (Manchester: Manchester University Press), 65; Priestly quoted in P. Panayi (1991) *The Enemy in Our Midst: Germans in Britain During the First World War* (New York: Berg/St Martin's Press), 20, also see 19.

38. Holmes, 'Historians and Immigration', 166; R. Ashton (1986) *Little Germany: Exile and Asylum in Victorian England* (Oxford: Oxford University Press).
39. On Baltic Germans, see T. Sowell (1996) *Migrations and Cultures: A World View* (New York: Basic), 5–7; on migrants' unstable identities, see A. Fahrmeir (2000) *Citizens and Aliens: Foreigners and the Law in Britain and the German States, 1789–1870* (New York: Berghahn), 232; Hoerder, 'From Migrants to Ethnics', 244–5. Nelli long ago made this point in 'Italians in Urban America', 51–2.
40. Quote from P. Panayi, *Germans in Britain Since 1500,* 1; also see R. Muhs, 'Jews of German Background', in Mosse, *Second Chance,* 178–9.
41. Panayi in *Germans in Britain Since 1500,* 7–8, 81–3; Zolberg, 'Global Movements, Global Walls', 285.
42. This reflected national patterns, per *1861 General Census Report,* PP1863 [3221] LIII, 39–40.
43. Brockie, *Family Names of the Folks of Shields,* 7; HO107/297/19 1841, f7v.
44. Hardy, HO107/2399 1851 f82; RG9/3789 1861 f52v; RG10/5037 1871 f26v; Hoyler, HO107/2399 1851 f392; RG9/3791 1861 f17v; RG10/5034 1871 f64v; Oiler, RG9/3791 1861 f11v.
45. Measer, RG9/3785 1861 f45; Lewis, RG9/378 1861 f66; Schroth and Sonenwolk, RG9/3793 1861 f81v; Frederick, RG9/3794 1861 f74; Velingley, RG9/3793 1861 f87.
46. Loewinsohn, RG9/3791 1861 f39; Levy, RG9/3794 1861 f54v; Gaskell, RG9/3787 1861 f91v. Baker, RG9/3793 1861 f66v.
47. Hertz, RG9/3786 1861 f99; John Brown, RG9/3788 1861 f119; John Young, RG9/3793 1861 73v; Emily Howse, RG9/3787 1861 f34; Jane Hardy, RG9/3789 1861 f52v.
48. On similar patterns among Welsh migrants, see C.G. Pooley and J.C. Doherty (1991) 'The Longitudinal Study of Migration: Welsh Migration to English Towns in the Nineteenth Century', in C.G. Pooley and I.D. Whyte (eds) *Migrants, Emigrants, and Immigrants: A Social History of Migration* (London: Routledge), 164, 166–70.
49. Schroth, RG9/3793 1861 f81v, also in *Ward's Directory 1859–60,* 152; Velingley, RG9/3793 1861 f87; Marks, 88 Wapping Street RG9/3793 1861 f83v, an outfitter in *Whelan's Directory 1865,* 427; Marks, Kirton's Quay, RG9/3793 1861 f81.
50. Levy, RG9/3794 1861 f63v. On ghostly apparitions there, see G.B. Hodgson (1996 [1903]) *The Borough of South Shields: From the Earliest Period to the Close of the Nineteenth Century* (South Shields: South Tyneside Libraries), 139.
51. Woolman, RG9/3794 1861 ff68–68v; Jackson, RG9/3794 1861 f72; Frederick, RG9/3794 1861 f74.
52. On stabilization, see A. Miles (1999) *Social Mobility in Nineteenth- and Early Twentieth-Century England* (New York: St Martin's Press), 63.
53. RG9/3790 1861 f6; RG10/5033 1871 f77v; RG11/5015 1881 f42v; Catherine reported herself a Fussinger in 1891, likely of Fussen, Bavaria. RG12/4158 1891 f4v; RG13/4733 1901 f125. See *Register of Electors* 1918, 2192d and 519f, among others, STCL.
54. Gillert, RG9/3788 1861 f94v, RG10/5033 1871 f17; Measer, RG9/3785 1861 f45, RG10/5027 1871 f42, RG11/5009 1881 f7; Hanson, RG9/3794 1861

f40, RG10/5032 1871 f 20, RG11/5015 1881 f67v, RG12/4160 1891 f11, RG13/4733 1901 f45vp.

55. Levy, RG12/4164 1891 f23v.
56. Gompertz, RG9/3794 1861CEB f58, RG10/5038 1871 f77, RG11/5020 1881 f48v, RG12/4164 1891 f26v; RG13/4729 1901 f41.
57. North Germans preponderated in 1881 also.
58. Sachse, RG10/5037 1871 f73v–74; also labourer and one-time seafarer Heinrich Vasen, RG10/5028 1871 f15v.
59. Hoerder emphasized regional and provincial affiliations' durability in 'From Migrants to Ethnics', 244–5.
60. Panayi, *The Enemy in Our Midst,* 14; H. Pollins, 'German Jews in British Industry', in Mosse, *Second Chance,* 362; on the Kulturkampf, see G.A. Craig (1978) *Germany 1866–1945* (Oxford: Oxford University Press), 71–8.
61. Carlberg, RG10/5037 1871 f53, RG11/5021 1881 f15, RG12/4164 1891 f91v.
62. Manson, RG10/5032 1871 f40 and RG11/5009 1881 f96v; RG13/4726 1901 f37v. Also see RG12/4157 1891 f16.
63. Rogers, RG10/5032 1871 f20 and RG11/5016 1881 f25v; RG12/4160 1891 f30; Hanson, RG10/5038 1871 f48 and RG11/5010 1881 f37; Carlberg, RG10/5037 1871 f53 and RG11/5021 1881 f15; also Brown, RG10/5038 1871 f61 and RG11/5020 1881 f47v.
64. Measer, RG9/3785 1861 f45; RG10/5027 1871 f42; RG11/5009 1881 f7.
65. Levy, RG9/3794 1861 f63v; RG10/5037 1871 f54; RG11/5020 1881 f39v.
66. Marks, RG9/3793 1861 f83v; RG10/5037 1871 f69v; RG11/5020 1881 f42. Also see Price, RG10/5037 1871 f73; RG11/5015 1881 f23v.
67. Rogers, RG10/5032 1871 f20 and RG11/5016 1881 f25v; RG12/4160 1891 f30.
68. Gjerde, 'Chain Migration from the West Coast of Norway'.
69. Brauninger, RG93790 1861 f6; RG10/5033 1871 f77v; RG11/5015 1881 f42v; RG12/4158 1891 f4v.
70. Dietrich, RG10/5038 1871 f69v; Birkett, RG11/5020 1881 f34, RG12/4164 1891 f29; Cook, RG11/5021 1881 f23, RG12/4154 1891 f137; Bruninger, RG11/5015 1881 f60v.
71. Hertrich, RG12/4153 1891 f82 and RG13/4727 1901 f152; Dietz, RG12/4158 1891 f101v–102; Hub, RG12/4158 1891 f77v. Also see RG13/4734 1901 f150v and RG13/4726 1901 f36.
72. Brokett, RG10/5037 1871 f54v.
73. Hertrich, RG12/4153 1891 f82; Kenzer, RG12/4153 1891 f81; Dietz, RG12/4158 1891 f101v–102. Dietz employed two British-born nephews, George Schroff of Blyth and Frank Dietz of Crewe. The Schroth/Sonenwolk household passed through South Shields in the 1860s.
74. These included Frederick Geiliz, RG12/4164 1891 f15; John and Marie Cook, RG12/4154 1891 f137; Louis and Minnie Romig, RG12/4155 1891 f7v; F. Fromhold, RG12/4160 1891 f29; and George and Margaret Miller, RG12/4161 1891 f82.
75. F. and W. Seitz, RG13/4729 1901 f111v; F. and M. Seitz, RG13/4737 1901 f133v; Dietrich, RG13/4735 1901 f101; Sieber, RG13/4727 1901 f151.
76. Wiehl, RG11/5015 1881 f103v; Shankle, RG11/5015 1881 f45v and 1891. Armstrong found many 'apparent lodgers' in actuality 'working servants', in 'Interpretation of the Census Enumerators' Books', 72.

77. Wiehl, RG11/5015 1881 f103v, RG12/4159 1891 f105.
78. Dietz, RG12/4158 1891 f101v–102; Steel, RG12/4153 1891 f81; Krafft, RG12/4156 1891 f68; Hub, RG12/4158 1891 f77v.
79. M. Walker (1964) *Germany and the Emigration, 1816–1885* (Cambridge: Harvard University Press), 35, 47, 71–6, 157, 161 and *passim*.
80. L. Tabili (2005) '"Having Lived Close Beside Them All the Time": Negotiating National Identities Through Personal Networks', *Journal of Social History* 39, 2 (Winter): 375–6.
81. 'Ueberblick über die Geschichte der Deutschen Evangelischen Gemeinde in South Shields von ihren Anfängen bis zum 1 Weltkrieg', undated typescript, Records of the South Shields German Church, TWAS C/SS28/11. The following account synopsizes this document. Also see Panayi, *Enemy in Our Midst*, 21, 23.
82. Carlberg, RG10/5037 1871 f53; RG11/5021 1881 f15; RG12/4164 1891 f91v.
83. Hornung, Ferry Street, RG12/4164 1891 f15–15v. Also see RG13/4726 1901 f35v.
84. 'Ueberblick über die Geschichte der Deutschen Evangelischen Gemeinde in South Shields'.
85. Kirchen-Ordnung der Deutschen Evangelischen Gemeinde in South Shields, 18 November 1906, C/SS28/4/1.
86. A German missionary Fritz Klein appeared in 1901, living at 83 Percy Street, but it remains unclear whether he was the cleric in question. RG13/4732 1901 f138v; Annual Report for 1913, C/SS28/8; 'Herr Singer', *Shields Gazette* (25 January 1919).
87. 'Ueberblick über die Geschichte der Deutschen Evangelischen Gemeinde in South Shields'.
88. 'Ueberblick über die Geschichte der Deutschen Evangelischen Gemeinde in South Shields'.
89. 'German Sailors' Mission for the Tyne District, 34th Annual Report, 1913' (Newcastle on Tyne: MS Dodds, 1914). TWAS C/SS28/8.
90. B.R. Hunter and G.K. Pollard, 'Seamen's Welfare in Ports', Appendix IX, South Shields, March 1939, 3, India Office Records (IOR) L/E/9/457.
91. '34th Annual Report', 3–5. See also O. Mortensøn (1992) 'Comment' on A. Kennerley, 'British Seamen's Missions in the Nineteenth Century', in L. Fischer, H. Hamre, P. Holm and J. Bruijn (eds) *The North Sea: Twelve Essays on Social History of Maritime Labour* (Stavanger: Stavanger Maritime Museum), 94–5; Dennis and Daniels, '"Community" and the Social Geography of Victorian Cities', 218–19.
92. Postcard to Rev. F. Singer, 7 Belgrave Terrace, South Shields, 9 March 1909, C/SS28/3/1.
93. '34th Annual Report', 5–7.
94. In the 1890s the congregation numbered perhaps 80, with an average attendance of 55 at services, and 63 communicants. 'Ueberblick über die Geschichte der Deutschen Evangelischen Gemeinde in South Shields'.
95. Sleege, 21 May 1879; Brauninger, 7 January 1884; also Breuninger, 14 September 1878 found in St Bede and St Cuthbert Marriages, TWAS C/SS29/3/1, microform 1936.
96. On christening, see E. Ross (1993) *Love and Toil: Motherhood in Outcast London, 1870–1918* (New York: Oxford University Press), 132–3.

97. Maria, May 1915, C/SS29/1/8 f5; Nora Eileen, 9 February 1919, C/SS29/1/8 f294; and several others, C/SS29/1/8 f5, f97, f122. Also see R. Lawless (1995) *From Ta'izz to Tyneside: An Arab Community in the North-East of England During the Early Twentieth Century* (Exeter: Exeter University Press), 12–13, 23, 49, 54, 56, 63, 72, 133, 152, 210.
98. Also see children and grandchild of Lorentz Larsson and Jacob Strybos baptized in Laygate Presbyterian (United Reformed) Church on 2 August 1891, 15 March 1908 and 10 February 1931. Baptismal Register TWAS C/SS/2/3; also Larsson, RG12/4159 1891 f117, HO144/430/B27593; Strybos, HO144/1033/176315.
99. M. Dombrow described the complexities not only of relating to Gentiles in early twentieth-century Gateshead, but even more to the self-confident Jewish community of Sunderland and the ultra-Orthodox who began to arrive in Gateshead at mid-century, in (n.d. *c.* 1988 [1972]) *They Docked in Newcastle and Wound Up in Gateshead* (Gateshead: Gateshead Libraries & Arts).
100. Feldman, *Englishmen and Jews,* 2; L. Olsover (1981) *Jewish Communities of North-East England* (Gateshead: Ashley Mark), 12; Williams, *Making of Manchester Jewry,* 1, 269; Panayi, *Immigration, Ethnicity and Racism,* 54–5, 106.
101. Feldman, *Englishmen and Jews,* 103, 147–8, 156–7, 162–3; J.P. Fox, 'British Attitudes to Jewish Refugees From Central and Eastern Europe in the Nineteenth and Twentieth Centuries', in Mosse, *Second Chance,* 472.
102. In T.M. Endelman (2002) *The Jews of Britain, 1656–2000* (Berkeley: University of California Press), South Shields is not mentioned, nor are Newcastle, Tyneside or Sunderland: Gateshead, despite possessing the largest Orthodox educational complex in postwar Europe (249), is mentioned only three times, in passing.
103. Olsover, *Jewish Communities of North-East England,* 13, 134; *Census 1851: Religious Worship, England and Wales* PP1852–53 [1690] LXXXI, Table F, ccixviii.
104. On occupations, see Williams, *Making of Manchester Jewry,* 358–60; Feldman, *Englishmen and Jews,* 162–3.
105. On this strategy, see D.R. Gabaccia and F. Iacovetta (2002) *Women, Gender, and Transnational Lives: Italian Workers of the World* (Toronto: University of Toronto Press), 13.
106. In a handful of cases such as that of Henry Jackson in 1871 and Wolff Singer in 1901, census-takers indicated Jewish identity gratuitously. Jackson, RG10/5038 1871 f76; Singer, RG13/4729 1901 f99; also Moses Markson, RG13/4729 1901 f105. On the challenges and pitfalls of identifying Jews by surname, see J.M. Ross (1974) 'Naturalisation of Jews in England', *Transactions of the Jewish Historical Society of England* 24: 70; on naming practices and Jewish identity, see D. Bering (1992) *The Stigma of Names: Antisemitism in German Daily Life, 1812–1933* (trans. Neville Plaice) (London: Polity).
107. Williams compiled a preliminary pool of possibly Jewish Mancunians based on 'basic sociological and historical premises' such as 'place of birth, surname, occupation, place of residence', *Making of Manchester Jewry,* 355. In South Shields' population the easiest tests to apply were common names

and occupations, corroborated with fuller information contained in some naturalization applications.

108. I have omitted households with peripheral members such as boarders or children with British parents. Williams defined the Jewish community more narrowly, counting only participants in communal institutions, in *Making of Manchester Jewry,* 356, but less formal affinities also bound co-religionists in South Shields, while anti-Semites ignored such distinctions. On discrimination against non-observant Jews, see Pollins, 'German Jews in British Industry', in Mosse, *Second Chance,* 363–4. Compare Williams' restrictive definition with Pooley and Doherty's inclusion in the Welsh community anyone in a household containing someone born in Wales. 'The Longitudinal Study of Migration', 150–2.
109. On south Germany, see Newman, 'German Jews in Britain' and Endelmann, 'German-Jewish Settlement in Victorian England', in Mosse, *Second Chance,* 32–3, 43. In any case, 70 per cent of German Jews lived in Prussia. M. Kaplan (1991) *The Making of the Jewish Middle Class: Women, Family, and Identity in Imperial Germany* (New York: Oxford University Press), 240 fn.62.
110. Feldman, *Englishmen and Jews,* 1, also see 147–54, 159.
111. An exception was Dutch slipper-maker Samuel Heilbron, married to London-born Jane. RG10/5029 1871 f86; RG11/5010 1881 f86v; RG12/4159 1891 f113; RG13/4730 1901 f17v.
112. See N.Z. Davis (1995) *Women on the Margins: Three Seventeenth-Century Lives* (Cambridge: Harvard University Press), 11–13.
113. Levy, RG9/3794 1861 f63v; RG10/5037 1871 f54; RG11/5020 1881 f39v; Mary Levy, RG12/4164 1891 f23v; RG13/4730 1901 f127v; Finn, RG10/5033 1871 f84v; RG11/5010 1881 f80; RG12/4155 1891 f7v; RG13/4726 1901 f24.
114. Taylor, RG9/3789 1861 f18; Karroskey, RG9/3790 1861 f19v; Marks, RG9/3793 1861 f83v; Simon, RG9/3794 1861 f58; Friend, RG9/3793 1861 f66v.
115. Pearlman served as President, Levy as Treasurer, and J. Gompertz as Secretary, per Olsover, *Jewish Communities of North-East England,* 256; on Gompertz, see Simon Arons, RG9/3794 1861CEB f58, RG10/5038 1871 f77; on Levy, see RG9/3794 1861 f63v, and Kossick, RG10/5038 1871 f77v; Joseph, RG11/5015 1881 f37, RG13/4730 1901 f130; Pearlman, RG12/4155 1891 f32, RG13/4730 1901 f7v.
116. Gompertz (Arons), RG9/3794 1861 f58; G10/5038 1871 f77 and RG11/5020 1881 f48v; *Ward's Directory 1899.*
117. Cohen, RG10/5037 1871 f51 and RG11/5020 1881 f48, RG12/4164 1891 f29.
118. Sager, RG11/5016 1881 f34; *Kelly's Post Office Directory 1873,* 157. On Marks, see RG10/5037 1871 f70v.
119. Rosenbaum, RG12/4153 1891 f75v–76.
120. Rosenberg, RG13/4730 1901 f46; Neuman, RG13/4733 1901 f16v.
121. Olsover, *Jewish Communities of North-East England,* 256–60.
122. Hamburg Hotel, RG9/3794 1861 f54v; D. Spour (comp.) (1979) *James Henry Cleet: A South Shields Photographer* (Newcastle: Side Gallery).
123. Olsover, *Jewish Communities of North-East England,* 258; D. Clark (1992) *We Do Not Want the Earth: The History of South Shields Labour Party* (Whitley

Bay: Bewick Press), 40. It remains unclear whether local Labour Party stalwart Aaron E. 'Ernie' Gompertz was descended from Aaron Simon Gompertz. Clark, 90, reports Gompertz moved to South Shields only in 1900. Also see 47, 69, 76, 80, 84, 88–91, 94–7.

124. Lawson, RG13/4734 1901 f89. Per Table 3.3, the fourth largest national group were Russians, followed by Danes.
125. Temperance Sailors' Home, RG13/4736 1901 f173v; Wachmeister, RG13/4737 1901 f5; Odgaard, RG13/4734 1901 f133; Theodorsen, RG13/4736 1901 f116; Egenson, RG13/4728 1901 f65. Hodgson mentioned a chapel for seamen with a Norwegian missionary from 1866, which I could not corroborate. *Borough of South Shields,* 284.
126. Kemp, RG11/5017 1881 f119.
127. Baker, RG10/5030 1871 f5.
128. Swedes, Danes and Norwegians also clustered in American cities, per Hoerder, 'From Migrants to Ethnics', 245.
129. Pooley and Doherty, 'The Longitudinal Study of Migration', 166. On housing relatives, see W.A. Armstrong, 'The Interpretation of the Census Enumerators' Books for Victorian Towns', in Dyos, *Study of Urban History,* 72.
130. O. Anderson (1911), HO144/1125/205128; Valentini (1919), HO144/1509/374925.
131. Olhaus, RG10/5034 1871 f55v; Nelson, RG11/5020 1881 f6; Rasmussen, RG12/4157 1891 f45v; Truwert, HO144/859/154029.
132. Cardiff City Police to Home Office, 5 November 1912, Madsen, HO144/1224/227482.
133. Bianchi, RG12/4158 1891 f46v. On such marriages in France, see Noiriel, *French Melting Pot,* 155. On Italian migration, see Samuel, 'Comers and Goers', 135–6, 149; Rosoli, 'Italian Migrants to European Countries'.
134. Williams, RG12/4729 1901 f16; Ryan, RG13/4727 1901 f144.
135. Dennis and Daniels suggest many lodgers might actually have been kin, in '"Community" and the Social Geography of Victorian Cities', 213.
136. Carlson, RG11/5020 1881 f7–7v; Nordberg, RG11/5020 1881 f108.
137. Vanakiotte, RG11/5017 1881 f94; RG12/4152 1891 f57–57v.
138. Erikson, RG11/5020 1881 f49v; Silversparre, RG11/5014 1881 f46.
139. Walters, RG11/5020 1881 f116v; Peterson, RG11/5021 1881 f18.
140. D.J. Rowe (1990) 'The North-East', in F.M.L. Thompson (ed.) *The Cambridge Social History of Britain 1750–1950 Vol. I: Regions and Communities* (Cambridge: Cambridge University Press), 421. Samuel, *Island Stories,* 57–60; Frost, 'Ambiguous Identities', 200; S. Rawnsley, 'Constructing "the North": Space and a Sense of Place', in Kirk, *Northern Identities,* 16–18.
141. N. Todd (1987) 'Black on Tyne', *Northeast Labour History Bulletin* 21: 17–27.
142. A. Blakeley (1997) 'Problems in Studying the Role of Blacks in Europe', *AHA Perspectives* 35, 5: 11–13.
143. Buettner, *Empire Families,* 83, 89.
144. Minutes of General Committee, 23 April 1879; letter from Dr William Burns Thomson, Superintendant Physician, Edinburgh Medical Mission Hospital and Dispensary, 20 March 1879, Ingham Infirmary Minutes, TWAS HO/ING/2/2.
145. Minutes of Special Meeting, 24 April 1879. HO/ING/2/2.

146. *Ingham Infirmary Annual Report for 1882,* 5, South Tyneside Central Library (STCL). Also see Rajaonah, RG11/5009 1881 f18v.
147. For contemporary racial debates, see D. Lorimer (1978) *Colour, Class, and the Victorians: English Attitudes to the Negro in the Mid-Nineteenth Century* (Leicester: Leicester University Press/Holmes & Meier); A. Burton (2000) 'Tongues Untied: Lord Salisbury's "Black Man" and the Boundaries of Imperial Democracy', *Comparative Studies in Society and History* 42, 3: 632–61.
148. Khan, Grammar School, Barker Terrace, RG12/4155 1891 f102; William George Morant, *Report of the Police Establishment 1896,* 5, STCL.
149. M. Anderson (1971) *Family Structure in Nineteenth-Century Lancashire* (Cambridge: Cambridge University Press).

## 4 Moving, Staying, Coming, Going: Migrants and Remigrants in Provincial Britain

1. HO107/2399 1851 f563; RG10/5034 1871 f65v; RG11/5017 1881 f129v; RG12/4161 1891 f19v.
2. RG11/5055 1881 f17; John Anderson, RG12/4160 1891 f24; Robert Anderson, RG12/4160 1891 f16; William Anderson, RG12/4160 1891 f75. On working-class parochialism, see R. Roberts (1971) *The Classic Slum: Salford Life in the First Quarter of the Century* (London: Penguin). For more positive views, see M. Anderson (1971) *Family Structure in Nineteenth Century Lancashire* (Cambridge: Cambridge University Press); M. Young and P. Willmott (1957) *Family and Kinship in East London* (Harmondsworth: Penguin).
3. E. Morawska (1991) 'Return Migrations: Theoretical Research Agenda', in R.J. Vecoli and S.M. Sinke (eds) *A Century of Europe Migrations, 1830–1930* (Urbana: University of Illinois Press), 277–92; D. Hoerder (ed.) (1985) *Labor Migration in the Atlantic Economies: The European and American Working Classes in the Period of Industrialization* (Westport: Greenwood). On emigration, see A. Murdoch (2004) *British Emigration, 1603–1914* (London: Palgrave Macmillan); E. Richards (2004) *Britannia's Children: Emigration from England, Scotland, Wales, and Ireland Since 1600* (London: Hambledon & London). On forced emigration, see P. Bean and J. Melville (1989) *Lost Children of the Empire* (London: Unwin Hyman); R. Hughes (1987) *The Fatal Shore* (New York: Knopf).
4. C.G. Pooley and J. Turnbull (1998) *Migration and Mobility in Britain Since the Eighteenth Century* (London: University College London), 298; D. Hoerder (1982) 'Immigration and the Working Class: The Remigration Factor', *International Labor and Working Class History* 21: 28–32; Morawska, 'Return Migrations', 277–8; S. Castles and G. Kosack (1973) *Immigrant Workers and Class Structure in Western Europe* (Oxford: Oxford University Press), 12.
5. H. Southall (1996) reported 6 per cent of politically active artisans left Britain in a three year period, frequently returning in 'Agitate! Agitate! Organize! Political Travelers and the Construction of a National Politics, 1839–1880', *Transactions of the Institute of British Geographers* new ser. 21, 1: 114, 123;

Durham miners' organizer Peter Lee emigrated to and from the United States and South Africa, John Wilson India and the United States, in H. Beynon and T. Austrin (1994) *Masters and Servants: Class and Patronage in the Making of a Labour Organisation: The Durham Miners and the English Political Tradition* (London: Rivers Oram), 85, 267–8. British subjects made up one-sixth to one-half of people born abroad at each census between 1851 and 1911, per *1911 Census General Report with Appendices* PP1917/18 [Cd.8491], XXV, Table CV, 217.

6. Compare these figures with Table 2.2.
7. Mackay, HO107/297/17 1841 f26v; Toshach, HO107/297/20 1841 f34; Stephenson, HO107/298/3 1841 f19 shared surnames, as discussed in Chapter 2.
8. D. Bryant (1971) pioneered the use of children's birthplaces to track women's mobility in 'Demographic Trends in South-Devon in the Mid-Nineteenth Century', in K.J. Gregory and W.L.D. Ravenhill (eds) *Exeter Essays in Geography in Honour of Arthur Davies* (Exeter: University of Exeter Press), 125–42, esp. 137–8, 141.
9. Beeson HO107/2399 1851 f222; Carl HO107//2399 1851 f673.
10. Taylor, RG9/3789 1861 f18. Ratios of children born overseas with parents of overseas versus British origin were 7:4 in 1841; 6:5 in 1851, 2:13 in 1861; 9:34 in 1871, 3:45 in 1881, 23:66 in 1891 and 63:106 in 1901.
11. 1871 Census General Report PP1873 [C.872-I] LXXI, Pt. II, Vol. IV expressed surprise that 'people born in different parts of the country are associated in the same family'. xxii.
12. R. Samuel (1973) 'Comers and Goers', in H.J. Dyos and M. Wolff (eds) *The Victorian City: Images and Realities* (London: Routledge & Kegan Paul), 124, 135–6, 138; A. Redford (1964 [1926]) *Labour Migration in England, 1800–1850* 2nd edn (W.H. Chaloner ed. and rev.) (Manchester: Manchester University Press), 123–4; Hoerder, 'Immigration and the Working Class', 30. In 1848 and the 1850s, French workers rioted against British labourers in France such as William Garbutt, A. Fahrmeir (2000) *Citizens and Aliens: Foreigners and the Law in Britain and the German States, 1789–1870* (New York: Berghahn), 172.
13. N. McCord (1995) 'Some Aspects of Change in the Nineteenth Century North East', *Northern History* 31: 249.
14. Mackay, HO107/297/17 1841 f26v.
15. Clasper, RG9/3785 1861 f60v, RG10/5029 1871 f54, RG11/5010 1881 f24, RG12/4155 1891 f69v, RG13/4730 1901 f54 p.1; Fairley, RG9/3788 f73v–74.
16. Betson, RG9/3794 1861f 59v; Lillico, RG9/3790 1861 f56.
17. Brown, RG10/5029 1871 f7; Wright, RG10/5029 1871 f71v; Richardson, RG10/5029 1871 f80; Bennett, RG10/5032 1871 f97.
18. Garrett, RG10/5032 f78v; Hawkes, RG10/5035 f91.
19. Also see G.B. Hodgson (1996 [1903]), *The Borough of South Shields: From the Earliest Period to the Close of the Nineteenth Century* (South Shields: South Tyneside Libraries), 278.
20. Bowes, RG11/5009 1881 f39v/p.20; Olditch, RG11/5011 1881 f4v.
21. Raven, RG10/5033 1871 f62; Alderson, RG10/5033 1871 f84v.
22. Cavnagh, RG11/5020 1881 f66v; Ross, RG11/5015 1881 f111v.
23. Gillie, RG11/5009 1881 #1 f12; Palmer, RG11/5009 1881 f92; Fox, RG11/5014 1881 f13v.

24. Felstead, RG12/4152 1891 f45v; Atkinson, RG11/5010 1881 f60v and RG12/4152 1891 f83.
25. Samuel, 'Comers and Goers', 153; E.J. Hobsbawm (1951) 'The Tramping Artisan', *Economic History Review* 2nd ser. 3: 310–16; S. Hochstadt (1999) *Mobility and Modernity: Migration in Germany, 1820–1989* (Ann Arbor: University of Michigan Press), 44–5.
26. F. Thistlethwaite (1960) 'Migration from Europe Overseas in the Nineteenth and Twentieth Centuries', reprinted in Vecoli and Sinke, *A Century of Europe Migrations*, 17–57.
27. Storey, HO107/2400 1851 f118v, RG10/5037 1871 f74v, RG11/5012 1881 f77, RG12/4154 1891 f82, RG13/4728 1901 f55v.
28. Richardson, RG10/5029 1871 f80; RG11/5009 1881 f24; RG12/4155 1891 f100; RG13/4730 1901 f59v. Also Clasper, RG9/3785 1861 f60v, RG10/5029 1871 f54, RG11/5010 1881 f24, RG12/4155 1891 f69v, RG13/4730 1901 f54.
29. None of these pit villages was contiguous with urban South Shields until after the Second World War. D.J. Rowe (1990) 'The North-East', in F.M.L. Thompson (ed.) *The Cambridge Social History of Britain 1750–1950 Vol. I: Regions and Communities* (Cambridge: Cambridge University Press), attributed such stereotypes to media exaggeration, but also noted mobility decreased in the twentieth century, after pit villages' nineteenth-century 'heyday' as 'social melting pot[s]', 425, 435–6. On stereotypes of miners, see critiques by Beynon and Austrin, *Masters and Servants*, 20–22; R. Colls and B. Lancaster (eds) (2005 [1992]) *Geordies: Roots of Regionalism* (Newcastle: Northumbria University Press), 10, 12–17; A. McClintock (1995) *Imperial Leather: Race, Gender and Sexuality in the Colonial Encounter* (London: Routledge), 115–16.
30. Craig, RG10/5035 1871 f44v; Harrison, RG10/5035 1871 ff83v–84; Good, RG10/5035 1871 f43.
31. Temple, RG12/4162 1891 ff138–137; Chiswell, RG12/4162 1891 f97; coalminers Knowles, RG12/4162 1891 f4v and Morris, RG12/4162 1891 f42v; joiner Thomas Oxley, RG12/4162 1891 f105v; and mariner Lionel Wilbert, RG12/4163 1891 f41.
32. Poole, RG12/4162 1891 f96.
33. But see Redford, *Labour Migration in England*, 176–8; J.W. House (1954) *North-Eastern England: Population Movements and the Landscape Since the Early Nineteenth Century* (Newcastle: Department of Geography, King's College, University of Durham), 50.
34. Hoerder confirms most migrants intended to return to their places of origin, 'Immigration and the Working Class', 28–9, 31–2. Pooley and Turnbull argued this discrepancy between intention and effect disrupts the dichotomy between temporary and permanent migration, in *Migration and Mobility*, 298.
35. Scholars differ as to whether children impeded mobility. See D.E. Baines (1972) 'The Use of Published Census Data in Migration Studies', in E A. Wrigley (ed.) *Nineteenth-Century Society: Essays in the Use of Quantitative Methods for the Study of Social Data* (Cambridge: Cambridge University Press), 322; D.I. Kertzer and D.P. Hogan (1989) *Family, Political Economy, and Demographic Change: The Transformation of Life in Casalecchio, Italy, 1861–1921* (Madison: University of Wisconsin Press), 90; Pooley and Turnbull, *Migration*

*and Mobility*, 326; R.J. Dennis (1977) 'Intercensal Mobility in a Victorian City', *Transactions of the Institute of British Geographers* new ser. 2: 357–8.

36. Redford, *Labour Migration in England*, 99–100, 111, 123–4, 169–73, 176–8; Hoerder, 'Immigration and the Working Class', 30.
37. This challenge came initially from E. Said (1993) *Culture and Imperialism* (New York: Vintage), xiv–xvi. Also see A. Thompson (2005) *The Empire Strikes Back? The Impact of Imperialism on Britain From the Mid-Nineteenth Century* (London: Pearson Educational/ Longman).
38. N. Chaudhuri (1992) 'Shawls, Jewelry, Curry and Rice in Victorian Britain', in N. Chaudhuri and M. Strobel (eds) *Western Women and Imperialism: Complicity and Resistance* (Bloomington: Indiana University Press), 231–46.
39. D. Douglass (1977) 'Pit Talk in County Durham', in R. Samuel (ed.) *Miners, Quarrymen and Saltworkers* (London: Routledge & Kegan Paul), 301; J. Kirkup (1996) *A Child of the Tyne* (Salzburg: University of Salzburg Press), 132.
40. Garbutt, HO107/2399 1851 f563; McLenahan, RG13/4736 1901 f24.
41. This proves consistent with patterns among rural-urban migrants' extended kin and co-villagers Anderson reported in *Family Structure in Nineteenth Century Lancashire*.
42. Thompson, HO107/2399 1851 f278.
43. M. and J. Phillips, HO107/2399 1851 f224, M.E. Phillips, HO107/2399 1851 f106v. Additionally, George Gibson (7, Prussia) was described as a 'visitor' in the household of George and Margaret Gibson, HO107/2399 1851 f621. Mary Elizabeth Phillips might have been the sister of Margaret and John Phillips as all were born in the West Indies within a few years of one another.
44. It also betrays the colonial practice of sending children 'home' to become 'pukka' Britons. E. Buettner (2004) *Empire Families: Britons and Late Imperial India* (Oxford: Oxford University Press).
45. Wikstrum, RG11/5009 1881 f37; Trotter, RG11/5009 1881 f40v.
46. Black Swan, RG10/5037 1871 f52v.
47. Canadians preferred boarders of similar race, religion, ancestry and occupation. P. Baskerville (2001) 'Familiar Strangers: Urban Families with Boarders, Canada, 1901', *Social Science History* 25, 3: 321–46. L. Davidoff (1995) found lodgers and landladies linked by occupational or kin networks, including builders lodging with their foremen, in *Worlds Between: Historical Perspectives on Gender and Class* (New York: Routledge), 163–4.
48. M. Rediker (1987) *Between the Devil and the Deep Blue Sea: Merchant Seamen, Pirates, and the Anglo-American Maritime World, 1700–1750* (Cambridge: Cambridge University Press); L. Tabili (1994) *'We Ask For British Justice': Workers and Racial Difference in Late Imperial Britain* (Ithaca: Cornell University Press).
49. J. Robinson (ed.) (1996) *Tommy Turnbull: A Miner's Life* (Newcastle: TUPS Books), 16.
50. Arguments for migration as culturally productive and integrative appear in Southall, 'Agitate! Agitate! Organize!', 177–93; and C. Stephenson (1979) 'A Gathering of Strangers? Mobility, Social Structure, and Political Participation in the Formation of Nineteenth-Century American Workingclass Culture', in M. Cantor (ed.) *American Workingclass Culture: Explorations in American Labor and Social History* (Westport: Greenwood), 39–40, 48–9, 51.

51. See Samuel, quoting Lady Bell, 'Comers and Goers', 125.
52. Inglis, HO107/2400 1851 f127v; Lloyd, HO107/2400 1851 f118; Levecque, HO107/2400 1851 f159v; Sales, HO107/2400 1851 f152; Nesbitt, HO107/2400 1851 f162v. Also see Doller, RG9/3787 1861 f45v; McDonald, RG9/3793 1861 f76.
53. Lillie, RG10/5031 1871 f61v; Sandeford, RG10/5038 1871 f6v.
54. In Boldon, Knowles, RG12/4162 1891 f4v; Morris, RG12/4162 1891 f42v. Also Bush, RG12/4160 1891 f6; Mills, RG12/4164 1891 f92v; Patrick, RG12/4164 1891 f96v; Gunderson, RG12/4164 1891 f36–36v; Anderson, RG12/4164 1891 f42.
55. St Bede's, RG11/5010 1881 f7v; Loarmount, RG11/5013 1881 f34.
56. In 1891 British households accommodated 17 visitors and seven employees originating overseas.
57. For the former interpretation, see N. McCord and D.J. Rowe (1977) 'Industrialisation and Urban Growth in North-East England', *International Review of Social History* 22: 57; C.G. Pooley (1977) 'The Residential Segregation of Migrant Communities in Mid-Victorian Liverpool', *Transactions of the Institute of British Geographers* 2nd ser., 2: 371; for the latter, Davidoff, *Worlds Between*, 155. On overcrowding, see M.J. Daunton (1985) *House and Home in the Victorian City: Working-Class Housing 1850–1914* (London: Edward Arnold), 79–82.
58. Quote from Davidoff, *Worlds Between*, 152, also see 161–2, 166, 168–9, 172–3; Baskerville, 'Familiar Strangers', 322, 333; W. Gamber (2005) found boarders created 'surrogate' familial relations including attending entertainments, playing music and card games, celebrating holidays, attending to the ill and the dead, quarrelling and making up. Many also maintained contact with ex-landladies and ex-fellow boarders, in *The Boardinghouse in Nineteenth-Century America* (Baltimore: Johns Hopkins University Press), 1–33.
59. M. Hunt (2004) 'Women and the Fiscal-Imperial State in the Late Seventeenth and Early Eighteenth Centuries', in K. Wilson (ed.) *A New Imperial History: Culture, Identity, and Modernity in Britain and the Empire, 1660–1840* (Cambridge: Cambridge University Press), 29–47.
60. On distinctions in intimacy between large boarding houses and private 'homes', see Gamber, *The Boarding house in Nineteenth-Century America*, 34–50. In the latter, lodgers might share rooms and even beds with family members.
61. Gadola, HO107/2399 1851 f115; Aitkin, HO107/2399 1851 f485.
62. Nadforth, HO107/2399 1851 f225v.
63. Paulding, HO107/2399 1851 f127; Lloyd, HO107/2400 1851 f118, RG9/3785 1861 f75v, RG10/5028 1871 f10, RG11/5013 1881CEB f30v; Nesbitt, HO107/2400 1851 f162v who may have survived in 1861 as Workhouse inmate W.N. RG9/3785 1861 f35v.
64. Sales at 23 Albion Street, HO107/2400 1851 f152; Reack at 24 Albion Street, HO107/2400 1851CEB f152v.
65. Gillespy, RG9/3786 1861 f51v; Ratcliff, RG9/3786 1861 f9; Kerr, RG9/3794 1861 f23; Chadwick, RG11/5011 1881 f63; Graham, RG11/5011 1881 f121.
66. Dish, HO107/2400 1851 f84, housing vocalist Thomas Miller of Fall River and a mariner from Croydon; Thompson, HO107/2400 1851 f118; Wood,

HO107/2400 1851 f159v. The town had six or seven commercial boarding houses in 1851.

67. Lawler, RG9/3793 1861 f65v; McManus, RG9/3793 1861 f77v.
68. Scrunger, RG9/3793 1861 f72v–73.
69. Clark, RG11/5020 1881 f43v–44.
70. Levitt and Arias, RG11/5020 1881 f47. Also McCalvey, RG11/5020 1881 f24v.
71. Samuel, 'Comers and Goers', 125. V.C. Burton (1987) cautions aggregate figures might be bloated by crews of ships, nearly all male, with little relationship to the proximate port, in 'A Floating Population: Vessel Enumeration Returns in Censuses, 1851–1921', *Local Population Studies* 28: 36–43.
72. Grigg, 'E.G. Ravenstein and the "Laws of Migration"', wrote of 'immigration fields',153; while J. Walvin (1973) argued Britain's Black community dispersed from London throughout the country with nineteenth-century expansion of maritime employment, in *Black and White: The Negro in English Society, 1555–1945* (London: Penguin), 204.
73. Hanson, seaman lodger, RG9/3794 1861 f40; lumper householder, RG10/5032 1871 f20; tailor and paterfamilias, RG11/5015 1881 f67v; Brown, seaman, RG9/3788 1861 f119; painter, RG11/5016 1881 f6v; Musgrave, mariner boarder, RG9/3793 1861 f53v; paterfamilias chemical labourer, RG11/5017 1881 f53.
74. Hanson, RG10/5033 1871 f71–71v, RG11/5014 1881 f48v; Vasey, RG10/5028 1871 f15v, RG11/5013 1881 f8v.
75. Johnson, RG10/5030 1871 f85v, RG11/5009 1881 f26; Brown, RG10/5038 1871 f61, RG11/5020 1881 f47v.
76. Three stokers and four coaltrimmers appeared in 1881. On the changing labour process, see E.W. Sager (1989) *Seafaring Labour: The Merchant Marine of Atlantic Canada, 1920–1914* (Kingston: McGill-Queen's University Press), 10–11, 246–9, 261–5; J.C. Healey (1969) *Foc'sle and Glory Hole: A Study of the Merchant Seaman and his Occupation* (New York: Greenwood), 24–39; T. Brassey (1871) *British Seamen* (London: Longmans, Green), 11, 17, 35–6.
77. See D.M. Williams (1992) 'The Quality, Skill and Supply of Maritime Labour: Causes of Concern in Britain, 1850–1914', and the comment by A. Thowsen, in L. Fischer, H. Hamre, P. Holm and J. Bruijn (eds) *The North Sea: Twelve Essays on the Social History of Maritime Labour* (Stavanger: Stavanger Maritime Museum), 41–58; Tabili, *'We Ask for British Justice'*, 41–57.
78. Hunt, 'Women and the Fiscal-Imperial State in the Late Seventeenth and Early Eighteenth Centuries'; V. Burton (1999) 'Whoring Drinking Sailors: Reflections on Masculinity From the Labour History of Nineteenth Century British Shipping', in M. Walsh (ed.) *Working Out Gender: Perspectives from Labour History* (Aldershot: Ashgate), 84–101, esp. 93.
79. Borough of South Shields, *Bye-Laws as to Seaman's Lodging-Houses* (1887), 3, 7. These measures partook of a nationwide social purity campaign equating lodging houses with prostitution. J. Walkowitz (1980) *Prostitution in Victorian Society: Women, Class, and the State* (Cambridge: Cambridge University Press), Chapter 3.
80. Hobsbawm, 'The Tramping Artisan', 310–16; Hochstadt, *Mobility and Modernity*, 44–5.

81. K. Jayawardena (1995) *The White Woman's Other Burden: Western Women & South Asia During British Rule* (London: Routledge); H. Callaway (1987) *Gender, Culture, and Empire: European Women in Colonial Nigeria* (London: Macmillan); M. Procida (2002) *Married to the Empire: Gender, Politics, and Imperialism in India, 1883–1947* (Manchester: Manchester University Press); Buettner, *Empire Families*.
82. Quote from Hoerder, 'Immigration and the Working Class', 34, also 37; Morawska, 'Return Migrations', 286–7; D.R. Gabaccia (1988) *Militants and Migrants: Rural Sicilians Become American Workers* (New Brunswick: Rutgers); Southall, 'Agitate! Agitate! Organize!'.
83. The phrase is from M. Baud and W. van Schendel (1997) 'Toward a Comparative History of Borderlands', *Journal of World History* 8, 2: 225.

## 5 Gentlemen of the Highest Character: Negotiating Inclusion with the People of South Shields

1. Memorial of Andrew Anderson, 1897, Home Office Aliens Department: The National Archives (hereafter TNA), HO144/407/B23795. Subsequent archival citations will be to this collection of case files or to the Duplicate Certificates of Naturalization, class HO334, also in TNA.
2. On manhood, honour and independence, see M.A. Clawson (1980) 'Early Modern Fraternalism and the Patriarchal Family' *Feminist Studies* 6, 2: 368–91; K. McClelland (1991) 'Masculinity and the Representative Artisan', in M. Roper and J. Tosh (eds) *Manful Assertions: Masculinities in Britain Since 1800* (London: Routledge), 74–91; S.O. Rose (1992) *Limited Livelihoods: Gender and Class in Nineteenth Century England* (Berkeley: University of California Press), 126–53.
3. R. Colls and B. Lancaster (eds) (2005 [1992]) *Geordies: Roots of Regionalism* (Newcastle: Northumbria University Press), xiv, 19–22; R. Samuel (1998) *Island Stories: Unravelling Britain,* Theatres of Memory, Vol. 2 (London: Verso), 153–71.
4. Pioneering works include L. Davidoff (1995) *Worlds Between: Historical Perspectives on Gender and Class* (New York: Routledge); A.L. Stoler (1991) 'Carnal Knowledge and Imperial Power: Gender, Race, and Morality in Colonial Asia', in M. di Leonardo (ed. and intro.) *Gender at the Crossroads of Knowledge: Feminist Anthropology in the Postmodern Era* (Berkeley: University of California Press), 51–101.
5. State-centred discussions include B. Anderson (1991 [1983]) *Imagined Communities: Reflections on the Origin and Spread of Nationalism* (London: Verso); G. Noiriel (1996 [1988]) *The French Melting Pot: Immigration, Citizenship, and National Identity* (Minneapolis: University of Minnesota Press); R. Brubaker (1992) *Citizenship and Nationhood in France and Germany* (Cambridge: Harvard University Press); R. Hansen (2000) *Citizenship and Immigration in Post-War Britain* (Oxford: Oxford University Press). Those stressing popular agency include V. Caron (1988) *Between France and Germany: The Jews of Alsace-Lorraine, 1871–1918* (Palo Alto: Stanford University Press); M. Kaplan (1991) *The Making of the Jewish Middle Class: Women, Family, and Identity in Imperial Germany* (New York: Oxford University Press); D. Ortiz (2000) *Paper*

*Liberals: Press and Politics in Restoration Spain* (Westport: Greenwood); S.O. Rose (2003) *Which People's War? National Identity and Citizenship in Britain, 1939–1945* (New York: Oxford University Press).

6. Notwithstanding L. Colley (1991) *Britons: Forging the Nation 1707–1837* (New Haven: Yale University Press); R. Price (1972) *An Imperial War and the English Working Class: Working-Class Attitudes and Reactions to the Boer War, 1899–1902* (London: Routledge & Kegan Paul). Also see M. Steinberg (1995) '"The Great End of All Government...": Working People's Construction of Citizenship Claims in Early Nineteeenth-Century England and the Matter of Class', *International Review of Social History* 40, Supplement 3: 19–50.
7. Quoted material is from G. Eley and G. Suny (eds) (1996) 'Introduction', in *Becoming National: A Reader* (Oxford: Oxford University Press), esp. 5, 9. Also see Noiriel, *The French Melting Pot,* 215–16; A. Burton (1997) 'Who Needs the Nation? Interrogating "British History"', *Journal of Historical Sociology* 10, 3: 227–48; A. Fahrmeir (2000) *Citizens and Aliens: Foreigners and the Law in Britain and the German States, 1789–1870* (New York: Berg), 231–3.
8. P. Panayi (1991) 'Middlesbrough 1961: A British Race Riot of the 1960s?', *Social History* 16, 2: 153, positing 'general hostility', 142, 'subconscious racial hostility...brought to the surface', 151; also P. Panayi (1996) 'Anti-German Riots in Britain During the First World War', in P. Panayi (ed.) *Racial Violence in Britain in the Nineteenth and Twentieth Centuries* (Leicester: Leicester University Press), on 'underlying...general xenophobia', 65; and recently G. Romain (2006) *Connecting Histories: A Comparative Exploration of African-Caribbean and Jewish History and Memory in Modern Britain* (London: Kegan Paul), on 'underlying' racism, 214.
9. L. Tabili (2005) 'Outsiders in the Land of Their Birth: Exogamy, Citizenship, and Identity in War and Peace', *Journal of British Studies* 44: 796–815.
10. On women's predominance, see E.G. Ravenstein (1885) 'The Laws of Migration', *Journal of the Royal Statistical Society* 48: 197; D.R. Gabaccia (1994) *From the Other Side: Women, Gender, and Immigrant Life in the United States, 1820–1990* (Bloomington: Indiana University Press), 21; notwithstanding D.B. Grigg (1994) 'E.G. Ravenstein and the "Laws of Migration"', in M. Drake (ed.) *Time, Family, and Community: Perspectives on Family and Community History* (Oxford: Blackwell/Open University Press), 154.
11. L. Tabili (2006) 'A Homogeneous Society? Britain's Internal "Others", 1800–Present', in C. Hall and S.O. Rose (eds) *At Home With The Empire: Metropolitan Culture and the Imperial World* (Cambridge: Cambridge University Press), 53–76. Also Noiriel, *The French Melting Pot,* 156–7.
12. H. Izdebski (1995) 'Government and Self-Government in Partitioned Poland', in M. Branch, J. Hartley and A. Maczak (eds) *Finland and Poland in the Russian Empire: A Comparative Study* (London: University of London), 77–89; E. Thaden (1984) *Russia's Western Borderland 1710–1870* (Princeton: Princeton University Press), vii–viii.
13. O. Jussila, 'How Did Finland Come Under Russian Rule?', in Branch et al., *Finland and Poland in the Russian Empire,* 61; F.H. Aarebrot (1982) 'Norway: Centre and Periphery in a Peripheral State', in D.W. Urwin and S. Rokkan (eds) *The Politics of Territorial Identity: Studies in European Regionalism* (Beverly Hills: Sage), 85.

14. G.A. Craig (1978) *Germany 1866–1945* (New York: Oxford University Press), 1–37; D.W. Urwin, 'Germany: From Geographical Expression to Regional Accommodation', in Rokkan and Urwin, *Politics of Territorial Identity*, 175–81.
15. D. Brower and E.J. Lazzerini (eds) (1997) *Russia's Orients: Imperial Borderlands and Peoples, 1700–1917* (Bloomington: Indiana University Press), xix.
16. J.E.O. Screen, 'The Military Relationship Between Finland and Russia, 1809–1917', 9–70 in Branch et al., *Finland and Poland in the Russian Empire*, and other essays in this volume especially V. Merkys, 'The Lithuanian National Movement: The Problems of Polonization and Russification', 271–82.
17. Merkys, 'The Lithuanian National Movement', 274–9; Izdebski, 'Partitioned Poland', 81; T. Polvinen (1995 [1984]) *Imperial Borderland: Bobrikov and the Attempted Russification of Finland, 1898–1904* (trans. Steven Huxley) (London: Hurst), 18, 271–2 and *passim*; Thaden, *Russia's Western Borderland*, 126, 142, 178–99, 231–3.
18. V.I. Lenin (1939 [1917]) *Imperialism: The Highest Stage of Capitalism* (New York: International); also Urwin, 'From Geographical Expression to Regional Accommodation', 179; Polvinen, *Imperial Borderland*, 6, 9.
19. T. Hamerow (1958) *Restoration, Revolution, Reaction: Economics and Politics in Germany, 1815–1871* (Princeton: Princeton University Press), 14–15, 246–8, 252–3, 255; R. Alapuro, 'Finland: An Interface Periphery', in Rokkan and Urwin, *Politics of Territorial Identity*, 113–64, esp. 120, 115–16; Merkys, 'Lithuanian National Movement', 274, 278–9; Thaden, *Russia's Western Borderland*, 141–2, 170, 193, 198–9, 213–14, 240. Analogously, R. Swift (2002) *Irish Migrants in Britain 1815–1914: A Documentary History* (Cork: Cork University Press), 4–6.
20. See D. Feldman (1994) *Englishmen and Jews: Social Relations and Political Culture 1840–1914* (New Haven: Yale University Press), esp. 2–3, 148–53; D. Bering (1992 [1987]) *The Stigma of Names: Antisemitism in German Daily Life, 1812–1933* (trans. N. Plaice) (London: Polity).
21. A. Zolberg (1978) 'International Migration Policies in a Changing World System', in W.H. McNeill and R.S. Adams (eds) *Human Migration: Patterns and Policies* (Bloomington: Indiana University Press), 242, 245, 266–71; E. Morawska and W. Spohn, 'Moving Europeans in the Globalizing World: Contemporary Migrations in Historical-Comparative Perspective (1955–1994 v. 1870–1914)', and A.R. Zolberg, 'Global Movements, Global Walls: Responses to Migration, 1855–1925', in G. Wang (ed.) (1997) *Global History and Migrations* (Boulder: Westview), 279–307 and 23–61.
22. Alprovich of Samiatage, Poland, HO144/356/B15315; L. and D. Josephs of Kalvaria, Poland, HO144/347/B13761 and HO144/414/B24920; brothers Pearlman from Kovno, HO144/406/1323675 and HO144/406/B23674.
23. Finn, HO144/38/83264; Epstein, HO144/883/B37681. See W. Fishman (1975) *Jewish Radicals: From Czarist Stetl to London Ghetto* (New York: Pantheon), 3–30. The eighth Russian subject, Alexander Sundstream, a merchant seaman from St Petersburg, appears as likely Swedish as Russian in affiliation. HO144/408/B23813.

24. Hamerow, *Restoration, Revolution, Reaction*, 255. This sample included one caulker, one shipchandler's clerk, one mariner, four pork butchers and eight master mariners.
25. Bruhn, HO144/400/B22378; Degn, HO144/424/B26415; Sonnichsen, HO144/115/A26293, Peterson, HO144/123/A3157. Fahrmeir found regional loyalties outweighed those to the German emperor, *Citizens and Aliens*, 233–4.
26. John Petersen, 69 Queens Road Jarrow on Tyne to the Home Office, n.d., *c.* June 1884, HO144/123/A3157.
27. A. Wawn, agent for Samuel Finn to the Home Office, 29 May 1879, HO144/38/83264.
28. M.S. Beerbühl (2003) 'British Nationality Policy as a Counter-Revolutionary Strategy During the Napoleonic Wars: The Emergence of Modern Naturalization Regulations', in A. Fahrmeir, O. Faron and P. Weil (eds) *Migration Control in the North Atlantic World: The Evolution of State Practices in Europe and the United States From the French Revolution to the Interwar Period* (New York: Berghahn), 55–70.
29. A. Kershen (1993) 'The Jewish Community in London', in N. Merriman (ed.) *The Peopling of London: Fifteen Thousand Years of Settlement From Overseas* (London: Museum of London), 140.
30. J.M. Ross (1974) 'Naturalisation of Jews in England', *Transactions of the Jewish Historical Society of England* 24: 65–8.
31. Finn, HO144/38/83264. Between 1801 and 1843 no one with a recognizably South Shields surname appeared, among a total of 171 cases, HO1/13 to HO1/18/88. No case originated in South Shields between 1843 and 1879. Handlist in TNA Catalogue Room Index to Denizations and Naturalizations, TNA.
32. Memorials typically included the applicant's name, British address, occupation, age, birthplace, marital status and nationality, as well as the nationality of the applicant's parents, names and ages of underage co-resident children and sometimes spouses, addresses of residences in Britain for at least five of the previous eight years and reasons for seeking naturalization. To obtain an 'Ordinary' Certificate 'A', applicants must demonstrate residence in Britain for five of the previous eight years. Index to Denizations and Naturalizations, 1801–1900, TNA. Other classes of Naturalization Certificates applied seldom to men resident in Britain, none to South Shields.
33. R. Kershaw and M. Pearsall (2004) *Immigrants and Aliens* (London: The National Archives), 62.
34. Referee statement for Edward Benson, 19 February 1912, HO144/1197/22 0525.
35. See agents for Nordberg, HO144/462/B32420.
36. Home Office internal minute regarding Erick Magnus Ahlstedt, *c.* April–May 1907, HO144/620/B35894.
37. A.R. Sundstream, aboard *SS Fountains Abbey* docked at Cardiff, to the Home Office, 15 November 1897, HO144/408/B23813.
38. James W. Browne, 13 King William Street, London to the Home Office, 11 December 1897 (Rupp), HO144/418/B25691.

39. See Home Office minute, 13 December 1913 (John Pearson), HO144/1293/244402; also Home Office internal minute, 7 June 1909 (Nyborg), HO144/916/180226.
40. Home Office minute on Ludvig Rasmussen's file, 11 February 1898, HO144/420/B25964; minute on Albert Jensen's file, 1909, HO144/876/16164/2.
41. Waterlow Brothers & Layton to Home Office, 29 January 1899, HO144/443/B2975. Also see Newlands and Newlands, for H.C.S.T. Christensen, 1 February 1899, HO144/437/B28754.
42. Young & Green to Home Office, 4 July 1894 (Anderson), HO144/346/B13674.
43. Home Office Undersecretary of State to South Shields Chief Constable, n.d., *c.* 23 March 1917 (Gabrielsen), HO144/1404/273678.
44. Relevant chief constables included Frederick George Miles Moorhouse, 1883–94, William George Morant 1894–1902 and William Scott, formerly chief detective inspector in Cardiff, appointed 1 December 1902. Hodgson, *Borough of South Shields*, 189. Scott's successor, William R. Wilkie, proved equally zealous.
45. On manhood and respectability, see K. McClelland (1996) 'Rational and Respectable Men: Gender, the Working Class, and Citizenship in Britain', in S.O. Rose and L.L. Frader (eds) *Gender and Class in Modern Europe* (Ithaca: Cornell University Press), 280–93; on women's critical role, see E. Ross (1985) '"Not the Sort that Would Sit on the Doorstep": Respectability in Pre-World War I London Neighborhoods', *International Labor and Working Class History* 27: 39–59.
46. Inspector William Proud, North Shields, 26 December 1908 and Home Office minute on file, 21 September and 28 October 1909; South Shields Chief Constable to Home Office, 23 March and 7 April 1914; Home Office minute, 17 April 1914, HO144/1030/171897.
47. Chief Constable to Home Office, 27 October 1906; Home Office minute 15 November 1906, HO144/835/145071.
48. Chief Constable to Home Office, 17 January 1923 (Putnin), HO144/1857/24 4467.
49. On licensed masculine aggression, see L. Roper (1994) *Oedipus and the Devil: Witchcraft, Sexuality and Religion in Early Modern Europe* (London: Routledge), 107–24.
50. Chief Constable to Home Office, 1 March 1913 (Anderson), HO144/1250/23 3759; correspondence 6 October 1913 (Auffinger), HO144/1289/243224; Chief Constable to Home Office 30 June 1912 (Parlow) HO144/1214/224479.
51. Chief Constable to Home Office, 17 September 1912 (Andreasen), HO144/1222/227162.
52. Chief Constable to Home Office, 3 April 1912, HO144/1197/220525.
53. On marriage, see J.R. Gillis (1985) *For Better, For Worse: British Marriages, 1600 to the Present* (New York: Oxford University Press); P. Corrigan and D. Sayer (1985) *The Great Arch: English State Formation as Cultural Revolution* (Oxford: Blackwell), 196–7 and *passim*.
54. Bruhn Memorial sworn October/November 1896, HO144/400/B22378.
55. Chief Constable to Home Office, 4 June 1904 (Buetow), HO144/759/118930.
56. Memorial, 27 May 1909 (Christensen), HO144/915/179711; also see Erickson, HO144/751/117129.

57. Minutes initialled JFU, 20.2.12 and WTK 14.3.12 (Jensen), HO144/1181/21 7650.
58. Olsen Memorial, 1883, HO144/126/A33400; Chief Constable to Home Office, 23 September 1901 (Bortner), HO144/1097/19739. Also Johnson Memorial, 10 November 1879, HO144/50/88815; Gompertz Memorial, *c.*1880, HO144/54/90701.
59. Fahrmeier, *Citizens and Aliens*, 179.
60. Nelson Memorial witnessed May 1896, HO144/394/B21323; Ahlstedt memorial, 13 March 1901, HO144/620/B35894.
61. Christensen Memorial, 19 September 1898, HO144/437/B28754.
62. Eggert Memorial, *c.* 1892, HO144/344/B13356; also Lorentz Larsson Memorial, 14 July 1898, HO144/430/B27593.
63. Nordberg Memorial 5 June 1900, HO144/4627/B32420; Rasmussen Memorial, 1887, HO144/297/B2410.
64. Morck Memorial, 17 January 1898, HO144/421/B26071. On *fin de siècle* xenophobia, see D. Feldman (1989) 'The Importance of Being English: Jewish Immigration and the Decay of Liberal England', in D. Feldman and G. Stedman Jones (eds) *Metropolis London: Histories and Representations Since 1800* (London: Routledge), 56–84; B. Gainer (1972) *The Alien Invasion: The Origins of the Aliens Act, 1905* (London, Heinemann).
65. Ahlstedt Memorial, 13 March 1901, HO144/620/B35894.
66. V. Burton (1999) 'Whoring, Drinking Sailors: Reflections on Masculinity from the Labour History of Nineteenth-Century British Shipping', in M. Walsh (ed.) *Working Out Gender: Perspectives from Labour History* (Aldershot: Ashgate), 87–93.
67. Also see Home Office minute on Segar's file, 27 May 1920, HO144/1738/39 4989; H.A. zur Nedden, HO144/443/B29751. On the Board of Trade examination system, see N. Cox (1972) 'The Records of the Registrar-General of Shipping and Seamen', *Maritime History* 2: 179.
68. Dabbert Memorial, witnessed 15 August 1898, HO144/432/B27865.
69. See, for example, the case of Andrew Anderson, forwarded 29 June 1894 from the Board of Trade to the Home Office, HO144/346/B13674. Louis Korner's case reveals the records were only available from 1890 onwards, although like many men, Korner had been working aboard British ships far longer. HO144/451/B30784.
70. On the vagaries of 'weekly boats' and discharges, see Chief Constable to Home Office, 13 March 1919 (Kreepse), HO144/1191/219929; cases of C. A. Nordberg, 1900, HO144/4621/B32420; H. Christensen, 1899, HO144/437/B28754; Isak Olsen, 1 August 1881, HO144/446/B3017.
71. Walter J. Howell to Home Office, 1 April 1901 (Ahlstedt), HO144/620/B35894.
72. On occupations closed to aliens, see Fahrmeir, *Citizens and Aliens*, 163–4. Although aliens were often nominated to the local offices, they were barred from holding them. See Beerbühl, 'British Nationality Policy as a Counter-Revolutionary Strategy', 67.
73. Chief Constable to Town Clerk, 6 July 1896 (Nelson), HO144/394/ B21323.
74. Josephs Memorial, 1893, HO144/347/B13761.
75. N. Pearson to Home Office, 21 December 1897, HO144/418/B25691. Also Chief Constable of County Durham to Home Office, 16 August 1911 (Abel), HO144/1152/211364.

76. Chief Constable to Town Clerk, 14 April 1904 (Jorgensen), HO144/752/11 7307; Chief Constable to Town Clerk, 15 June 1904 (Junala), HO144/ 761/119318.
77. Memorial, January 1897, HO144/391/B20840.
78. Nagel Memorial, 29 April 1914, HO144/1319/252762; Kragh Memorial, *c.* 1897, HO144/415/B25160.
79. Josephs Memorial, 1893, HO144/347/B13761; Finn Memorial, *c.* May 1879, HO144/38/83264.
80. Home Office minute, *c.* April 1919 (Jacobson), HO144/1390/269393; Chief Constable to Home Office, 7 September 1892 (Andersson), HO144/341/ B12737.
81. Chief Constable to Home Office, 22 August 1908 (Andersen), HO144/879/ 65505.
82. Daglish to Home Office, 4 December 1883 (Petersen), HO144/123/A3157.
83. These reasons echo older traditions of settlement including binding in apprenticeship, fulfilling a year's service, marrying a local woman, property ownership, paying taxes or holding public office. See D. Feldman (2003) 'Migrants, Immigrants and Welfare from the Old Poor Law to the Welfare State', *Transactions of the Royal Historical Society* 6th ser. 13 (Cambridge: Cambridge University Press), 85–7.
84. McClelland, 'Masculinity and the Representative Artisan', 74–91.
85. Referees for Samuel Finn, 1879, HO144/38/83264; referees for James Meier, n.d. *c.* 12 February 1885, HO144/148/38473;
86. Chief Constable, 24 July 1912, forwarding oath, HO144/1197/220525. Also see Chief Constable to Home Office, 17 March 1902 (Epstein), HO144/642/B37681.
87. South Shields' Chief Constable, 2 June 1919, HO144/1499/366544.
88. Feldman likewise found many Liberals dismissed formal naturalization as 'a miserable but expensive technicality', in 'The Importance of Being English', 67; also see J. Torpey (2000) *The Invention of the Passport: Surveillance, Citizenship, and the State* (Cambridge: Cambridge University Press), 190 n.21.
89. For a sample of the Home Office's form letter specifying 'respectability' see file of Charles Bernhard Andersson, 3 September 1892, HO334/341/B12737.
90. William George Morant to Home Office, 6 July 1896 (Nelson), HO144/394/B21323.
91. Detective Report, Newcastle-upon-Tyne Constabulary, 23 March 1898 (Rasmussen), HO144/420/B25964. Byker is a suburb of Newcastle.
92. Chief Constable to South Shields Town Clerk, 10 April 1899 (Anderson), HO144/407/B23795.
93. Chief Constable to Home Office, 4 October 1916, HO144/915/353871; and see Chief Constable to Home Office, 7 January 1915 (Wold), HO144/1349/260392.
94. Chief Constable to Home Office, 3 October 1921 and 13 May 1922 (Stephan), HO144/1798/418429.
95. South Shields' Chief Constable to Home Office 25 April 1912 and subsequent correspondence (Benson), HO144/1197/220525.
96. Chief Constable Morant to Home Office, 23 November 1895 (Herder), HO144/382/B19564.

97. W. Pearson, Mayor of Jarrow to Home Office, 21 December 1897 (Rupp), HO144/418/B25691.
98. Just as men accounted for the vast bulk of those naturalized between 1879 and 1939, men almost exclusively served as referees.
99. John Fenwick, medical botanist, referee for Ernest Götz, 28 January 1889, HO144/308/B5833; Stephenson Fletcher, Jr, tallowchandler, referee for Peter Sonnichsen, HO144/115/A26293; Joseph Edward Sleightholme, private enquiry agent and furniture dealer, referee for Samuel Schenker, Chief Constable to Home Office 16 November 1916, HO144/1420/279696. There were a total of 739 identifiable referees, but some vouched for more than one applicant, discussed below, so they totalled 676 persons.
100. Compare M. Banton (1955) *The Coloured Quarter: Negro Immigrants in an English City* (London: Jonathan Cape), who argued that only 'neurotics' and social outcasts fraternized with 'immigrants', 13, 150–1, 170–3, 185, 228.
101. Not all referees described relationships in detail, but the chief constable was increasingly called on to report their precise origin and content to the Home Office.
102. See D.F. Crew (1979) *Town in the Ruhr: A Social History of Bochum, 1860–1914* (New York: Columbia University Press), 6.
103. See Clawson, 'Early Modern Fraternalism and the Patriarchal Family'.
104. William Sketheway, innkeeper, 1897 (Pearlman), HO144/406/B23675.
105. Also see the cases of Paul Eggert, 1893, HO144/344/B13356, and Charles Henry Phaffley, 1896, HO144/388/B20462.
106. Declared 1916 (Schenker), HO144/1420/279696.
107. Chief Constable of Newcastle, 8 November 1897 (Kragh), HO144/415/B25160.
108. Frederick James Boyd, declared 14 June 1920; Swansea Borough Police C.I.D. to Home Office, 22 December 1920 (Bilbao), HO144/1660/264299.
109. John Christoph Petterson, HO144/123/A31517; George Adolf Christensen, HO144/915/179711; Emil Granlund, HO144/1499/366544.
110. Declaration, 15 June 1900 (Nordberg), HO144/462/B32420.
111. Memorial of J. William Wood McAlister for John Pettersen (who spelled his own name Petersen), 1883, HO144/123/ A31517.
112. Chief Constable to Home Office, 2 June 1919 (Granlund), HO144/1499/366544.
113. Doctors: Anderson, HO144/346/B13674; Jacobson, HO144/420/B25957; Levy, HO144/1258/235889. Union representatives: Fye, HO144/1498/364777; Johnson, HO144/1678/385429; Stephan, HO144/1748/418429. Burdon: Gabrielsen, 19 March 1917, HO144/1404/273678; Sundstream, HO144/408/B23813.
114. Referees' declarations, *c.*1893 (Anderson), HO144/346/B13674.
115. Chief Constable to Home Office, 7 June 1916 (Pearlman), HO144/1451/310568; Chief Constable to Home Office, 10 April 1899 (Anderson), HO144/407/B23795; Declaration of Reference for G. E. Anderson, 20 December 1919, HO144/1591/382304.
116. Chief Constable to Home Office, 21 February 1898 (Morck), HO144/421/B26071; Affidavit of Jane Eales regarding Charles Wahlquist, *c.* August/September, HO144/431/B27852; Chief Constable to Home Office, 6 July 1896 (Nelson), HO144/394/B21323.

117. Chief Constable to Home Office, 25 October 1896 (Voss), HO144/391/B20840.
118. Chief Constable to Town Clerk, 4 April 1905 (Erickson), HO144/751/117129. Also see Nordberg, supported by his landlord, HO144/462/B32420.
119. Herder, HO144/382/B19564.
120. Durham County Constabulary, Jarrow-upon-Tyne, 1 September 1907 (Klotz), HO144/862/155506.
121. Chief Constable to Home Office, 4 July 1910 (Netz), HO144/1085/193688.
122. Chief Constable to Home Office, 13 November 1907 (Erickson), HO144/867/158611.
123. Chief Constable to Town Clerk, 3 April 1898 (Degn), HO144/424/B26415; also see Anderson, 1897, HO144/407/B23795; and Christensen, 1899, HO144/437/B28754.
124. Affidavit of William Suckling, 9 April 1897; Chief Constable to Home Office, 1 February 1898 (Sundstream), HO144/408/B23813.
125. Chief Constable to Home Office, 4 March 1906 (Trapp), HO144/811/136730.
126. Declaration of Reference, 10 December 1919 (Anderson), HO144/1591/382304.
127. Declared 1922 (Rasmussen), HO144/1760/428719.
128. James William Southern, referee for Augustus Lundean, 1894, HO144/369/B17382.
129. Chief Constable's report, 11 January 1910 (Keith), HO144/556/185506.
130. Chief Constable to Home Office, 8 April 1913 (Levy), HO144/1259/235951.
131. Chief Constable to Home Office, 1 April 1919 (Valentini), HO144/1509/374925.
132. Chief Constable to Town Clerk, 9 January 1903 (Hub), HO144/688/103348.
133. South Shields Chief Constable, 29 June 1914 (Nagel), HO144/1319/252762.
134. Thomas Oliver Stewart, 27 May 1909 (GA Christenson), HO144/915/179711.
135. Carl Christian Bruhn Memorial, 1896, HO144/400/B22378.
136. Town Clerk to Home Office, 21 September 1898 (Larsson), HO144/430/B27593.
137. Chief Constable to Home Office, 18 February 1915 (Alder), HO144/1356/261603.
138. Declared 8 December 1919 (G.E. Anderson), HO144/1591/382304.
139. Chief Constable, 7 June 1916 (Pearlman), HO144/1451/310568.
140. Chief Constable to Town Clerk, 4 June 1904 (Buetow), HO144/759/118930.
141. Martin Putnin, HO144/1857/244467; Markus Bortner, HO144/1097/19739; Chief Constable to Home Office, 28 May 1921 (Danielson), HO144/1704/418430.
142. Charles Wahlquist, HO144/431/B27852; George Edwin Anderson, HO144/1591/382304.
143. Referees for Paul Arthur Eggert, 1892, HO144/344/B13356.
144. Declaration, 26 May 1902 (Klebert), HO144/649/B38143.
145. Memorial, 23 February 1918; Chief Constable to Home Office, 10 April 1918, enclosing special report from Sergeant Henry Wood, Durham County Constabulary, 9 April 1918 (Magnan), HO144/1490/355342.
146. Chief Constable to Home Office, 6 July 1896 (Nelson), HO144/394/B21323.
147. W. Pearson, Mayor of Jarrow to Home Office, 21 December 1897, regarding Michael Friedrich Rupp, HO144/418/B25691. Also see Memorial,

5 June 1900 of Nordberg, HO144/462/B32420; Herder, HO144/382/B19564; Gompertz, HO144/54/90701.

148. Memorial of Henry Levy, declared 17 March 1913; Chief Constable to Home Office, 8 April 1913, HO144/1258/235889.
149. Chief Constable to Home Office, 1 April 1919; Valentini Memorial, dated 15 January 1914, HO144/1509/374925.
150. Memorial of Moses Netz, 1 June 1910, HO144/1085/193688.
151. See, for example, the case of P.J. Trapp, on which the Home Office commented, 'The papers have been prepared not by Waterlow but by a country firm for whom Waterlows act as London agents'. Minute *c.*1906, HO144/811/136730.
152. On this distinction, see M.J. Hickman (1999) 'Alternative Historiographies of the Irish in Britain: A Critique of the Segregation/Assimilation Model', in R. Swift and S. Gilley (eds) *The Irish in Victorian Britain: The Local Dimension* (Dublin: Four Courts), 251.
153. On constricted communities of obligation, see Feldman, 'Migrants, Immigrants and Welfare'.
154. Memorial, 1883, HO144/123/A31517.
155. E. Ross (1983) 'Survival Networks: Women's Neighbourhood Sharing in London Before World War I', *History Workshop Journal* 15: 4–27; E. Ross (1982) '"Fierce Questions and Taunts": Married Life in Working-Class London, 1870–1914', *Feminist Studies* 8: 575–602. On daily practice as cultural production, see E.P. Thompson (1991) *Customs in Common* (New York: New Press), esp. 1–15.

## 6 His Wife Must Surely Know: Women and Migrants' Integration

1. Memorial of Emeterio Bilbao, n.d., *c.* 1 June 1920; Metropolitan Police to Home Office, 20 April 1921; South Shields Chief Constable to Home Office, 8 June 1921; Home Office minute *c.* 28 January 1921; Athertons Ltd, Solicitors, to Home Office, 28 June 1921, The National Archives (hereafter TNA), HO144/1660/264299.
2. South Shields Chief Constable to Home Office, 30 November 1920, HO144/1660/264299; Mary and Enrique Zarraga, Spring 1922, Burgess Rolls, Holborn Ward, p. 16, 753e and 754e, South Tyneside Central Library (hereafter STCL). Zarraga himself was naturalized in January 1914, HO334/62 and HO144/1297/245672. On Basque boarding houses, see J. Echeverria (1999) *Home Away From Home: A History of Basque Boardinghouses* (Reno: Nevada). On her sole European case, in Liverpool, see 234–5.
3. Exceptions include E.G. Ravenstein (1885 and 1889) 'The Laws of Migration', *Journal of the Royal Statistical Society*, Pt. I, 48: 167–227, esp. 196–7, 199, 218, 220, and Pt. II, 52: 241–301, esp. 249, 252, 259, 263, 266–70, 273, 288; A. Rossiter (1991) 'Bringing the Margins into the Centre: A Review of Aspects of Irish Women's Emigration', in S. Hutton and P. Stewart (eds) *Ireland's Histories: Aspects of State, Society, and Ideology* (London: Routledge), 234–5. Most historical scholarship has emerged from

US history: D. Gabaccia has pioneered attempts to globalize the discipline. See, for instance (1994) *From the Other Side: Women, Gender, and Immigrant Life in the United States, 1820–1990* (Bloomington: Indiana University Press); C. Harzig (ed.) (1997) *Peasant Maids-City Women: From the European Countryside to Urban American* (Ithaca: Cornell University Press). On the state of the discipline early in the century, see the editors' 'Introduction', in D.R. Gabaccia and F. Iacovetta (2002) *Women, Gender, and Transnational Lives: Italian Workers of the World* (Toronto: University of Toronto Press), 3–41.

4. Analogously, see L. Norling (1996) 'Ahab's Wife: Women and the American Whaling Industry, 1820–1870', in M.S. Creighton and L. Norling (eds) *Iron Men, Wooden Women: Gender and Seafaring in the Atlantic World, 1700–1920* (Baltimore: Johns Hopkins University Press), 70–91; L. Norling (2000) *Captain Ahab Had a Wife: New England Women and the Whalefishery, 1720–1870* (Chapel Hill: University of North Carolina Press); S. van Kirk (1980) *Many Tender Ties: Women in Fur-Trade Society, 1670–1870* (Norman: Oklahoma), 53–76 and *passim.*
5. Chief Constable, 12 November 1906 (Johanson), HO144/837/145705.
6. Sprogas, HO144/1692/410208. Also see Chief Constable, 3 November 1910 (Jessen), HO144/1025/167950; Chief Constable, County Durham to Home Office, 10 July 1912 (Kursacoff), HO144/1208/223106; Chief Constable Morant, 2 February 1898 (Morck), HO144/421/B26071.
7. Detective Inspector William Tanner to Head Constable Police Office, Town Hall, Newport, 10 December 1908 (Pestana), HO144/893/172225.
8. Home Office minute, 28 December 1911 (P.J. Jensen), HO144/1181/217650.
9. C. Dixon (1984) 'The Rise and Fall of the Crimp', in S. Fisher (ed.) *British Shipping and Seamen, 1630–1960: Some Studies* (Exeter Papers in Economic History), 55; W. Gamber (2005) *The Boardinghouse in Nineteenth-Century America* (Baltimore: Johns Hopkins University Press), 141–5.
10. S. Collins (1957) reported landladies were revered in Britain's postwar communities of colour for precisely this reason in *Coloured Minorities in Britain: Studies in British Race Relations Based on African, West Indian and Asiatic Immigrants* (London: Lutterworth), 56–7.
11. William Tanner, Detective Inspector, Newport Police, to Head Constable, 6 November 1908 (Andriotis), HO144/885/168327.
12. Truwert, HO334/45 and HO144/859/154029.
13. L. Davidoff (1995) discussed the complexities of lodging as housing, labour and social relation in *Worlds Between: Historical Perspectives on Gender and Class* (New York: Routledge), 151–79. Also see Gamber, *The Boardinghouse in Nineteenth-Century America*; Gabaccia, *From the Other Side*, 62–3; H. Beynon and T. Austrin (1994) *Masters and Servants: Class and Patronage in the Making of a Labour Organisation: The Durham Miners and the English Political Tradition* (London: Rivers Oram), 176.
14. Ravenstein, 'The Laws of Migration', I, 220. Also see G. Noiriel (1996 [1988]) *The French Melting Pot: Immigration, Citizenship, and National Identity* (Minneapolis: University of Minnesota Press), 100, 152.
15. V. Burton (1987) 'A Floating Population: Vessel Enumeration Returns in Censuses, 1851–1921', *Local Population Studies* 28: 36–43.

16. Nationally the ratio was 105 women to 100 men. Ravenstein, 'The Laws of Migration', I, 220, 218. By 1931 County Durham ranked sixth from the bottom among British counties in percentage of women, with 984 women for each 1000 men, while in many other counties women outnumbered men. *1931 Census of England and Wales: Preliminary Report* (London: HMSO, 1931), xx.
17. H.A. Mess (1928) *Industrial Tyneside: A Social Survey* (London: Ernest Benn), 36. Durham remained the 'most married county in England and Wales', 35.
18. E. Knox (2005 [1992]) '"Keep Your Feet Still, Geordie Hinnie": Women and Work on Tyneside', in R. Colls and B. Lancaster (eds) *Geordies: Roots of Regionalism* (Newcastle: Northumbria University Press), 94. Also J. Foster (1979 [1974]) *Class Struggle and the Industrial Revolution: Early Industrial Capitalism in Three English Towns* (London: Methuen), 261, 336; A. Miles (1999) *Social Mobility in Nineteenth-Century England* (New York: St Martin's), 154.
19. R. Bartlett (1993) *The Making of Europe: Conquest, Colonization and Cultural Change, 950–1350* (Princeton: Princeton University Press), 55–6; T.E. Sheridan (1992) *Los Tucsonenses: The Mexican Community in Tucson, 1854–1941* (Tucson: University of Arizona Press), 146.
20. Hodgson, *The Borough of South Shields*, 21–2; also see *Archaeologia Aeliana* x: 239. Archaeological evidence suggests this practice was widespread. See B.R. Hartley and R.L. Fitts (1980) *The Brigantes* (Gloucester: Alan Sutton), 56; H. Jewell (1994) *The North-South Divide: The Origins of Northern Consciousness in England* (Manchester: Manchester University Press), 21.
21. G. Rubin (1975) 'The Traffic in Women: Notes on the "Political Economy" of Sex', in R.R. Reiter (ed.) *Toward an Anthropology of Women* (New York: Monthly Review), 157–210; van Kirk, *Many Tender Ties*, 28–9.
22. Bartlett, *Making of Europe*, 55–6; P. Carrasco (1997) 'Indian-Spanish Marriages in the First Century of the Colony', in S. Schroeder, S. Wood and R. Haskett (eds) *Indian Women of Early Mexico* (Norman: University of Oklahoma Press), 89–90, 97–8, 102–3; van Kirk, *Many Tender Ties*, 29–31, 41–2.
23. Also see Davidoff, *Worlds Between*, 172.
24. Chief Constable to Home Office, 20 September 1910 (Lindemann), HO144/1096/197353. This *entrée* may also have afforded his brother Harold Lindemann access. Memorial of Harold Lindemann, 13 July 1911, HO144/1154/211663.
25. Home Office minute, 25 July 1911 (Eklund), HO144/1150/210753.
26. Chief Constable to Home Office, 5 June 1911 (Moiraghi), HO144/1140/208446.
27. J. Gillis (1985) *For Better, For Worse: British Marriages, 1600 to the Present* (New York: Oxford University Press).
28. On marriage as 'a gamble', see E. Ross (1993) *Love and Toil: Motherhood in Outcast London, 1870–1918* (New York: Oxford University Press), 56, quoting Emmie Durham, in P. Thompson (1985 [1975]) *Edwardians: The Remaking of British Society* (Chicago: Academy Chicago), 167. On landladies stereotypically scheming to effect such unions, see Gamber, *The Boardinghouse in Nineteenth-Century America*, 106.
29. Chief Constable, County Durham to Home Office, 10 July 1912 (Kursacoff), HO144/1208/223106.

30. Chief Constable to Home Office, 4 November 1912 (Feldman), HO 144/1239/229518.
31. Putnin Memorial dated 27 September 1920, HO144/1857/244467. Due to husbands' absence at sea, mariners' wives often remained in their parents' homes. Norling, *Captain Ahab Had a Wife*, 223–7.
32. See Norling, *Captain Ahab Had a Wife*.
33. South Shields Chief Constable to Undersecretary of State, Home Office, 23 May 1905 (Nielsen), HO144/789/128937.
34. Memorial, February 1898 (Morck), HO144/421/B26071.
35. Lind Memorial, HO144/1225/227892. See also Frederick Koster, bereaved in 1901 and naturalized in 1904, HO334/39 and HO144/771/122697.
36. Fothel Ali, 8 February 1940, HO334/156 AZ15207. Also Abdul Ali, HO334/143/AZ8503 (1936); Sofian Doyal, HO334/143 AZ8757 (1936). To avoid confusion, Arabic names will be reported with the family name last, as they appear in British records.
37. Chief Constable to Town Clerk, 25 November 1903 (Schelin), HO144/732/11 3253.
38. For women referees, see 1 March 1892 (G.A. Petterson), HO144/337/B12099; Chief Constable to Town Clerk, 2 April 1904 (Glusich), HO144/743/115542.
39. Home Office minute (Mogensen), HO45/7399.
40. (Wiberg) HO144/423/B26303; (Sonnichsen) HO144/115/A26293. With reversion to conventional, more rigorous processes in the years 1915–24, of 34 men naturalized only eight remained unmarried, each with substantial wartime service, and between 1925 and 1930, only 3 of 13 men were unmarried.
41. Quote from Edmund J. Taylor, Bristol Town Clerk, to Home Office, 24 February 1904 (Makevit), HO144/743/115455.
42. Home Office minute, 26 May 1910 (Kerrick), HO144/1058/18874. Also see Home Office minute *c.* June 1906 (Amans), HO144/820/139375.
43. They cited as precedent the case of Peter Julius Jensen, Home Office minute, Summer 1912 (Möhle), HO144/1218/225674.
44. Home Office minute, n.d., *c.* December 1912–January 1913 (Strom), HO144/1236/230140.
45. Home Office minute, 1906 (Amans), HO144/820/139375.
46. Home Office minute, 3 September 1904; John Wannag to Home Office, 30 March 1904; South Shields Chief Constable, 16 February 1904, HO144/743/115539.
47. Home Office minute, 1904; Chief Constable, 28 November 1903 (Jensen), HO144/732/113319.
48. Chief Constable to Home Office, 6 March 1909 (Petirs), HO144/901/174804; Home Office minute, 12 May 1910 (Roemeling), HO144/1071/190913. Also see Chief Constable to Home Office, 17 February 1906 (Frank), HO144/812/136918; Chief Constable, 8 August 1905 (Lindstrom), HO144/795/131460.
49. Knox, 'Keep Your Feet Still, Geordie Hinnie', 102; Norling, *Captain Ahab Had a Wife*, 214–37.
50. Phrase is from Knox, disputing it, in 'Keep Your Feet Still, Geordie Hinnie', 94–7, 99, 102–6.

51. L.T. Ulrich (1982) *Good Wives: Image and Reality in the Lives of Women in Northern New England, 1650–1750* (New York: Knopf).
52. Norling, 'Ahab's Wife', 81; M. Hunt (2004) 'Women and the Fiscal-Imperial State in the Late Seventeenth and Early Eighteenth Centuries', in K. Wilson (ed.) *A New Imperial History: Culture, Identity, and Modernity in Britain and the Empire, 1660–1840* (New York: Cambridge University Press), 29–47.
53. M.L. Wong (1989) *Chinese Liverpudlians: A History of the Chinese Community in Liverpool* (Birkenhead: Liver Press), 36–40. On working-class survival strategies, see E. Ross (1979) '"Fierce Questions and Taunts": Married Life in Working-Class London, 1870–1914', *Feminist Studies* 8, 3: 575–602.
54. On fisherfolk, see R. Byron (1994) 'The Maritime Household in Northern Europe', *Comparative Studies in Society and History* 36, 2: 271–92; P. Thompson with T. Wailey and T. Lummis (1993) *Living the Fishing* (London: Routledge & Kegan Paul), 167–81; B. Berggreen (1992) 'Dealing with Anomalies? Approaching Maritime Women', and A. van der Veen, 'Independent Willy-Nilly: Fisherwomen on the Dutch North Sea Coast, 1890–1940', in L.R. Fischer, H. Hamre, P. Holm and J. R. Bruijn (eds) *The North Sea: Twelve Essays on Social History of Maritime Labour* (Stavanger: Stavanger Maritime Museum), 111–26, 181–96.
55. Chief Constable to Home Office, 3 June 1913 (Eilertsen), HO144/1267/23 7978.
56. Alternatively, it may have indicated the family had been abandoned, per Sheridan, *Los Tucsonenses*, 145. Some absent husbands appeared in the electoral rolls.
57. Hughes, RG10/5034 1871 f64v; Tommy Turnbull described in daunting detail the heavy labour involved in keeping Durham miners fit to work, in J. Robinson (ed.) (1996) *Tommy Turnbull: A Miner's Life* (Newcastle: TUPS), 6, 16, 134, 248–9 and *passim*.
58. Chief Constable William Morant to Home Office, 9 November 1897; Dorothy Kragh to Home Office, 18 October 1897, HO144/415/B25160.
59. Chief Constable, 31 October 1896 (Bruhn), HO144/400/B22378.
60. Louise Anderson to Mr W. Young, 29 June 1894 (A. Anderson), HO144/346/B13674. On similar practices, see S.F. Collins (1951) 'The Social Position of White and "Half-Caste" Women in Colored Groupings in Britain', *American Sociological Review* 16: 801.
61. Chief Constable to Home Office, 9 January 1904 (Johnson), HO144/739/11 4566; Chief Constable to Home Office, 5 May 1904 (Larson), HO144/755/118072; Chief Constable, 13 November 1903 (A.C. Anderson), HO144/729/112844; Chief Constable to Home Office, 16 February 1904 (Knudsen), HO144/742/115541.
62. Chief Constable to Home Office, 29 August 1905 (Gustafson), HO144/796/ 131913.
63. Home Office minutes, 13 February and 17 March 1904 (Kristofferson), HO144/756/118374.
64. Home Office minutes, 16 and 22 January 1912 (Hesse), HO144/1180/ 217279; Chief Constable to Home Office 26 March 1910 (A. Johansen), HO144/599/184070; Chief Constable to Home Office, 9 July 1911 (Strybos), HO1344/1033/176315.

65. Chief Constable, 26 March and 8 April 1904 (A. Anderson), HO144/750/11 6806. Also see Chief Constable to Home Office, 12 May 1904 (A.G. Anderson), HO144/756/118368.
66. Hannay and Hannay, Solicitors, to Home Office, 13 January 1923 (Putnin), HO144/1857/244467.
67. Chief Constable to Home Office, 6 December 1921 (Segar), HO144/1420/39 4989.
68. Chief Constable, 20 May 1914; Mary Ann Erickson to Home Office, 13 July 1916, HO144/1365/263487.
69. Chief Constable, 6 May 1905, HO144/788/12835.
70. Chief Constable to Home Office, 16 December 1913 (Zarraga), HO 144/1297/245672.
71. D. Frost (2000) reported wives of West Africans, identifying fiercely with the African community, still passed undetected into the white milieu for employment, shopping and other functions, in 'Ambiguous Identities: Constructing and De-constructing Black and White "Scouse" Identities in Twentieth-Century Liverpool', in N. Kirk (ed.) *Northern Identities: Historical Interpretations of 'The North' and 'Northernness'* (Aldershot: Ashgate), 205–8. Thompson, Wailey and Lummis found women's importance enhanced their authority, in *Living the Fishing*, 177–8.
72. Knox, 'Keep Your Feet Still, Geordie Hinnie', 103–6.
73. Chief Constable, 6 May 1905 (Hermanson), HO144/788/128635.
74. Chief Constable to Home Office, 22 February 1900 (Korner), HO144/451/B3 0784; Chief Constable to Town Clerk, 20 August 1900 (Nordberg), HO144/462/B32420.
75. Chief Constable to Home Office, 23 September 1910 (Bortner), HO144/1097/197439. Swedish mariner Per Albin Johnson similarly acquired bona fides from a married sister, Mrs Gabrielson, living nearby in Blyth. Chief Constable Morpeth, 26 April 1912, HO144/1197/220638.
76. 'Shields Murder', *Shields Gazette* (Wednesday, 12 March 1919).
77. Note regarding visit of Mrs Ahmed on 11 August 1930, and letter from Clara Bellanato to Colonial Office, 3 September 1930, both in Colonial Office papers CO725/21/8, TNA.
78. On women's bodies as points of social as well as sexual entry, see J. McCulloch (2000) *Black Peril, White Virtue: Sexual Crime in Southern Rhodesia, 1902–1935* (Bloomington: Indiana University Press), 182.
79. A. McFarlane in collaboration with S. Harrison and C. Jardine (1977) *Reconstructing Historical Communities* (London: Cambridge University Press), 159.
80. Koster, HO334/39 and HO144/771/122697; household of Casper Diehl, RG11/5015 1881 f32v. Also Kerrick, decribed above. HO144/1058/18874 and the Bianchi-Taroni household in Chapter 4, RG12/4158 1891 f46v. Also see Noiriel, *The French Melting Pot*, 155, 191; E.D. Steele (1976) 'The Irish Presence in the North of England, 1850–1914', *Northern History* 12: 220–1.
81. On working-class matrilocality, see M. Young and P. Willmott (1957) *Family and Kinship in East London* (Harmondsworth: Penguin).
82. Chief Constable of South Shields to Home Office, 30 June 1921 (A. Johnson), HO144/1678/385429, Certificate HO334/92.

83. Erickson married German John Hanson, per Memorial 1 May 1917 HO144/1473/329558 and HO334/81; Swan married John Bengston, a Swede, per Memorial 29 October 1919 HO144/1504/371562 and HO334/83; Malanson married Christian Thorius, a Dane, per Memorial 16 October 1918, HO144/1503/370770 and HO334/83.
84. Wilhelmina and Abdul Ali lived at 43 1/2 Albion Street in Shields Ward, per the electoral register for 1930, 1492a and 1493a, STCL. Also see Wong, *Chinese Liverpudlians*, 68–9, 73.
85. Ali, electors 3391l and 3392l; Deen, electors 979 and 980, Register of Electors, STCL. Musleh was naturalized in 1937, per HO334/146 AZ10191.
86. Rossiter, 'Bringing the Margins into the Centre', 234–5. An exception is L. Marks (1994) *Model Mothers: Jewish Mothers and Maternity Provision in East London, 1870–1939* (Oxford: Clarendon).
87. Gabaccia, *From the Other Side*, 6, 29–30.
88. On related questions, see Ravenstein, 'The Laws of Migration', Pt. 1, 196; C.G. Pooley (1977) 'The Residential Segregation of Migrant Communities in Mid-Victorian Liverpool', *Transactions of the Institute of British Geographers* 2nd ser., 2: 374; F. Thistlethwaite (1960) 'Migration from Europe Overseas in the Nineteenth and Twentieth Centuries', reprinted in R.J. Vecoli and S.M. Sinke (eds) (1991) *A Century of Europe Migrations, 1830–1930* (Urbana: University of Illinois Press), 46 n. 44; Noiriel, *The French Melting Pot*, 191.
89. Formal political status, of course, remains a crude measure: Alexander Sleege and his wife Euphrosina came from opposite ends of the German Empire formed after their birth, Danzig and Baden. RG12/4157 1891 f53v. See also Andreas and Margaret Ros from Hanover and Hamburg, RG12/4158 1891 f76v.
90. Exceptions included Phillip Hornung, missionary and manager of the German Sailors Home in Ferry Street, and his wife Luise, of Iqiqe, Peru (possibly Iquitos, Peru or Equique, Chile), RG12/4164 1891 f15–15v. Also see Randolph, RG12/4154 1891 f45v.
91. Alprovich, RG11/5015 1881 f34v.
92. Harild, HO144/738/114109.
93. Common origin hardly guaranteed harmony. See J. Gjerde, 'Chain Migration from the West Coast of Norway', in Vecoli and Sinke, *A Century of European Migrations, 1830–1930*, 158–81.
94. Rachel Levy, RG9/3794 1861 f54v; Brauninger, RG9/3790 1861 f6; RG10/5033 1871 f77v; RG11/5015 1881 f42v; RG12/4158 1891 f4v; Levy, RG10/5037 1871 f54; RG11/5020 1881 f39v; RG12/4164 1891 f23v; also the Birkett-Katzenberger household in Chapter 3.
95. Gabaccia, *From the Other Side*, 19–20.
96. On women's economy of makeshift, see J. Robinson (1997 [1975]) *Francie* (Newcastle: TUPS), 5–29 and *passim*.
97. S.O. Rose (1992) *Limited Livelihoods: Gender and Class in Nineteenth-Century England* (Berkeley: University of California Press), 80–8; E. Higgs (1987) 'Women, Occupations and Work in the Nineteenth Century', *History Workshop Journal* 23: 64, 67–8, 70 and *passim*; D.J. Rowe (1973) 'Occupations in Northumberland and Durham, 1851–1911', *Northern History* 8: 124.

98. On the relationship between family resources and women's labour, see A. August (1999) *Poor Women's Lives: Gender, Work, and Poverty in Late-Victorian London* (Madison: Fairleigh Dickinson), 114–15; Foster, *Class Struggle and the Industrial Revolution*, 312 n. 3. Also Gabaccia and Iacovetta, 'Introduction', 15; Gabaccia, *From the Other Side*, 152 fn. 3.
99. M. Kaplan (1991) *The Making of the Jewish Middle Class: Women, Family, and Identity in Imperial Germany* (New York: Oxford University Press), esp. vii–63; Gabaccia, *From the Other Side*, xi.
100. Bowes, RG11/5009 1881 39v/p.20; Olditch, RG11/5011 1881 f4v/p.2.
101. Women long-distance migrants normally migrated as members of families, Gabaccia, *From the Other Side*, 29–30; D. Feldman (1994) *Englishmen and Jews: Social Relations and Political Culture* 1840–1914 (New Haven: Yale University Press), 157.
102. During the Napoleonic era, Shields mariner Jack Nastyface encountered an Englishwoman from Poole, Dorset in the Dutch port of Flushing. W. Robinson (2002 [1973]) *Jack Nastyface: Memoirs of an English Seaman* O. Warner (Intro.) (London: Chatham), 122–3.
103. Hughes, RG10/5034 1871 f64v.
104. Jeffreson, RG12/4152 f62; Forde, RG12/4153 1891 f126; Fairles, RG12/4158 1891 f61.
105. Olsen, RG12/4154 1891 f7.
106. Brown, RG12/4156 1891 f88.
107. Norman, RG12/4154 1891 f102v; Newton, RG12/4159 1891 f74; Hagen, RG12/4159 1891 f74v.
108. J. Gillis (1979) 'Servants, Sexual Relations, and the Risks of Illegitimacy in London, 1801–1900', *Feminist Studies* 5, 1: esp. 151–3, 157. 163; Davidoff, *Worlds Between*, esp. 18–40, 104–13.
109. Higgs, 'Women, Occupations and Work in the Nineteenth Century', 69.
110. Chevallier, RG10/5036 1871 f17; Hay, RG10/5030 1871 f59v.
111. Knox, 'Keep Your Feet Still, Geordie Hinnie'. In 1891, 11.5 per cent of the town's population were domestic servants, nearly all women. J.W. House (1954) *North-Eastern England: Population Movements and the Landscape Since the Early Nineteenth Century* (Newcastle: Department of Geography, King's College, University of Durham), 60. Vivid descriptions of women's meagre employment options appear in Robinson, *Francie*.
112. Johnson/Black Swan, RG10/5037 1871 f52v.
113. Taylor, RG10/5034 1871 f53, RG11/5017 1881 f134; RG12/4163 1891 f103.
114. Longfield, RG12/4164 1891 f47; Kaiser, RG12/4152 1891 f98v.
115. Gabaccia, *From the Other Side*, xv.
116. Rubin, 'The Traffic in Women'; N. Yuval-Davis (1993) 'Nationalism and Racism', *Cahiers de recherche sociologique* 20: 183–202; D. Nirenberg (1996) *Communities of Violence: Persecution of Minorities in the Middle Ages* (Princeton: Princeton University Press), 166–99.
117. L. Bland (2005) 'White Women and Men of Colour: Miscegenation Fears in Britain After the Great War', *Gender and History* 17, 1: 29–61.
118. Gabaccia, *From the Other Side*, xv.
119. See A.F. Hill (2002) 'Insider Women With Outsider Values', *New York Times* (6 June).

120. On class exogamy, see Miles, *Social Mobility in Nineteenth and Early Twentieth Century England,* Ch. 7, esp. 153–4, 162; D. Mitch (1993) '"Inequalities Which Every One May Remove": Occupational Recruitment, Endogamy, and the Homogeneity of Social Origins in Victorian England', in A. Miles and D. Vincent (eds) *Building European Society: Occupational Change and Social Mobility in Europe* (Manchester: Manchester University Press), 140–64.
121. Scholars differ as to whether the First World War stimulated social change, as argued in A. Marwick (1965) *The Deluge: British Society and the First World War* (Boston: Little, Brown), esp. Ch. 3, 87–112; or backlash as per S.K. Kent (1993) *Making Peace: The Reconstruction of Gender in Interwar Britain* (Princeton: Princeton University Press); M.L. Roberts (1994) *Civilization Without Sexes; Reconstructing Gender in Postwar France, 1917–1927* (Chicago: University of Chicago Press).

## 7 Men of the World: Casualties of Empire Building

1. Discharge Papers of Robert Sherman, Tyne and Wear Archives Service (TWAS), 1400/1–80.
2. Before 1908 maritime jobseekers need produce no documentary evidence of their origins or seafaring experience, not even discharges. See *Parliamentary Debates* (Commons) CLXXXV, cols 618–655 (3 March 1908).
3. On everyday resistance, see J.C. Scott (1990) *Domination and the Arts of Resistance: Hidden Transcripts* (New Haven: Yale University Press); E.P. Thompson (1975) *Whigs and Hunters: The Origin of the Black Acts* (New York: Pantheon); C. Ginzburg (1982 [1976]) *The Cheese and the Worms: The Cosmos of a Seventeenth Century Miller* (trans. J. and A. Tedeschi) (Harmondsworth: Penguin); J. Yoors (1977) *The Gypsies* (New York: Simon & Schuster), esp. 50–9, 88, 108–13.
4. J. Scott (1985) *Weapons of the Weak: Everyday Forms of Peasant Resistance* (New Haven: Yale University Press). On names, see J. Caplan (2001) '"This or That Particular Person": Protocols of Identification in Nineteenth-Century Europe', in J. Caplan and J. Torpey (eds) *Documenting Individual Identity: The Development of State Practices in the Modern World* (Princeton: Princeton University Press), 49–66.
5. A. Fahrmeir, O. Faron and P. Weil (eds) (2003) *Migration Control in the North Atlantic World: The Evolution of State Practices in Europe and the United States From the French Revolution to the Interwar Period* (New York/Oxford: Berghahn).
6. O.J. Martinez (1994) *Border People: Life and Society in the U.S.-Mexico Borderlands* (Tucson: University of Arizona Press), 20–1, citing P. Sahlins (1989) *Boundaries: The Making of France and Spain in the Pyrenees* (Berkeley: University of California Press), 222–7, 268–9, 292.
7. On France, see G. Noiriel (1996 [1988]) *The French Melting Pot: Immigration, Citizenship, and National Identity* (Minneapolis: University of Minnesota Press), 47–51. For a rollicking account of governments' futile efforts to curb forgery, see A. Fahrmeir (2001) 'Governments and Forgers: Passports in

Nineteenth-Century Europe', in Caplan and Torpey, *Documenting Individual Identity*, 218–34.

8. Quotes from M. Rediker (1987) *Between the Devil and the Deep Blue Sea: Merchant Seamen, Pirates, and the Anglo-American Maritime World, 1790–1750* (Cambridge: Cambridge University Press), 10. Also see G. Horne (2005) *Red Seas: Ferdinand Smith and Radical Black Sailors in the United States and Jamaica* (New York: New York University Press), 83, 93 and *passim*; I. Land (2007) 'Tidal Waves: The New Coastal History', *Journal of Social History* 40, 3: 731–43.
9. Quotes from D. Arnold (1979) 'European Orphans and Vagrants in India in the Nineteenth Century', *Journal of Imperial and Commonwealth History* 7, 2: 114–17; V. Burton (1999) 'Whoring Drinking Sailors: Reflections on Masculinity From the Labour History of Nineteenth Century British Shipping', in M. Walsh (ed.) *Working Out Gender: Perspectives from Labour History* (Aldershot: Ashgate), 84–101; M. Creighton (1995) *Rites and Passages: The Experience of American Whaling, 1830–1870* (Cambridge: Cambridge University Press), esp. 139–61.
10. See Noiriel, *French Melting Pot*, 156–9.
11. Quote from A.R. Zolberg (1978) 'International Migration Policies in a Changing World System', in W.H. McNeill and R.S. Adams (eds) *Human Migration: Patterns and Policies* (Bloomington: Indiana University Press), 270, also 251–4 and *passim*; J. Torpey (2000) *The Invention of the Passport: Surveillance, Citizenship, and the State* (Cambridge: Cambridge University Press), 3, 62, 68–9, 73–9, 87–9, 91; L.P. Moch (1992) *Moving Europeans: Migration in Western Europe since 1650* (Bloomington: Indiana University Press), 10–11, 107; D. Gabaccia (1994) *From the Other Side: Women, Gender, and Immigrant Life in the United States, 1820–1990* (Bloomington: Indiana University Press), 5, 8.
12. R. Brubaker (1992) *Citizenship and Nationhood in France and Germany* (Cambridge: Harvard University Press); A. Fahrmeir (2000) *Citizens and Aliens: Foreigners and the Law in Britain and the German States, 1789–1870* (New York: Berghahn); Torpey, *Invention of the Passport.*
13. J.R. Gillis (1985) *For Better, For Worse: British Marriages, 1600 to the Present* (New York: Oxford University Press); also see G. Frost (1997) 'Bigamy and Cohabitation in Victorian England', *Journal of Family History* 22, 3: 286–306.
14. I. Land (2005) 'Bread and Arsenic: Citizenship From the Bottom Up in Georgian London', *Journal of Social History* 39, 1: 89–110, esp. 104.
15. R. Bartlett (1993) *The Making of Europe: Conquest, Colonization and Cultural Change, 950–1350* (Princeton: Princeton University Press), 146, 278.
16. D. Bering (1992) *The Stigma of Names; Antisemitism in German Daily Life, 1812–1933* (trans. N. Plaice) (Cambridge: Polity), 28–35 and *passim.*
17. W. Brockie (1857) *Family Names of the Folks of Shields Traced to their Origins, with Brief Notice of Distinguished Persons, to Which is Appended a Dissertation on the Origin of the Britannic Race* (South Shields: T.F. Brockie & Co.), 6.
18. C. Dixon (1980) 'Legislation and the Sailors Lot, 1660–1914', in P. Adam (ed.) *Seamen in Society* (Bucharest: Commission Internationale d'Histoire Maritime), III, 97.
19. Chief Constable to Home Office, 3 December 1912, The National Archives (TNA), HO144/1237/230347.

20. Chief Constable to Home Office, 29 September 1911 (Wilhelm), HO144/1167/214143. Also see Noiriel, *The French Melting Pot*, 74–5, 124; Bering, *The Stigma of Names*, 217, 236–7.
21. Jacobson, HO334/40 certificate 15443 and HO334/46/18016; Bjerkin, HO334/42/16065; Jokelsohn (1910), HO334/51/19611; Grinfelds, HO334/138/AZ6070; Mosley (1938), HO334/147/AZ10800.
22. Bering, *Stigma of Names*, 188–98. On the 'cultural work' of renaming, see D. Ghosh (2004) 'Decoding the Nameless: Gender, Subjectivity, and Historical Methodologies in Reading the Archives of Colonial India', in K. Wilson (ed.) *A New Imperial History: Culture, Identity and Modernity in Britain and the Empire, 1660–1840* (Cambridge: Cambridge University Press), 310.
23. Papers of Christopher Metcalfe Swainston, TWAS DX244/3, 21. On name changes as a 'barometer of pressure', see Bering, *Stigma of Names*, 13 and *passim*.
24. Erickson, RG12/4160 1891 f117, HO144/751/117129. Also Josephs, RG11/5015 1881 f34, HO144/414/B24920. On informal acquisition of citizenship rights, see D. Feldman (1989) 'The Importance of Being English: Jewish Immigration and the Decay of Liberal England', in D. Feldman and G. Stedman Jones (eds) *Metropolis London: Histories and Representations Since 1800* (London: Routledge), 67.
25. Rogers household, RG10/5032 1871 f20; Isabella Rogers naturalization petition, HO334/81 and HO144/1473/329550.
26. T. Hamerow (1958) *Restoration, Revolution, Reaction: Economics and Politics in Germany, 1815–1871* (Princeton: Princeton University Press), 246–8, 252–3, 255; R. Alapuro (1982) 'Finland: An Interface Periphery', in D.W. Urwin and S. Rokkan (eds) *The Politics of Territorial Identity: Studies in European Regionalism* (Beverly Hills: Sage), 113–22; E. Thaden (1984) *Russia's Western Borderland 1710–1870* (Princeton: Princeton University Press), esp. 121, 199–200, 213, 231–9.
27. Compulsory military service became widespread in Continental Europe. F. Caestecker (2003) 'The Transformation of Nineteenth-Century West European Expulsion Policy, 1880–1914', in Fahrmeir, Faron and Weil, *Migration Control in the North Atlantic World*, 120, 123–7, 134 n. 10; Torpey, *Invention of the Passport*, 1–16.
28. T. Polvinen (1995 [1984]) *Imperial Borderland: Bobrikov and the Attempted Russification of Finland, 1898–1904* (trans. S. Huxley) (London: Hurst), 43, 124, 214, 273; J.E.O. Screen (1995) 'The Military Relationship between Finland and Russia, 1809–1917', in M. Branch, J. Hartley and A. Maczak (eds) *Finland and Poland in the Russian Empire: A Comparative Study* (London: University of London Press), 262–3.
29. On migration as resistance, see D.R. Gabaccia (1988) *Militants and Migrants: Rural Sicilians Become American Workers* (New Brunswick: Rutgers). On what historians can glean from objectively untrue stories, see A. Portelli (1991) *The Death of Luigi Trastulli and Other Stories: Form and Meaning in Oral History* (Albany: State University of New York Press).
30. Chief Constable William Scott to Home Office, 16 February 1904; Wannag to Home Office, 30 March 1904; Mercantile Marine Superintendant to Home Office, 21 December 1903, HO144/743/115539.

31. Affidavit by Karl Tomson, 1 November 1916; minute on file, *c.* 1916, HO144/1015/152437.
32. Minute, 12 January 1910, HO144/1053/187550.
33. Moch, *Moving Europeans*, 11; Gabaccia, *Militants and Migrants*, 80; Fahrmeir, *Citizens and Aliens*, 183.
34. The Home Office wordlessly altered Erickson's documents to identify him and his parents, like Junala and Nyborg's, as 'subjects of Russia'. HO144/751/117129 and HO334/38/14369. Junala, 4 June 1904, HO144/761/119318 and HO334/38/119318; Nyborg, HO144/916/180226 and HO334/47 /18269. Also Grönberg, HO144/1086/193920 and HO334/51/19820; Strom, Home Office minute, *c.* 1909, HO144/1236/230140.
35. Polvinen, *Imperial Borderland*, 168, 130–1, 183–4 and *passim*; also Branch, Hartley and Maczak, *Finland and Poland in the Russian Empire*, 61–73, 91–109, 283–7; Thaden, *Russia's Western Borderlands*, 121, 199–200, 213, 231–9.
36. The Home Office insisted Apiht and his parents were Russian subjects. HO144/821/140089 and HO334/42/16037. On Baltic Germans, see Thaden, *Russia's Western Borderlands*, 4.
37. Further evidence appeared in the eagerness of newly autonomous subject peoples to shed Russian nationality after the First World War. See cases of Latvians Robert Upmal, 1919 HO144/1591/38166; John Sprogas, 1920, HO144/1092/410208; Martin Putnin,1922, HO144/1857/244467; Finn George Edwin Anderson, 1920, HO144/1591/382304.
38. Moch, *Moving Europeans*, 10–11; Torpey, *Invention of the Passport*, 18.
39. Quote from John Torpey, 'Passports and the Development of Immigration Controls in the North Atlantic World During the Long Nineteenth Century', 83; also see F. Caestecker, 'The Transformation of Nineteenth-Century West European Expulsion Policy, 1880–1914', 120, 123–4, both in Fahrmeir, Faron and Weil, *Migration Control in the North Atlantic World*. See also A.R. Zolberg (1997) 'Global Movements, Global Walls: Responses to Migration, 1855–1925', in G. Wang (ed.) *Global History and Migrations* (Boulder: Westview), 279–85.
40. C. Guerin-Gonzalez and C. Strikwerda (1993) (eds) *The Politics of Immigrant Workers: Labor Activism and Migration in the World Economy Since 1830* (London: Holmes & Meier), 12; U. Herbert (1990 [1986]) *A History of Foreign Labor in Germany, 1880–1980: Seasonal Workers/Forced Laborers/Guest Workers* (trans. W. Templer) (Ann Arbor: University of Michigan Press), xvii.
41. Zolberg, 'International Migration Policies in a Changing World System', 271–75.
42. D. Feldman (2003) 'Migrants, Immigrants and Welfare from the Old Poor Law to the Welfare State', *Transactions of the Royal Historical Society* 6th ser. 13 (Cambridge: Cambridge University Press), 79–104; Caestecker, 'The Transformation of Nineteenth-Century West European Expulsion Policy', 124–31; Torpey *Invention of the Passport*, 1–21, 80–1, 154, 158 and *passim*.
43. D. Feldman (1994) *Englishmen and Jews: Social Relations and Political Culture 1840–1914* (New Haven: Yale University Press); Zolberg, 'International Migration Policies in a Changing World System', 275–6. The 1905 Act applied to steerage passengers only, Fahrmeir, *Citizens and Aliens*, 242. On France, see Noiriel, *French Melting Pot*, 214.

44. W.H. Poole of the Shipowners' Parliamentary Committee, an industry pressure group, to the Rt Hon. Gerald Balfour, President of the Board of Trade, 23 June 1903, Board of Trade papers, TNA MT9/756.M12074; 'Report of the Committee Appointed by the Board of Trade to Inquire into Certain Questions Affecting the Mercantile Marine with Minutes of Evidence, Appendices and Index', 17 May 1903 (HMSO 1903), Cd. 1607, found in MT9/756.12917. On Anglo-German tension, see P. Panayi (1991) *The Enemy in Our Midst: Germans in Britain During the First World War* (New York: Berg), 36–41.
45. The language test was aimed largely although not exclusively at Chinese mariners. *Parliamentary Debates* (Commons) CLXXXV col. 640 and *passim* (3 March 1908). On these abusable tests, see Feldman, *Englishmen and Jews*, 371–2.
46. For the French analogue, see Noiriel, *French Melting Pot*, 156. Also see xix, 50, 78–9.
47. Cd.1607, clause (7), xi.
48. Mariner forms were suspended in March 1915, Board of Trade to Home Office, 18 October 1915, HO45/10943/255778/43. Service under the Crown had been grounds for naturalization since at least 1870, but no one residing in South Shields had pursued this option. See Index to Denizations and Naturalizations, 1801–1900, f100, TNA.
49. The sixth was the United States. See Table 3.1.
50. This process appears transparently in (Pestana), HO144/899/173955.
51. Home Office minute, *c.* 28 May 1909 (G. A. Christensen), HO144/915/17 9711.
52. Minute on 'Mariner form' (Weide), HO144/865/156788.
53. Detective Department, Central Police Station, Cardiff, 20 May 1904 (Kristofferson), HO144/756/118374.
54. Home Office minute, March/April 1914 (Masur), HO144/1308/249465. Also minute, case of Voss, 1896, HO144/391/B20840.
55. Home Office minute and South Shields Chief Constable to Home Office, 28 January 1910 (Poulson), HO144/538/186332.
56. Newport County Borough Police Detective Inspector William Tanner to Chief Constable, C.E. Gower, Esq., 17 February 1914 (Henricks), HO144/1299/246542.
57. Moiraghi Memorial, 3 May 1911, HO144/1140/208446; Kohler Memorial, 13 March 1913, HO144/1203/221337. Also see Strybos, 1911, HO144/1033/176315; Olson, 1913, HO144/1252/234220.
58. John Bull, 4 June 1904 (Jansson), HO144/762/120136. Also see cases of Larsen, 1904, HO144/755/118072; Koster, 1904, HO144/771/12 2697.
59. Home Office minute, 13 March 1910, HO144/922/182168.
60. South Shields Chief Constable, 4 August 1913 (Gustafson), HO144/1280/24 0708.
61. Home Office minute, *c.* 1914 (Hanson), HO144/1306/248946.
62. Carlberg Memorial 2 February 1914, HO144/1307/249192.
63. Morck Memorial, *c.* January 1898, HO144/421/B26071.
64. On similar atomized, lone men, see J. Gjerde (1991) 'Chain Migration from the West Coast of Norway', in R.J. Vecoli and S.M. Sinke (eds) *A Century of*

*European Migrations, 1830–1930* (Urbana: University of Illinois Press), 161, 166, 174–5.

65. See, for example, 'Application and Declaration' of Christian Warrer, 29 March 1905, HO144/786/127822.
66. South Shields Chief Constable to Home Office, 3 December 1912; Home Office minute, 20 November 1912 (Anderholm), HO144/1237/230347.
67. Frederick Koster, Master, *SS Tynemouth* to Home Office, 25 October 1912; South Shields Chief Constable to Home Office, 3 December 1912, HO144/1237/230347. Koster was naturalized in 1904, HO334/39 and HO144/771/122697.
68. Home Office minute, 2 March 1913 (Enlund), HO144/1258/235715.
69. Home Office minute, *c.* 1913 (Birkedal), HO144/1278/240305.
70. Home Office minute, 15 May 1911 (Mattison), HO144/1085/193725.
71. See, for example, James Krause, HO144/776/124261; and C. Dixon (1984) 'The Rise and Fall of the Crimp', in S. Fisher (ed.) *British Shipping and Seamen, 1630–1960: Some Studies* (Exeter: Exeter Papers in Economic History), 55.
72. Cardiff Police, 28 November 1904; Metropolitan Police CID, 24 September 1904, Home Office minute (Ketchen), HO144/769/121869.
73. Chief Constable to Town Clerk, 25 November 1903 (Lagerberg), HO144/732/113255.
74. Chief Constable to Home Office, 8 and 30 July 1910 (Grönberg), HO144/1086/193920.
75. Mercantile Marine Office, Hull, 8 November 1911 (Lindgren), HO144/1111/201884.
76. Detective Department Cardiff City Police, 12 and 25 January 1913; South Shields' Chief Constable, 30 December 1912 (Persson), HO144/1227/228338.
77. Chief Constable to Town Clerk, 15 June 1904 (Junala), HO144/761/119318.
78. Chief Constable to Home Office regarding Lewis Peter Bremer, 19 September 1905, HO144/867/158611.
79. Cardiff City Police to Home Office, 12 November 1912 (Feldman), HO144/1234/224518.
80. See Chief Constable to Home Office, 4 January 1904, regarding Olof Mauritz Emil Cervin's landlord, HO144/739/114417; Chief Constable to Home Office, 4 February 1910 (Magnuson), HO144/1054/187972; Chief Constable, 6 October 1906 (Weide), HO144/820/139522; Glamorgan Constabulary to Cardiff Chief Constable, 19 January 1912 (Cejka), HO144/1179/217164; cases of Apiht, HO144/821/140089; Pestana, HO144/893/172225; Pehrsson, HO144/826/141676.
81. Chief Constable to Home Office, 15 September 1906; Home Office minute, HO144/833/144153.
82. On mobility as a masculine attribute and privilege, see C. Cockburn (1990) *Machinery of Dominance: Women, Men, and Technical Know-How* (Boston: Northeastern); M. Duneier (1992) *Slim's Table: Race, Respectability, and Masculinity* (Chicago: University of Chicago Press).
83. Chief Constable to Home Office, 31 August 1910 and 31 May 1911; Procurator Fiscal of Glasgow, 29 July 1910; Merchant Marine Superintendant, Glasgow, 19 September 1911; Glamorgan Constabulary,

1 July 1910, HO144/1085/193725. 10 Market Place was a Temperance Hotel in 1912 per HO144/1233/229405 case of Dux.

84. Chief Constable, 31 May 1911, HO144/1085/193725. Typographical errors in the quote have been corrected.
85. Robson, Supervisor, Mercantile Marine Office, South Shields, 19 September 1911; Home Office minutes, 15 May 1911, 1 August 1911, 22 September 1911, HO144/1085/193725.
86. Stenwick Memorial, 10 May 1910; John W. Huish, Chief Constable of North Shields to Home Office, 12 June 1909; Chief Constable of South Shields, 19 May and 12 November 1909; Cardiff City Police, 3 December 1909 and 17 February 1910, HO144/1034/177307. Also see the case of Mauritz Berndsson, Sgt Albert Davies, Cardiff City Police Detective Department, 3 July 1913, HO144/1274/239334.
87. Torpey, *Invention of the Passport*, 166. The Continuous Certificate of Discharge was introduced in 1900 to curb skyrocketing desertion rates: mates held men's certificates during voyages, leaving deserters uncredentialled. Dixon, 'Legislation and the Sailors Lot', 100.
88. Chief Constable to Home Office, 29 May 1909 (Olsen), HO144/1029/170796. Also see Spalwitz, HO144/760/119261.
89. John Wannag to Home Office, 30 March 1904, HO144/743/115539. Mengel household, RG13/4736 1901 f107.
90. Putnin Memorial, 22 October 1913, HO144/1857/244467.
91. George Wood, Police Constable, 31 August 1906; Home Office minute, 3 September 1906 (Pehrsson), HO144/826/141676.
92. Chief Constable to Home Office, 23 December 1907 (Busto), HO144/868/15 9175; Chief Constable to Home Office, 18 April 1906 (Schulz), HO144/820/139363.
93. Gabaccia, *From the Other Side*, 32; Moch, *Moving Europeans*, 149; also Noiriel, *French Melting Pot*, 158–9.
94. Chief Constable to Home Office, 1 April 1909 (Strybos), HO144/1033/176 315; Chief Constable to Home Office (Moiraghi), HO144/1140/208446.
95. Warrer Memorial dated 29 March 1905, HO144/786/127822. Also see Chief Constable to Home Office regarding Ernest Feldman, HO144/1234/229518; Chief Constable to Home Office, 1 April 1919, regarding Giovanni Valentini, HO144/1509/374925.
96. 'Application and Declaration' of Christian Warrer, 29 March 1905, HO144/786/127822. Sea service added up to six years, one month and 20 days, while time ashore totalled four months in South Shields and perhaps six months in Hartlepool.
97. Noiriel described a similar process whereby French citizenship became valuable only when the Third Republic made entitlements conditional on it, *French Melting Pot*, xix, 50, 78–9.
98. Home Office minute on Christensen, 1 June 1909; Memorial declared 27 May 1909; South Shields Chief Constable to Home Office, 7 June 1909, HO144/915/179711. Christensen had served in British ships since age 14.
99. Mercantile Marine Superintendant's communication reported in Home Office minute, 23 May 1910; Chief Constable to Home Office, 29 April 1910; JP [John Pedder] Home Office minute, 26 April 1910 (Johnson), HO144/1065/189640.

100. G. Eley and R.G. Suny (eds) (1996) *Becoming National: A Reader* (New York: Oxford University Press), 9.
101. S. Castles and G. Kosack (1973) *Immigrant Workers and Class Structure in Western Europe* (Oxford: Oxford University Press), 21–2; J. Torpey (2001) 'The Great War and the Birth of the Modern Passport System', in Caplan and Torpey, *Documenting Individual Identity*, 256–70. On this broader context, see L. Lucassen (1998) 'The Great War and the Origins of Migration Control in Western Europe and the United States (1880–1920)', in A. Böcker, K. Groenendijk, T. Havinga and P. Minderhoud (eds) *Regulation of Migration: International Experiences* (Amsterdam: Het Spinhius), 44–72.
102. Panayi, *The Enemy in Our Midst*, 45, 60, 64 and *passim*, which offers the fullest treatment of wartime aliens policy.
103. Panayi, *Enemy in Our Midst*, 8, 46–52; S. Yarrow (1990) 'The Impact of Hostility on Germans in Britain, 1914–1918', in T. Kushner and K. Lunn (eds) *The Politics of Marginality: Race, the Radical Right and Minorities in Twentieth Century Britain* (London: Frank Cass), 98–9.
104. Aliens and Nationality Committee, 16 May 1917, HO45/10776/276521. On prohibited areas, see Panayi, *Enemy in Our Midst*, 50–6, 261.
105. Copy, letter from Norwegian Charge d'Affaires to Foreign Office, n.d., *c.* 6 June 1916; Home Office to Foreign Office, 12 June 1916 (Henricksen), HO144/1299/246192.
106. HO334/87/5992, Chief Constable to Home Office, 29 February 1920; Home Office minute *c.* 1920 (Kwist), HO144/1581/324689. Also see the case of John Zinnis, a Russian residing for 22 years in South Shields, who had claimed to be German for 11 years: 'Question of Nationality. Russian Who Went to Sea as a German. Charge Dismissed at Shields Court', *Shields Gazette* (29 April 1915), back page.
107. On performativity, see S. Maza (1996) 'Stories in History: Cultural Narratives in Recent Works in European History', *American Historical Review* 101, 5: 1493–1515.
108. 'Aliens Restriction Act', *Shields Gazette* (30 April 1915). See other cases in this issue; Panayi, *Enemy in Our Midst*, 48, 60.
109. Chief Constable to Home Office, 15 June 1915 (Erickson), HO144/1365/26 3487.
110. Mrs Mary Ann Erickson to the Home Secretary, 13 July 1916; Grunhut & Gill to the Home Office, 13 July and 21 August 1916, HO144/1365/263487.
111. Grunhut & Gill to the Home Office, 19 March 1917; Home Office to Chief Constable, South Shields, *c.* 23 March 1917 (Gabrielsen), HO144/1404/273678.
112. Memorial, *c.* 20 March 1917; Home Office minute, 30 May 1919 (Hüttmann), HO144/915/353871.
113. Memorial, 23 February 1918; Durham County Constabulary, 9 April 1918; Home Office minute, spring 1918 (Magnan), HO144/1490/355342.
114. Anderson had resided in Britain since age four, minute HO144/1591/382304; and Tubanski since age three. Chief Constable to the Home Office, 11 July 1919, HO144/1370/264514.
115. On the Defence of the Realm Act, or D.O.R.A., and other repressive measures, see Panayi, *Enemy in Our Midst*, 52, 60. Many measures directed at aliens also constrained citizens and subjects. See Torpey, 'Great War and the

Birth of the Modern Passport System'; K. Saunders (2003) ' "The Stranger in our Gates": Internment Policies in the United Kingdom and Australia during the Two World Wars, 1914–1939', *Immigrants and Minorities* 22, 1: 23, 26–7.

116. S. Auerbach (2007) 'Negotiating Nationalism: Jewish Conscription and Russian Repatriation in London's East End, 1916–1918', *Journal of British Studies* 46: 594, 609. On citizenship, military service and German Jewry, see Bering, *Stigma of Names*, 129, 210–12, 243–54.
117. J. Bush (1980) 'East London Jews and the First World War', *London Journal* 6, 2: 153; J.M. Ross (1974) 'Naturalisation of Jews in England', *Transactions of the Jewish Historical Society of England* 24: 68. A prescribed form for 'Friendly Aliens' serving with His Majesty's Forces replaced concessions for mariners. See similar measures in the United States. Horne, *Red Seas*, 86.
118. Leslie Joseph Pearlman, who had lived in Britain since age nine, was refused by the Chief Recruiting Office in Sunderland because he was not naturalized. L.J. Pearlman Memorial, 20 April 1916, HO144/1451/310568. Also see D. Cesarani (1990) 'An Embattled Minority: The Jews in Britain During the First World War', in Kushner and Lunn, *The Politics of Marginality*, 65–6. Jews resisted fighting against German co-religionists in alliance with the hated Russian Empire, in conditions precluding religious observance. Bush, 'East London Jews and the First World War', 148–51, and Auerbach, 'Negotiating Nationalism', 611, 619. On Jews and Czarism, see W.J. Fishman (1974) *Jewish Radicals: From Tsarist Stetl to London Ghetto* (New York: Pantheon).
119. Chief Constable to Home Office, 18 March 1915; Home Office minute, 24 March 1919; Home Office to Chief Constable, 14 April 1919; Chief Constable to Home Office, 18 April 1919; Hannay and Hannay to Home Office, 24 March 1919 (Alder), HO144/1356/261603.
120. Scott to Home Office, 22 March 1915, 2 August 1916, 12 December 1916, 19 January 1917, 5 February 1917, 28 April 1920, 16 November 1925 (David Saville), HO144/5609/262573. Duplicate certificates of naturalization for Leslie Saville, HO334/115/A19545; Emanuel Saville, HO334/133/AZ3790; Leopold Saville, HO334/133/AZ3791.
121. Some 3000 Russians who refused to fight were 'repatriated'. Auerbach, 'Negotiating Nationalism', 601, 609, 613–15, 617; Bush, 'East London Jews', 153–5 and *passim*; Cesarani, 'Embattled Minority', 67–9.
122. Panayi, *Enemy in Our Midst*, 57–8, 153, 181; Cesarani, 'Embattled Minority', 75.
123. Yarrow, 'Impact of Hostility on Germans', 98, 100–2; Panayi, *Enemy in Our Midst*, 41, 52–3, 57, 97, 129, 251–2; Panayi (1996) 'Destruction of the German Communities in Britain during the First World War', in P. Panayi (ed.) *Germans in Britain Since 1500* (London: Hambledon), 119–20, 124–9.
124. 'Ueberblick über die Geschichte der Deutschen Evangelischen Gemeinde in South Shields von ihren Anfängen bis zum 1 Weltkrieg', undated typescript, Records of the South Shields German Church, TWAS C/SS28/11.
125. Charles Rennoldson, 'Herr Singer', letter to the editor of the *Shields Gazette* (23 January 1919).
126. Panayi, 'Anti-German Riots', 66.
127. Panayi, *Enemy in Our Midst*, 235–53; Panayi, 'Anti-German Riots', 70–87; 'Germans Mobbed', *Shields Gazette* (13 May 1915).

128. 'Alien Enemies: Premier's Announcement in the Commons', *Shields Gazette* (14 May 1915); Panayi, *Enemy in Our Midst*, 249–50. On violence elsewhere in the Northeast, see 'Rioting at North Shields' *Shields Gazette* (15 May 1915), back page; 'Charges at North Shields Court: Not Playing the Game', *Shields Gazette* (17 May 1915).
129. 'Mischief in the Air', *Shields Gazette* (17 May 1915); 'The Anti-German Riots', *Shields Gazette* (18 May 1915). Also see Panayi's account, *Enemy in Our Midst*, 251–3.
130. Testimony of Superintendant Young, Inspector Jagger and Chief Constable Scott at the subsequent trial, 'The Anti-German Riots at South Shields', *Shields Gazette* (17 May 1915).
131. 'Turbulent Scenes on Saturday Night', *Shields Gazette* (17 May 1915).
132. Depositions of James Armstrong, P.S. 16, and George V. Bell, P.C. 39, Police Constable James Anderson, Special Constable Joseph Lumley and Constable Alfred Key, 24 August 1915, Claims Under Riot Damages Act, 1886, Town Clerk's Department, South Shields County Borough Corporation, TWAS T95/172. Twelve South Shields merchants sought compensation, most of them naturalized British subjects.
133. Nationally the Unionist press and politicians instigated violence while unions, Labour and the Liberals denounced it. Panayi, *Enemy in Our Midst*, 233–4, 274–8.
134. 'The Anti-German Riots', *Shields Gazette* (15 May 1915), 3.
135. Panayi, 'Anti-German Riots', 89–90; N. Gullace (2005) 'Friends, Aliens, and Enemies: Fictive Communities and the Lusitania Riots of 1915', *Journal of Social History* 39, 2: 362.
136. 'Turbulent Scenes on Saturday Night', *Shields Gazette* (17 May 1915); 'The Anti-German Riots in Shields', *Shields Gazette* (Thursday, 20 May 1915).
137. Saunders, 'The Stranger in our Gates', 27, 40 n. 26; Sir Edward Troup, memorandum: 'Treatment of Alien Enemies', n.d., *c.* June 1918, War Cabinet Documents, TNA CAB24/55 (GT4931) ff129–132.
138. Panayi, 'The Destruction of the German Communities', 121–3; Panayi, *Enemy in Our Midst*, 77–80, 91; Panayi, *Immigration, Ethnicity and Racism*, 106, 124. For a poignant account of internees' hardships, see Gullace, 'Friends, Aliens, and Enemies', 357–60.
139. (Gustinger), HO144/1076/192256. The United States, of course, proved only a temporary haven. By March 1928, Frank Zaganowsky resided in Eldon Street, South Shields, HO144/1244/231776. His wife appeared in the electoral rolls for 1934 living at 5 South Eldon Street in Rekendyke Ward, holding the married woman's franchise. The couples may have been acquainted as the license for 11 Nelson's Bank passed from Zaganowsky to Gustinger, *Council Minutes* 18 September 1901, 1066. On Speyer, see Yarrow, 'Impact of Hostility on Germans', 112 n. 51.
140. Panayi, 'Destruction of the German Communities', 118–20; Saunders, 'The Stranger in our Gates', 23, 31–2.
141. Panayi, *Enemy in Our Midst*, 95–8; Yarrow, 'The Impact of Hostility on Germans', 101, 109–10.
142. *1911 Census Report: Birthplaces* PP1913 [Cd.7017] IX, Table 3, 121; *1921 Census of England and Wales* (London: HMSO, 1923), County of Durham, Table 22, 99.

143. D. Clark (1992) *We Do Not Want the Earth: The History of South Shields Labour Party* (Whitley Bay: Bewick Press), 25, 35, 39–44, 47, 57–8.
144. Yarrow, 'Impact of Hostility on Germans', 96–112; Saunders, 'Stranger in our Gates', 27–8, 40 n. 30; Cesarani, 'Embattled Minority', 61–81. *1911 General Census Report with Appendices* PP1917–18 [Cd.8491] XXXV, 219.
145. Zolberg, 'International Migration Policies in a Changing World System', 276. Except for military cases and widows of aliens recovering their British nationality, naturalization was effectively suspended during the war. Ross, 'Naturalisation of Jews in England', 68. In South Shields, nearly all 54 persons naturalized between 1915 and 1924 were widows, soldiers, in jeopardy of their jobs or men who had lived in Britain since childhood.
146. 'Admiralty Work and Foreign Employees', TWAS 1826/45/1.
147. Zolberg, 'International Migration Policies in a Changing World System', 280.
148. A. Miles (1999) *Social Mobility in Nineteenth- and Early Twentieth-Century England* (New York: St Martin's Press); D. Feldman (1989) 'The Importance of Being English: Jewish Immigration and the Decay of Liberal England', in D. Feldman and G. Stedman Jones (eds) *Metropolis London: Histories and Representations Since 1800* (London: Routledge), 56–84; D.A. Lorimer (1978) *Colour, Class, and the Victorians: English Attitudes to the Negro in the Mid-Nineteenth Century* (Leicester: Leicester University Press).
149. S. Hochstadt (1999) *Mobility and Modernity: Migration in Germany, 1820–1989* (Ann Arbor: University of Michigan Press), 10, 35–49; B. Studer (2001) 'Citizenship as Contingent National Belonging: Married Women and Foreigners in Twentieth-Century Switzerland' (trans. K. Sturge) *Gender and History* 13, 3: 622–54.

## 8 I Give My Missus the 28 Shillings: Everyday Forms of Accommodation

1. Depositions of Nagi Mohamed, 24 May 1929, and Lauretta Clarice Lee, 1 July 1929, Durham Autumn Assizes, Rex v. Nagi Mohamed, The National Archives (hereafter TNA) ASSI45/89/10.
2. On acculturation, see D. Hoerder (1996) 'From Migrants to Ethnics: Acculturation in a Societal Framework', in D. Hoerder and L.P. Moch (eds) *European Migrants: Global and Local Perspectives* (Boston: Northeastern), 211–17. On strategic use of local dialect, see S.K. Phillips (1994) 'Natives and Incomers: The Symbolism of Belonging in Muker Parish, North Yorkshire', in M. Drake (ed.) *Time, Family, and Community: Perspectives on Family and Community History* (Oxford: Blackwell), 225–39; R. Colls and B. Lancaster (eds) (2005 [1992]) *Geordies: Roots of Regionalism* (Newcastle: Northumbria University Press), 22, 145.
3. Some made the historical and conceptual linkages, but as sociologists or anthropologists could not perform fieldwork with nineteenth-century migrants. See K. Little (1972 [1948]) *Negroes in Britain: A Study of Race Relations in an English City* (London: Routledge & Kegan Paul); M.P. Banton (1955) *The Coloured Quarter: Negro Immigrants in an English City* (London: Jonathan Cape), 18–36.

4. Duffield (1993) 'Skilled Workers or Marginalised Poor? The African Population of the United Kingdom, 1812–52', *Immigrants and Minorities* 12, 3: 49–87, offered a pithy assessment of the literature to 1993. Also D. Killingray (1993) 'Africans in the United Kingdom: An Introduction', *Immigrants and Minorities* 12, 3: 2–27, esp. 11, 17; J. Green (1998) *Black Edwardians: Black People in Britain 1901–1914* (London: Frank Cass); M.H. Fisher (2004) *Counterflows to Colonialism: Indian Travellers and Settlers in Britain, 1600–1857* (Delhi: Permanent Black).
5. D. Lorimer (1978) *Colour, Class, and the Victorians: English Attitudes to the Negro in the Mid-Nineteenth Century* (Leicester: Leicester University Press/Holmes & Meier), 13, 16–17, 38–43 and *passim.*
6. On these centripetal forces, see L. Tabili (1994) *'We Ask for British Justice': Workers and Racial Difference in Late Imperial Britain* (Ithaca: Cornell University Press).
7. S.F. Collins (1957) *Coloured Minorities in Britain: Studies in British Race Relations Based on African, West Indian and Asiatic Immigrants* (London: Lutterworth); N. Todd (1987) 'Black on Tyne', *Northeast Labour History Bulletin* 21: 17–27.
8. D. Bean (1971) *Tyneside: A Biography* (London: Macmillan), 186–7.
9. Carr, 'Black Geordies', 136, 138–9, 144, 146.
10. D. Byrne (1976–77) 'The 1930 "Arab Riot": A Race Riot That Never Was', *Race and Class* 18: 261–77.
11. R. Lawless (1995) *From Ta'izz to Tyneside: An Arab Community in the North-East of England During the Early Twentieth Century* (Exeter: Exeter University Press), esp. 1, 5, 86–92.
12. C.F. El-Solh (1993) '"Be True to Your Culture": Gender Tensions Among Somali Muslims in Britain', *Immigrants and Minorities* 12, 1: 24, 31; Shamis Hussein (1993) minimized intermarriage yet interviewed Marian Abdullahi whose great-grandmother was Welsh, in 'Somalis in London', in N. Merriman (ed.) *The Peopling of London: Fifteen Thousand Years of Settlement From Overseas* (London: Museum of London), 163.
13. C. Cookson (1971 [1968]) *Colour Blind* (London: Corgi); Lawless, *From Ta'izz to Tyneside,* esp. Chapters 3 and 4; Carr, 'Black Geordies', esp. 136, 138–9, 144, 146.
14. Tabili, *'We Ask for British Justice'.*
15. Although P. Panayi (1991) acknowledged anti-Germanism paved the way for the 1919 riots in *The Enemy in Our Midst: Germans in Britain During the First World War* (New York: Berg), 288, elsewhere (1994) he defined racism as a 'constant' punctuated by 'peaks' of large-scale open conflict in *Immigration, Ethnicity and Racism in Britain, 1815–1845* (Manchester: Manchester University Press), 125; a 'universal', 'underlying' 'background' an 'ever-present factor' (1996), begging the question of causality, in *Racial Violence in the Nineteenth and Twentieth Centuries* (Leicester: Leicester University Press), 15, 18–20; while N. Evans (1985) attributed discrimination and violence in Cardiff to 'racist urges', in 'Regulating the Reserve Army: Arabs, Blacks and the Local State in Cardiff, 1919–1945', in K. Lunn (ed.) *Race and Labour in Twentieth Century Britain* (London: Frank Cass), 68. In contrast, A. Dunlop (1990) pointed out that racist discourses directed against Indians echoed prior hostility to the Irish and Lithuanians, in 'Lascars and

Labourers: Reactions to the Indian Presence in the West of Scotland during the 1920s and 1930s', *Scottish Labour History Society Journal* 25: 49. Thanks to Anna Clark for this article.

16. P. Wolfe (2001) 'Land, Labor, and Difference: Elementary Structures of Race', *American Historical Review* 106: 866–905, esp. 894; B.J. Field (1990) 'Slavery, Race and Ideology in the United States of America', *New Left Review* 181: 95–118.
17. D. Nirenberg (1996) *Communities of Violence: Persecution of Minorities in the Middle Ages* (Princeton: Princeton University Press), 3, 5, 9–11, 13, 15, 35.
18. J. Robinson (ed.) (1997) *Francie* (Newcastle: TUPS); J. Kirkup (1996) *A Child of the Tyne* (Salzburg: University of Salzburg Press).
19. J. Carney, R. Hudson, G. Ive and J. Lewis (1976) 'Regional Underdevelopment in Late Capitalism: A Study of the Northeast of England', in I. Masser (ed.) *Theory and Practice in Regional Science* (London: Pion/Academic), 20.
20. As the manuscript censuses are closed for 100 years, those for 1911, 1921 and 1931 will not be open for some time.
21. Before 1918, 28 per cent of men in South Shields remained unenfranchised, 76 per cent of single men nationally. D. Clark (1992) *We Do Not Want the Earth: The History of South Shields Labour Party* (Whitley Bay: Bewick), 48.
22. See R.J. Johnson (1971) 'Resistance to Migration and the Mover/Stayer Dichotomy: Aspects of Kinship and Population Stability in an English Rural Area', *Geografiska Annaler* ser. B, 53: 16–27, and discussion about identifying Jews in Chapter 3.
23. On Frederick Sveden, see RG13/4728 1901 f93; on Samuel Camilleri, see RG13/4734 1901 f43. Common Lodging Houses became regulated in the 1890s. South Shields Corporation, *Minutes of Proceedings*, 24 May 1894, 324; hereafter *Corporation Minutes*, South Tyneside Central Library (hereafter STCL.).
24. G.B. Hodgson (1996 [1903]) *The Borough of South Shields: From the Earliest Period to the Close of the Nineteenth Century* (South Shields: South Tyneside Libraries), 207–8; John Spear, Medical Officer of Health, *Report on the Health of South Shields for the Year 1876* (South Shields: Joseph R. Lackland, 1877), 20, hereafter *Medical Officer of Health Report*, STCL.
25. *Medical Officer of Health Reports* for 1890, vi, and 1903, 20.
26. William George Morant, *Report of the Police Establishment 1896*, 7; William Scott, *Report of the Police Establishment 1910*, Table 21, 31, STCL.
27. D. Feldman (1994) *Englishmen and Jews: Social Relations and Political Culture 1840–1914* (New Haven: Yale University Press).
28. H. Southall (1996) 'Agitate! Agitate! Organize! Political Travellers and the Construction of a National Politics', *Transactions of the Institute of British Geographers* new ser. 21, 1: 177–93; C. Stephenson (1979) 'A Gathering of Strangers? Mobility, Social Structure, and Political Participation in the Formation of Nineteenth-Century American Workingclass Culture', in M. Cantor (ed.) *American Workingclass Culture: Explorations in American Labor and Social History* (Westport: Greenwood), 31–60.
29. Local pulmonary tuberculosis rates had actually remained relatively stable for 40 years. *Medical Officer of Health Report, 1916*, 12; quoted matter from *Medical Officer of Health Report, 1920*, 24. Also see W. Campbell Lyons' report to the Health Committee on *The Prevalence of Tuberculosis*

*in South Shields*, March 1930, 7–11, 14, 25, 32; and his *Annual Report of the School Medical Officer for the Year 1933*, 73–6. The local newspaper, the *Shields Gazette*, helped publicize these spurious views, Lawless, *From Ta'izz to Tyneside*, 190–4. Also see M. Worboys (1999) 'Tuberculosis and Race in Britain and its Empire, 1900–50', in W. Ernst and B. Harris (eds) *Race, Science and Medicine, 1700–1960* (London: Routledge), 144–66; A.M. Kraut (1994) *Silent Travelers: Germs, Genes and the 'Immigrant Menace'* (New York: Basic); Evans, 'Regulating the Reserve Army', 93–5.

30. High Northeastern tuberculosis rates correlated to overcrowded housing, H.A. Mess (1928) *Industrial Tyneside: A Social Survey* (London: Ernest Benn), 92, 111. Figures for Jarrow and Hebburn appear on 110–11.
31. 'Brewster Sessions', *Shields Gazette* (5 February 1919), 5. Also 'Foreigners and Drink', *Shields Gazette* (1 February 1919), 2.
32. Shiavux Cawasje Driver, who operated laundries in 15 1/2 Green Street and 73 Mile End Road was likely a Parsi or Zoroastrian, found in *Ward's Directory 1932*. See C. Geshekter (1985), on Parsi family Cowasji Dinshaw in Somalia, 'Anti-Colonialism and Class Formation: The Eastern Horn of Africa Before 1950', *International Journal of African Historical Studies* 18: 19.
33. Byrne, 'The 1930 "Arab Riot" ', 265. Also see T. Lane (1986) *Grey Dawn Breaking: British Merchant Seafarers in the Late Twentieth Century* (Manchester: Manchester University Press), 17–18, 32.
34. Based on analysis of Duplicate Certificates of Naturalization, 1935–39, HO334, TNA.
35. On Faid and Nassar Abdula, see 'Shields Murder', *Shields Gazette* (25 February 1919), 3; on Ghulam Rasul, Home Office papers, HO45/15774/607696/16; Samuel Grant to Commissioner of Police, Freetown, 16 February 1936, CO323/1365/55; Perla, HO334/143/AZ8722.
36. R.B. Serjeant (1981 [1968]) *Studies in Arabian History and Civilization* (London: Varorium Reprints), 207–8, 214; R.L. Playfair (1859) *An Account of Aden*, repr. from *A History of Arabia Felix* (Aden: Printed at the Jail Press for Cowasjee Dinshaw), 2–29, 36, 51–6, 60.
37. 'Evacuation of Somaliland, November–December 1940', CO535/136/4621 3/6, TNA; F.M. Hunter (1968 [*c.* 1870s]) *An Account of the British Settlement of Aden in Arabia* (London: Frank Cass), 42.
38. F. Halliday (1992) *Arabs in Exile: Yemeni Migrants in Urban Britain* (New York: Tauris), 12.
39. Governor of Aden to Colonial Office, 16 March 1938, CO725/54/9. Also see Lawless, *From Ta'izz to Tyneside*, 29–46.
40. Aden Resident to the Government of India, 27 November and 24 December 1929, and telegram, 11 January 1930, India Office Records, (c) British Library Board, hereafter IOR, L/E/9/954.
41. Halliday, *Arabs in Exile*, 8–16, esp. 12.
42. G.H. Summers (1924) 'Somaliland', in C. Lucas (ed.) *Empire at War*, Vol. 4 (London: Humphrey Milford), 565.
43. Colonial Office minute, 'Destitute Somali Seamen', September 1921, CO535/68/45715; also see B.A. Byatt, Somaliland Commissioner's Office, 21 November 1910, CO535/20/36983; E.A. Alpers (1986) 'The Somali Community at Aden in the Nineteenth Century', *Northeast African Studies* 8: 143–5; Lane, *Grey Dawn Breaking*, 18.

44. Hunter, *An Account of the British Settlement of Aden*, 28, 31, 35, 40–2; Alpers, 'The Somali Community at Aden', 143–4, 150–1. C. Geshekter (1985) 'Anti-Colonialism and Class Formation: The Eastern Horn of Africa Before 1950', *International Journal of African Historical Studies* 18: 20; Lawless, *From Ta'izz to Tyneside*, 18–19.
45. Brown, RG13/4727 1901 f14; also Aden-born James Best, RG13/4737 1901 f163.
46. Correspondence from Ahmed Alwin, 19 January 1926, and Syed Mehdi, 21 January 1926, IOR L/E/9/953.
47. *Corporation Minutes*, 18 August 1909, 257. Ali Said claimed in 1917 to have arrived in 1896, Lawless, *From Ta'izz to Tyneside*, 10.
48. *Corporation Minutes*, 17 July 1912, 61, and 18 September 1912, 418.
49. *Corporation Minutes*, 19 December 1917, 660; 20 February 1918, 146. On Ruddock, see HO45/11897/332087.
50. See Samuel Camelleri, RG13/4734 1901 f43. Zaganowsky operated 20 Nelson's Bank as late as 20 September 1905, per *Corporation Minutes*, 425, but Muckble held the license by 13 October 1915, per *Corporation Minutes*, 446.
51. On this strategy, see D.R. Gabaccia and F. Iacovetta (2002) *Women, Gender, and Transnational Lives: Italian Workers of the World* (Toronto: University of Toronto Press), 13.
52. Warrant and Commitment Books, 1914–28, South Shields Constabulary, Tyne & Wear Archives Service (hereafter TWAS) T151/152 and /153. Documents were available for these years only. On arbitration, see Lawless, *From Ta'izz to Tyneside*, 51, 61–5.
53. Also see prosecutions by Mohamed Muckble, 15 September 1917 and 24 August 1918, T151/152 and /153.
54. This despite Ali Said's somewhat self-serving assertions to the contrary. Lawless, *From Ta'izz to Tyneside*, 53, 190.
55. Cardiff Chief Constable to the Home Office, 18 June 1919; and newscutting from *Manchester Guardian* (13 June 1919), both in HO45/11017/377969.
56. The quote is from R.J. Parker, Principal Admiralty Transport Officer, Cardiff, 28 June 1916, CO535/44; the figure 700 comes from 'The Arab', *Shields Gazette* (11 March 1919); Minute, 'Destitute Somali Seamen', September 1921, CO535/68/45715.
57. These included Mahomet Salim for 24 Long Row; Faid Abdula for 63 Thrift Street; Abdul Abraham for 81 East Holborn; Mary Ellen Said for 79a East Holborn. *Corporation Minutes*, 22 March 1916, 295; 19 April 1916, 438; 29 May 1916, 544; 21 June 1916, 648. Also see 13 October 1915, 443; 19 January 1916, 48; Lawless, *From Ta'izz to Tyneside*, 11.
58. South Shields Immigration Officer to Home Office, 23 January 1920, HO11897/332087/17.
59. *Medical Officer of Health Reports* for 1919, 8; 1920, 24. Also see Lawless, *From Ta'izz to Tyneside*, 11, 15.
60. L. Tabili (1994) 'The Construction of Racial Difference: The Special Restriction (Coloured Alien Seamen) Order, 1925', *Journal of British Studies* 33: 54–98.
61. Corresponding figures for Cardiff can be found in Little, *Negroes in Britain*, 98; also see Evans, 'Regulating the Reserve Army', 68–9, 86.

62. PC R.J. Hetherington to South Shields Chief Constable, 17 September 1935, CO3232/1323/13.
63. Samuel Grant aka Joe Fanday to Commissioner of Police, Freetown, 16 February 1936, CO323/1365/5.
64. In contrast, Newcastle had only four Jamaicans and four Sierra Leoneans. 'North East England District: Summary of Returns Furnished by Superintendants of the Numbers of Coloured Seamen Unemployed, etc.', 29 July 1930, CO725/21/8.
65. Mess, *Industrial Tyneside*, 35. The 1931 census showed 258 Scandinavians as opposed to 123 men from the Indian Empire and 419 'Other Asians', most of them likely Arabs. Fifty German men and 29 women also appeared. *Census of England and Wales 1931—General Tables: Population, Institutions, Ages and Marital Conditions, Birthplace and Nationality, Welsh Language* (London: HMSO, 1935), Table 30, 187.
66. For instance, Wilhelmina and Abdul Ali, HO334/149 (1938); Wilhelmina and Mohamed Musleh, HO334/146 (1937) discussed above.
67. A ship's runner 'obtained crews of Arab and Indian ships', per Eva Gertrude Martin. Depositions of Jane Macey, Frederick Elder and Eva Gertrude Martin, 1 August 1929, Rex v. Nagi Mohamed, ASSI/45/89/10. Franklin was reputedly a Maori from New Zealand. Lawless, *From Ta'izz to Tyneside*, 65.
68. On working-class matrifocality, see M. Young and P. Willmott (1957) *Family and Kinship in East London* (Harmondsworth: Penguin).
69. Fareh, HO334/139. Ahmed Sherrif resided at 74 Wapping Street in 1925. Also see Mohamed Logan, residing at 25 East Holborn in 1918.
70. Mahomed and Isabella Mosley, HO334/146/AZ10191; Ahmed and Christine Awad, HO334/140/AZ7378; Ali and Mary Mathewson Nasin, HO334/141/AZ7951, July 1936; Hamad and Jenny Sherrif, HO334/142/AZ 8438, July 1936; Abdul and Wilhelmina Ali, HO334/149/AZ11783.
71. Ahmed and Abdulla in *Ward's Directory 1932*; Cassem in *Ward's Directory 1924*.
72. Mackmute, *Ward's Directory 1920*; Alwin, *Ward's Directory 1920* and *1924*.
73. Single men estimated by subtracting women from men.
74. 1925 Parliamentary Electoral Rolls, STCL. Also see households containing Abdulla Raga, 25 Alderson Street, 1930; Aron and Frances Sayeed, 42 Maxwell Street, 1930 and 1936, Hilda Ward; Ahmed Ali, 38 Dock Street, Tyne Dock, 1936.
75. Rex v. Ali Said and others *c.*, August 1930, TWAS T95/152.
76. Lawless, *From Ta'izz to Tyneside*, 195, 205; Carr, 'Black Geordies', 138–9.
77. On Liverpool's 'no-go' areas, see D. Frost (2000) 'Ambiguous Identities: Constructing and De-constructing Black and White "Scouse" Identities in Twentieth Century Liverpool', in N. Kirk (ed.) *Northern Identities: Historical Interpretations of 'The North' and 'Northernness'* (Aldershot: Ashgate), 204; on Cardiff, Evans, 'Regulating the Reserve Army', 73; N. Sinclair (1993) *The Tiger Bay Story* (Cardiff: Butetown History and Arts Project), 34–6. Thanks to Anna Davin for this source. For a different view, see S. Collins (1955–56) 'The British-Born Coloured', *Sociological Review* 3: 83–4.
78. For 1930 estimates from the *Shields Gazette*, see Lawless, *From Ta'izz to Tyneside*, 175, 188; and for 1934 figures, 195, 201.

79. Nine Arab households were sole occupiers of their buildings, and 48 Arab families lived in ten buildings occupied solely by other Arabs, amounting to 24 per cent of such families. Mohammed Salleh owned one of a small handful of properties entirely occupied by Arabs, a shop and other premises at 27–29 East Holborn. 'Register of Houses in Clearance Areas, 1931–1935', TWAS T/28/20–24.
80. On these complaints, see Collins, *Coloured Minorities in Britain*, 157, also 152–9; Lawless, *From Ta'izz to Tyneside*, 194–206.
81. Lawless, *From Ta'izz to Tyneside*, 195–201.
82. 'Funeral of the Victim', *Shields Gazette* (21 February 1919), 4.
83. Grunhut, Grunhut & Makepeace to Town Clerk, 15 and 17 April 1936, Watch Committee Minutes, TWAS 229/58.
84. See Collins, *Coloured Minorities in Britain*, 210; Lawless, *From Ta'izz to Tyneside*, 53.
85. *Medical Officer of Health Report* for 1928, 101.
86. Lawless, *From Ta'izz to Tyneside*, 208.
87. Also see Collins, *Coloured Minorities in Britain*, 207; Register of licenses of Slaughter-men, 1936–1950s, TWAS T179/538. Compare to postwar brouhaha over halal school meals, C. Husband (1994) 'The Political Context of Muslim Communities' Participation in British Society', in B. Lewis and D. Schnapper (eds) *Muslims in Europe* (London: Pinter), 91–2.
88. Lawless, *From Ta'izz to Tyneside*, 210, 212, 221, 228, 284 fn. 7. Also see Lane, *Grey Dawn Breaking*, 120–1.
89. 'Behind the Invasion by Destitute Arabs', *The Seaman* (22 October 1930), 5; S.F. Collins (1951) 'The Social Position of White and "Half-Caste" Women in Colored Groupings in Britain', *American Sociological Review* 16: 798.
90. Quotes from Lawless, *From Ta'izz to Tyneside*, 221–3; Collins, *Coloured Minorities in Britain*, 184–7; Collins, 'The British-Born Coloured', 80. On Salford's similarly capricious press, see J. Jenkinson (1988) 'The Black Community of Salford and Hull, 1919–1921', *Immigrants and Minorities* 7, 2: 171.
91. For the former, see Lawless, *From Ta'izz to Tyneside, passim*; for for the latter, see Halliday, *Arabs in Exile*, 47–9.
92. Case of Abdullah Ahmed aka Hasan Karika discussed in Home Office minute, 20 March 1924, HO45/11897/332087/86. On James Muir Smith, councillor for Westoe Ward in the 1890s, see *Corporation Minutes*, 9 November 1894, 657, STCL; Byrne, 'The 1930 "Arab Riot" ', 116; on Grunhut, RG12/4155 1891 f75v, RG11/5010 1881 f4, RG13/4730 1901 f161; Lawless, *From Ta'izz to Tyneside*, 176.
93. N. McCord (1980) 'Early Seamen's Unions in North East England', in P. Adam (ed.) *Seamen in Society* (Bucharest: Commission Internationale d'Histoire Maritime), III, 91.
94. Dictated letter from Seamen's Mission, Sunderland to High Commissioner for India, 13 March 1936, CO725/34/8. Also see South Shields PC Hetherington, 17 April 1935, CO535/111/46017.
95. Byrne alleged the National Maritime Board reinforced the divisive preference for 'local men' in 'The 1930 "Arab Riot" ', 264, but my point is that it was not racially exclusive.

96. On women as victims and perpetrators in the *Lusitania* riots, see P. Panayi (1996) *Racial Violence in Britain in the 19th and 20th Centuries* (Leicester: Leicester University Press), 79–87. Also see L. Tabili (2005) 'Outsiders in the Land of Their Birth: Exogamy, Citizenship, and Identity in War and Peace', *Journal of British Studies* 44: 796–815.
97. Lawless, *From Ta'izz to Tyneside*, 174–84.; L. Bland (2005) 'White Women and Men of Colour: Miscegenation Fears in Britain after the Great War', *Gender and History* 17, 1: 29–61; Frost, 'Ambiguous Identities', Evans, 'Regulating the Reserve Army', 86–95.
98. Principally Sydney Collins, who observed and analysed women's role in these settlements with insight and sensitivity, and without the invective found in other such works, in 'Social Position of White and "Half-Caste" Women', 801; Collins, *Coloured Minorities in Britain, passim.*
99. Lawless, *From Ta'izz to Tyneside*, 174–206 and *passim.*
100. Frost, 'Ambiguous Identities', 206–7; Collins, *Coloured Minorities in Britain*, 23–4, 61–6, 160, 180.
101. M.L. Wong (1989) *Chinese Liverpudlians: A History of the Chinese Community in Liverpool* (Birkenhead: Liver Press), 66–73.
102. Collins, *Coloured Minorities in Britain*, 163, 165, 205; also Wong, *Chinese Liverpudlians*, 68.
103. Collins, *Coloured Minorities in Britain*, 202; Collins, 'Social Position of White and "Half-Caste" Women', 801.
104. Tabili, *'We Ask for British Justice'*, 75, 101, 106, 108, 144–5.
105. Analogously, see A. Miles (1999) *Social Mobility in Nineteenth- and Early Twentieth-Century England* (New York: St Martin's Press), 145–75.
106. Collins, *Coloured Minorities in Britain*, 162–7 and *passim*; Collins, 'Social Position of White and "Half-Caste" Women', 797–802. Unnamed Cardiff police detective, quoted in *Daily Herald* (11 January 1929), found in HO45/13392/493912/95. Also see Wong, *Chinese Liverpudlians*, 66–73; Sinclair, *The Tiger Bay Story*, esp. 34; L. Tabili (1996) 'Women "of a Very Low Type": Crossing Racial Boundaries in Late Imperial Britain', in L.L. Frader and S.O. Rose (eds) *Gender and Class in Modern Europe* (Ithaca: Cornell University Press), 165–90; J. Jenkinson (1985) 'The Glasgow Race Disturbances of 1919', in Lunn (ed.) *Race and Labour in Twentieth Century Britain*, 62; on exogamy see Noiriel, *The French Melting Pot*, 152.
107. Deposition of Lauretta Lee, ASSI45/89/10.
108. Collins, *Coloured Minorities in Britain*, 162, 167. In contrast, see S. Westwood (1985) *All Day, Every Day: Factory and Family in the Making of Women's Lives* (Urbana: University of Illinois Press), 102–28.
109. See R.S. Parreñas (1998) ' "White Trash" Meets the "Little Brown Monkeys": The Taxi Dance Hall as a Site of Interracial and Gender Alliances Between White Working Class Women and Filipino Immigrant Men in the 1920s and 1930s', *Amerasia* 24, 2: 129–30; M. Nava (2007) *Visceral Cosmopolitanism: Gender, Culture and the Normalisation of Difference* (London: Berg), 115–16 and *passim.*
110. 'Koran' is an Anglicized version of the Arabic 'Qur'an'.
111. Collins, *Coloured Minorities in Britain*, 55–8, 155–8, 162, 166–7, 211; also D. Frost (1999) *Work and Community Among West African Migrant Workers in the Nineteenth Century* (Liverpool:Liverpool University Press), 203.

112. Deposition of Lauretta Lee, ASSI45/89/10; Collins, *Coloured Minorities in Britain*, 202; also Lawless, *From Ta'izz to Tyneside*, 92–8.
113. 'An Eye-Witness', *Shields Gazette* (14 May 1919), 3.
114. 'Boarding House Tragedy', *Shields Gazette* (11 March 1919), 3.
115. 'Another Stage in Arab Tragedy', *Shields Gazette* (12 March 1919), 3.
116. 'Inquest Resumed', *Shields Gazette* (11 March 1919), 3.
117. Collins, *Coloured Minorities in Britain*, 178–80.
118. Yussif Hersi Sulliman to the BBC in Newcastle, 26 November 1938, CO725/66/17. On Sulliman, also see minute CO323/1365/5; 'Status of Somali Seamen in U.K', CO535/135/3.
119. Lawless, *From Ta'izz to Tyneside*, 92–8, 184–7, 203. Also see Collins, *Coloured Minorities in Britain*, 23; Frost, 'Ambiguous Identities', 204–7.
120. See M. Conte-Helm (1989) *Japan and the North East of England: From 1862 to the Present Day* (London: Athlone).
121. 'Holborn Disturbance', *Shields Gazette* (18 February 1919), back page.
122. *Shields Gazette* (14 January 1919), 3; Extract from Police Occurrence Book, Thursday, 9 January 1919, and statements of Thomas George Young and Detective Sergeant Wilson, 'Claims Under Riot Damages Act, 1886', TWAS T95/172.
123. Collins, *Coloured Minorities in Britain*, 57.
124. Quote from 'Another Stage in Arab Tragedy', *Shields Gazette* (12 March 1919), 3; 'Shields Murder', *Shields Gazette* (19 February 1919), 3; 'Shields Murder', *Shields Gazette* (25 February 1919), 3; 'Boarding House Tragedy', *Shields Gazette* (11 March 1919), 3. The brothers were Cairenes. 'Shields Murder', *Shields Gazette* (25 February 1919), 3. On this unsolved murder, see Lawless, *From Ta'izz to Tyneside*, 52–3.
125. L. Tabili (2005) 'Empire is the Enemy of Love: Edith Noor's Progress and Other Stories', *Gender and History* 17, 1: 5–28. For contrasting policy, see N. Myers (1992) 'In Search of the Invisible: British Black Family and Community, 1780–1830', *Slavery and Abolition* 13, 3: 166; I. Land (2005) 'Bread and Arsenic: Citizenship from the Bottom Up in Georgian London', *Journal of Social History* 39, 1: 102.
126. H.W. Smith (1998) 'The Talk of Genocide, the Rhetoric of Miscegenation: Notes on Debates in the German Reichstag Concerning Southwest Africa, 1904–14', in S. Friedrichsmeyer, S. Lennox and S. Zantop (eds) *The Imperialist Imagination: German Colonialism and its Legacy* (Ann Arbor: University of Michigan Press), 110–23. Two such couples did return to Canada and Barbados, Jenkinson, 'The Black Community of Salford and Hull', 182.
127. 'Shields Arab Tragedies', *Shields Gazette* (26 June 1919), 6 o'clock edition, 3.
128. Quote is from by Mr Logan, MP, in Parliamentary Debates (Commons) Vol. 34, cols 970–971, 983 (10 July 1935). On 25 March 1924 alone, dependents of 18 Arabs applied for relief as the breadwinner had been deported. South Shields Poor Law Union, Relief Committee Minute Book April 1919–May 1925, TWAS T81/81.
129. Figures tabulated from duplicate certificates of naturalization, TNA HO334.
130. Collins, *Coloured Minorities in Britain*, 152–3, 160–1.
131. Colonial Office minute by W.J. Bigg, 20 August 1934, CO535/105/6; Joe Fanday aka Samuel Grant to Commissioner of Police, Freetown, 16 February 1936, CO323/1365/5. See also D. Frost (1993) 'Ethnic Identity, Transience,

and Settlement: The Kru in Liverpool Since the Late Nineteenth Century', *Immigrants and Minorities* 12, 3: 95.

132. See also D. Frost, 'Ethnic Identity, Transience, and Settlement', 89.
133. Exceptions included a handful of Latvians and the lone Indian States subject.
134. On intermarriage as a 'measure of relative integration', see D.F. Crew (1979) *Town in the Ruhr: A Social History of Bochum, 1860–1914* (New York: Columbia University Press), 171; J. Foster (1979 [1974]) *Class Struggle and the Industrial Revolution: Early Industrial Capitalism in Three English Towns* (London: Methuen), 125–6; C.G. Pooley (1977) 'The Residential Segregation of Migrant Communities in Mid-Victorian Liverpool', *Transactions of the Institute of British Geographers* 2nd ser., 2: 74–5.
135. Collins, *Coloured Minorities in Britain*, 18, 164–5. On boarding housekeepers, see Lawless, *From Ta'izz to Tyneside*, 47–73; Tabili, *'We Ask for British Justice'*, 141–3, 147, 151–4.
136. Lawless, *From Ta'izz to Tyneside*, 69–70; deposition of Lauretta Lee, ASSI45/89/10. On postwar continuities, see Collins, *Coloured Minorities in Britain*, 211.
137. D. Lawless (1995) 'The Role of Seamen's Agents in the Migration for Employment of Arab Seafarers in the Early Twentieth Century', in D. Frost (ed.) *Ethnic Labour and British Imperial Trade: A History of Ethnic Seafarers in the UK* (London: Frank Cass), 34–58.
138. Minutes of meeting, 19 March 1919, *Corporation Minutes* (January–June 1919), 345.
139. Aden Resident's telegram to the Colonial Office, 11 April 1935, CO725/33/6.
140. 'Minute of a Conference 3 May 1929', IOR L/E9/954; Collins, *Coloured Minorities in Britain*, 156, 183, 194–5, 209–10, 216; Little, *Negroes in Britain*, 60–3; Lawless, *From Ta'izz to Tyneside*, 51, 61–5.
141. Letter from T. Lally of the India Office, 11 January 1928, 24 January 1928, HO45/13392/493912/41. On the rota, see Tabili, *'We Ask for British Justice'*, 106–9.
142. Quote from Victor Grunhut, 'Shields Murder', *Shields Gazette* (25 February 1919), 3. Also see Collins, 'British-Born Coloured', 80.
143. High Commissioner for India to the Home Office, *c.* January 1928, HO45/13392/493912; minute, n.d., winter 1931–32, 'Status of Somalis in Great Britain', 1931, CO535/94/38610.
144. 'Seaport Town's Problem', *Public Assistance and Health and Hospital Review* (10 October 1930), 1281, cutting in IOR L/E/9/954; Byrne, 'The 1930 "Arab Riot" ', 273–4; Lawless, *From Ta'izz to Tyneside*, 161–5. For the policy change withholding outdoor relief, see Relief Committee Minute Book, Shields District, 25 September 1930, TWAS T81/84.
145. Draft Colonial Office to Ministry of Health, 1 October 1930, enclosing correspondence from Ali Hamed Dheli, CO725/21/8, ff40, 45. Also see CO725/21/9 ff113–119.
146. Lawless, *From Ta'izz to Tyneside*, 53.
147. Relief Committee Minute Book, Shields District, 9 June 1925–15 November 1932, TWAS T81/84. PAC policy varied however. See Jama Hussein,

21 November 1921, CO535/68/25119; J. Robinson (ed.) (1996) *Tommy Turnbull: A Miner's Life* (Newcastle: TUPS), 175.

148. On the rota and the campaign against Arab mariners, see Tabili, *'We Ask for British Justice'*, 106–9, 152–5 and *passim*.
149. Lawless, *From Ta'izz to Tyneside*, 49.
150. William Wilkie, *Report of the Police Establishment 1929*, TWAS151/42.
151. Register of Seamen's Lodging Houses, 1929–1965, T151/88 TWAS.
152. John Reid, Borough Engineer to Town Clerk, 29 December 1933; Town Clerk to Ministry of Health, 14 February 1934; Ministry of Health to Town Clerk, 21 February 1934, TWAS T95/101.
153. Even the union recognized their influence: while reviling the boarding housekeepers, the union approached them to assist in persuading their clients to join the rota. Byrne, 'The 1930 "Arab Riot" ', 270.
154. Lawless, *From Ta'izz to Tyneside*, 21–3, 25–6, 32.
155. Collins, *Coloured Minorities in Britain*, 197; Lawless, *From Ta'izz to Tyneside*, 54–6, 60–5.
156. Byrne, 'The 1930 "Arab Riot" ', 263; Lawless, *From Ta'izz to Tyneside*, 22–3, 58–60.
157. Quote from minute, 1920, HO45/11897/332087/17; minute, 29 January 1931, CO535/91/38286; internal minute, n.d., *c.* winter 1931–32, CO535/94/38610; Home Office official, 3 November 1924, HO45/11897/332087/94.
158. J.W. Oldfield, Assistant Superintending Immigration Officer, Newcastle, to the Home Office, 23 January 1920, HO45/11897/332087/17; Lawless, *From Ta'izz to Tyneside*, 65–7.
159. Baines of the India Office to F.J. Adams of the High Commissioner for India, 20 May 1930, IOR L/E/9/954. On the coasting trade, see Lane, *Grey Dawn Breaking*, 12.
160. See Tabili, *'We Ask for British Justice'*, 106–9, 113–34, 152–5.
161. Home Department minute and letter to Chief Constable of South Shields, 14 March 1917; A.W. Ruddock to Thomas Cook's representative, 12 March 1917; Chief Constable of South Shields, 3 April 1917; Home Office circular, 28 February 1917, HO45/11897/332087/2 and /5.
162. Also see Superintending Aliens Officer at Cardiff to the Home Office, 31 March 1917, HO45/11897/332087/7.
163. Like those in Glasgow, the conflicts in South Shields differed from the riots in Liverpool and Cardiff in June, arising from labour competition rather than revulsion against interracial couples. On Glasgow, see Jenkinson, 'The Glasgow Race Disturbances', 43–67; on those in June, see Bland, 'White Women and Men of Colour'; and for a general summary, see J. Jenkinson (2009) *Black 1919: Riots, Racism and Resistance in Imperial Britain* (Liverpool: Liverpool University Press). On 1930, see Byrne, 'The 1930 "Arab Riot" '; and on 1919, 1930 and racial tension in South Shields generally, see Lawless, *From Ta'izz to Tyneside*, esp. Chapters 4 through 7.
164. Home Office to Clerk to Justices for Borough of South Shields, 11 April 1924; S. Ormond, Immigration Officer, to the Home Office, 24 March 1924; minute on front of file, n.d., HO45/11897/332087/86.

165. One common lodging house was prosecuted during the same period. *Report of the Police Establishment* for 1925, 1926 and 1927, TWAS T151/39, /40, /41.
166. *Report of the Police Establishment* for 1929, William Wilkie, 2.
167. Collins found the postwar community intimidated by memories of interwar deportations and violence, compounded by ongoing police harassment, *Coloured Minorities in Britain*, 161–2, 213–15.
168. *Corporation Minutes* (January–June 1933), 961; Town Clerk to Borough Engineer, 21 March 1934, 'Holborn Clearance', TWAS T95/101.
169. For heated press and Town Council debates, see Lawless, *From Ta'izz to Tyneside*, 194–206. Also Collins, *Coloured Minorities in Britain*, 156–7. On racial segregation as a technology of colonialism, see L. Spitzer, *The Creoles of Sierra Leone: Responses to Colonialism, 1870–1945* (Madison: University of Wisconsin Press, 1974).
170. Lawless, *From Ta'izz to Tyneside*, 201–6; Collins, *Coloured Minorities in Britain*, 156.
171. Caution by Pooley, 'The Residential Segregation of Migrant Communities', 373.
172. Hannay and Hannay to South Shields Town Clerk, 12 March 1935, 'Holborn Clearance Areas—Claims for Compensation', TWAS T95/362.
173. Collins, *Coloured Minorities in Britain*, 19, 151, 153–4, 157, 158–9, 171–2. The terms 'centripetal' and 'centrifugal' come from Collins. On Liverpool, see Frost, 'Ambiguous Identities', 204.
174. On elite-sponsored religious revival as a vehicle of depoliticized social discipline, see Lawless, *From Ta'izz to Tyneside*, 217–37, esp. 220, 226; Collins, *Coloured Minorities in Britain*, 91, 174–80, 185–6. On religious revival as a response to political disempowerment, see J. Gump (1997) 'A Spirit of Resistance: Sioux, Xhosa, and Maori Responses to Western Dominance, 1840–1920', *Pacific Historical Review* 66, 1: 21–52.
175. Frost, 'Ethnic Identity, Transience and Settlement', 92–3, 96–7, 100–1.

# Index

Note: The letter 'n' followed by the locators refers to endnotes.